Having The

ETHICS AND CULTURE

Ethics in Comedy: Essays on Crossing the Line
(Steven A. Benko, editor, 2020)

Ethics After Poststructuralism: A Critical Reader
(Lee Olsen, Brendan Johnston and
Ann Keniston, editors, 2020)

*Having Their Say: Athletes and Entertainers and
the Ethics of Speaking Out* (Kristie Bunton, 2021)

Having Their Say

*Athletes and Entertainers and
the Ethics of Speaking Out*

KRISTIE BUNTON

ETHICS AND CULTURE

Series Editor James M. Okapal

McFarland & Company, Inc., Publishers
Jefferson, North Carolina

This book has undergone peer review.

ISBN (print) 978-1-4766-8098-9
ISBN (ebook) 978-1-4766-4375-5

LIBRARY OF CONGRESS AND BRITISH LIBRARY
CATALOGUING DATA ARE AVAILABLE

Library of Congress Control Number 2021011554

© 2021 Kristie Bunton. All rights reserved

*No part of this book may be reproduced or transmitted in any form
or by any means, electronic or mechanical, including photocopying
or recording, or by any information storage and retrieval system,
without permission in writing from the publisher.*

Front cover image of a pregame football
player © 2020 RobMattingley/iStock

Printed in the United States of America

*McFarland & Company, Inc., Publishers
Box 611, Jefferson, North Carolina 28640
www.mcfarlandpub.com*

Table of Contents

Preface   1

Introduction: Who Gets to Say What? Identifying Questions About
    Speaking Out by Celebrity Athletes and Entertainers   5

Part I—Ethical Territory to Consider

1. What's the Cultural Landscape for Speaking Out? Connecting
    Celebrity Speakers and Public Issues   16

2. What Counts as Speaking Out? Defining the Ethical Construct   33

3. What Ethical Issues Surround Speaking Out? Exploring Power,
    Privilege, Harm and Justification   48

Part II—Ethical Questions to Answer

4. What Is the Relationship of the Speaker to the Topic?   64

5. What Is the Motivation for Speaking Out?   77

6. What Is the Nature of Any Harm Created?   90

7. Does Speaking Out Promote Dialogue?   105

Part III—Ethical Actors and Topics to Evaluate

8. Shut Up and Play? Athletes Speaking Out About Inequality   122

9. Raise a Fist or Take a Knee? Athletes Speaking Out
    Symbolically About Injustice   138

10. Who's an Expert? Celebrities Speaking Out During
    a Pandemic   156

11. Shut Up and Listen? Ethical Responses to Speaking Out   173

Conclusion: How Do We Speak Out Ethically When We're Not Famous?   188

Chapter Notes   197

Works Cited by Chapter   231

Index   261

Preface

Over the years, I sometimes have explained my outspoken family and our spirited discussions by joking, "We never met an opinion we couldn't have." I've enjoyed our ability to be our own marketplace of competing ideas. Over those same years, in my many communication ethics classes, I've also enjoyed encouraging students to recognize the power and promise of free expression of competing ideas to serve the common good. Yet as the rancorous 2018 midterm election season lurched to a close, I did not feel exhilarated by freewheeling expression conveyed through multiple channels. Instead, I felt exhausted by what seemed like the noise of opinion all around me in the news and commentary I ordinarily enjoyed reading and felt a duty to monitor. I wondered: Does everybody get to say something publicly these days? Do they all have to shout—or whatever is the equivalent of shouting on social media—and disagree with one another? Why are news organizations reporting some of these ill-expressed ideas? Do I have to listen to them all? Should I respond to some?

As I looked ahead to what I imagined would be an even louder and more contentious 2020 presidential election season, I craved quiet to think about public noise, and I recalled an essay my colleague Dr. Wendy Wyatt and I wrote several years before. Our essay, "The Ethics of Speaking Out," appeared in *Ethics and Entertainment: Essays on Media Culture and Media Morality*, published by McFarland and edited by Howard Good and Sandra L. Borden in 2010. Dr. Wyatt and I examined three episodes in the early 2000s when singers and actors shocked audiences by speaking out about political and social issues. Dr. Wyatt and I proposed a test that could be used to justify when celebrities ethically could transcend audiences' role-related expectations for artistic or athletic performance to express serious views about public issues. I wondered how our speaking-out test might apply in the social media environment that had flourished since we published our essay in 2010.

I soon learned I wasn't alone in wondering. Serendipitously, McFarland editor Layla Milholen contacted Dr. Wyatt and me to ask whether our ideas about speaking out applied to the examples proliferating in today's fully digital environment. Dr. Wyatt's other scholarly projects prohibited her from joining me to pursue a new examination of speaking out, but I decided to go ahead. I couldn't shake the conclusion that the noise of today's communication environment begged for an ethical analysis of when and how speaking out by famous people is justifiable. Digital platforms empower anyone with an internet connection to speak out publicly, nearly instantly to worldwide audiences, and in a way that persists over time. To me, this meant all of us as moral agents—but especially those with the ability to command widespread public attention—should think before speaking out about how our proposed speech might harm or help other stakeholders or issues.

As I approached anew the topic of speaking out, I collected more examples than I possibly could analyze, perhaps because mainstream news coverage so often amplified the voices of celebrities who spoke out through social media platforms. After all, when professional basketball superstar LeBron James tweets that U.S. President Donald Trump is a "bum," it makes news. I quickly decided to use national news coverage of speaking out to help me winnow the many examples available to examine. I also began to focus more closely on superstar athletes and entertainers than on other public figures who speak out because I observed these athletes' and entertainers' ubiquity in popular culture and what seemed to me to be their increasing participation in political culture. As I worked on this project throughout 2019 and into the early months of 2020, I found more and more examples of these celebrity athletes and entertainers speaking out with compelling force about the political implications of such issues as health care, policing and criminal justice, and racial and gender discrimination.

I finished the first draft of this book in March 2020. Within mere weeks, a series of dramatic public crises unfolded, convincing me I must revise the manuscript to include new and even more compelling cases of speaking out. The partisan cleavages that had so characterized public discourse in the United States since the 2016 presidential campaign and had played out so rancorously in the 2018 midterm election had by spring and early summer 2020 become louder and louder, as a coronavirus pandemic swept around the world, infecting and killing scores of people. Authorities rapidly closed factories, schools, restaurants, stores, offices and sports arenas to try to stop the virus from spreading. The economy cratered, leaving millions of workers without jobs and prompting acts of speaking out that blamed employers and politicians, while the simple act of wearing a face mask to prevent viral transmission prompted still more contentious and politicized speaking out.

Each of these three crises—escalating political divisions, a pandemic of unprecedented impact and the resulting economic devastation—produced much speaking out that I wanted to analyze as I revised this project. But a fourth crisis generated even more important speaking out to analyze. That crisis began on May 25, 2020, in Minneapolis, Minnesota, when police officers arrested a Black citizen named George Floyd, who was accused of using a counterfeit $20 bill to buy cigarettes and soon was restrained face down on a street by the police. A white officer knelt on George Floyd's neck for nearly nine minutes while he pleaded for help and lay dying. Horrific video of Floyd's killing was recorded by witnesses who soon shared the video in a variety of media channels. The video became a viral sensation and helped prompt millions of people around the world to speak out using social media and to join demonstrations for racial justice and police reform. As were so many observers, I was awed by the moral courage of people who risked exposing themselves to the life-threatening coronavirus by leaving the self-isolation of their homes to demonstrate in ways these protestors believed were essential for escalating awareness of the corrosive, life-threatening virus of racism and injustice.

Writing a book about speaking out is not an act of moral courage, but it is my attempt to focus the ethical analysis lens I acquired in graduate school and honed in professional life onto the acts of others, who may be morally courageous in speaking out. I hope my analysis will help readers of this book consider their own ability to speak out when appropriate.

With a nod to the ethical principle of transparency, I want to offer context about my ethical analysis lens. As an undergraduate, I trained to be a journalist because I was curious about people and wanted to tell their stories. I pursued graduate education because I wanted to better understand the ethical responsibilities involved in reporting people's stories—especially the power and privilege journalists possess to shape their audiences' understanding of people. Ultimately, I became a professor because I wanted to help budding journalists prepare to carefully exercise these serious responsibilities. I remain fundamentally convinced that reporting people's stories can be a powerful way to help us learn about and understand one another, even as we differ. Yet I must acknowledge that the way I frame and analyze these stories of speaking out may be sincere but undoubtedly is imperfect. I am white, female, middle-class, academically trained, Christian and politically moderate, among other characteristics. I have tried to recognize how my own identity and experiences affect the ways I tell stories of people who speak out, but I realize I may be blind to my own biases. I regard each of us as a person worth dignity, so I have tried to tell with respect and fairness these stories of people who speak out.

Finally, I want to express my gratitude for the kindness of my circle of colleagues, friends and family members who cared about this project simply because it mattered to me. Wendy Wyatt offered excellent comments on the book proposal. My colleague Jean Stayton effectively covered the physical and mental absences I needed to think and write, and she became a quick and accurate proofreader, too. My dear friends Margaret Howard and Wendy Wehr graciously listened and asked good questions every time I expounded on this project, and Margaret doubled as a thoughtful manuscript reader. My siblings and their spouses—my "favorite eight"—cared and prayed for my ability to complete this work. So, too, did many of my cherished nieces and nephews. My creative and generous niece Molly Bunton and her mother Cathy Bunton organized a shower of handwritten notes to cheer me through finishing the first draft. "Sister mine" Katie Proctor and brother-by-marriage Matt Proctor went even further, reading and discussing everything from outline to proposed examples to completed chapters. If this book is my own way of speaking out, I am responsible for its shortcomings, but it is better because my circle listened and questioned.

Introduction:
Who Gets to Say What?

*Identifying Questions About Speaking Out
by Celebrity Athletes and Entertainers*

*"In the past I've been reluctant to publicly voice my political
opinions."*

Pop music superstar Taylor Swift got political with her fans one Sunday in October 2018 in a way she'd never been before. Some of the many
Grammy-winning and Billboard chart-topping songs Swift had written
and sold over the previous decade to millions of music fans around the
world alluded to her views about gender and power, but until her Instagram
post that October Sunday, Swift never had revealed a political identity or
endorsed specific candidates.

That day, Swift told her 112 million Instagram followers why she was
speaking out about the 2018 midterm elections. Noting she would vote in
the state of Tennessee, where she and her family moved when she was a
teen trying to break into the music business, Swift wrote, "In the past I've
been reluctant to publicly voice my political opinions, but due to several
events in my life and in the world in the past two years, I feel very differently
about that now." Swift, who won a symbolic $1 verdict in a 2017 counter-suit
for sexual assault and battery by a Colorado radio show host who groped
her,[1] explained the issue motivating her political views in 2018. She wrote,
"I always have and always will cast my vote based on which candidate will
protect and fight for the human rights I believe we all deserve in this country." Swift said she opposed discrimination on the basis of gender, race and
sexual orientation, declaring, "I cannot vote for someone who will not be
willing to fight for dignity for ALL Americans, no matter their skin color,
gender or who they love." Therefore, Swift wrote, she would not vote for
Marsha Blackburn, a Republican seeking a U.S. Senate seat in Tennessee,

5

and explained that Blackburn's "voting record in Congress appalls and ter-rifies me." Swift said while Blackburn served in the U.S. House of Represen-tatives, she did not vote for equal pay for women or for legislation intended to protect women from domestic violence and sexual crimes, and she did not support equal rights for same-sex couples. "These are not MY Tennessee values," Swift proclaimed, before endorsing the Democratic candidate for U.S. Senate, Phil Bredesen, and naming the Democratic candidate for U.S. House of Representatives, Jim Cooper, for whom she said she'd also vote.

At the conclusion of her Instagram post, Swift spoke directly to her younger social media followers, encouraging them to register and to vote in the hotly contested midterm elections across the United States, writing, "So many intelligent, thoughtful, self-possessed people have turned 18 in the past two years and now have the right and privilege to make their vote count. But first you need to register, which is quick and easy to do." She ended her post by directing followers to the website vote.org to learn how to register in their own states. The post soon was "liked" by more than two million Instagram users.[2]

Swift made her attention-getting post the day after ending a North American concert tour and two days before voter registration closed in her home state of Tennessee. In less than 48 hours after Swift's post, vote.org officials reported more than 166,000 new voters had registered across the country and that some 42 percent of those new registrants were between the ages of 18 and 24. "We have never seen a 24- or 36- or 48-hour period like this," vote.org spokeswoman Kamari Guthrie told *The New York Times*. "This is leaps and bounds beyond what we typically see."[3]

Before her Instagram statement, Swift had been scrupulously apoliti-cal, carefully managing her public image and digital identity. In 2008, for instance, when she was first eligible to vote as an 18 year old, she declined to say how she voted in the presidential election that sent Democrat Barack Obama to the White House. *People* magazine reported that because Swift would be in Los Angeles on Election Day, she stood in line for an hour and a half on the last day of Tennessee's early voting period and signed auto-graphs while waiting. All Swift would tell the magazine was, "I wavered back and forth the entire time I was waiting in line and when I got into the voting booth, I said, 'That's the one I'm voting for,' and I pressed the button. And I feel good about it!"[4]

At age 22, Swift again declined to reveal which presidential candidate she supported, telling *Time* magazine just before the 2012 presidential elec-tion that gave Barack Obama a second term in the White House, "I try to keep myself as educated and informed as possible. But I don't talk about politics because it might influence other people. And I don't think that I know enough yet in life to be telling people who to vote for."[5]

Four years later, Swift was photographed wearing a top with cut-out shoulders to the polls, which caused some observers to speculate she supported 2016 Democratic candidate Hillary Clinton, who had been photographed in younger years wearing something similar. Despite that sort of speculation about her political leanings, Swift did not reveal for whom she voted in the election that sent Republican Donald Trump to the White House. Some commentators took her to task for remaining steadfastly silent about her politics, noting she was the world's best-selling pop artist and had expressed feminist views in her music but declined to join fellow artists in speaking out to support Hillary Clinton, the country's first female major-party presidential nominee. Nearly two years later, Swift explained she didn't endorse Hillary Clinton because Donald Trump "was weaponizing the idea of the celebrity endorsement" during the 2016 campaign, and she feared she would hurt Clinton's candidacy more than help it.[6]

Swift's 2018 midterm election Instagram post therefore stunned observers with its newly specific political message. Thousands of Swift's fans, perhaps especially those who had thought she was a closet Republican, engaged in a flurry of speculation about her decision to speak out.[7] Swift's post, and people's reactions to it, also reminded some observers of the episode 15 years before when another singer at the height of her popularity spoke out about U.S. politics. A typical observation connecting Swift with that episode was this tweet observing, "I'm old enough to remember when Republicans banned the Dixie Chicks for criticizing America while overseas."[8]

> *"We're ashamed that the president of the United States is from Texas."*

In 2003, the Dixie Chicks, an American country music trio, were enjoying worldwide popularity before speaking out led to their vilification. Composed of lead singer Natalie Maines and sisters Martie Maguire and Emily Robison, the Dixie Chicks had soared to success by updating traditional country music with what a *New York Times* music writer called "assertive, irreverent femininity."[9] Their song "Goodbye Earl," for instance, suggested a woman was justified in killing a husband who repeatedly abused her. With multiple Grammy-winning songs to their credit, at one point the Dixie Chicks reigned as the best-selling female group of all time.[10] Just days before the United States invaded Iraq in 2003, the Dixie Chicks were touring in Europe, playing a gig at the Shepherd's Bush Empire theater in London.[11] That evening in March, Natalie Maines stood on stage chatting with the audience as the trio readied to perform its chart-topping song "Travelin' Soldier," which mourned a young American man killed while serving in Vietnam.[12] As she strummed her guitar, Maines, a Texas native, told the audience, "Just so you know, we're on the good side with y'all. We do not want this war, this violence, and we're ashamed that the president of the United States is from Texas."[13]

Her comments were included in a concert review in *The Guardian* newspaper in London. They spread quickly to the United States, where public reaction to them landed the Dixie Chicks in what *The Guardian* later called "the center of a massive political firestorm."[14] In an America where patriotism prevailed two years after the 9/11 terror attacks, criticism of President George W. Bush was not popular, especially among country music fans who were listening to radio stations that showcased songs—such as Toby Keith's "Courtesy of the Red, White and Blue for instance—that one critic described as "steeped in earnestly patriotic drum-banging."[15] The Dixie Chicks rapidly were boycotted by country music fans and radio stations, and in Louisiana, a group of fans smashed the trio's CDs with a bulldozer.[16] The Dixie Chicks' "Travelin' Soldier" single quickly plunged from number 1 to number 63 on the country music charts,[17] and soon the corporate sponsor of the trio's U.S. concert tour bailed out.[18] Just weeks before, on the first day of sales for that tour, the group had shattered a music industry record by selling $49 million worth of tickets, but by the time the trio began playing those sold-out concerts, death threats to the women concerned them enough to hire 24-hour armed security guards.[19]

As the women continued touring, they tried to clarify their position of supporting U.S. military members while remaining opposed to the war in Iraq, but their efforts seemed futile. Journalist Howard Bryant noted, "Even money couldn't save the Dixie Chicks. The band attempted to make a million-dollar donation to the American Red Cross, which, too scared to challenge the perceived public sentiment or find itself at the center of a possible boycott, rejected the money. One sentence about a war that would soon be historically discredited ruined the Dixie Chicks' careers."[20]

Three years later, the Dixie Chicks released "Taking the Long Way," an album with a single pointedly titled "Not Ready to Make Nice," which featured equally pointed lyrics suggesting death threats against Maines were an overreaction to the words she spoke in London.[21] The album won all five Grammy awards for which it was nominated, including the top three Grammy categories. Yet the Dixie Chicks still found their songs banned by politically conservative country music radio stations.[22] The Academy of Country Music awards show audience laughed heartily when host Reba McEntire joked about the Dixie Chicks singing with "their foot in their mouth," for instance.[23] In 2006, a documentary titled *Shut Up and Sing* depicted the Dixie Chicks picking up the pieces of their lives after Maines' remarks on the London stage. In the film, the women said they stood by

Maines' decision to speak out, despite the costs to their careers and the threats to their safety.[24]

Ethical Questions Raised When Celebrities Speak Out

Why did Taylor Swift's political Instagram post leave her largely unscathed, while Natalie Maines' political comment to a concert audience destroyed the Dixie Chicks' career? Should constraints apply when celebrity athletes and entertainers speak out about serious public issues? This book examines ethical issues that arise when these famous people speak out on issues often unrelated to the performances that brought those figures to public attention. Taylor Swift, for instance, rose to fame for writing and singing songs about breakups with boyfriends, not for endorsing political candidates, and many of her fans expected her to continue to fulfill that entertaining role. Natalie Maines and the Dixie Chicks rose to prominence with sometimes-provocative lyrics and big-voiced ballads, but politically conservative country music fans didn't expect Maines to criticize the U.S. president while touring abroad. In fact, audiences expected the trio to "shut up and sing."

Both Taylor Swift and Natalie Maines are U.S. citizens with legal rights under the First Amendment to the U.S. Constitution to express themselves freely. Yet, as their cases show, when entertainers speak out about public issues of great import, their views quickly can be magnified and criticized significantly more than ordinary citizens' words will be. Natalie Maines expressed her opposition to the Iraq War and President Bush in a country music concert, where audiences typically have expected female performers to look and sound good, and to tackle nothing more controversial than a song about a romance gone wrong. What ethical responsibilities did Maines bear as a public figure when she defied her audience's role-related expectations? Some critics said Maines had no right to subject her ticket-buying concert audience to political views they might not share. "There's a contract that binds country singers to their fans, and the Dixie Chicks have broken it," noted a *New York Times* music critic.[25] Swift, too, defied role-related expectations for a female pop singer who ascended to fame while remaining scrupulously apolitical.

Did Swift and Maines possess ethically justifiable motives for speaking out? Although Maines appeared to speak spontaneously as she riffed with the concert audience before launching into a song, the trio said in later interviews they had discussed the U.S. invasion of Iraq several times. "We were about to go to war, and before we went on that night we talked about how silly we felt having to go out and entertain when our hearts were so heavy with what was about to happen," Maguire said.[26] "It felt pretty trite" not to speak out "on what was supposed to be the eve of the war," Maines said. "At that stage too everyone in Europe, or everyone outside of the U.S., talked about the U.S. like we all thought one way. So it was important for me to let them know that you can't group us all into one."[27]

In standing by their anti-war position, in the face of a country music establishment that favored President Bush's invasion of Iraq, did Maines and her fellow Dixie Chicks display moral courage? Did Swift display moral courage in making her Instagram post?

> *"I saw how one comment ended such a powerful reign, and it terrified me."*

Two years after she spoke out about the 2018 midterm elections, Swift was the subject of a documentary film titled *Taylor Swift: Miss Americana*, which, in the words of *Variety* magazine, depicted "how gradually, and sometimes reluctantly, Swift came to place herself into service as a social commentator."[28] The documentary debuted at the Sundance Film Festival, and some critics found its most telling scene one in which Swift was seen on camera arguing with her father and a group of unnamed male advisors about whether to make her Instagram post endorsing Democratic candidates in Tennessee. The advisors worried Swift's proposed post "could have the effect of halving her audience on tour." Swift's father worried the post would pose risks to her personal safety, saying, "I'm terrified. I'm the guy that went out and bought armored cars." Swift conceded her father was not wrong about stalkers and others who routinely threatened her safety, but she indicated she erred by not publicly opposing Donald Trump and endorsing Hillary Clinton in 2016. In 2018, she said, "I need to be on the right side of history," and asked her father's forgiveness before making the post.[29]

In interviews she gave to promote the documentary's premiere at Sundance, Swift further explained her motivation for speaking out: "This was a situation where, from a humanity perspective, and from what my moral compass was telling me to do, I knew I was right, and I really didn't care about repercussions."[30] Her decision to speak out doesn't mean she failed to understand the possible repercussions of her speech. As an emerging musician, Swift had observed the Dixie Chicks' fall from grace. "I saw how one comment ended such a powerful reign, and it terrified me," she said. "These days, with social media, people can be so mad about something one day and then forget what they were mad about a couple of weeks later. That's fake outrage. But what happened to the Dixie Chicks was *real* outrage. I registered it—that you're always one comment away from being done being able to make music."[31]

Ethical Obligations When Speaking Out

In addition to considering possible harm to themselves or their careers, how should celebrity athletes and entertainers work to minimize harm to the subjects of speech or the audiences who receive it? It's perhaps relatively harmless for a powerful U.S. president such as George W. Bush to find himself criticized from a concert stage by a country singer. He can find a platform through which to respond, should he choose to. In fact, when President Bush was asked in a network television interview about the Dixie Chicks, he said he supported their right to speak freely and added that "if some singers or Hollywood stars feel like speaking out, that's fine. That's the great thing about America."[32] A president also can choose, as Donald Trump apparently did, not to engage in a tit-for-tat on social media, of which he was a prolific user, with a music superstar such as Swift. But what if the subject of the celebrity athlete's or entertainer's speech is a more private, less powerful person? Does the athlete or entertainer bear extra ethical care for speaking out about those people or for speaking out about particularly sensitive, potentially offensive topics? What ethical obligations do athletes or entertainers who speak out have for wielding their public platforms in ways that foster dialogue with the recipients of their views? What about audiences? Do recipients of athletes' and entertainers' speech bear any affirmative ethical obligation to respond? If they disagreed with Swift's post endorsing Democratic candidates, for instance, were her followers ethically obliged to speak out and disagree with her publicly? What are the limits to audience response? Although listeners and radio stations hired a bulldozer to smash Dixie Chicks CDs, there was no evidence the dramatic display of opposition harmed anyone. Issuing death threats to the trio and their young children who typically traveled with them while on tour, however, clearly raised the possibility of physical and emotional harm to them. How might respect for the dignity of all people be a required ethical element of speaking out and of response to speaking out?

Finally, and perhaps most crucially, what can we as ordinary people learn from cases of celebrity athletes and entertainers who speak out? How can we speak out ethically and with moral courage in our own spheres of influence? Few of us will find ourselves sharing political views with 112 million Instagram followers or chatting with a crowd from a concert stage. Even so, we will experience situations in our workplaces, our schools, our houses of worship and our neighborhoods, and in our e-mail inboxes, our Twitter feeds, our Facebook pages and our Instagram accounts when we might want to defy the expectations people have for our personal and professional roles to speak out about public issues important to us. If we do so, we want to speak out effectively and ethically.

Social media platforms, whether Twitter, Facebook, Instagram or others, and the digital devices we use to post, read and view content on those platforms, now are omnipresent in our lives. Many of us rarely tuck our smart phones and tablets farther away than our pockets, tote bags and bedside tables so we can check digital content incessantly during our days—and nights. These devices and social media platforms arguably offer the most sophisticated means of communication any people in human history have possessed. We adroitly use our devices to communicate our stories and perspectives quickly and widely, with little constraint from the old filters of religious, educational, government, business or journalistic authorities.

This book is written with the conviction that these powerful human communication tools available to so many of us today can enlighten and encourage all of us who seek a better world. The more communication tools we have to speak out and wisely share a panoply of human views and experiences, the better off we all will be in seeking a common good. Yet these remarkably powerful communication tools—especially social media platforms favoring short bursts of attention-getting opinion and rapid "likes" or "dislikes" over sustained discourse and careful argumentation—also present great power to harm and offend other people, whether with untruthful or deceitful content, ill-considered views, or disrespect for others' human dignity. In that context, then, this book examines ethical challenges facing all of us when we speak out publicly. Serious ethical responsibilities attach to famous athletes and entertainers in a digital world in which many audience members equate celebrity status with authority and expertise about shared public issues. In applying ethical principles to examples of speaking out by athletes and entertainers, this book attempts to help all of us understand our ethical responsibilities for when and how we speak out about public topics in our spheres of influence.

Parameters That Shape the Ethical Analysis of Speaking Out

Before the book moves to a fuller examination of these ethical responsibilities for speaking out, it's useful to first identify five parameters that guide the selection of the examples of speaking out that this book presents and analyzes.

First, this book emphasizes examples of speaking out that occur in a specific American context. These examples involve athletes and entertainers speaking out in the United States during the first two decades of the 2000s, when increasingly polarized speech has focused on the political and social effects of race, gender and class—speech that includes some Americans' jubilation at electing the country's first Black president, other Americans' disdain for the country's first female presidential nominee, and yet other Americans' fear of losing status in a country of fast-changing demographics. As polarizing rhetoric escalated during the 2020 presidential election season, a viral pandemic infected and killed hundreds of thousands of American people, and the related shutdown of the U.S. economy left millions of workers without jobs. The effects of the pandemic and the economic crash were heightened early in the summer of 2020 by a crisis about racism and police brutality. That crisis exploded after millions of Americans saw a video recording of a white police officer kneeling for nearly nine minutes on the neck of a Black citizen named George Floyd, who lay dying on a Minneapolis, Minnesota, street where he had been arrested.[33] Coming after years of unjustified killings of Black people[34] by American police, and at a time when Black people were disproportionately victimized by the viral pandemic and the economic crash, Floyd's death provoked thousands of people to join demonstrations against systemic racism. The resulting attention to the Black Lives Matter movement by celebrities, politicians, businesses, media organizations and sports leagues created what a longtime *Washington Post* sports columnist called "an avalanche" of activism and speaking out[35] that merits ethical analysis.

Second, this book examines examples of speaking out in which athletes and entertainers question power and privilege. Speaking out typically generates more controversy and criticism—and thus may require more moral courage—when speakers question the status quo than when they defend it. For generations, from baseball legend Jackie Robinson to football quarterback Colin Kaepernick, controversy and criticism have faced Black athletes who found the moral courage to speak out against racial injustice even while their very presence in sports was derided. In the context of that history, this book considers many contemporary Black athletes' use of social media posts and symbolic gestures to question racial injustice, as well as the consequences Black athletes particularly may endure for speaking out.

Third, this book analyzes examples of speaking out that raise ethical questions both through an initial act of speaking out and through news coverage that amplifies it. Most of the speaking out analyzed here comes from athletes and entertainers who first became famous through what scholars call "achieved" celebrity derived from great skill and talent, as opposed to "ascribed" celebrity derived from family background or "attributed" celebrity derived through media attention alone.[36] Achieved celebrities who transcend their athletic or artistic accomplishments to speak out about unrelated public issues bear ethical responsibilities for that speech that are worth examining. So too do the journalists who decide to report on speaking out by achieved celebrities instead of reporting on other public issues and who frame that speaking out in specific ways that may affect our understanding of the issues. For example, the book considers both professional tennis superstar Serena Williams' remarks about racism and sexism, and news coverage about her remarks that promulgated the very stereotypes she opposed.

Fourth, this book focuses on examples of speaking out that tend more toward "right doing" than wrongdoing. Arguably, many books and articles about ethical responsibility devote too much space to analyzing cases of unethical behavior that tempt us to think doing right is impossible. This book doesn't devote much space to wrongdoing. For instance, this book does not analyze celebrities unethically speaking out about their opposition to childhood vaccinations or their support for alternative health and wellness treatments. Those books have been written, and they are commendable.[37] This book also doesn't present moral agents as singular moral exemplars. The entertainers and athletes examined here are flawed humans just as we all are. But this book finds their behavior in speaking out more right than wrong in the circumstances, which is what studying ethics is fundamentally about: learning to do as much right as possible in situations that don't offer one right answer.

The fifth and final parameter shaping this book is intended to relate to all of us who read it. We're not famous, and we're probably not trained to excel as speakers, but we can deduce ethical principles from examples of celebrities speaking out and apply those principles to our ordinary lives. Therefore, this book emphasizes examples of speaking out by celebrities who primarily became famous as they honed their talents and training to achieve elite status as athletes and entertainers, and then only secondarily became famous for speaking out about issues that might not be connected to their previous achievements. For instance, when we read about world-class sprinter Allyson Felix summoning the courage to reject an endorsement contract and speak out about the treatment of female athletes after they give birth, we can consider whether we have the moral courage to stand up and say "no" in our own work lives, or whether we would use our own stories to make a point in our communities. We also can think about the ethical responses we might provide as listeners to speaking out, especially if the speaker reveals a deeply personal experience. How might we be respectful and humble listeners? When do we need to be skeptical listeners who talk back? Above all, this book intends to derive from famous examples several principles of practical ethics that we can employ as we speak and listen in our own circles.

PART I

Ethical Territory to Consider

1

What's the Cultural Landscape for Speaking Out?

Connecting Celebrity Speakers and Public Issues

Years before the Dixie Chicks were excoriated by country music fans for saying from a London concert stage that they opposed President George W. Bush and the U.S. invasion of Iraq in 2003, and years before musical mega-star Taylor Swift used social media both to exhort young Americans to register to vote in the 2018 midterm elections and to endorse Democratic Party candidates, famous entertainers and athletes spoke out about public issues and political campaigns. In fact, perhaps more than in other countries, politics in the United States has been distinguished by connections to celebrity,[1] and this chapter explores those historical connections as a way to understand the context in which celebrity athletes and entertainers speak out today.

Celebrity Athletes and Entertainers in Political Campaigns

By the mid–20th century, American electoral campaigns regularly focused more on individual candidates' charisma than on candidates' issue platforms or records of public accomplishment. If style matters as much or more than substance in winning an election, then popular entertainers and athletes may have just the right qualifications to help candidates gain voters' attention.

Candidates for years have linked their campaigns to celebrities.[2] In 1920, Republican nominee Warren Harding recruited vaudeville, Broadway and film stars such as Al Jolson, Douglas Fairbanks and Mary Pickford to campaign for him. In the 1930s and 1940s, Democrat Franklin Roosevelt's

16

campaigns deployed film and music stars such as Humphrey Bogart, Judy Garland, Rita Hayworth and Frank Sinatra.[3] In 1960, Democrat John F. Kennedy's campaign worked hard to convince the popular Black singer and actor Harry Belafonte to endorse JFK after baseball legend Jackie Robinson, who was famous for breaking that sport's color barrier, said he was likely to endorse Kennedy's Republican opponent, Richard Nixon, because he had a stronger record of support for civil rights measures.[4] Belafonte ended up making a campaign ad with JFK that celebrity politics scholar Mark Wheeler calls "unusual" for that era because the ad portrayed the candidate "mostly listening" while Belafonte "pleaded the candidate's case for him."[5] Actor John Wayne endorsed Nixon in the 1960 and 1968 elections, while actor and director Warren Beatty initiated the use of lucrative fundraising concerts for several Democratic candidates, starting with George McGovern in 1972.[6] Singer, actor and director Barbra Streisand, who accepted Beatty's invitation to sing for McGovern, subsequently became a fundraising force for Democratic presidential candidates, notably raising millions of dollars in 1992 for a relatively unknown Arkansas Democrat named Bill Clinton.[7]

Perhaps the most powerful support of a presidential candidate by an entertainment icon was bestowed on 2008 Democratic candidate Barack Obama by talk show host, actress, magazine publisher, film and television producer Oprah Winfrey—or simply Oprah, as the world knows the media magnate. Winfrey is the only person to have been named 10 times to *Time* magazine's list of the 10 most influential people in the world,[8] and her overwhelming influence on audiences is reflected by the very existence of a term invented to describe it: the "Oprah effect." The "Oprah effect" covers at least three types of power attributed to Winfrey: her influence on people's attitudes and behaviors about the political and social issues she examined on her long-running daytime television show[9]; her career-making impact on lifestyle experts such as financial counselor Suze Orman, psychologist "Dr. Phil," physician "Dr. Oz" and interior designer Nate Berkus after she launched them from her television, magazine and online venues to platforms of their own; and her "turn-to-gold touch" on the sales of products ranging from books to bedroom slippers after they were featured on her media channels.[10] When Winfrey made her first public political endorsement with her support of Obama,[11] the "Oprah effect" on his campaign was significant. One academic study, which generated headlines during the election season, suggested Winfrey's endorsement alone accounted for the one million additional votes for Obama that secured the Democratic Party presidential nomination for the lesser-known junior U.S. senator from Illinois over Hillary Clinton, the better-known U.S. senator from New York and former First Lady.[12]

Entertainers who approach the endorsement super-power of Winfrey are considered powerful speakers on behalf of campaigns and are eagerly courted by candidates. In turn, entertainers often are eager to speak out and endorse, raise money for or campaign with candidates, perhaps because they genuinely support candidates' platforms and want to be as involved in politics as any other citizen—and, skeptics might note, perhaps because involvement in politics may enhance an entertainer's reputation as a "serious" artist. Whatever their reasons for allying themselves with campaigns, celebrities have become such frequent endorsers of candidates that during the 2016 presidential campaign, *The Los Angeles Times* produced a "celebrity endorsement tracker"—a scorecard of sorts—to regularly report on which celebrities had written statements of support, raised funds or campaigned in person for which candidates in the primary and general elections.[13] (Obviously, celebrities' involvement in a campaign may generate attention for candidates, but that involvement cannot guarantee victory. In 2016, one website calculated that Democratic Party presidential nominee Hillary Clinton was endorsed by Hollywood celebrities who had 195.6 million social media followers, while the eventual victor, Republican Party nominee Donald Trump, was endorsed by Hollywood celebrities who had merely 21 million followers.[14])

Entertainers and athletes who care about politics don't use their celebrity just to endorse candidates. They also may have all the charisma and popularity to transcend their roles as speakers for someone else's candidacy into roles as speakers for their own candidacies. Most notably, two celebrities whose endorsements previously were sought by presidential candidates ultimately became U.S. presidents themselves. Former Hollywood movie studio "B list" actor Ronald Reagan was elected president in 1980, after he had been California governor, and Donald Trump, who perhaps was better known for hosting and producing reality television's *Celebrity Apprentice* series than for his career as a New York real estate developer, was elected president in 2016.

Athletes and entertainers have been elected state governors, as with former television wrestler Jesse Ventura in Minnesota, and former body building champion and action movie star Arnold Schwarzenegger in California. Entertainers and athletes have been elected to Congress, as with former Buffalo Bills professional football player Jack Kemp representing New York in the U.S. House of Representatives before becoming U.S. secretary of housing and then the Republican nominee for vice president, and former singer and variety show host Sonny Bono representing California in the U.S. House. Entertainers and athletes have been elected to the U.S. Senate, as with former New York Knicks basketball player and Hall of Fame member Bill Bradley representing New Jersey, and former comedian and

Saturday Night Live cast member Al Franken representing Minnesota. Certainly, not all entertainers who seek public office are elected—*Sex and the City* actress Cynthia Nixon's 2018 Democratic primary election bid for the New York governorship is among recent notable celebrity campaign defeats—but by virtue of their candidacies, these celebrities have injected their views about politics into public discourse.

Celebrities Speaking Out from High-Profile Stages

The same goes for other celebrities who have not sought elective office. They, too, have turned attention to political issues and affected public discourse about issues by speaking out. For example, during the civil rights movement of the 1960s, six popular Black entertainers—singer and actor Harry Belafonte, Broadway and Hollywood actors Ossie Davis, Ruby Dee and Sidney Poitier, comedian Dick Gregory, and singer, comedian and actor Sammy Davis, Jr.—became "the movement's most outspoken, effective, and consistent celebrity activists, seemingly unafraid of the potential consequences to their careers," according to historian Emilie Raymond.[15] With their participation in such pivotal civil rights events as the 1963 March on Washington and the 1965 "Bloody Sunday" March in Selma, Alabama, these entertainers whom Raymond calls "the leading six" stars "changed the racial climate in Hollywood and helped establish a blueprint for celebrity politics."[16]

"There's a great deal to say and I'm not going to say it tonight."

In 1972, actress Jane Fonda famously expressed her opposition to the Vietnam War by visiting U.S. foes in North Vietnam, recording radio messages to U.S. troops asking them to question their superiors' orders and posing for photos atop an anti-aircraft gun while clad in North Vietnamese gear.[17] Curiously, the actress who had been outspoken at anti-war protests around the United States—and who seemed never to resist an opportunity to share her controversial views—declined to say anything political from the Academy Awards ceremony stage when she won a "Best Actress" Oscar for her performance in *Klute*. Instead, she accepted her Oscar statue and simply said, "Thank you. Thank you very much, members of the Academy. And thank all of you who applauded. There's a great deal to say and I'm not going to say it tonight. I would just like to really thank you very much."[18]

Actor Marlon Brando, however, used the next year's Academy Awards ceremony to draw attention to a cause that was important to him: society's treatment of Native American Indians, as characterized by a long-running standoff between activists and federal agents at Wounded Knee, South

Dakota. Brando sent an activist dressed in tribal clothing to the awards ceremony stage, where she was to read a statement and refuse the "Best Actor" Oscar statue Brando won for *The Godfather*. Before the activist forcibly was walked off stage, she managed to tell the audience that Brando declined his Oscar, "the reasons for this being … the treatment of American Indians today by the film industry … and on television in movie reruns, and also with recent happenings at Wounded Knee."[19] The Associated Press reported that Brando's act of symbolically speaking out had the effect of "upending a decades-long tradition of tears, nervous humor, thank-yous and general good will" at the Academy Awards.[20] Political scientist Greg Rabidoux suggests that even if the audience attending the awards ceremony didn't hear all of Brando's prepared statement that night, "the symbolism of Brando's refusal to accept the Academy's highest award … was not lost on over sixty-five million viewers"[21] watching on television.

Nor was Brando's powerful expression of his political views lost on performers subsequently honored with Hollywood's biggest award. According to the Associated Press, before Brando's "truly groundbreaking" display, Oscar winners "avoided making news even if the time was right and the audience never bigger,"[22] and even if the film for which they were honored was political. In 1963, for instance, Gregory Peck received the "Best Actor" Oscar for his *To Kill a Mockingbird* portrayal of Atticus Finch, the attorney who defends a Black man wrongly accused and convicted of raping a white woman. When Peck accepted his Oscar statue, he thanked author Harper Lee, who wrote the Pulitzer Prize–winning novel on which the film was based, as well as the film's director, producer and studio, the movie critics who covered his work, and his family and friends.[23] Peck did not say a word about the issues of racism and injustice that were the focus of both the film and the novel—issues he had discussed when he was interviewed about the film.[24]

After Brando's response to winning an Oscar, however, entertainers' appearances on awards ceremony stages became more openly political, even if controversial and uncomfortable for some in the ceremony or television audiences. In 1993, for example, actor Richard Gere was supposed to present the Oscar for art direction, but he first spoke from the stage about human rights abuse in Tibet. The same year, actors Susan Sarandon and Tim Robbins were supposed to present the Oscar for best film editing, but they first protested the United States' internment at Guantanamo Bay of Haitian immigrants who tested positive for HIV.[25] The next year, when comedian and actress Whoopi Goldberg hosted the Academy Awards, she joked in her opening monologue about all the political and social causes entertainers might mention from the Oscars stage: "Save the whales. Save the spotted owl. Gay rights. Men's rights. Women's rights. Human rights.

Feed the homeless. More gun control. Free the Chinese dissidents. Peace in Bosnia. Health care reform. Choose choice. ACT UP. More AIDS research."[26]

> *"When the powerful use their position to bully others we all lose."*

By the Hollywood awards season of 2017, after Donald Trump's election to the U.S. presidency, some entertainers seemed to regard it more as an obligation than an option to speak out, with both speech and symbols, as they picked up awards at the televised ceremonies for the Oscars, Grammys and Tonys. When actress Meryl Streep received a lifetime achievement award at the Golden Globes ceremony that year, she pointedly rebuked President Trump. Streep began her remarks by acknowledging her professional role and saying, "An actor's only job is to enter the lives of people who are different from us, and let you feel what that feels like. And there were many, many, many powerful performances this year that did exactly that. Breathtaking, compassionate work."

Then, without mentioning Trump's name, she departed from her role as an actress and chastised the president for mocking a journalist with a physical disability who covered a Trump campaign event. Streep said, "But there was one performance this year that stunned me. … It was that moment when the person asking to sit in the most respected seat in our country imitated a disabled reporter. Someone he outranked in privilege, power and the capacity to fight back. It kind of broke my heart when I saw it, and I still can't get it out of my head, because it wasn't in a movie. It was real life. And this instinct to humiliate, when it's modeled by someone in the public platform, by someone powerful, it filters down into everybody's life, because it kinda gives permission for other people to do the same thing. Disrespect invites disrespect, violence incites violence. And when the powerful use their position to bully others we all lose."[27]

> *"What I know for sure is that speaking your truth is the most powerful tool we all have."*

Soon, *The New York Times* observed, openly criticizing the president had become "standard fare at Hollywood-centric events."[28] At the 2018 Golden Globes ceremony, Oprah Winfrey received a lifetime achievement award, and she aimed her remarks at President Trump and other powerful men in film, television and politics who had been accused of sexual assault and sexual harassment by the many women who publicized their experiences through the Me Too movement. Winfrey said, "What I know for sure is that speaking your truth is the most powerful tool we all have. And I'm especially proud and inspired by all the women who have felt strong enough and empowered enough to speak up and share their personal stories. Each of us in this room are celebrated because of the stories that we tell. And this year we became the story. But it's not just a story affecting the entertainment industry. It's one that transcends any culture, geography, race, religion, politics or workplace." She concluded, "I want all the girls watching here and now to know that a new day is on the horizon!"[29] Winfrey's remarks so electrified the audiences attending the ceremony and watching on television that the next day, *The New York Times* reported how quickly people used the internet to agitate for her to run against President Trump in 2020.[30]

Entertainers over the years also became increasingly inclined to use awards ceremonies to speak out symbolically by wearing buttons, ribbons or specific colors of clothing that would show television viewers the entertainers' support for particular causes. In the 1990s, for instance, entertainers wore red ribbons to the Academy Awards to signify support for HIV and AIDS patients, and in 2003, entertainers wore dove-shaped peace pins to protest the war in Iraq.[31]

> "We are a canvas for no expression other than the words our
> voices have chosen to speak."

In 2018, actresses wore black clothing to the Golden Globes to speak out symbolically in support of the Me Too and Time's Up movements against sexual assault and abuse. Actress and director Amber Tamblyn explained in an essay before the awards ceremony, "I have often wondered what would happen if actresses stood in solidarity with a singular, powerful choice for just one night. What would that even look like? To uniformly reject our lifelong objectification and say: Enough. We belong to no one. We are a canvas for no expression other than the words our voices have chosen to speak. Tonight, you will see just such an experiment as myself and hundreds of women from the Time's Up movement will reject colorful gowns for black ones on the Golden Globes' red carpet and at related events across the country. Wearing black is not all we will be doing. We will be doing away with the old spoken codes in favor of communicating boldly and directly: What we are wearing is not a statement of fashion. It is a statement of action. It is a direct message of resistance. Black because we are powerful when we stand together with all women across industry lines. Black because we're starting over, resetting the standard. Black because we're done being silenced and we're done with the silencers. Tonight is not a mourning. Tonight is an awakening."[32]

In August 2020, four actresses used another high-profile venue to speak out with their political views. Because the highly infectious coronavirus pandemic then gripping the United States dictated that no-large scale public gatherings that might spread the virus should occur, the Democratic Party abandoned its traditional presidential nominating convention for a virtual event that included four nights of recorded video presentations and live-streamed speakers.

Convention planners notably did not choose politicians to host each night's proceedings. Instead, actresses familiar from long-running popular television shows—Eva Longoria, Kerry Washington, Tracee Ellis Ross and Julia Louis-Dreyfus—each hosted a night of the convention from a Los Angeles sound stage. Convention planners worked with the actresses to ensure that their on-air remarks allowed them to speak out with their own views, as well as the Democratic Party's views. *The New York Times* noted that these entertainers spoke on screen for significantly more minutes each night than did most of the politicians a party's convention usually is designed to showcase. While the actresses were not the first celebrities to participate in a presidential nominating convention, that they were afforded significant air time during the first-ever virtual convention was a notable example of the influential voice of celebrity in electoral politics.[33]

Another notable example of influential celebrity voice came on the virtual convention's final night, when Joseph Biden was feted as the Democrats' candidate for president. *The New York Times* noted that "one of the highest-profile athlete appearances at a political convention for either party in history" occurred when National Basketball Association superstar Stephen Curry and his wife Ayesha Curry, a popular cookbook author and television food show host, appeared in a three-minute prime-time video with their two young daughters to endorse Biden's candidacy.[34] CNN noted that the basketball star brought "real cultural cachet with young voters" to the candidacy of 77-year-old Biden,[35] who needed to secure the voters of citizens much younger than he. Biden quickly gained some 54,000 "likes" and 9,000 comments when he tweeted the Currys his thanks immediately after their video aired.[36] Other social media accounts also quickly liked and commented on the Currys' endorsement, causing MSN to report that "Twitter went ballistic" and "wild" in reaction to the upbeat video of the family.[37]

Stars' Freedom to Speak Out on Their Own Platforms

With the power to generate reactions such as those, celebrity athletes and entertainers show no signs they will speak out or become involved in politics less often. In fact, entertainers today are perhaps freer than ever to speak out about public issues. By the second half of the 20th century, movie and television studios' or powerful recording labels' abilities to tightly control stars' images and public comments had waned with the demise of rigid studio contracts that were the only way some entertainers previously could get work.[38]

By the early 21st century, stars' ability to control their work and images through digital platforms gave them added power. They could post photos, videos and comments directly to people who followed their social media channels, and thus stars with political positions potentially exerted more unfiltered influence on audiences than in previous eras. Political scientist Greg Rabidoux suggests, "Today, would-be politicos are far more public in their support for causes, charitable fundraising, and unabashed mixing of who they are and what they represent to their fans with their politics than ever before. What was once taboo, especially under the Hollywood studio system—taking on unpopular issues, inevitably dividing audiences over volatile issues like same-sex marriage, guns, stem-cell research, religion, war, unwed motherhood—has become rather standard now in Tinseltown."[39]

Public expression of views by stars has become standard in the sports world, too—and to potentially greater effect, given how much attention people pay to sports and how strongly they identify with their favorite athletes. Six of every 10 Americans (male or female, white or non-white, old or young, possessing college degrees or not) called themselves sports fans during the 2000s, according to a Gallup poll.[40] Even while those fans' live television viewing declined, as people downloaded content at their convenience and watched it on phones, tablets and computers, overall sports viewing remained strong. In 2017, for instance, 86 of the top 100 U.S. telecasts were live sports events, pre- and post-game shows, and analysis programs, and many of those telecasts focused on professional football.[41] That such strong viewership came in 2017 is notable not least because of the attention-getting headlines about sports, race and politics generated that year by the protest of National Football League quarterback Colin Kaepernick, who in 2016 and 2017 symbolically spoke out about racial injustice by taking a knee when the national anthem was played before his San Francisco 49ers games—and who repeatedly attracted the ire of President Donald Trump for doing so.[42]

Of course, Kaepernick's protest, which was an act of moral courage that cost him his NFL career when no team in the league would extend him a contract, was not the first costly stand against racial and social injustice by a prominent athlete. In 1967, heavyweight boxer Muhammad Ali was stripped of his title for refusing to serve in the U.S. Army during the Vietnam War, and in 1968, on a podium at the Olympic Games, U.S. sprinters Tommie Smith and John Carlos raised their fists in what was construed as a Black power salute and promptly were dismissed from the Olympics.[43]

"Athletes have always been political. But until recently they rarely possessed the means to explain themselves so directly to their fans," staff writer Hua Hsu observes in *The New Yorker* magazine.[44] Now, however, social media platforms give professional athletes a direct voice to express views to fans. Add to that the security that comes with the dollar value of many athletes' contracts and the knowledge that team owners need to attract the athletes' fans to live events and telecasts to keep the sports economy thriving, and the result is that "today's athletes possess a relative freedom when it comes to speaking their minds, taking risky political stands, or acting with a kind of blunt directness," Hsu notes.[45]

Many sports fans weren't especially surprised or upset in 2012 when National Basketball Association superstar LeBron James tweeted a photo of his Miami Heat teammates paying tribute to the young victim of a controversial murder they believed was racially motivated, or when NBA players in 2014 spoke out in such opposition to a team owner's racist remarks that he was forced to sell his ownership stake, or when James and three of his fellow NBA players in 2016 took the stage at the glitzy ESPY (Excellence in Sports Performance Yearly) awards in Los Angeles, like so many actors at Oscars and Emmys ceremonies, to speak out about racial injustice.[46] In 2016, some 50 years after he was ostracized for symbolically speaking out at the Olympics, John Carlos called athletes who speak out with words or gestures "an extension of a life-long relay."[47]

Connections Between Speaking Out and Racial Injustice

Four years later, athletes—and millions of other people—used words and gestures to speak out with historic fury about racial injustice after they were enraged by video that burst onto social media feeds and into news reports in late May 2020. The video showed a white police officer calmly kneeling for almost nine minutes on the neck of Black citizen George Floyd, who lay dying after his arrest for trying to use a counterfeit $20 bill in a Minneapolis, Minnesota, neighborhood store.[48] Black Lives Matter protests quickly emerged across the country, and star athletes and entertainers were seen in several cities joining crowds of protesters to speak out. On a Saturday two weeks after Floyd's killing, half a million people participated in Black Lives Matter demonstrations in 550 U.S. locations. Within a month, between 15 million and 26 million people in the United States had joined the protests. Data scientists said the number of marches and demonstrations plus the number of people participating in them made Black Lives Matter the largest protest movement in U.S. history.[49] Political protest scholars attributed these historic levels of participation to several factors. One factor was that scores of Americans' isolation at home to avoid contracting the coronavirus that had shut down the U.S. economy gave them time to watch the video of George Floyd's killing, to see news about who was responding to the injustice and to decide to join protests. Another factor was protest organizers' savvy use of social media to quickly spread details about when and where to protest. A third and perhaps surprising factor was broad public support for protesting from athletes and such sports organizations as the National Football League and NASCAR (the national stock car racing organization).[50] After years of dodging issues of race in the league, and edging Black quarterback Colin Kaepernick out of football after he protested racial injustice by kneeling during the national anthem before games, the NFL in 2020 had no choice but to support Black Lives Matter. A video featured football star after football star demanding the league "condemn racism and systematic oppression of black people" and "admit wrong in silencing our players from peacefully protesting." Within 24 hours, the NFL's commissioner released his own video announcing the league's support and acknowledging its past wrongdoing.[51]

Just weeks after George Floyd's killing, the landscape for speaking out by famous athletes and entertainers had shifted seismically. Most of us in the audience now expect these celebrities will speak out about serious public issues such as racial injustice, as they did in droves when they either joined the Black Lives Matter protests or used their social media platforms to amplify the Black Lives Matter message. We may wonder whether, with each of their acts of widely publicized and rapidly disseminated speech, these celebrity speakers represent increasing influence over complex public issues by figures who are not traditionally qualified as experts. In the dismal view of a critic such as the Pulitzer Prize–winning journalist Chris Hedges, we live in a society in which "our gods are celebrities"[52] and "knowledge is confused with how we are made to feel" by those celebrities.[53]

Concerns About Celebrity Influence on Public Issues

Concerns about whether celebrities exercise disproportionate influence on public life are not new. These concerns notably were raised by historian Daniel Boorstin in the early 1960s. Boorstin's influential book on imagery's power to shape culture, *The Image: A Guide to Pseudo-Events in America*, suggested celebrities were people famous for being famous, as opposed to people who were famous for accomplishing great things.[54] Therefore, if we look to celebrities who endorse candidates as our role models for voting, Boorstin suggested we are looking to imitations of a role model, rather than looking to a real role model who possesses expertise relevant to public affairs.

Scholars since Boorstin have extended his assessment, suggesting we equate celebrity with authority and expertise more than ever. Sociologist Frank Furedi notes, "The ascendancy of the celebrity is one of the distinctive features of late twentieth and early 21st century western culture," especially because our confidence in traditional authorities to serve as our sources of guidance has eroded.[55] People who don't trust government officials, religious leaders or academic experts to guide us may now trust celebrities, who "are often recycled as moral and political leaders who possess the authority to lecture people about how to conduct their life," Furedi writes.[56] If LeBron James or Taylor Swift, who seem "real" to us (despite how carefully they may curate their public images on social media), tell us via Twitter that we should vote, or post an Instagram photo of themselves in line at a polling place, perhaps we will be influenced to go stand in line at our own polling places and vote—maybe even for the candidates these celebrities told us they support. Are their endorsements ill-informed? Well, so what? Even if some of us deride these celebrity speakers, many of us seem disposed to allow celebrities the opportunity to influence us without much regard for expertise or consequence. "These quasi-charismatic figures do not have to justify their moral status," Furedi argues. "Nor does society hold celebrities to account. When we become disappointed in their performance we simply look for a fresh face and a more convincing personality."[57]

In other words, we don't much look for expertise when we look to famous people for cues about public issues—and we do look to them. Culturally, we seem preoccupied today with celebrities who command global attention for their views on a wide array of topics that may not relate to their perceived expertise or professional role. "The nature of constant, instantaneous and frenzied topic discussions over the global internet in the 21st century seems to have found a perfect match with the accelerating and expanding role of global celebrities," according to marketing scholars Chong Ju Choi and Ron Berger.[58]

> *"We're literally hunted EVERYDAY/EVERYTIME we step outside the comfort of our homes."*

For instance, in early May 2020, basketball stars James and Curry raised awareness among their millions of social media followers about a 25-year-old Black man named Ahmaud Arbery who was chased and fatally shot by two armed white men in February 2020 while he was out jogging through their Georgia neighborhood. After a video of the killing emerged months afterward, James and Curry expressed outrage that authorities had made no arrests or charges in the case. James was furious about yet another shooting of an unarmed Black man, posting to social media, "We're literally hunted EVERYDAY/EVERYTIME we step outside the comfort of our homes."[59] Curry called the killing "sickening" and implored his social media followers not to view the video but to respect and remember Arbery.[60] A *Washington Post* sports writer said the basketball stars' posts helped create "fury on social media,"[61] and an NBA writer said their posts "reinvigorated the outcry for the victim."[62] People who did not subscribe to the basketball stars' Instagram and Twitter feeds and see their messages nevertheless learned of their outrage over Arbery's killing because mainstream news organizations quickly deemed the athletes' statements worth reporting.

The Power of Social Media to Magnify Speaking Out

Like James and Curry, today's celebrities have more frequent and easier access to—and control over—the digital platforms they use to distribute messages instantly and globally. Thus, their opinions may be magnified, whether well-informed or false. In mid–2020, the photo-sharing social network Instagram boasted more than 1 billion monthly active users worldwide, including 105 million users in the United States, more than half of whom were 34 years or younger. Millions of those users followed athletes and entertainers, who owned nine of the top 10 most-followed Instagram accounts. (Instagram's own Instagram account occupied the top spot on the list.) The Portuguese footballer Cristiano Ronaldo attracted the largest Instagram following of any individual in the world, with 244.56 million followers. The remaining eight most-followed individuals were singers Ariana Grande, Selena Gomez and Beyonce, actor and professional wrestler Dwayne "The Rock" Johnson, reality television stars Kylie Jenner and her sister Kim Kardashian West, and footballers Leo Messi and Neymar.[63]

Twitter, which is primarily used to distribute 280-character "tweets" of text, has been described as "a near-instant access channel to celebrities," who use the platform to publicize their latest endeavors to fans "and work on their public image." In mid–2020, Twitter boasted 152 million daily active users worldwide, and with 110.09 million followers, former President Barack Obama topped the list of the 10–most followed Twitter accounts. With 80.46 million followers, President Donald Trump ranked eighth on the list. From the beginning of his term in office, President Trump habitually bypassed traditional news conferences and interviews to send "tweetstorms" of his views several times a day—and those tweetstorms frequently included President Trump's views about entertainers and athletes—making his Twitter feed a must-follow source of news about and from the president. The other individuals on Twitter's top 10 list were singers Katy Perry, Justin Bieber, Rihanna, Taylor Swift, Lady Gaga and Ariana Grande, and *The*

Ellen Show, a syndicated television daytime talk show hosted by comedian Ellen DeGeneres.[64]

Facebook, the world's most-used social media platform, boasted 2.7 billion monthly active users in mid–2020,[65] when six of its 10 most popular fan pages were occupied by brands (Facebook itself was first, followed by the electronics company Samsung, and further down the list, Coca-Cola and two European football clubs), but the four individuals who cracked Facebook's top 10 were entertainers and athletes: Footballer Cristiano Ronaldo, with 122.28 million Facebook fans, owned the most popular individual Facebook page, just as he owned the world's most popular individual Instagram account. He was followed on the Facebook list by singer Shakira, action movie star Vin Diesel and footballer Leo Messi.[66]

Obviously, then, social media followers are interested in the entertainers and athletes who are often their role models.[67] The scope and speed of social media platforms such as Instagram and Twitter provide entertainers and athletes who initially become famous through their artistic or physical talents more power than ever to expand their images and identities into all-encompassing international fame. Oprah Winfrey and Taylor Swift, to name two examples of stratospheric fame, are recognized around the world for their exceptional talents at telling stories through television, film and music, but they also are famous for social and cultural views they represent, whether they speak them from an awards ceremony stage or post them on an Instagram page.

In fact, societal attention to fame seems so pervasive today that we barely can imagine a world in which stars would refrain from speaking out about public issues. Just as we take it for granted that film, television, music and sports stars will endorse products or put their names on products of their own, we take it for granted they will speak out about public issues—and that their views on the issues are worth our consideration. It's not just those of us with Facebook fan pages who pay attention to athletes' and entertainers' views, either. If the politicians who carefully monitor every nuance of voter preference thought citizens didn't care about entertainers' or athletes' endorsements and views about public issues, the politicians likely wouldn't invite athletes to the White House or showcase entertainers as part of their campaigns.

The blurred lines between politics and entertainment—as evidenced by the serious consideration world leaders have given the rock musician Bono as an authority on poverty and debt relief—have existed for many years and perhaps are becoming blurrier. Today's opinion leaders (or "influencers," in the language of social media) may be highly skilled as athletes or entertainers, or famous for association with an event or other personality. Less often are they elected or appointed officials, or intellectual authorities. Today's opinion leaders are well-known people with widely available, even if carefully curated, public personas. We can define these public opinion leaders or influencers as people who have fans of some sort, whether those fans are voters, followers, donors, ticket buyers or collectors of memorabilia. We trust these figures, not the political authorities of old, and we have greater confidence now in celebrities who insert themselves into politics.[68] Sociologists Nick Couldry and Tim Markham assert that we simply expect that celebrity speakers will be "an essential component of public debate about the issues that require public resolution."[69]

Perhaps we like listening to star athletes speak out about issues because we watch them achieve fame through their physical accomplishments. Sports scholars David Andrews and Steven Jackson suggest that while we understand actors are playing scripted roles on stage or screen, we understand athletes as "*real* individuals participating in unpredictable contests," which gives them "an important veneer of authenticity"[70] that can make us likely to listen to them.

Perhaps we like listening to star entertainers speak out because they excel at casting issues into stories we easily understand. When Taylor Swift uses the storytelling power she usually brings to her music to tell us she was groped by a radio deejay, we get it: Sexual assault in the workplace can happen to anyone, no matter how influential, and it's not acceptable.

Celebrity Speakers Stand in for Citizens in Public Discourse

Today's influencers—these entertainers and athletes who speak out—increasingly stand in for citizens in the discourse about public issues. Sometimes, entertainers and athletes thrust themselves into the discourse, as James and Swift did in the 2020 presidential election season. Other times, news organizations and journalists thrust entertainers and athletes into the discourse. These celebrities often are available for journalists' interviews, thanks to the work of publicists, and these celebrities often are happy to comment on issues in ways they and their publicists hope will contribute to a public perception of gravitas. Yet speaking out only to enhance reputation is questionable, and not just on the celebrities' part. The motive of publicists who push unqualified or uninformed celebrities to speak out is an ethical question worth examining, as is the motive of journalists for interviewing these public figures. In too many cases, news reporters interview athletes or entertainers about a pressing public issue, rather than finding citizens who are affected by that issue. When they do so, reporters take an ethical bypass from the journalism practices that should offer voice to the voiceless.

Public discourse weighted toward celebrities' views can raise additional ethical concerns. After all, public issues are important for the health and welfare of our society. They are "things or issues regarded as of shared concern, not purely private concern, matters that in principle citizens *need* to discuss in a world of limited resources," according to Couldry and Markham.[71] When they speak out on serious public issues, celebrity speakers may stand in, although in an imbalanced or imperfect manner, for less powerful people with whom they have little experience.

By virtue of their privileged status, celebrity speakers possess "certain discursive power" that makes theirs "a voice above others, a voice that is channeled into the media systems as being legitimately significant," argues media scholar P. David Marshall.[72] Through their public speech, these celebrity speakers may teach the public, rightly or wrongly, about issues under consideration. Celebrity speakers may lack sufficient expertise on an issue to be the stand-in or teacher, yet they possess disproportionate power both to attract media attention, thus magnifying the weight of their views, and to influence opinions and behavior of the public.[73] Ethicist William F. May suggests that unlike teaching authorities of old—religious authorities and intellectuals—who possessed advanced training in the subjects about which they spoke publically, today's celebrities have become "unordained teaching authorities" who influence the public. May argues that these celebrities "have overshadowed religious leaders and academicians as the authorities to whom people turn for their views and cues."[74] Furthermore, Couldry and Markham suggest celebrities' views are so welcomed—indeed, expected—in the public arena today that they have become "an essential component of public debate about the issues that require public resolution."[75]

"If you are going to speak out, try to do your homework."

Singer and actor John Legend is an example of a celebrity who has become a regular contributor to public debate. Legend made entertainment history in 2018 when he became the first Black man to join the ranks of the only 15 entertainers who each have won an Emmy award, a Grammy award, an Oscar award and a Tony award.[76] While he was earning this superstar status as an entertainer, Legend also earned a reputation for speaking out about politics, especially through social media. A prolific user of Twitter, Legend has used the platform to advocate for such issues as criminal justice reform and voters' rights, as well as to campaign for Democratic Party candidates and to ferociously criticize Republican President Donald Trump. Legend's views have been frequent sources for media coverage, and in 2020 he gave an *Esquire* magazine interview that described an ethical duty to speak out. "It's an important part of our culture, especially black culture, for black artists to stand up for justice; to speak out," he said.[77] A few weeks later, Legend mused on Twitter about whether other performing artists should speak out about politics as much as he did. "Reporters always ask me if more artists should speak out about politics," Legend wrote. Then he answered, "I always say ummmmmm not necessarily." Legend went on to tweet his advice for artists who do want to speak out, and that advice seemed to echo the concerns of William F. May and other scholars about celebrities serving as teachers of the public. Legend advised his fellow artists: "If you are going to speak out, try to do your homework. Read about it. Talk to activists and organizers and people impacted. Be open to evolution and changing your mind. Be intentional and strategic. And think about the impact of your words on the real lives of real people."[78]

Legend seemed to understand the ethical duties he and his fellow celebrities should consider when speaking out. The next chapter further explains how speaking out is an ethical construct that celebrity athletes and entertainers should understand before they speak out about important public topics.

2

What Counts as Speaking Out?

Defining the Ethical Construct

As a high school senior, Stephen Curry was a self-described "under-rated" basketball player given a "courtesy" opportunity to try out for the Virginia Tech team only because his father played college basketball there.[1] Ultimately snubbed by college basketball powerhouses such as Virginia Tech that he had hoped to attend, Curry enrolled at Davidson College, a small North Carolina liberal arts school.[2] As a sophomore, Curry led the Davidson Wildcats on a national attention-getting run to the NCAA tournament's "elite eight," where they lost to the perennial champion Kansas Jayhawks. As a junior, Curry led all NCAA players in scoring points per game and decided to forego his senior year to enter the National Basketball Association draft.

At age 20, Stephen Curry was a "slender, baby-faced prospect" picked in the NBA draft's seventh place by the Golden State Warriors.[3] Almost no one would have predicted that by the time he entered his early 30s, Curry would be "a transcendent figure on the NBA landscape" who "reshaped the way basketball is played."[4] Almost no one also would have predicted that over that period, Curry would become a powerful speaker for public issues he deemed important. Stephen Curry's career in the NBA is both a story of basketball prowess derived from being called "underrated" and a story of public advocacy derived from his faith and values. This chapter uses this second aspect of the Stephen Curry story to illustrate the elements of speaking out that make it an ethical construct worth examining.

At age 28, Curry cemented his place among the NBA elite, becoming the first player in league history unanimously elected its Most Valuable Player. Curry earned the honor by winning both the NBA fan vote and all 130 votes from the U.S. and Canadian sports journalists eligible to vote for the winner. Curry's first MVP title came the year before, so his unanimous selection in 2016 made him one of just 11 players in the 61 years since the award's inception to win consecutive MVP titles.[5] The award vaulted Curry into the company of basketball legends such as Bill Russell, Wilt Chamberlain, Kareem Abdul-Jabbar, Larry Bird, Magic Johnson, Michael Jordan and LeBron James.[6]

His success also vaulted Curry, who led the Golden State Warriors to three NBA championships in his first decade in the league, to the top of the list of best-paid NBA players. The Golden State Warriors offered him a new record-setting five-year $201 million contract, which at the time was the biggest deal in NBA history.[7] No doubt the Warriors organization was willing to pay a stratospheric salary for Curry because his skill in shooting three-point baskets from far outside positions on the court was transforming the way professional basketball is played. No doubt the team also appreciated Curry's popularity with millions of fans, who liked both his ability to make three-point baskets and his determination early on to transcend the sport's view that he was too small to compete successfully at basketball's highest level.

"I can do all things."

After the two MVP awards, three league championships and six all-star game appearances, one social media list ranked Curry as the second-most popular player in the NBA, at least in terms of his social media following. (The only current player more popular was the NBA's "King" LeBron James.) At the end of 2019, Curry's 42 million social media followers included 21.1 million Instagram users, 12.7 million Twitter users and 8.2 million Facebook users.[8] On his social media platforms, Curry emphasized more than his status as an elite professional basketball player. On Twitter, for instance, his profile first described him as a Christian and family man: "Believer. Husband to @ayeshacurry, father to Riley, Ryan and Canon, son, brother." Next, Curry's profile listed his NBA team and his college alma mater: "Golden State Warriors guard. Davidson Wildcat." The profile continued with another reference to his Christian faith: "Philippians 4:13," which Christians worldwide know as the Bible verse "I can do all things through Christ who strengthens me." The profile ended with the hash tag #IWILL, an advertising slogan linked to Curry's endorsement deal with Under Armour, the sports and fitness shoe and apparel retailer.[9]

Fans liked Curry for several of the reasons outlined in his Twitter profile, not just for his basketball prowess. Many fans liked his public emphasis on family and faith: His wife was a successful cookbook author, television cooking show host and restaurateur; his father was a 16-year NBA player; his brother also played in the NBA; his mother was known to send him uplifting scriptures in text messages before and after his games; and his adorable young children were seen in news reports, on magazine covers and in social media messages, such as the videos of his two-year-old daughter charming sports writers at post-game news conferences during the 2015 NBA finals.[10]

Some of Curry's popularity—not just with fans, but also with the NBA and advertisers who sought his endorsements—stemmed from his ability to avoid public missteps with alcohol, drugs or sexual impropriety that sometimes befall highly paid young professional athletes in major media markets such as the San Francisco Bay Area the Golden State Warriors call home. In his early years in the NBA, Curry seemed to focus his public image on his wife and the children they soon had, as well as on his Christian faith and the lucrative endorsement deal he made with Under Armour for his own line of basketball shoes.

Never shy about communicating his Christian faith, whether through spoken words or symbolic gestures such as raising his arm toward heaven after making a basket, Curry began writing Bible verses, especially Philippians 4:13, on his athletic shoes before he took the court for Davidson College basketball games. He continued writing on his shoes in the NBA, where television cameras often magnified his and other players' shoe-based messages. When he signed a deal with Under Armour, Curry and the company linked his Christian beliefs with the shoes that carried his name.[11] Incorporating scripture into Curry's shoe line worked well with Under Armour's "ambition to infuse its products with meaning—with stories about the histories and traits of the celebrity athletes they were created for—in hopes of deepening its connection to the athletes and inspiring customers to buy more gear."[12] Several versions of Curry shoes sold to the public by Under Armour were manufactured with a Philippians 4:13 "I can do all things" message somewhere on the shoe, and for Curry himself, the company made one-of-a-kind versions of his shoes leaving a space purposely blank for his scripture writing before games.[13]

> *"It'll hopefully inspire people to find something that drives them."*

Curry told a reporter he wrote scripture on his shoes as "a mantra that I live by and something that drives me every single day." He said he intended his scripture display to speak to basketball watchers: "It'll hopefully inspire people to find something that drives them, whether that's a verse or some other motivating force that keeps you hungry and keeps you driven. That's mine, and you can pick whatever yours is and let that drive you, too, as you continue with basketball or whatever field you're in in your life."[14]

Clearly, Curry wrote scripture on his shoes to influence people besides himself, but as his fame grew, Curry became known more for silence than speech on topics beyond basketball. A national basketball writer once observed, "Stephen Curry isn't exactly known for speaking his mind. In fact, a case could be made that he is as adept from beyond the three-point line as he is at avoiding controversy away from the court."[15] Another sports columnist suggested Curry deliberately decided when to speak out, especially with regard to his Christian faith, writing: "There is a reason you don't hear Stephen Curry preaching into every microphone in his face. It's a calculated decision to elude religious rhetoric like he does aggressive defenders. He is fine with the subtle gestures—scriptures on his shoe, points upward after baskets, blessed being a regular in his vocabulary—and letting how he lives do the talking. He will answer when asked, dialogue person-to-person. But Curry much prefers being an example over a spokesperson."[16]

When, as a young NBA player, Curry did begin to speak out on a serious public issue, he endorsed a cause no one with compassion for fellow human beings could oppose: the prevention of a deadly disease. At Davidson College, Curry's roommate had organized a "Buzz Kill" basketball tournament that introduced Curry to efforts to curb malaria around the world.[17] Malaria, which is transmitted by tiny mosquitoes that bite at night, is particularly devastating in sub-Saharan Africa, where some 300 million people lack insect-resistant bed nets that would safeguard them. Malaria also is especially cruel to children younger than five years, who comprise 70 percent of the more than 429,000 people worldwide who die from the disease annually.[18]

Starting in 2012, Curry donated to the United Nations Foundation "Nothing But Nets" program three insect-resistant malaria bed nets for each three-point shot he sank in an NBA game. Curry became a "Nothing But Nets" program ambassador and traveled to Tanzania to deliver bed nets to children and families.[19] In late 2017, Curry and his partners at Under Armour issued a limited edition Curry sneaker featuring a pattern of nets, and he donated a bed net for every pair sold.[20] When he celebrated his 30th birthday in 2018, Curry issued a Facebook challenge to raise $30,000 for the purchase of bed nets. He raised more than $45,000 in less than 24 hours after issuing his challenge,[21] and he ultimately raised more than $82,000 for bed nets, becoming the first professional athlete to raise money for a non-profit organization using a Facebook Fundraiser.[22] By the end of the 2017–2018 NBA season, Curry's record-setting number of three-point baskets meant he had donated some 5,400 bed nets to "Nothing But Nets."[23]

Curry's advocacy for malaria prevention afforded him an opportunity for speaking out that raised his profile beyond basketball. In 2015, just months before he won his first NBA MVP title, Curry was invited to the White House to make a short talk about his "Nothing But Nets" work. Rear Admiral Timothy Ziemer, who chaired President Barack Obama's malaria initiative, introduced Curry to Obama's staff and the journalists who were there to report on Curry's talk. Ziemer thanked Curry for his advocacy, saying, "When someone of his stature and reputation steps up and not only articulates the problem of malaria, but also provides time and resources, it sends a resounding message." After his talk, Curry was invited into the Oval Office, where he met President Obama and discussed the malaria issue with him—before talking hoops with the president, a well-known college and professional basketball fan.[24] Subsequently, the men "formed a close friendship over their shared passion for sports and civic engagement."[25]

A year later, Curry appeared in two public service videos, one with President Obama to promote his "My Brother's Keeper" campaign for community role models to mentor young people, and one with First Lady Michelle Obama to promote her campaign for better health through fresh food options.[26]

Four Ethically Salient Characteristics of Speaking Out

These early choices by Curry about speaking out on public issues, such as preventing malaria, mentoring young people and promoting healthy eating, illustrate what separates speaking out from other forms of public expression by celebrity athletes and entertainers. Speaking out is not chatter, gossip, casual comment or commercial endorsement. Speaking out may be accomplished with words, gestures or symbols, but whatever its form, the concept of speaking out means speaking one's mind in the best sense of that phrase.

Four ethically salient characteristics distinguish speaking out, and these characteristics may ethically oblige the speaker to perform moral justification for speaking out:

1. *The speaker's role*: When a celebrity athlete or entertainer speaks out, the speaker transcends or defies the public's role-related expectations for the speaker. Audience members, especially those who are the speaker's fans, typically expect the entertainer or athlete to continue to demonstrate the artistic or athletic skill that generated his or her fame and to communicate about subjects directly related to that skill. Speaking out does not occur if a professional athlete such as Stephen Curry is interviewed about his own basketball performance or his teammates' or opponents' play. Speaking out does not occur if Curry posts a social media message congratulating a fellow player or commending a video clip of an outstanding play. Audiences fully expect professional athletes to speak in pre- or post-game interviews and news conferences, and to actively communicate on social media platforms.

Nor is a professional athlete such as Curry speaking out when he is paid to endorse a product or service. Audiences fully expect professional athletes to appear in advertising messages and promotional campaigns touting the shoe and apparel lines that bear their names and earn them money, but audiences may not expect the athlete or entertainer to speak out about serious public issues that do not seem directly related to the sport or the art form. In effect, when audiences believe the speaker's primary ethical duty is to perform athletically or artistically, the speaker who upends the audience's role-related expectations may be ethically obliged to justify assuming the new and unrelated role.

2. *The speaker's subject*: The speaker addresses an issue of significant social or political concern to the public. Speaking out is speech about weighty societal topics—human rights, conflict and peacemaking, public health and education, racial and gender equity are a few examples—and the speech ought to be less about the speaker's self-interests and more about the public's shared concerns. The speaker is of course philosophically and legally free to express controversial views on serious subjects. However, depending on the subject's gravity, and the related possibilities of misunderstanding the subject's complexity or offending the audience's sensibilities, the speaker may be morally required to justify speech that is potentially harmful to the subject or the audience.

3. *The speaker's intent*: The speaker intends to interject herself or himself into the public conversation and thinking about a social or political issue of concern to the public. Speaking out is not accidental speech. Speaking out is a deliberate choice. The athlete or entertainer must accept that choosing to speak out may create some risk for maintaining either or both reputation and livelihood (and, in some instances, may create some risk to the livelihoods of all the people whose incomes depend on the celebrity's economic success). In speaking out about some especially controversial or sensitive subjects, the speaker may not only need to justify taking on risk, but may need to deploy real moral courage in defying risk to speak out.

4. *The speaker's platform*: The speaker uses a public platform or venue to speak out. Speaking out is not using the speaker's influence to speak privately with authorities or experts on the topic, although private speech also may be used effectively and ethically by athletes and entertainers advocating for a cause. In speaking out, the speaker acknowledges using a platform or venue or occasion often intended for something other than social or political speech. Thus, the speaker's use of the platform may compound the audience's role-related expectations for the occasion. Over the years, a Hollywood awards show's television

audience has come to expect some entertainers will use the stage for political remarks, but until recently, a crowd of sports fans usually did not expect a basketball arena's floor to become the site of a protest about police brutality. The greater the departure from a platform's typical use, the greater the need for the speaker to justify creating that departure.

Stephen Curry's Speaking Out as Ethically Salient

In Curry's case, when he began to advocate for malaria prevention, he moved at least slightly outside the public's role-related expectations for a professional basketball player. The public primarily expects someone in Curry's role to help his team win NBA games. The public is not surprised these days when professional athletes endorse causes, especially causes related to public health or education, but the public typically does not demand athletes take up those causes. Therefore, Curry's advocacy for malaria prevention, which is a cause almost anyone could support, placed him slightly outside the primary role-related expectations for a professional basketball player, but not dramatically so. His participation in the Obama videos moved him slightly further outside the public's role-related expectations, not because of the subject of the causes endorsed in the videos, but because they were causes promoted by an obviously partisan president and first lady with whom Curry was willing to associate. Therefore, Curry at least minimally met the first ethically salient characteristic of speaking out: the speaker's placement into a different role.

Preventing malaria, a deadly disease that victimizes children in some of the world's poorest nations, is an obviously significant issue of social and political concern to world citizens, so Curry's advocacy on the topic complied with the second ethically salient characteristic of speaking out: the speech's serious social or political subject. Curry's advocacy via videos for President Obama's "My Brother's Keeper" project that focused on finding role models for young men of color and for Michelle Obama's initiative to improve the nutrition of young people both also met the second ethically salient characteristic of speaking out. The plight of young Americans, especially those disadvantaged by race and income disparities, is a topic obviously worth public attention.

Curry did not accidentally become affiliated with malaria prevention. He chose to announce publicly he would donate insect-resistant bed nets for baskets he scored in NBA games, he chose to travel to Africa to distribute bed nets, he chose to speak about his work to a gathering of White House advisors, and he chose to use a Facebook platform to raise money for bed nets on the occasion of his 30th birthday. Thus, Curry met the third ethically salient characteristic of speaking out: the speaker's deliberate intent to enter public discourse about the serious public issue. Nor did Curry accidentally participate in President Obama's and Mrs. Obama's videos. As an experienced subject of news coverage and veteran of public appearances, he knew cameras were rolling. Curry willingly clowned around with President Obama in the "My Brother's Keeper" video. Likewise, Curry willingly participated in Michelle Obama's video on healthy eating, which featured Curry, his wife and Mrs. Obama waggling turnips grown in the first lady's White House garden.[27] A media-savvy professional athlete such as Curry had to know the videos would attract news coverage and social media attention. Speaking out on these relatively inoffensive yet important causes—preventing malaria, mentoring young people and encouraging good nutrition—required little if any moral courage on Curry's part, but demonstrating moral courage is not required to verify the speaker's intent. The speaker's intent to enter the public conversation is sufficient.

Curry also met the fourth ethically salient characteristic of speaking out: the speaker's use of a public platform. A professional athlete who routinely played in major media markets and who was well on his way to an MVP season in the NBA, as Curry was when he began speaking out about causes important to the Obamas, would know every day that he was the subject of sports news coverage. He also would know accepting an invitation to speak at the White House occupied by a basketball-obsessed president would result in national news coverage in venues beyond sports pages and sportscasts. Curry's talk about malaria prevention to Obama's advisors did just that. So, too, did his participation in the Obama videos.

As Curry's behavior illustrates, then, speaking out is public, it is intentional, and it may blur established role boundaries. Examining the second half of Curry's first decade in the NBA further illustrates speaking out as an act that may raise ethical questions and require moral justification.

In February 2016, after the Golden State Warriors won the 2015 NBA championship, their first league title in 40 years, Curry and his teammates visited the White House for what has become a traditional rite of passage for college and professional sports teams that win national championships. By then, Curry had been tagged publicly as President Obama's "friend," perhaps because they had golfed together during the president's previous summer vacation, but nothing about the White House visit could be characterized as speaking out by Curry. The president teased Curry about being "a pretty good shooter" who had to cede the limelight to his daughter Riley at news conferences after the championship series games.[28] All Curry had to say for the cameras and journalists was that during his 2015 White House visit to discuss malaria prevention, he had asked to see the East Room, so he could be prepared to enter the setting where championship visits with the president typically occurred.[29] This sort of public appearance by a public figure in a role related to his fame may involve public comments to journalists or observers, but that doesn't make it an act of speaking out. This occasion was innocuous, focusing on a basketball-fanatic president praising a group of exemplary athletes.

> *"That's not the way that I'll do it, but I support him and his attempt to start a conversation."*

On later occasions, however, the Golden State Warriors' NBA championships would present powerful instances of speaking out about race and politics by Curry and his teammates. About six months after the team's visit to the White House, Curry endorsed President Obama's former Secretary of State, former New York Senator and former First Lady Hillary Clinton, in her 2016 campaign for president. Curry issued his endorsement as a one-word answer—"Hillary"—to a moderator's short "Hillary or Trump?" question during a technology conference panel. One journalist called it "about the most understated endorsement possible of Hillary Clinton."[30]

Curry, who appeared at the conference to promote his own business investments in the technology industry, also answered a question about his fellow San Francisco professional athlete Colin Kaepernick, the National Football League quarterback who was generating controversy for kneeling when the national anthem was played before San Francisco 49ers games. Curry said he would keep standing for the anthem before Golden State Warriors games, but he endorsed Kaepernick's use of symbolic speech to draw attention to racial injustice: "That's not the way that I'll do it, but I support him and his attempt to start a conversation and continue a conversation to try to better a terrible situation," Curry said, noting he had "been part of certain conversations off the grid in finding different ways to make our community better, especially for African Americans."[31] Both Curry's one-word endorsement of Hillary Clinton's candidacy for president and his longer comments about Kaepernick's race-related protest were obvious acts of speaking out that transcended Curry's role as professional basketball player and voluntarily used a public venue in which political speech was not expected or required.

> *"Nothing but respect!"*

Unlike other athletes and entertainers—notably NBA super-star LeBron James—Curry did not campaign with Clinton, but his political views became more public in November 2016. Late on election night, when Republican Donald Trump was declared victorious, the Democratic Party activist, author and CNN commentator Van Jones expressed despair. He

told CNN viewers the election outcome had been swayed by racial preju-
dice against outgoing President Obama, saying, "This was a white-lash. This
was a white-lash against a changing country. It was a white-lash against a
black president, in part." Jones also said Trump's victory was a "deeply painful moment" for many Black people, including Jones.[32] Subsequent news
reports noticed that "non-political, uncontroversial family man" Stephen
Curry agreed with Jones' assessment when Curry proclaimed on Twitter,
"Van Jones … nothing but respect!"[33]

Curry's endorsement of Clinton and his tweet of disappointment at
President Trump's election are obvious acts of speaking out. They placed
Curry in a role apart from his generally expected one, they were about an
issue of political significance for the public, they were intentional inter-
jections into public discourse about the country's future, and they used
public venues that were almost certain to be amplified by news coverage
of the messages. They also seemed to forecast the possibility of more overt
political speaking out from Curry, although on some topics he remained
circumspect.

> *"I've got a platform and I've got to be able to use it and take it
> all in stride."*

The politics of discrimination on the basis of sexual identity was one
of those topics. In 2016, the NBA revoked its decision to play the league's
2017 All-Star Game in Curry's home town of Charlotte, North Carolina.
The president and general manager of Curry's Golden State Warriors
team was Rick Welts, who was called by *USA Today* "the most prominently openly gay NBA executive" and "considered the father of the modern All-Star Game."[34] Welts influenced the NBA to abandon Charlotte after
North Carolina adopted House Bill 2, which *USA Today* described as an
"anti–LGBTQ law that required people to use bathrooms of their birth gender and omitted gay and transgender people from discrimination protections."[35] The decision was a costly blow to North Carolina, not just because
of the revenue lost when the NBA pulled its All-Star Game and related fes-
tivities, but because the league's decision influenced the NCAA and other
college sports organizations to yank their events from the state, which historically had hosted and profited from many marquee basketball events.[36]

Because Curry grew up in North Carolina and played college basketball there, and because his team's executive was instrumental in organizing the boycott, news reporters logically asked Curry's opinion about
the politics of the All-Star Game. His response was measured. "I think it's
unfortunate for our city and our state to be under the microscope with HB2
and how it's unfolded," he said. "I'm all for equal and fair rights and treatment for everybody. Until it gets addressed, until some changes are made,

this could be a recurring theme in North Carolina."[37] Curry also expressed regret that the basketball tournaments that "would bring so much joy and support to the city" were being moved to other states, but he admitted, "I don't have any answers" about whether North Carolina should amend its law. He went on to tell a reporter he was "still getting used to the idea" that his views were important enough for reporters to ask him about politicized controversies such as the North Carolina boycott. Now that he was a two-time league MVP and his team had won its first NBA championship in 40 years, Curry acknowledged he had obtained a platform for speaking out. He was learning how to use his platform to speak out appropriately, he said: "Other than being under a huge microscope, I don't see it as a negative at all and I am not too sensitive to not think I can say a certain thing, or have a certain belief, and meet some resistance. Or even face certain repercussions. But it is different, because four, five years ago, what I said, nobody cared. It's kind of weird just because I hit a bunch of shots, I've got a platform and I've got to be able to use it and take it all in stride."[38]

Curry's measured perspective on the North Carolina boycott was not enough for some observers, who wanted him to speak out more forcefully against the state law. For instance, one sports writer observed Curry had achieved "global heights of popularity" with his basketball skill, marketing influence and social media presence, which were "testaments to his dogged work ethic, his love of family, his charity, and the deep Christian faith that binds them all together." However, the writer chided Curry, saying his "lack of a concrete answer" to questioning about the North Carolina boycott was "unfocused" and failed to uphold his reputation "for being a breaker of barriers" and "a paragon for the underdog."[39] Essentially, the writer assigned Curry an ethical duty to speak out on a controversial public topic and even went so far as to suggest that because Curry played basketball for a team located in the San Francisco Bay Area, "one of the most pro–LGBT rights regions of the country," he had a special obligation to speak out in opposition to the North Carolina law.[40] But none of Curry's roles—as an NBA player, a shoe seller, a self-identified Christian and a Black man—categorically required him to express a specific position on a public issue. Speakers have the legal freedom to speak out, but their speech cannot be ethically compelled.

"I agree with that description, if you remove the 'et.'"

By 2017, Curry appeared confident of his ability to use his speaking-out platform on topics that mattered to him. Early that year, Kevin Plank, the chairman of the Under Armour athletic apparel and equipment company, gave an interview in which he called President Donald Trump a "bold," "decisive" and "pro-business president" who was "a real asset for this country."[41] As one of the most prominent professional athletes with an Under Armour deal, Curry was asked for his reaction to the Under Armour chairman's description of Trump as an "asset." Curry said, "I agree with that description, if you remove the 'et.'"[42]

That Curry could effectively call the U.S. president an "ass," and do so while disagreeing with the company that paid him handsomely to help sell its products, reflected Curry's power, as a *Washington Post* journalist observed: "The fortunes of a company and its endorsers are closely tied. Curry owns equity in Under Armour as part of his lucrative UA endorsement deal. His shoe is key to the company's success."[43] The journalist went on to point out that Curry's security as "one of the best and most marketable athletes in the world" meant he could candidly share his view of President Trump with little fear of jeopardizing his Under Armour deal; both Curry and the company had to be know he had "innumerable other companies, particularly athletic footwear and apparel companies, waiting in line for him to endorse their brand."[44]

In that context, Curry's act of speaking out about the president involved relatively little risk. Reportedly, however, Curry had managed even that small risk by engaging in some private speaking that suggested careful thought before his public speaking out. According to *The Washington Post,* "By the time he'd said it ['if you remove the "et"'], he'd spent time on the phone with Plank and others at Under Armour, and the company quickly put out a statement explaining it was a diverse one that respects people from all walks of life."[45]

The Golden State Warriors won their second NBA championship with Curry in June 2017. Asked shortly afterward if he would join the team in a traditional celebratory visit to the White House, Curry said he did not want to visit with President Trump, and by autumn, Curry's dim view of the president's politics became better known. In August, President Trump was criticized soundly for his belated and tepid condemnation of a violent white supremacist rally in Charlottesville, Virginia, during which a counter-protestor was killed by a neo–Nazi who drove his car into the crowd.[46] Among those objecting to the president's response to the Charlottesville violence was Under Armour's chairman Kevin Plank, who just months before had called President Trump an asset to business. In the wake of Charlottesville, Plank resigned from the president's advisory panel on American manufacturing.

"I don't want to go. That's my nucleus of my belief."

In September, as the Golden State Warriors prepared for a new season, reporters again asked Curry if he would join the team at the White House to celebrate its championship. Curry unequivocally said no: "I don't want to go. That's my nucleus of my belief."[47] He mentioned President Trump's disparaging remarks about Black athletes' protests of racially motivated violence and injustice, and added, "We're trying to do what we can using our platform and using our opportunities to shed light on that. That's where I stand on it. I don't think us not going to the White House will miraculously make everything better. But that's my opportunity to voice that."[48] A sports columnist wrote of Curry's remarks about President Trump and the White House visit, "What's notable here is not only Curry being willing to speak about this forcefully, but to do so in a direct affront to President Trump, whose administration has proved to be about as divisive as any issue roiling the nation. It's a stark change from how Curry has historically comported himself. It's also one that everyone, given the nature of the topic, will notice."[49]

President Trump noticed. Early on the morning after Curry's remarks, before the Golden State Warriors could hold that day's team meeting for players to decide about going to the White House, the president took to his Twitter account to un-invite the team and to single out Curry. President Trump tweeted, "Going to the White House is considered a great honor for a championship team. Stephen Curry is hesitating, therefore invitation is withdrawn!"[50]

If Curry had any doubts about the heights to which his influence and views had been elevated, surely they were eliminated after President Trump's message, which "ignited an early morning storm" at Curry's house.[51] Curry told reporters it was "surreal, to be honest,"[52] to awaken and learn about the president's tweet, which a San Francisco Bay Area sports writer said "reverberated around the sports world" and made Curry the subject of thousands of social media comments that "streamed in on Twitter as fast as the Warriors' pace of play."[53]

Commenters heatedly agreed and disagreed with Curry's views about President Trump, politics and race.[54] Among the commenters agreeing with Curry were the NBA's top current player, LeBron James, whose tweet called the president a "bum" and pointed out Curry had said since June he did not want to visit the Trump White House.[55] Adam Silver, the NBA's commissioner, also weighed in. He expressed regret that President Trump's tweet meant Curry and his Golden State Warriors teammates would not get to state their views in person to the president, but Silver said, "I am proud of our players for taking an active role in their communities and continuing to speak out on critically important issues."[56]

Finding themselves unwelcome at the White House, the Golden State Warriors issued a statement saying, "In lieu of a visit to the White House, we have decided that we'll constructively use our trip to the nation's capital in February to celebrate equality, diversity and inclusion—the values that we embrace as an organization."[57] During their Washington visit, team members accompanied school children on a visit to the National Museum of African American History and Culture.[58]

> *"People want to hear what you have to say. We shouldn't shy away from it."*

When they won the NBA championship again in 2018, "there was less drama" about the Golden State Warriors' decision to eschew the Trump White House.[59] The team's Washington visit emphasized "community outreach" projects aimed at helping local young people. Curry visited the historically Black Howard University to screen a documentary film about the racially motivated killing of nine Black people at a Charleston, South Carolina, church in 2015. The film was the first effort from a media production company Curry had established. At a question-and-answer session at the film screening, he discussed how his Christian faith influenced his view of the death penalty for a crime such as that committed in Charleston. "Just in terms of what I believe in humanity and the redeeming qualities of my lord and savior and what that means for somebody going through the worst, nothing's impossible," he said, and added, "There are situations where an individual can be redeemed or be healed."[60]

By then, whether on perennially controversial public topics such as race, crime or religion, Stephen Curry, the 30-year-old two-time MVP, seemed to have become fully confident in his ability to speak out and be heard. He seemed comfortable interjecting himself into public discourse about serious public issues—and perhaps to accept speaking out as akin to an ethical duty for a professional athlete of his stature. During the Howard University film screening session, he said: "Athletes in general, especially in the NBA, guys are educated. They know what they're talking about. They know what they believe. And there's a reason when you say something there are headlines. People want to hear what you have to say. We shouldn't shy away from it."[61] He went on to explain, "We have a league that supports each other. We have a commissioner that supports us in using our voice to speak for those who can't speak for themselves. And I think this era of athlete is unafraid to be unapologetically themselves, whatever that means."[62]

Ethicist Patrick Plaisance defines ethics "as a form of inquiry concerned with the process of finding rational justifications for our actions when the values that we hold come into conflict."[63] Ethical reasoning is the process in which we resolve those conflicts of equally compelling moral principles, duties and loyalties. In the instance of speaking out about White House visits and President Donald Trump, Stephen Curry balanced his professional role-related duty to effectively represent and play for his team and employer, the Golden State Warriors, with the conflicting moral principle of personally telling the truth as he saw it about politics, race and discrimination. In speaking out, Curry balanced the conflicting professional role and personal principle by clearly expressing his views about the president in a calm and rational manner that avoided inflammatory language and did not incite further argument.

Subsequently, Curry continued using his status as an influential and admired athlete to speak out more and more forcefully about issues of racism and injustice. The next chapter uses his example to illustrate ethical limits to speaking out, especially with regard to the issues of power, privilege and harm that often surround powerful speakers.

3

What Ethical Issues Surround Speaking Out?

*Exploring Power, Privilege,
Harm and Justification*

A decade into his career with the National Basketball Association's Golden State Warriors, two-time league Most Valuable Player Stephen Curry "remained gleefully free of controversy."[1] Off the basketball court, Curry was known for—and spoke out about—his Christian faith, his wife and her career in the restaurant and television food world, their adorable young children, and his popular Under Armour athletic shoe line. U.S. president Donald Trump had targeted Curry in 2017 for publicly and pointedly speaking out about his unwillingness to visit the White House to celebrate the Golden State Warriors' league championship, because he disagreed with President Trump's stances on racially motivated violence and injustice. However, Curry's generally measured comments on such public issues kept his reputation untarnished, his fan base loyal and his huge social media following intact.

"I don't want to just be noise."

The sports network ESPN described Curry as speaking out thoughtfully about select political, social and religious views "while navigating the rarefied air of being one of the most recognizable athletes on the planet."[2] Unlike other athletes whose intemperate or thoughtless comments sometimes landed them in public hot water, Curry seemed to stay out of speaking trouble, not least because of his reticence to comment on topics not closely related to his experiences as a professional athlete, a Christian, a husband and father, and as a Black man concerned about racial and social inequities. In a November 2017 "Player's Tribune" essay, Curry articulated self-awareness about "what it means to have a platform." He vowed, "I don't want to just be noise." Instead, he said he wanted to use his platform "to talk about real issues, that are affecting real people."[3]

His essay portrayed Curry as a public figure who understood the power of his speaking-out platform, and he seemed equipped to use it responsibly—until the day about a year later when Curry said he did not believe the U.S. space agency had landed astronauts on the moon.[4] The almost immediate critical response of basketball fans, journalists, historians and scientists to Curry's denial of U.S. space history illustrates ethical concerns about power, privilege and harm that surround speaking out by celebrity athletes and entertainers. To examine those concerns and how they necessitate ethical justification for speaking out, this chapter compares the ethical lapse in Curry's speaking out about U.S. space history with the ethical strength of Curry's speaking out about the coronavirus pandemic that devastated the United States some two years later.

The First Amendment Context for Speaking Out

The First Amendment to the Constitution legally safeguards the right of all U.S. citizens, whether they are famous or not, to speak out, especially about public issues. Free expression is an essential element of representative democracy, which succeeds only if citizens are able to express themselves—and to hear others express themselves—on issues of shared concern without fear of government reprisal. In its landmark 1964 First Amendment ruling *New York Times vs. Sullivan*, the U.S. Supreme Court upheld "a profound national commitment to the principle that debate on public issues should be uninhibited, robust, and wide-open."[5] All citizens may engage in the democratic process by expressing themselves and listening to others, before making decisions about what government should do on citizens' behalf. All citizens, including basketball star Stephen Curry, legally *can* speak out, but ethically *should* they? When athletes and entertainers use their legal rights as citizens to speak out, what corresponding ethical responsibilities do these influential public figures have for the social, cultural, political or financial effects of their comments on other, often less powerful, people, institutions or causes? Curry's comment denying the U.S. moon landings shows how speaking out may become an unethical use of the power and privilege public figures enjoy, may create harm for issues and audiences, and may require moral justification by speakers. By contrast, Curry's comments about the coronavirus pandemic show how speaking out may become an ethical use of power and privilege to raise awareness about a crucial issue and prevent harm to audiences.

"We ever been to the moon?"

Curry's comment about the moon landings came in December 2018, when he joined three fellow NBA players and a moderator on a podcast interview program called "Winging It," which *The Guardian* reported was "more of a hang session than a proper interview" whose purpose was "to give listeners a sense of conversations that players actually have when scoop-hungry reporters aren't parsing their every word."[6] A bit more than halfway through the program, when the "hang session" topics had ranged from up-and-coming basketball players to favorite golf clubs to random thoughts about the sounds dinosaurs might make, Curry abruptly asked his fellow players, "We ever been to the moon?" His three fellow players quickly answered no, they did not believe so. The program's moderator soon asked Curry to elaborate on his view, and he said he did not believe the United States had landed astronauts on the moon. Then he said, "Sorry, I don't want to start conspiracies,"[7] and the group briefly discussed popular conspiracy theories that suggested the moon landings had been staged.[8]

The topic accounted for only a short portion of the entire 70-minute podcast episode, but Curry's denial of the moon landings seemed as if it landed from outer space. (Pun intended.) Upon the podcast's distribution, "the blowback to Curry's throwaway thought was swift and strong"[9] and "eclipsed any other Curry talk on social media," according to national news reports.[10] As one sports columnist pointed out, "with his trips to the National Museum of African American History and Culture and astute-sounding quotes on national politics," Curry had "fashioned a brand of a thoughtful and informed athlete. ... And then that same athlete said he thought the 1969 moon landing (and all subsequent moon landings) was faked."[11]

Fans and critics immediately expressed dismay. Curry had failed to deliver the kind of informed comment audiences expected of him when speaking out. Curry confounded the role-related expectations audiences had for him, based on a decade of increasing prominence in the NBA and in public venues away from the basketball court.

"Don't do this. You guys are too smart."

Perhaps the most severe rebuke of Curry's statement came on the ESPN network's popular "Pardon the Interruption" program, where hosts Tony Kornheiser and Michael Wilbon, longtime sports journalists and analysts, upbraided Curry and his fellow basketball players for denying history. Wilbon said, "Don't do this. Don't come out and say, 'These pictures are kinda grainy. They're black and white. Happened before I was born.' Because does that mean you don't believe in slavery? You don't believe in the Revolutionary War? ... Don't do this. You guys are too smart. ... If you are as woke as you say, you are as technologically savvy as you appear to be, don't do this. Because you're saying, 'I don't believe in history.'"[12] Kornheiser further condemned Curry's moon landing denial, saying, "It's a very small step to becoming a Holocaust denier or a slavery denier." Labeling the denial "anti-intellectual" and "anti-science," Kornheiser suggested Curry should be embarrassed by his statement and its reflection on him, his family, his college and the NBA.[13]

In effect, Wilbon and Kornheiser were asking Curry to wield with ethical care the extraordinary power his status as a highly popular professional athlete afforded him for sharing his opinion. Wilbon's and Kornheiser's linkage of Curry's moon landing denial to denials of slavery also suggest the commentators may have been placing a burden of racial representation on Curry because he is Black. We cannot clearly deduce whether representation factored into Wilbon's and Kornheiser's motive for calling out Curry, because they did not state their intent. We can deduce that when celebrity athletes and entertainers such as Curry speak out, they command more attention in public arenas than do ordinary citizens. These celebrities possess the power to make their voices and views heard. With their comments, these celebrities can turn the attention of news outlets, talk shows, social media platforms and huge audiences to seemingly random issues that strike the fancy of the celebrities. In December 2018, the public was not paying any particular attention to the history of the six U.S. moon landings some 50 years before—until Curry suddenly said the landings were a hoax. A few words on his part set off days of public attention.

One reason Curry's words generated attention was because they followed another popular NBA player's public statement of belief in a hoax, and together, the two incidents suggested NBA players were ignorant of fundamental scientific history. Not quite two years earlier, on a different players' podcast chat in February 2017, Cleveland Cavaliers guard Kyrie Irving said he believed Earth is flat. Irving repeated his view three times on that podcast and said "no concrete information" existed to prove Earth is round.[14] Despite receiving many questions from journalists and much information from scientists and teachers attempting to shake his belief in a flat Earth, Irving publicly persisted in defying scientific evidence about Earth for more than a year and a half. In October 2018 he finally apologized for the effect of his flat Earth comments, especially on susceptible young people. Explaining that "at the time, I was huge into conspiracies" he found on internet YouTube videos, Irving did not say explicitly he no longer believed in a flat Earth.[15] Instead, what he said was, "For all of the science teachers, everybody coming up to me like, 'You know, I have to reteach my whole curriculum,' I'm sorry. I apologize."[16]

"Sad to see … role models to millions of kids promote idiotic conspiracy theories."

When Curry denied U.S. space history two months after that apology, he seemed about to become a public laughingstock similar to Irving. Just days after Curry's remarks, the NBA's Sacramento Kings mocked him by projecting video footage of moon-walking astronauts in their arena before a game with Curry's Golden State Warriors.[17]

A wide variety of social media users also teased Curry. For instance, he was lampooned by the general manager of the NBA's Houston Rockets, who used Twitter to send Curry an archival photograph of staff members in the U.S. space agency's mission control room emblazoned with the heading, "Today we congratulate the 400,000 people involved in faking six moon landings for keeping their mouths shut for 49 years."[18]

A California space and science center near the Golden State Warriors' San Francisco Bay Area home used Twitter to invite Curry to "drop by any time" and offered him a "fun fact" that pointed out "if the moon was scaled down to the size of a tennis ball, the Earth would be the exact same size as a basketball!"[19] Of course, some of the social media posts aimed at Curry were less good-natured. For instance, retired U.S. astronaut Jose Hernandez sent a stern tweet about Curry's failure to realize the potential power of his public remarks: "Sad to see folks that command big social media presence & are role models to millions of kids promote idiotic conspiracy theories."[20]

Kyrie Irving, who had been criticized similarly, came to his fellow player's defense. Irving said news outlets were to blame for using their coverage to blow Curry's statement out of proportion. In response, one national writer conceded Irving was "right to point out that there are more pressing matters to consider than whatever far-out notions that he and his fellow sports celebrities kick around in their safe spaces," but the writer suggested Irving and Curry failed to take responsibility for the power of their role and the impact of their speech, arguing, "he and Curry should know better than anyone the weight that their endorsements carries. If sports heroes can sell sneakers and sugar water, odds are they can pretty much sell anything."[21]

Celebrities as Unordained Teaching Authorities

The idea of "selling anything" speaks to the power of celebrity athletes such as Curry and Irving to educate the public—for good or ill—about the issues these public figures choose to address. Public figures who casually speak out on topics that take their fancy may be no better educated and no better qualified than members of the public to address a topic, yet the public figures' power gives them a megaphone for their views and credibility with many impressionable people who hear and may believe those views.

Public figures are "unordained teaching authorities,"[22] according to ethicist William F. May. "Only occasionally encumbered by knowledge, the celebrity helps signal to the people what it looks like to be in the know, what attitudes to adopt, and what to prize and what to despise in the courage of managing their lives."[23] This influence can make celebrities' voices louder than the voices of trained experts, such as the historians and scientists who were appalled by Curry's and Irving's ignorance of scientific history.

Public figures' power bestows on them more than the privilege of being heard when they speak out. It also often bestows on them the privilege of being invited into a legitimate role in the public discourse about a topic and of being treated with at least a modicum of respect on that topic, even if they're ill-informed about it. Most people who deny history and endorse conspiracy theories are labeled crackpots. Yet when Stephen Curry denied history and suggested conspiracy theories about faked moon landings were true, his comments were reported as newsworthy, and he quickly was invited to see the government's collection of moon rocks and to fly in a rocket crew capsule. He even enjoyed the privilege of having his ignorance laughed off by no less than the head of the U.S. space agency.

The day after Curry's comments became public, the National Aeronautics and Space Administration invited Curry for a personal tour of NASA's space center. A NASA spokesperson said, "We'd love for Mr. Curry to tour the lunar lab at our Johnson Space Center in Houston, perhaps the next time the Warriors are in town to play the Rockets. We have hundreds of pounds of moon rocks stored there, and the Apollo mission control. During his visit, he can see firsthand what we did 50 years ago, as well as what we're doing now to go back to the moon in the coming years, but this time to stay."[24]

NASA head Jim Bridenstine echoed the invitation and laughed off Curry's apparent belief in conspiracy theories. He called Curry's moon landing denial "funny" and said, "I can't imagine he really believes that." Bridenstine went on to say his son was among Curry's fans and NASA would be glad to host Curry's visit to the Johnson Space Center as a way of turning him into a space exploration advocate. "If we can get him involved in space, I'm for it!" the NASA head said.[25]

The Boeing Company also sent an invitation to Curry, offering to augment his space center visit with a chance to learn how to fly a Starliner space crew capsule Boeing was manufacturing for a NASA rocket and testing at the space center. In a tweet that said, "We'll teach you how to fly the #Starliner to the @Space_Station," Boeing joked with the basketball player, "Wonder how much vert you can get in zero gravity?"[26]

The invitations suggested more red-carpet treatment for Curry than the tours the ticket-buying public usually receives, and he accepted the offers. "I'm going to go to NASA and I'm going to enjoy the experience wholeheartedly," he said.[27]

Ordinary citizens enjoy the freedom of speech to deny moon landings or to say Earth is flat, but they do not enjoy the privilege of good-humored invitations to tour NASA facilities and test rocket capsules to correct their ignorance of scientific history. Nor do they enjoy the privilege of offers from distinguished scientists and astronauts to teach them space facts. Curry did.

> "Steph, so much respect for you, but re the moon-landing thing, let's talk."

Upon learning about Curry's denial of the moon landings, retired U.S. astronaut Scott Kelly quickly reached out to the basketball player via Twitter. Kelly's tweet said, "Steph, so much respect for you, but re the moon-landing thing, let's talk."[28] The offer to talk about Curry's ignorance of space history came from an astronaut who made his own space history by serving on four missions into space and spending a total of 520 days there, including 340 days aboard the International Space Station so scientists could study whether extended time in space alters a person's DNA.[29] The social media-savvy Curry, who by then was "using everything short of rocket boosters to walk back" his denial of the moon landings,[30] soon took Kelly up on his "let's talk" tweet and invited him to join an Instagram Live video chat session. In the subsequent chat Curry shared with his social media followers, Kelly explained the potential harm of Curry's and Irving's remarks: convincing people to doubt science and history. Kelly said, "When people believe [flat Earth or moon landing conspiracies], they believe the other things that are more important like climate change not being real or vaccines and 9/11 being a conspiracy theory."[31] As had the ESPN hosts Wilbon and Kornheiser, Kelly essentially was asking Curry to take ethical responsibility for the potential harm his remarks could create.

> "When a superstar athlete, says it, anybody ... will believe whatever he has to say."

The potential harm of Curry's remarks also was noted by science teachers. One of them was a Philadelphia teacher, who had told National Public Radio in 2017 his middle school students considered "flat Earther" Kyrie Irving more of an authority on Earth's nature than their science teacher. "How have I failed these kids so badly they think the Earth is flat just because a basketball player says it?" asked teacher Nick Gurol. "They think that I'm part of this larger conspiracy of being a round-Earther. That's definitely hard for me because it feels like science isn't real to them."[32]

In 2018, Gurol said he thought his students would think the U.S. moon landings weren't real, either—just because they heard Stephen Curry thought the landings were a hoax. "When someone like that, a superstar athlete, says it, anybody that follows basketball will believe whatever he has to say," Gurol told a science website. "That's mostly the young men in my class, and also plenty of the girls too. It could be anywhere from half to 75% of my class believing whatever he says."[33]

The ESPN analysts, the retired astronauts and the science teachers who criticized Curry's remarks were asking him to understand the importance of the context in which he spoke out. Curry's moon landing denial came during an era in which many people seemed more vocal than ever about distrusting scientific facts and institutions, and in which people's distrust could be shared easily and widely through social media platforms. A *Guardian* columnist explained: "It used to be that conspiracy theorists hewed to a type. They wore tinfoil hats, babbled incoherently to themselves and, by and large, were little more than a nuisance to the onlookers with the curiosity or the compassion to engage them. But in the current post-truth era, where crowdsourced information has replaced peer-reviewed research and confirmation bias stands in for intellectual curiosity, the truthers congregate online to double down on old conspiracy theories (like the Earth being flat) and breathe life into new ones (like Hillary Clinton being a lizard person). Science can't hold a candle to celebrity, and sports personalities seem keener than ever to stir the pot."[34]

Famous athletes who speak out about science and history, as Curry and Irving did, enjoy both the power to make their voices heard and the privilege of being heard by a variety of audiences. When they speak out about issues, these athletes' power to command the attention of news reporters and public officials can outweigh the power of ordinary citizens to determine what issues ought to command attention in the news and public arenas. The athletes' power to attract attention also can outweigh the power of the public to respond. A science teacher who objects to professional basketball players' opinions about science never will be heard as loudly or treated as deferentially as these elite athletes will. Therefore, public figures such as Curry and Irving bear an ethical obligation to use their power and privilege wisely, and to consider the potential harm their speaking out may create. Sometimes, that may mean they should not speak out, especially if they are not experts or authorities on the topic, and if their role-related expertise is not connected to the topic.

"Obviously I was joking when I was talking on the podcast."

After his moon landing denial became public, and NASA officials, former astronauts, scientists, teachers and sports analysts immediately responded to it via social media channels, Curry didn't explain his denial for two days, which is an eon in the world of instant communication via digital media.

When he did give an interview to ESPN, Curry said, "Obviously I was joking when I was talking on the podcast."[35] He added, "I was silently protesting how stupid it was that people actually took that quote and made it law as 'Oh my God, he's a fake-moon-landing truther,' whatever you want to call it, yada, yada, yada. So I was silently protesting that part about it, how the story took a life of its own."[36]

To assert he was "obviously joking" and "silently protesting" seems disingenuous on Curry's part. If his denial of the moon landings was a joke, why didn't he clearly say on the podcast that he was joking or being sarcastic? Failing to do so, and upon realizing how many people took his moon landing denial seriously, why didn't Curry use his social media platforms, which he wielded with skill and frequency, to say he had been joking? Or why didn't Curry immediately give an interview to any of the many sports journalists who would have jumped to report an explanation of his headline-grabbing comment? Curry's status as an influential professional athlete would have afforded him the privilege of attention if he sought to quickly correct his moon landing denial.

> *"We want you to understand the weight of your words. They matter. So does truth."*

As an elite athlete, Curry repeatedly had acknowledged responsibility to use his public platform wisely, and in this case, he seemed not to fully recognize the public context into which his comments played. In North Carolina, his hometown newspaper, *The Charlotte Observer*, published an editorial sharply reminding Curry of that context. "Truth has already taken a beating in 2018," the newspaper's editorial board wrote. "Does it matter if one more person makes one more ludicrous statement? It does, if that person is an NBA star and Charlotte son whom children and others look up to. It matters in an era where people are being encouraged not to believe that which is plainly reality. It matters in a cultural and political landscape in which the distinction between true and false is becoming more difficult to discern. It threatens our public discourse, and more." The newspaper concluded its address to Curry with a pointed reminder of his power: "Not to lay all that on one dumb remark—or, we hope, joke—about the moon. But we'd all be better off with fewer loony remarks from public figures. It's not that we want you to shut up and dribble. The opposite, in fact. We want you to understand the weight of your words. They matter. So does truth."[37]

The Need for Moral Justification

As a moral agent in this case, Curry seemingly failed to resist the urge to endorse false conspiracy theories, failed to understand the context into which his moon landing comment would fall, failed to anticipate the harmful effect of his comment on susceptible people, and failed to predict critical responses to the comment.

Analyzing cases of speaking out after they fail or succeed helps future speakers practice the principle of moral justification required of moral agents. Moral agents are people who can understand moral principles and who possess enough autonomy to decide whether to comply with those moral principles in choosing how to act. Moral agents are the opposite of moral patients, who are not sufficiently rational to be considered morally accountable for their actions.[38]

Curry qualifies as a moral agent in two necessary ways. First, he is an individual capable of acting on his own behalf or on behalf of an organization he represents. Second, he is an individual capable of making a defensible ethical decision. Curry is not a child; he is an autonomous adult possessed of mature reasoning powers to make sense of the events occurring around him. To make an ethical decision about how to act, a moral agent is required to consider his or her motives for acting or speaking, the relevant stakeholders who may be affected by her or his action or speech, the moral duties to which he or she owes loyalty, and the potential consequences of the ethical decision she or he reaches.

As a moral agent, Curry must look outside himself to test his ethical resolution, present rational reasons to support it, and consider who would be affected by his proposed resolution and how those affected would perceive the resolution. In other words, a moral agent must engage in the work of justification. Philosopher Sissela Bok explains, "To justify is to defend as just, right, or proper, by providing adequate reasons. It means to hold up to some standard, such as a religious or legal or moral standard. Such justification requires an audience: it may be directed to God, or a court of law, or one's peers, or one's own conscience; but in ethics it is most appropriately aimed, not at any one individual or audience, but rather at 'reasonable persons' in general."[39]

A Test for Moral Justification of Speaking Out

Ethicists Wendy Wyatt and Kristie Bunton propose a specific test of moral justification for speaking out by public figures that can be applied to Curry's case. The Wyatt and Bunton test asks four questions:

1. What is the relationship of the celebrity to the issue he or she is speaking out about?
2. What is the motivation for speaking out?
3. What is the nature of any harm created?
4. Does speaking out promote dialogue?[40]

The justification test requires all four parts be satisfied to justify whether public figures should speak out. Examining Curry's speaking out about U.S. moon landings against all four parts of the test confirms his ethical lapse.

Applying the Speaking Out Test

First, no relationship between Curry and the topic of moon landings apparently existed. He was known for speaking out about his family, his sport, his Christian faith, his charity work to prevent malaria, and occasionally, his views about racial and social injustice. When he spoke out about preventing malaria, for instance, his comments seemed steeped in knowledge gained over years of commitment to the cause. When he denied the moon landings, he had demonstrated no particular interest in or expertise about scientific history.

Second, although we obviously cannot get inside Curry's head and decidedly confirm his motive for denying the moon landings, we can reasonably deduce from the situation in which the basketball players' podcast was recorded that the motivation for the comment was humor. The players had been joking about sounds dinosaurs might have made before Curry wondered aloud about moon landings. The podcast was a lighthearted "hang session" the players were enjoying, and the two players who host the podcast said that as they recorded the conversation, they didn't think Curry was seriously doubting space history.[41] Assuming humor was the motive for the comment, it seems an inadequate reason to deny historical fact in a public message distributed to a wide audience. Promoting truth about scientific history should outweigh using humor to gain attention or seem cool. However, absent a clear indication of motive to mislead listeners, we can give Curry some benefit of the doubt and consider his comment an example of "willful ignorance," which is less ethically grievous than a lie that intends to deceive. Philosopher Lee McIntyre suggests a willfully ignorant comment occurs "when we do not really know whether something is true, but we say it anyway, without bothering to take the time to find out whether our information is correct."[42] We must scrutinize Curry's willfully ignorant comment because "if the facts are easily available, the person who states a falsehood seems at least partially responsible for any ignorance," McIntyre contends.[43]

Third, Curry's comment created unfortunate harms. Most seriously, his critics charged that despite the casual environment of the podcast, Curry failed to understand the danger of denying scientific history in any public venue in a "post-truth" world in which "feelings sometimes matter more than facts," according to McIntyre,[44] and in which factual reality is under attack, to the detriment of science.[45] Curry's critics particularly worried a denial might influence susceptible young fans who idolize the basketball player more than they trust their science teachers. Effects on vulnerable audiences require extra ethical care from moral agents.

Fourth, although his comment did generate attention, Curry's denial of the moon landings did not promote much dialogue about relevant issues that could have been debated. For instance, meaningful dialogue might have involved citizens discussing why people's beliefs in conspiracy theories about science persist, or why young people easily are convinced history is not true, or even why journalists and the public turn their attention to silly comments by professional athletes. No dialogue of that sort occurred, although his video chat with astronaut Scott Kelly was a helpful attempt by Curry to rectify his misunderstanding about the importance of scientific history and share his new understanding with his social media followers.

> *"Understand that you should not believe something just because somebody says it."*

Failing all four parts of the speaking-out test, Curry's comment about the moon landings cannot be ethically justified. Furthermore, he did not actually apologize for misleading people about the moon landings. A public apology—which ethicists Nikki Usher and Janel Schuh define as a "distinct apology from one to many"[46] delivered in a truthful, sincere, timely and voluntary manner[47]—could have helped restore trust among sports fans, journalists, historians and scientists who were dismayed by his remarks. To Curry's credit, he did seem to quickly learn a lesson about his power and privilege as a speaker, as an accountable moral agent should. Philosophers Nicholas Bunnin and Jiyuan Yu suggest, "Moral agents can react to the acts of other moral agents. Accordingly they are responsible for their acts and the subject of blame or praise."[48] In Curry's case, within a few days of his statement denying the moon landings, he said, "I am going to educate myself firsthand on everything that NASA has done and shine a light on their tremendous work over the years. And hopefully people understand that education is power, informing yourself is power. For kids out there that hang on every word that we say ... understand that you should not believe something just because somebody says it. You should do your homework and understand what you actually believe."[49]

Curry also put his money where his mouth had been, arranging with his partners at Under Armour to customize a pair of his Curry 6 basketball shoes into a "moon landing" version he wore in an NBA game less than a month after his podcast comment. He autographed the shoes, which turned them into a collector's item, and then put them up for auction online. They sold for $58,100 that Curry donated to science, technology, engineering and mathematics education programs in the San Francisco Bay area.[50] In those subsequent comments and his fundraising work, Curry attempted to address his ethical lapse in speaking out to deny U.S. space history.

"What are the chances? Could this really happen?"

A year and a half later, when the United States was falling into the grip of a devastating coronavirus pandemic, a different case of speaking out by Curry was an ethical success in both its use of power and privilege to educate thousands of people about the virus, and its exercise of ethical duty to prevent harm to an issue or audience. In fact, *USA Today* called Curry's speaking out about the pandemic the "most significant move of his career."[51]

Americans watched the pandemic devastate regions of Asia and Europe before arriving in the United States in early 2020. By March, officials closed schools, offices, retail stores, factories, restaurants, gyms, hair salons, houses of worship, public parks, museums and sports venues to encourage people to isolate themselves in their homes, where they could avoid contracting the viral illness called Covid-19 and thus "flatten the curve" of sharply rising cases that were filling hospital beds too quickly to manage. Unfortunately, the rapid closure of the U.S. economy resulted in the loss of millions of Americans' jobs.[52]

Curry was the first NBA player tested for the virus, and he described his experience in an essay for *Time* magazine, writing: "March 6. That's when it all became very real. I had just played my first basketball game in months the night before, and conversations were swirling about what this virus might mean for the league. That night, I started to feel sick. The fever set in. First at 100. Then 101. My first thought was, 'What are the chances? Could this really happen?' After months of waiting to get back on the court following a broken hand and two surgeries, I just wanted to play. But the threat of this mystery virus locked me in my bedroom to protect everyone I cared about: wife, kids, teammates, fans. ... Thankfully, my test came back negative. But that experience hit me, and it hit me hard."[53]

Curry then expressed a responsibility to help other people being hit by the virus. He wrote, "I'm fortunate to have the job I do, and not have to worry about all the many things crippling families across the country during this pandemic: unemployment, hunger, housing. How couldn't I use all of my resources and the full power of the platform my wife and I have built to help those desperately in need during this time?"[54]

Curry said he and his wife had directed their "Eat. Learn. Play" foundation in the first month of the economic shutdown to provide a million meals to families in Oakland, California, where the Currys live. Subsequently, the foundation would work with Oakland schools and community food banks to reopen local restaurants to provide meals for impoverished Oakland residents, while restoring workers to their restaurant jobs.[55]

"To hopefully reach a different demographic or people that are interested in the facts."

Another way Curry used the power of his platform was to arrange an interview with Dr. Anthony Fauci, the nation's leading infectious disease expert. Fauci often was seen on televised briefings taking White House reporters' questions alongside President Donald Trump, but he agreed to be interviewed on Instagram Live by Curry. The athlete followed by scores of young sports fans on social media asked Fauci questions about how the coronavirus spread, why young people who felt healthy should nevertheless practice physical distancing from one another to slow the viral spread, and why self-isolation at home was another important way to slow viral spread even if isolation grated on normally active young people.

Curry explained his reason for conducting the interview, saying he wanted "to hopefully reach a different demographic or people that are interested in the facts of what's going on."[56] He seemed to succeed, as nearly 50,000 viewers watched the Instagram Live interview, and many more viewers were expected to watch the recorded version.

USA Today sports columnist Mark Medina praised Curry's effort to inform those viewers, writing, "Either way, they will have witnessed something that does not usually match what they see on social media. They digested actual information instead of fake news. They watched something substantial on a platform that often highlights the day-to-day minutia. They became informed about an issue that could either help calm their anxieties or realize they should take this virus and the subsequent social distancing rules seriously. Though there are already a reported 82,404 cases and 1,100 deaths involving COVID-19 in the United States, Curry's interview with Fauci could lead more people to help flatten the curve and save lives."[57] Medina heaped further praise on Curry's performance, writing, "Viewers walked away much more informed about the COVID-19 than they could have by witnessing any White House briefing. There, President Donald Trump has either misstated the severity of COVID-19 or what he has done to address the problem. He has often contradicted Fauci's advice on the use of certain untested drugs or when it is safe for businesses to open."[58] Fauci, too, praised Curry's effort, complimenting him for asking well-prepared and "intelligent" questions about the pandemic.[59]

Examining Curry's pandemic speaking against Wyatt and Bunton's four-part test for the moral justification of speaking out confirms his ethical success on the topic.

First, some relationship between Curry and issues of public health existed. He had done a great deal of previous speaking out, grounded in facts, about prevention of the deadly disease of malaria. (See Chapter 2.)

Second, in his magazine essay about the need to feed homeless and impoverished people suffering from the pandemic's economic devastation, Curry expressed a motivation for using his privilege to help others. In his Instagram Live interview with Dr. Fauci, he expressed motivation for trying to reach social media followers who needed factual information about the coronavirus.

Third, no harm was created by Curry's pandemic speaking, whether that was his speaking out in his magazine essay about helping less-privileged people or his speaking out by interviewing Fauci to share information about viral spread with young people. Rather, both these acts of speaking out likely prevented harm. In an environment in which much misinformation about viral spread was confusing and scaring people, or lulling them into thinking the need to "flatten the curve" was overblown, the recipients of Curry's speech received helpful facts.

Fourth, Curry's interview with Fauci created dialogue about the pandemic in the way he organized the session, inviting social media followers before the interview to tweet him questions they wanted to see answered and during the interview to post questions and comments on the Instagram Live platform.[60] In closing his magazine essay about the need to help other people, Curry exhorted readers who might not possess the same privileges he did nevertheless to speak out and act in their own ways to help others, writing that "our small gestures in times of crisis can end up being the big gestures that made the difference."[61]

The next four chapters analyze behavior by two famous speakers to more deeply illustrate each of these four elements of the speaking-out test, as well as the potential harms and benefits associated with speaking out by celebrity athletes and entertainers.

PART II

Ethical Questions
to Answer

4

What Is the Relationship
of the Speaker to the Topic?

*"Sick and dying, they brought themselves down here to speak
to no one."*

In June 2019, comedian Jon Stewart showed audiences a glimpse of himself they'd rarely seen in the 16 years he presented *The Daily Show* on late night television. Testifying before a committee in the U.S. House of Representatives to advocate for extending medical benefits for 9/11 first responders, Stewart abandoned the sarcasm that made him popular with television viewers. The satirist for years had refused to be characterized as a trusted source of information, even as *The Daily Show* gained significant influence in political and journalistic circles, but now he spoke with a seriousness unlike his sardonic television persona.

As he addressed members of Congress seated before him on a two-tiered dais, Stewart paused periodically to blink back tears and clear his throat. He described the heroism of firefighters, paramedics and police officers who responded within minutes to the September 2001 terrorist attacks in New York and worked for weeks atop the pile of rubble created when the World Trade Center towers crashed to the ground. He explained that working in the rubble's toxic environment left many first responders with cancer and other debilitating conditions. He demanded Congress renew the fund that helped first responders and their families pay medical and funeral bills.

Looking up at several empty chairs on the dais, Stewart thanked the hearing's organizers and said, "But as I sit here today, I can't help but think what an incredible metaphor this room is for the entire process that getting health care and benefits for 9/11 first responders has come to. Behind me, a filled room of 9/11 first responders, and in front of me, a nearly empty Congress." Of the first responders crowded into the hearing room, Stewart said, "Sick and dying, they brought themselves down here to speak to no one."

He chastised members of Congress who did not attend the hearing, saying, "Shameful. It's an embarrassment to the country and it's a stain on this institution. And you should be ashamed of yourselves for those that aren't here. But you won't be because accountability doesn't appear to be something that occurs in this chamber." He went on to say, "There is not a person here, there is not an empty chair on that stage that didn't tweet out 'Never forget the heroes of 9/11. Never forget their bravery. Never forget what they did, what they gave to this country.' Well, here they are." Then he asked about the missing members of Congress, "And where are they?" Accusing Congress of "callous indifference and rank hypocrisy," Stewart said the failure of Congress to renew the benefits program was costing many gravely ill first responders "their most valuable commodity: Time. It's the one thing they're running out of."[1]

The effects of Stewart's powerful statement were immediate. Video of his testimony went viral online and was included in scores of news stories.[2] After covering Stewart's testimony, journalists scurried to ask powerful politicians, especially U.S. Senate Majority Leader Mitch McConnell, why they had not renewed the first responders' funding program. The next day, the House of Representatives committee that heard Stewart's testimony approved the funding bill and sent it to the full House for a vote. Within two weeks, a delegation of first responders emerged from a meeting with McConnell with his promise that the Senate he controlled would vote to renew funding by summer's end. Stewart's advocacy was credited for helping pressure McConnell into that promise.[3]

Stewart's June 2019 advocacy was not the first time he was credited for helping 9/11 first responders. His advocacy on their behalf had been credited for pushing Congress to initially approve and then renew the September 11th Victim Compensation Fund in 2010 and 2015. For nearly a decade, first responders' benefits had been the only significant topic on which Stewart personally spoke out, especially after he departed *The Daily Show* and began avoiding the limelight. This chapter uses Stewart's sustained pattern of speaking out on behalf of first responders' health needs to understand the ethical parameters of the relationship between speakers and the topics on which they speak out.

Ethical Salience and Role-Related Expectations in Speaking Out

Speaking out is distinguished by four ethically salient characteristics, and these characteristics oblige the speaker to perform moral justification for the act of speaking out. (See Chapter 2.) Each of these characteristics occurs in Stewart's acts of speaking out in support of 9/11 first responders.

The first ethically salient characteristic of speaking out occurs when speakers transcend the role-related expectations of their audiences. In 2015, when Stewart signed off after 16 years at the helm of *The Daily Show* on Comedy Central, the show had been the subject of more articles, television reports and books assessing its influence on politics and journalism than perhaps any American political comedy to date.[4] One study found equal substance in the news presented on *The Daily Show* and on nightly network news broadcasts.[5] A national poll found audiences considered political comedian Stewart as trusted a news source as marquee television journalists Tom Brokaw, Anderson Cooper, Dan Rather and Brian Williams.[6] Pundits and analysts assigned significant political sway to Stewart and *The Daily Show*, suggesting it provoked political action.[7] Yet Stewart never accepted being described as politician or journalist. He told *New York Times* political columnist Maureen Dowd that late night comedians "are not warriors in anyone's army," and said, "I don't view us as people who lead social movements."[8] Stewart's most prominent role was that of political comedian, he repeatedly insisted, and, most likely, that's how his audience understood him. Audiences paid attention to Stewart because he was hilarious when skewering politics and journalism. When Stewart assumed the role of advocate in Congress, he transcended both the public's general role-related expectations for political comedians to offer pithy observations about politics, rather than to engage in politics, and the public's more specific role-related expectations for Stewart to remain uninvolved in politics, given all he had said about his limited role over the years.

Role-related expectations are crucial to consider in ethical analysis. Like the "prescribed pattern of behavior for an actor in a given part in a play," a societal role "carries with it a repertoire of expected behavioral regularities," according to philosophers Nicholas Bunnin and Jiyuan Yu.[9] We all expect people—others, as well as ourselves—to behave according to the expectations set out for the roles we have assumed or been assigned. Understanding the expectations that come with those roles helps us interact with one another in personal and professional contexts. "Since a person may assume a multitude of roles, it is inevitable that sometimes his different roles will conflict with one another. Such conflicts may pose serious moral problems," Bunnin and Yu suggest.[10] As a moral agent able to decide autonomously how to act ethically,[11] a speaker who is a famous public figure bears some responsibility for balancing what may be the audience's previous expectations for the public figure with the new role as speaker.

The second ethically salient characteristic of speaking out occurs when speakers address an issue of significant concern to the public.

Addressing the ongoing health expenses of first responders who worked in the dangerously polluted environment of lower Manhattan after the terrorist attacks is undoubtedly such a significant public concern. *The Washington Post* reported, "According to the World Trade Center Health Program, more than 9,400 registered responders developed cancer after the attacks. Thousands more experience mental-health conditions, airway ailments and other health issues. As of March 2019, at least 2,100 responders and 182 survivors registered with the program have died. That death toll does not reflect those who did not register with the program before their deaths, or who died before the program came into existence in 2011. New health ramifications, such as an emerging trend of memory problems among responders, are still coming to light."[12] From the opening of the victims' compensation fund in 2011 to its pending renewal in 2019, some $5 billion of the $7.3 billion allocated by Congress had been paid to 21,000 claimants, but more than 19,000 unpaid claims still were pending, and the fund was supposed to quit taking new claims in December 2020 because it was likely to be depleted.[13]

Of course, Stewart's advocacy for replenishing the 9/11 first responders' program competed with views expressed by other citizens and politicians. Some people argued first responders were no more important than military veterans or other Americans who also needed government assistance. Some people argued government instead should spend money on education, the environment or national defense, and some people argued government funding overall should be kept in check. All of these views, including Stewart's, addressed the serious issue of citizens' concern about their government's priorities.

The third ethically salient characteristic of speaking out occurs when speakers who have transcended role-related expectations intentionally interject their voices into the public discourse about serious issues. Ethically justifiable speaking out is not accidental. Moral agents are responsible for the consequences of their behavior,[14] so they should consider possible consequences carefully before acting. Stewart's speaking out easily qualifies as an intentional interjection into the public conversation. Scheduling hearings that involve multiple members of Congress, their staffs and various witnesses obviously requires advance notice to get them all to Washington. As an astute observer of American politics who had testified in Congress, Stewart knew how the legislative process worked. He participated deliberately. Ethically, he would be required to accept any resulting criticism of his role as a speaker on behalf of 9/11 first responders.

The fourth ethically salient characteristic of speaking out occurs when speakers use a public platform or venue to speak out. Planning congressional committee hearings involves multiple arrangements for public exposure. Committee staffs work with media outlets to televise and livestream congressional hearings, and to make space for news photographers and reporters in crowded hearing rooms. As a savvy public figure, Stewart knew his name on the docket of citizens who were to testify about the first responders would ensure headline-making coverage of the hearing. He knew his role in the hearing was to bring the weight of his celebrity to bear on the first responders' legislation. Stewart also knew he could parlay his fame into interviews before and after the hearing with political journalists who eagerly would report his views, as they had done on his previous lobbying visits to Congress. Thus, he would be required ethically to bear any consequences for choosing to speak out as publicly as possible.

Accordingly, Stewart's testimony in support of 9/11 first responders meets all four of the ethically salient characteristics for speaking out, and thus requires ethical justification using Wyatt's and Bunton's four-part test, which asks about the relationship of the speaker to the topic of the speech, the speaker's motivation for speaking, the nature of any harm created by speaking, and the tendency of the speech to promote dialogue about the topic.[15]

Justifiable Relationships Between Speakers and Topics

This chapter focuses on the test's first element: an ethically justifiable relationship between speaker and topic. Famous entertainers and athletes may demonstrate they are well-suited to speak about a topic by showing a specific stake in the issue, by establishing a long-term commitment to the issue, by possessing particular expertise about it, and by speaking from an informed perspective with an understanding of any repercussions that may result from speaking.[16] A crucial point for ethical analysis is that justifiable speaking out requires speakers who are well-informed and take seriously their responsibility for accurate communication.

"I try not to remember, to be honest with you."

Stewart's case provides evidence of a strong and sustained, and thus ethically justifiable, relationship between the speaker and his topic. The relationship began on the morning of Tuesday, September 11, 2001, when Al-Qaeda terrorists flew airplanes into New York's World Trade Center and Washington's Pentagon, killing nearly 3,000 people. Stewart, a New Jersey native who had lived most of his life in and around New York, was at home in lower Manhattan when the attacks occurred. "I heard the first plane hit while I was in bed. It felt like a bomb. It rattled the place pretty good," he said.[17] Soon, Stewart and his wife went out to check on family, and Stewart said while they were on the street they saw one of the World Trade Center towers collapse. "That's when just everything started spinning," he said.[18] Of the days after the attack that devastated his neighborhood, Stewart said, "I just remember us bursting into tears on a constant basis, as everybody was. The smell is the thing that I'll never forget.... I try not to remember, to be honest with you."[19]

Television networks provided 24-hour news and analysis about the terrorism that shook America to its core, and no one was in any mood for late night comedy shows to poke fun at news and politics. Late night shows, including *The Daily Show*, went on hiatus. Stewart and his staff questioned how they ever could return to air with the irony and absurdity that were his show's signature.[20]

"But you know what the view is now? The Statue of Liberty."

When "The Daily Show" did resume on September 20, Stewart delivered a nine-minute monologue that suggested he had decided the answer was to speak straight from his broken heart. He called the show's freedom to produce political satire a "privilege" and said, "This is a country that allows for open satire, and I know that sounds basic and it sounds as though it goes without saying—but that's really what this whole situation is about. It's the difference between closed and open. It's the difference between free and ... burdened and we don't take that for granted here by any stretch of the imagination."[21] Choking back tears, sniffling repeatedly and taking long pauses to compose himself, Stewart said he would not despair over the terrorist attacks. "And the reason I don't despair is because this attack happened. It's not a dream. But the aftermath of it, the recovery, is a dream realized," he said. "Any fool can blow something up. Any fool can destroy. But to see these guys, these firefighters, these policemen and people from all over the country, with buckets, rebuilding. That, that—that is—that's extraordinary. That's why we've already won. It's light. It's democracy."[22]

Stewart finished with words that would be quoted often by writers who later called the monologue among the most compelling performances of his career on *The Daily Show*.[23] He said, "The view from my apartment was the World Trade Center, and now it's gone. And they attacked it. This symbol of American ingenuity and strength and labor and imagination and commerce, and it's gone. But you know what the view is now? The Statue of Liberty. The view from the south of Manhattan is now the Statue of Liberty. You can't beat that."[24] Stewart said he walked off *The Daily Show* set afterward and "just bawled." Delivering the monologue was "an incredibly emotional experience," he said. "We all knew people who had been down there and had lost people."[25] This "intensely personal" connection[26] between Stewart and the terrorist attacks, which he first expressed in that monologue, demonstrates a specific stake in the 9/11 issue that helps ethically justify his subsequent speaking out about first responders' health benefits.

Nine years after the attacks, in December 2010, Stewart and his staff were, as usual, sifting through current news and political events for items to lampoon on *The Daily Show*, when they noticed the U.S. Senate's Republican majority, led by Senator Mitch McConnell, had passed a tax cut to benefit wealthy Americans while stalling a bill to fund 9/11 first responders' increasing medical expenses. Stewart and his staff also noticed television news programs had failed to cover the bill. Stewart decided *The Daily Show* would tackle the situation, which typified the political inertia and journalistic inattention he often showcased, but he decided to treat the issue differently on air. He became "an overt advocate, something he'd avoided doing for eleven years," according to a history of the show.[27] Stewart opened his December 16, 2010, show with a segment that called Congress "worst responders," accused Republicans of "an outrageous abdication" of their responsibility and challenged the news networks' failure to report on the bill. Then, *The New York Times* observed, "he donned a newsman hat himself, inviting four first responders to discuss the need for medical care. For nine minutes—an eternity on television, particularly on 'The Daily Show'— the men said they were fighting for their health. Mr. Stewart had edged into an advocacy role."[28]

> *"I don't even know if there was a deal, to be honest with you, before his show."*

Stewart's advocacy gave the stalled first responders' bill traction. The next day, major news networks began covering the bill.[29] Less than a week later, Congress passed the bill, and President Barack Obama signed it into law on January 2, 2011.[30] Many voices gave Stewart credit. "Jon shining such a big, bright spotlight on Washington's potentially tragic failure to put aside differences and get this done for America was, without a doubt, one of the biggest factors that led to the final agreement," said New York mayor Michael Bloomberg, who also had lobbied for the bill.[31] Firefighter Kenny Specht, one of the first responders Stewart interviewed on *The Daily Show*, gave Stewart even more credit, saying, "I don't even know if there was a deal, to be honest with you, before his show."[32] Notably absent among the voices giving or taking credit afterward, however, was Jon Stewart's. He did not comment on the bill's passage and reportedly told *The Daily Show* staff not to, either.[33] We cannot know why Stewart chose not to comment, but we might interpret his silence as a gesture of humility intended to re-focus attention on 9/11 community members who needed government benefits.

Political and television analysts soon asked how Stewart's newly successful role as a political advocate might affect his ongoing role as a comedian. A British columnist pointed out, for instance, that although Stewart regularly insisted he was neither politician nor journalist, his influence had been "laid bare for all to see" and suggested that meant he now carried "a burden of responsibility" for using it wisely.[34] But while Stewart continued to skewer politicians and government on his television show, he did not take up speaking out on public issues. That is, until five years later, when the first responders' legislation signed into law in 2011 was about to expire.

In September 2015, about a month after he had departed *The Daily Show* for private life, the otherwise reclusive Stewart traveled to Washington to join tens of 9/11 first responders as they walked the halls of congressional office buildings to buttonhole legislators and staff members about why they had not yet renewed the benefits program.[35] He used his fame to attract cameras and reporters to a news conference and then reportedly insisted first responders do "most of the talking in dozens of private meetings with members [of Congress] and staff."[36]

The Washington trip was not an impulse on Stewart's part. He knowingly interjected himself into public discussion about the first responders' legislation once again. Two months before, just days before he left *The Daily Show*, Stewart interviewed New York's Democratic U.S. senator Kirsten Gillibrand, a longtime sponsor of the first responders' bill, and promised to "schedule a ritual shaming" of the legislation's opponents with her.[37] Hearing about Stewart's on-air promise, at least one Republican Congress member dismissed the possible power of the comedian's advocacy. Arizona's Republican U.S. Congressman Trent Franks said, "What Jon Stewart does I'd hope would never affect my vote in the slightest. ... I'll shake hands and say 'how are you sir?,' listen politely and that'll be the end of it."[38]

First responders, however, thought Stewart's advocacy on their behalf would affect congressional votes, and they needed those votes for the 2015 renewal. "The police officers and firefighters and construction workers were sicker and more disheartened than they'd been in 2010—some 33,000 people had developed 9/11-related ailments, including at least 4,166 cases of cancer; more cops had died of illnesses linked to the attack than had perished in it—and the bill was on the verge of lapsing. So when Stewart returned to D.C. that day to walk the halls with the responders, and again use his bully pulpit to shame lawmakers in a very public way for failing to reauthorize an act that had been underfunded in the first place, they were especially grateful," *HuffPost* reported.[39]

As the autumn continued and the bill's expiration date drew closer without a congressional vote, Stewart continued displaying long-term commitment to the first responders' legislation. He devised "a backup plan" to prod Congress.[40] Although reluctant to intrude on his successor at *The Daily Show*, Stewart asked for air time on his old show. Then he took a camera crew to Washington to again buttonhole lawmakers, especially the Senate's Republican majority leader, Mitch McConnell, who agreed to meet with first responders but not with Stewart. The resulting video of first responders being ducked by lawmakers and their staff members "made for a sharp eight minutes of satire" that aired in early December on *The Daily Show*. What made the program truly compelling, however, was Stewart's attempt to reconvene the panel of four first responders who had joined him on air in 2010. "The fact that it wasn't possible made the segment even more of a gut punch," noted a history of the show. "Only Kenny Specht, a former NDNY lieutenant suffering from thyroid cancer, was able to return, sitting next to Stewart and three empty chairs."[41] Specht said two of the first responders were too ill to appear on air, and the other had died of 9/11-related cancer.[42]

"It took a comedian to shed light on such a serious issue."

After that poignant episode of *The Daily Show*, Stewart continued demonstrating a commitment to speaking out about the first responders' bill. He drew more attention by appearing unannounced three days later on fellow comedian Stephen Colbert's CBS *Late Show*. Tapping into the media's growing preoccupation with Republican presidential candidate Donald Trump and his propensity to use Twitter, Stewart donned a bad wig and orange makeup to parody Trump, as he had done to great effect many times on *The Daily Show*. Then, at Colbert's command to "Bring 'da Trump!" Stewart mimicked a crazy Trump voice to urge audience members to tweet "worst responders" to their Congress members and insist they pass the bill.[43] The segment attracted journalists' attention and quickly generated headlines. The next day, journalists reported McConnell's promise the Senate would act. One headline read "Mitch McConnell gives Jon Stewart what he wants," and a week later, the bill passed.[44] John Feal, the leader of a prominent first responders' lobbying organization, credited Stewart. Feal said first responders had made some 300 lobbying trips to Washington over 12 years. "But it took a comedian to shed light on such a serious issue," Feal said. "Would the bill have passed without Jon Stewart? Probably. Don't know. But I don't think I would've wanted to take that chance."[45]

"It's a shared moment."

Later, Stewart said he regarded lobbying for the first responders' bill as typical of a theme that occupied *The Daily Show* under his direction. A history of *The Daily Show* contended the "subtext of the whole show, the whole sixteen years" was "bewilderment" over unresolved issues government should resolve for citizens. Stewart didn't take credit for the first responder bill's passage, however. He said, "But it's something. It's a shared moment."[46] Then Stewart disappeared again from the public eye, described by a biographer as "a content homebody" who rarely sought publicity.[47]

"This is a man who could have had anything," a *Los Angeles Times* writer observed. "He could still be on Comedy Central every night. He probably could've moved to HBO for a weekly show, or cashed out on Netflix. CNN would surely have hosted his talking head a few times a week. Any publication would welcome regular op-eds under his byline. He could sell out arena after arena on a national stand-up tour. He could command an army of social media followers. But he doesn't." Instead, the writer argued, Stewart spoke out "only in moments of dire need ... tackling a problem surely all Americans can stand behind yet which still goes unaddressed."[48]

"I didn't mean to interrupt them—with their jobs."

In 2019, Stewart again left his private life and demonstrated long-term commitment to the first responders' cause. Using his star power to draw attention to the cause, Stewart visited Capitol Hill in the spring to lobby for another extension of the first responders' fund and in June to testify before a congressional committee to exert pressure anew on stalling lawmakers. "His anger as incisive as it was indiscriminate, he took the entirety of Congress to task," reported *The Los Angeles Times*. "He—like always— spoke truth to power, rather than point fingers at pawns or the powerless. He avoided partisan pot-shots to avoid lowering the argument into partisan terms. He didn't condescend and he never breathed an air of arrogance. Appealing to equal measures of pathos and logic, Stewart did what he always has done: put a spotlight on feckless cynicism and made sure we all saw."[49]

Days after his congressional testimony, Stewart showed further commitment to the first responders' bill—and strategic understanding of how to use his celebrity voice to maintain pressure on Senate Majority Leader McConnell. Stewart appeared on *Fox News Sunday*, where Republican audiences and politicians would hear him castigate McConnell. Stewart pulled no punches, saying, "I want to make it clear that this has never been dealt with compassionately by Senator McConnell. ... He has always held out until the very last minute, and only then, under intense lobbying and public shaming, has he even deigned to move on it." McConnell responded to Stewart's pressure the next morning with his own appearance on Fox News, saying Congress would "take care of the 9/11 victims compensation fund" and explaining that "many things in Congress happen at the last minute." McConnell also said he didn't know why Stewart was "all bent out of shape" and that it seemed to McConnell as if Stewart was "looking for some way to take offense."[50]

Stewart turned up his pressure another notch. That night, he turned again to Stephen Colbert's CBS *Late Show*, where for seven minutes he and Colbert hammered McConnell. Colbert played a video clip of McConnell saying congressional inaction on the first responders' bill could be explained "because members have a lot of things going on at the same time," to which Stewart feigned surprise and sarcastically said, "You know what, Stephen? Now I feel stupid. This is a huge misunderstanding. I didn't know that they were busy. I didn't mean to interrupt them—with their jobs." He went on, "Honestly Mitch McConnell, you really want to go with the 'We'll get to it when we get to it' argument for the heroes of 9/11?"[51] Stewart then turned McConnell's own words on him: "You know what, if you're busy, I get it. Just understand the next time we have a war, or you're being robbed, or your house is on fire and you make that desperate call for help, don't get bent out of shape if they show up at the last minute with fewer people than you thought were going to pay attention and don't actually put it out. ... I'm sure they'll put it out for good when they feel like getting around to it. No offense."[52]

Early the next morning, the *Late Show* video clip of Stewart blasting McConnell already had been viewed more than 1.1 million times on Twitter and YouTube.[53] A few days later, McConnell met with first responders and promised Congress would vote on the bill before the end of the summer.[54]

> *"Jon's at his best when he's articulating our pain and suffering and agony."*

First responders' organizer John Feal again praised Stewart for his advocacy. Feal told National Public Radio that over the decade they'd worked together on behalf of first responders, he and Stewart had become good friends, and they had learned how best to use Stewart's voice on behalf of the first responders. "Jon's at his best when he's articulating our pain and suffering and agony," Feal said. He also called Stewart a "humble," "compassionate" and "low maintenance" person who wanted "to be embedded in the teams" that Feal organized to lobby in Washington, rather than a celebrity who wanted to stand out.[55]

Of course, not everyone heaped praise on Stewart for speaking out about the first responders' bill. For instance, after reading about Stewart's war of words with McConnell in *The Hill*, a newspaper and website that cover Capitol Hill, some readers were suspicious of Stewart's motives. "Stewart has made his living trashing Republicans. However noble he pretends his goals are, he is not to be taken seriously," wrote one. "Stewart was just being a show-biz hotdog, whining about something that was going to be taken care of without all of his noise," wrote another. Yet another wrote, "Stewart grandstanded and accomplished nothing. The Senate was going to address this anyway." Another worried about Stewart's role in public affairs, writing, "The fact that comedians are our moral compass bodes ill for our nation."[56]

The Need for Strong Evaluation by Moral Agents

These commenters are absolutely free to enter the conversation about the first responders' bill and Stewart's advocacy for it. As did the commenters, we may support or oppose Stewart's involvement, but no evidence suggests Stewart tried to quash others' views about the bill. In fact, the evidence for an ethically justifiable relationship between Stewart as speaker and the first responders' bill as his topic is strong. Stewart showed a personal stake in the issue just days after the 9/11 terrorist attacks. He displayed a decade-long commitment to the issue that included lobbying Congress multiple times and speaking out about the issue in media interviews and on news and comedy programs. He spoke from an informed perspective, sharing facts about the first responders' quick arrivals at the World Trade Center, the many months they worked there, the toxic conditions of the rubble in which they worked, and the resulting illnesses they contracted. He participated respectfully in the democratic process, championing the view with which he fervently agreed.

Thus, Stewart's relationship to his topic exemplifies the kind of "strong evaluation" philosopher Charles Taylor argues moral agents are obliged to make. "Responsible moral agents are precisely that by virtue of their ability to distinguish the good from the bad and the better from the good. The goal of the self's moral life is to produce a person capable of exercising practical reason in order to make moral decisions. Strong evaluation is the key to this ability," explains Taylor scholar Peggy Bowers.[57] Taylor contends moral agents who understand strong evaluation are both authentic and deep in their commitment to a decision.[58] The evidence of Stewart's relationship to his topic suggests a commitment authentic and deep enough that he was willing to shed "the comedic safety blanket he once had" and to take up the role of advocacy, observes media and politics scholar Allaina Kilby. "What Stewart has shown us is that comedy and satire have limited capabilities. They can draw our attention to a problem, but the ability to create real political change is dependent on passion, tenacity and sustained engagement in the democratic process."[59]

Stewart's entry into the democratic process as an outspoken advocate is an example of an essential moral role identified by moral philosopher

Thomas McCullough, who argues that public life must attend to ethical claims made by engaged citizens. McCullough writes, "The view of political life as a policy-making process, with decisions made by a democratic elite employing policy analysts (experts), has two fateful consequences. First, public discussion of the ethical issues is devalued and is seen as extraneous to policy making. Ethics enters into the process only as an arbitrary function of the individual decision maker. Second, the citizen is rendered remote, powerless, alienated, apathetic, and hopeless."[60] In speaking out for first responders' assistance, Stewart made an ethical claim as a citizen demanding respect from his fellow Americans for the first responders' service and sacrifice.

Ascribing motive to a moral agent is tricky territory, of course, because no one aside from the moral agent truly knows her or his motive for behavior. In Stewart's case, however, all available evidence suggests he possessed an ethically justifiable motive to help direct government health care benefits to gravely ill public servants and that his sustained relationship to the topic of advocacy for first responders ethically justifies his speaking out. The next chapter examines the second element of the ethical justification test for of speaking out—the speaker's motivation—in greater detail.

5

What Is the Motivation for Speaking Out?

In July 2019, U.S. president Donald Trump stepped into the White House Rose Garden to address an audience gathered to see him sign into law the reauthorization of the 9/11 Victims Compensation Fund, which assisted first responders and other victims who became ill after the September 11, 2001, terrorist attacks in New York, Washington, D.C., and Pennsylvania. President Trump said the firefighters, police officers and emergency workers who "raced into smoke, fire, and debris" at the attack sites were "selfless patriots of unmatched character and devotion."

After the attacks, many first responders contracted cancers and other serious illnesses from working in the toxic conditions created by the collapse of the World Trade Center in New York, and President Trump said that for nearly 20 years first responders "endured hardship with amazing grace and incredible grit." He noted that more than 2,000 first responders or other people who lived and worked near the World Trade Center had died from 9/11-related illnesses and that additional thousands were living with those illnesses. The law that would extend compensation through the year 2092 for medical or burial expenses and lost wages to those victims or their families was the nation's way of honoring its "solemn duty to America's best, bravest, and finest," President Trump said.[1]

As he concluded his remarks, the president asked several dozen first responders and family members of those who had died from 9/11 illnesses to gather around him at the desk where he would sit to sign the bill. Many of the 9/11 community members who surrounded President Trump had lobbied for the compensation fund for years, helping secure its authorization in 2010, its reauthorization in 2015 and what they hoped was its final reauthorization in 2019. The bill now was named the "Never Forget the Heroes: James Zadroga, Ray Pfeifer and Luis Alvarez Permanent Authorization of the September 11th Victim Compensation Fund Act." Police detective James Zadroga's name had been placed on the 2010 bill authorizing the fund because his fatal respiratory disease was one of the first illnesses connected to post–9/11 recovery work at the World Trade Center.[2] The two names that joined Zadroga's on the 2019 bill honored first responders who spent their dying days lobbying for the fund: Firefighter Ray Pfeifer died from 9/11-related kidney cancer in 2017,[3] and police detective Luis Alvarez died from colorectal cancer just days after he testified for the 2019 bill in the U.S. House of Representatives.[4]

> *"There's no celebration, knowing that people are sick and dying."*

After the president signed the Zadroga, Pfeifer and Alvarez Victim Compensation Fund, the families and 9/11 community members gathered in the White House Rose Garden clapped, shook the president's hand, exchanged high-fives, hugged one another, wiped away tears and posed for photos. President Trump handed one of the bill-signing pens to John Feal, a "ramrod activist" who as a demolition supervisor lost half his left foot working in the World Trade Center rubble and originally was denied victims' compensation because his injury occurred too long after the 9/11 attacks.[5] Feal had led nearly 300 trips to the nation's capitol for first responders to lobby for the compensation program over 18 years, making him one of the 9/11 community's most visible advocates.

In 2019, Feal was especially vocal in television news interviews to advocate for the fund's reauthorization, as its progress stalled on Capitol Hill. After the bill signing ceremony, journalists again sought out Feal for comment on the law's importance. Noticeably more subdued in interviews than he was on the day the bill was passed by the U.S. Senate and referred to the president for signature, Feal said he was relieved rather than jubilant over the bill signing. Clutching the pen he had been given by President Trump, Feal said, "There's no celebration, knowing that people are sick and dying. The bill isn't going to save anybody's lives. We're going to offer financial relief."[6]

Standing alone in the Rose Garden for a cable TV news interview, Feal referred to the notable absence of the highest-profile long-term partner with whom he had advocated for the compensation fund: "To Jon Stewart, if you're watching, you're my best friend and I love you," Feal said.[7]

Stewart, the well-known television political satirist, for years stood beside Feal, advocating for 9/11 first responders' fund and calling on Congress to re-authorize the fund. In 2019, for instance, as Congress considered extending the fund for 70 years, Stewart spoke out forcefully and shamed members of Congress for failing to pass the extension, and he skewered Republicans for paying more attention to President Trump than to the bill. Perhaps, therefore, Stewart was absent from the bill signing ceremony in the Rose Garden because he did not want to be in the presence of a president whose posturing he disrespected. Perhaps Stewart was absent because President Trump did not invite Stewart, whose unflattering satire the president probably disliked. Perhaps Stewart was absent because he was on a previously scheduled family vacation, as some news sources reported.[8] Perhaps Stewart was absent because after some 18 years of speaking out for the first responders, he regarded passage of the law as the end of his advocacy on the topic. Perhaps, knowing his presence would attract news coverage, Stewart was absent so cameras would focus instead on 9/11 community members, such as Feal, who attended the bill-signing ceremony.

Motivation as a Key Aspect of Justification for Action

The previous chapter established an ethically justifiable relationship between Stewart and speaking out on behalf of the first responders' fund, showing his long-term commitment to the 9/11 community and his informed perspective about the compensation fund. This chapter turns to the question of whether Stewart's motivation for speaking out on the topic was ethically justified. Examining a speaker's motivation is the second requirement in Wyatt's and Bunton's four-part test a famous entertainer or athlete can use to ethically justify transcending role-related expectations to speak out about a serious issue of public importance. The test examines the relationship of the speaker to the topic of the speech, the speaker's motivation for speaking, the nature of any harm created by speaking, and the tendency of the speech to promote dialogue about the topic.[9]

Motivation is a crucial element of ethical justification for action. Philosophers Lawrence Becker and Charlotte Becker define motive as a reason or cause for a moral agent's action: "An agent will be judged to have acted well or to be morally good as she acts from the right motives."[10] Immanuel Kant's duty-based philosophy suggests a moral agent's good will—or motivation, we may call it—must be pure if the moral agent's action is to be justifiable. In Kantian philosophy, good will is the only true moral good and is "esteemed beyond comparison as far higher than anything it could ever bring about."[11] Good will outweighs other moral goods, according to Kant. "Intelligence, wit, judgment, and other talents of the mind we may care to name, or courage, resolution, and constancy of purpose, as qualities of temperament, are without doubt good and desirable in many respects; but they can also be bad and hurtful when the will is not good," he wrote.[12] In other words, Kantian philosophy requires motivation that stems from good intention for an action. No matter what good consequences an action might produce, the action is not ethically justifiable unless it is rooted in good intention. Kant stated, "A good will is not good because of what it effects or accomplishes—because of its fitness for attaining some proposed end: it is good through its willing alone."[13]

Obviously, ascertaining moral agents' motivation for decisions to act is a risky endeavor. Only moral agents themselves truly know why they make particular ethical decisions. We cannot get inside their heads. In cases of famous athletes and entertainers who transcend role-related expectations to speak out, only the speakers know with certainty their motives for speaking, and unless speakers share that motivation publicly, we should remember that we enter tricky territory when we attempt to assign motivation to moral agents. Furthermore, all of us often have more than one motive for acting as we do, so even if a moral agent discloses a motive for speaking out, we cannot be certain it is the speaker's primary motive. "Since agents may have many layers of motive, there is some question about how to specify 'the motive' from which an agent acts," Becker and Becker point out.[14] Therefore, while our ethical analysis of speaking out will be incomplete unless we attempt to understand moral agents' motivations for speaking, we must approach that task with humility.

Ethically Suspect Motivations for Speaking Out

Numerous motivations for superstar entertainers and athletes to speak out are ethically suspect. Foremost among them is motivation rooted in vanity. These celebrities are as human as the rest of us, and human nature suggests any of us can be flattered when others look to us for our opinions and judgments. But speaking out to boost one's ego, to enhance one's public reputation, to gain visibility or to rehabilitate an image are self-centered motives lacking Kantian good will.

Celebrity athletes and entertainers with easy access to public platforms may risk little when they speak out, and in many instances, adoring fans may welcome these public figures' speech. *Guardian* columnist Marina Hyde asserts that we live in a "celebocracy, which means that a celebrity's voice is worth approximately 10,000 times" that of a regular person's voice.[15]

Sometimes, however, these celebrities should resist the temptation to use their popularly valued voices. When they imagine speaking out on topics about which they are not expected or expert sources, celebrities might wisely consider a number of questions before speaking, such as:

- Why me?
- Just because I can speak out, should I?
- Do I have something useful to say on this subject?
- Should I use my platform not to share my views but to direct my audience to experts' views?

Of course, asking these questions would require celebrities to exercise a self-restraint that does not exist in Hyde's "celebocracy," which takes for granted celebrity affiliation with public causes. "In fact, if a star or upcoming ingénue does not have a cause to endorse, a charity to raise awareness and bucks for, or a politician he or she is associated with, well, questions get asked and eyebrows raised (you know, more than the usual) and the seriousness of the up-and-comers is scrutinized," writes political scientist Greg Rabidoux. "Part of a service provided by some savvy Hollywood agents today is media advice on picking the right cause or issue to get in front of as a way to demonstrate caring and sincerity to one's fans."[16]

Cross-Expertise Violations

Speaking out about good causes because it enhances connections with fans is not ethically justifiable. Avoiding speech motivated by self-centered purposes is crucial when celebrity speakers do not possess sufficient knowledge about a topic and therefore may misinform those fans, even potentially harming them with misinformation that stems from lack of expertise. Our contemporary digital culture offers instant access to more information—and misinformation—than at any point in human history, and yet, international affairs scholar Tom Nichols argues "we are witnessing the *death of the ideal of expertise* itself, a Google-fueled, Wikipedia-based, blog-sodden collapse of any division between professionals and laypeople, students and teachers, knowers and wonderers—in other words, between those of any achievement in an area and those with none at all."[17]

Nichols criticizes "cross-expertise violations" that occur when people who are well-informed or skilled in one field veer into other fields in which they possess little if any expertise. He finds entertainers especially guilty of these cross-expertise violations, which may be motivated by factors ranging from naiveté to ego. "Sometimes, however, the motivation is as simple as the opportunity provided by fame. Entertainers are the worst offenders here. (And yes, in their field, they are experts. Acting schools are not run by chemical engineers.) Their celebrity affords them easy access to issues and controversies, and to actual experts or policymakers who will work with them," Nichols suggests. "This creates bizarre situations in which experts in one field—entertainment—end up giving disquisitions on important questions in other fields."[18] At their worst, Nichols argues, cross-expertise violations by celebrities who disseminate uninformed or misinformed views "push fads, create false alarms, and change the daily habits of millions of gullible fans."[19]

Ethically Justifiable Motivations for Speaking Out

To be fair, public figures may produce ethically justifiable motivations for speaking out. First among them is the fundamental principle that public figures possess the same legal rights to free expression as anyone else does and are entitled to use those rights. High-profile public figures, especially the entertainers and athletes who achieve superstar status and command social media platforms that reach millions of followers, "are often objectified, discussed, and ridiculed with little consideration for who they are as people," asserts digital media scholar danah boyd,[20] but these celebrities are citizens with viewpoints, too.

In the United States these public figure citizens enjoy the same First Amendment rights as the rest of us to start or join a public conversation on topics of shared concern. The Constitution doesn't require citizens to be well-informed. Rather, the Constitution extends to all citizens the right to speak freely without fear of government censorship, as long as they do not cause the kinds of harm to reputation and safety that come from slandering others or yelling "fire!" in a crowded public place. Superstars who are motivated to speak out because they want to exercise their basic right of free speech are as legally free to do so as any citizen would be.

Ethical Fitness

Additional ethically justifiable motivations exist. In acting from these additional motivations, thoughtful celebrities are not just speaking out because they *can* do so as citizens, but are speaking out as more fully cognizant moral agents because they *ought* to do so. In this way, celebrity speakers overcome the problem of moral muteness. Ethicist Frederick Bruce Bird writes, "To be morally mute is to be silent about one's moral convictions in settings where it would be fitting to give voice to them."[21]

Morally aware speakers overcome the moral blindness and moral deafness that might render them impervious to issues. Rather, the moral agent sees and hears a moral issue, and then abandons moral silence to act on a duty to speak out about that issue.[22] In essence, the moral agent becomes what professional ethics scholars Minette Drumwright and Patrick Murphy call a "seeing, talking practitioner" of ethics who speaks out.[23] Another way to put it is that the moral agent who speaks out may be an example of "ethical fitness," which ethicist Rushworth Kidder calls the "capacity to recognize the nature of moral challenges and respond with a well-tuned conscience, a lively perception of the difference between right and wrong, and an ability to choose the right and live by it."[24]

Ethically fit moral agents may justify speaking out by demonstrating a motivation to use their citizen free speech rights to tell the truth. Here, celebrities are motivated by a moral duty to tell the truth about an issue of shared public concern when the truth is not known, is being ignored or is drowned out. This motivation to tell the truth may be strongly justified if these world-famous entertainers and athletes are using their public platforms to tell the truth about important issues of public concern that are being neglected by powerful authorities or institutions. Celebrity entertainers' or athletes' social media channels may attract hundreds of thousands of, if not millions, of followers, and entertainers' or athletes' social media messages may generate news coverage that will reach additional hundreds of thousands.

Of course, in using their popular platforms to tell the truth, these famous people must act with care. Truth is central to the basic human condition of trusting the other people with whom we share our society, according to philosopher Sissela Bok. She notes, "This is why some level of truthfulness has always been seen as essential to human society, no matter how deficient the observance of other moral principles."[25] Influential famous people who speak out must intend to be truthful and not to mislead. Audiences need to trust the truth of messages they receive.[26]

Preventing or Rectifying Harm

Influential famous people also may be justifiably motivated to use their citizen rights to free speech to tell the truth, especially to powerful authorities, because drawing attention to the subject may rectify or prevent a harm. Here, celebrities again are ethically fit moral agents who believe speaking out may right a wrong. "The basic reason for acting morally is to avoid causing harm to other people,"[27] according to philosopher Bernard Gert. He identifies 10 harms as "evils" all moral agents seek to avoid and want others to avoid: killing, causing pain, disabling or depriving of ability, depriving of freedom, depriving of pleasure, deceiving, breaking promises, cheating, disobeying the law, and failing to exercise one's duty.[28] Gert writes, "All human beings are vulnerable; not only can they suffer all the harms mentioned, but they can be caused to suffer these harms by the actions of others. People can be killed, caused to suffer pain, be disabled, and be deprived of freedom and pleasure by the actions of other people. No rational person wants to suffer any of these harms unless he has an adequate reason for suffering it. In fact, all rational persons seek to avoid death, pain, disability, loss of freedom, and loss of pleasure unless they have an adequate reason not to avoid them."[29]

Speaking out from the motivation to prevent or rectify one or more of these harms to self or others is ethically justifiable, especially if famous speakers are motivated to address harms to less powerful and more vulnerable people who may lack the agency to speak effectively for themselves. The motivation to prevent or rectify harm, especially to vulnerable parties, naturally may be connected with a motivation to help create or further dialogue on the important issue of shared public concern that affects those parties, and with the motivation to stimulate discussion of potential solutions.

These related motivations capitalize on celebrity athletes' and entertainers' abilities to command widespread public attention that may be used for good. Television satirist Jon Stewart's years of speaking out about first responders' needs for government benefits to defray expenses created by illnesses resulting from their 9/11 service exemplifies these motivations.

The Principle of Loyalty

Acting out of loyalty, especially a long-term loyalty such as that displayed by Stewart to the 9/11 first responders, also is an ethically justifiable motivation for speaking out. Philosopher Josiah Royce identifies loyalty as the central concept around which moral agents may organize their "entire moral world."[30] So that they do not fall into blind loyalty to immoral causes, moral agents need to possess "a rational conception of loyalty,"[31] Royce writes. Thus, he defines loyalty as the "willing and practical and thoroughgoing devotion of a person to a cause,"[32] which involves three elements. The moral agent must identify the cause, be "willingly and thoroughly" devoted to the cause, and, perhaps most importantly, take "sustained and practical" actions on behalf of the cause.[33]

Royce cautions that moral agents cannot justifiably declare loyalty to a cause simply because it pleases them, or because it serves moral agents' own purposes. A loyalty is "much larger than your private self,"[34] Royce declares. Furthermore, "loyalty is social" and may involve "fellow-servants."[35] Speaking together from loyalty to a public cause, as Jon Stewart and John Feal repeatedly did on behalf of the 9/11 first responders, fits Royce's criteria and thus is an ethically justifiable motivation for speaking out.

Moral Consistency

Another ethically justifiable motivation for speaking out is acting from what Kidder calls "moral consistency" and explains as "a clear congruence" between ethical actions and underlying moral values. "The truly consistent individual, the one who generally wins our highest praise as an exemplar of virtue, is the one whose actions in public and private are morally identical."[36]

Here, moral agents may use their First Amendment rights to speak out, to tell the truth, to prevent or rectify harm, to stimulate dialogue and to explore solutions because moral consistency demands speaking out. Jon Stewart made his name as a television satirist by pointing out government's failure to serve citizens, so extending his on-camera criticisms into advocacy that called out failures to help 9/11 first responders is morally consistent. Nichols notes, "Activism is the right of every person in an open and democratic society."[37] A celebrity such as Stewart who is motivated toward activism ethically can justify his advocacy if he is truthful, authentic and consistent in speaking out. The 9/11 first responders' situation was the one issue Stewart spoke out about for a decade.

> "Today I am in our nation's capital. I don't particularly enjoy coming down here."

In early 2019, the 9/11 community saw a dire need to extend benefits that had been authorized in 2010 and funded again in 2015. In February 2019, the fund's administrator announced that $5 billion worth of claims from the $7.3 billion fund already had been paid and that additional payments to victims and their families must be cut by 50 to 70 percent because the number of people eligible for the remaining funding had skyrocketed. In the previous two years alone, claims for benefits had been submitted by some 20,000 additional victims whose 9/11-related cancers and other serious illnesses only recently had been diagnosed.[38] Upon learning how quickly the fund was being depleted and how many additional claimants needed benefits, John Feal and his FealGood Foundation colleagues returned to Washington, arranging for 9/11 first responders to walk the halls of Congress to lobby for more funding and a permanent extension to the program.

To draw attention to first responders' needs, Feal again recruited Jon Stewart, who had been out of the public eye after retiring from *The Late Show*. In retirement, Stewart made only a rare comedy appearance here or there, but when Feal needed him, Stewart emerged from private life, apparently demonstrating Royce's unswerving loyalty to a cause. When Stewart resumed his advocacy in 2019, *The Washington Post* noted his consistency on the issue, reporting, "Stewart's fury on the issue has been nearly unparalleled among other public figures, emerging louder than arguably anyone else on Capitol Hill or in the media each time money for first responders' health care has been at risk of evaporating."[39]

As Stewart joined the first responders lobbying in Washington, D.C., he published an opinion piece in *The New York Daily News,* writing, "Today

I am in our nation's capital. I don't particularly enjoy coming down here." Yet, he said, "I am walking the halls of Congress with injured and ill 9/11 responders and survivors, looking to see if 'Remembering 9/11' is more than a cheap obligatory slogan senators and representatives tweet out." Stewart displayed his knowledge of the facts about the issue, writing that 45,000 people had been certified by the World Trade Center Health Program with post–9/11 chronic health conditions and more than 10,000 people had been certified with 9/11-related cancers. He went on to suggest that voting for a permanent reauthorization of the Victim Compensation Fund was a bipartisan issue that should matter to every member of Congress, because victims whose 9/11-related illnesses made them eligible for the fund lived in each of the 50 U.S. states and 434 of the 435 U.S. congressional districts. Stewart ended his essay with these simple yet powerful words: "We ask so much of our Nation's first responders and volunteers. Let us not repay their selflessness with apathy."[40]

"Are the cameras on? Is everybody on me?"

While on Capitol Hill that February day, Stewart and Feal also gave interviews to several national cable television news networks. Stewart and Feal obviously calculated that Stewart's fame would open congressional doors and attract news coverage, but Stewart never seemed to dominate the advocacy. Feal told a reporter later that Stewart could have used his fame to seek special treatment but was instead a "low-maintenance" advocate who wanted "to be embedded in the teams" of first responders lobbying together.[41] A mutual respect among Stewart, Feal and other first responders seemed evident, as did a shared fervor for their cause. Stewart could have commanded television time alone, but he sat beside Feal for interviews, and they spoke as colleagues. Both men seemed sincerely motivated to keep their focus on first responders and other victims of the 9/11 attacks' toxic aftermath, and not on their personal experiences. When Feal told CNN, "There are men and women, uniform and nonuniform, responders and survivors, that are panicking" over their 9/11-related health care expenses, Stewart added, "The idea that 18 years later they're still tugging on the hemline on the government to get this bill through and get it funded properly is truly beyond comprehension."[42]

Stewart also participated in a news conference with Feal, other first responders and the New York members of Congress sponsoring the bill. Playing on his well-documented reputation as what *The New York Daily News* called "no fan of President Trump,"[43] Stewart spoke words he knew would create headlines and focus attention on congressional inaction. "Are the cameras on? Is everybody on me?" Stewart asked reporters covering the news conference. "The Trump Justice Department is doing an excellent job administrating this program. The claims are going through faster, and the awards are coming through. … The program works exactly like it's supposed to, so now it's Congress' job to fund it properly and let these people live in peace."[44]

Stewart's assessment that a pro–Trump remark would generate attention for the first responders' bill was a savvy use of his news conference appearance. President Trump soon posted messages to his millions of Twitter followers about Stewart's praise of the Trump administration's support of the first responders' program, which also put some pressure on President Trump's fellow Republicans in Congress to vote for the program's reauthorization.[45]

> *"None of these people want to be here. And they're not here for themselves."*

Stewart, Feal and first responders returned to Capitol Hill in June 2019 to testify for the bill before a subcommittee of the U.S. House of Representatives, and Stewart's "game-changing outrage"[46] about the urgency of first responders' needs spoke volumes to the public and to Congress. "Stewart hadn't planned to unleash on the lawmakers in quite the way he did," *The Daily Beast* reported.[47] But John Feal knew that Stewart's relationships in the 9/11 community were deep and sincere. Feal also remembered that Stewart strongly connected with firefighter Ray Pfeifer when they lobbied for the 2015 reauthorization of the 9/11 fund and that Stewart gave the eulogy at Pfeifer's 2017 funeral.[48] *The Daily Beast* reported that "Pfeifer left a deep impression on Stewart,"[49] so shortly before the first responders' delegation entered the congressional hearing room to testify for the 2019 reauthorization, Feal gathered the group and gave Stewart the fireman's coat Pfeifer wore on his first job.[50] "I don't deserve this but I will treasure it like I treasure Ray and our friendship," a teary-eyed Stewart said as he received the coat. "We're going to do it today. Not just for Ray but all you guys and all the people that he was fighting for. This is beautiful. Thank you."[51] Feal hoped the gesture would help Stewart speak from his authentic personal concern for his first responder friends.[52]

Once the hearing was under way, "Feal kept working on Stewart, pointing to the packed audience and empty chairs of representatives."[53] Afterward, Feal told an interviewer that the most compelling way to use Stewart to build momentum for the bill's passage was to encourage him to speak authentically.[54] "Jon had a prepared written statement. And if Jon would've read that statement, we wouldn't be here talking today," Feal said. "And from the heart … it was a lot better than coming from a piece of paper."[55]

As he testified, Stewart seemed to speak with no motive other than helping first responders to whom he had become loyal since he watched them respond heroically to the devastation of his lower Manhattan neigh-borhood in 2001. Stewart could not have been more truthful or convinc-ing when he thumped the hearing room table with his fist and blinked back tears to say he was outraged that several members of the congressional committee were absent from the hearing. "I'm sorry if I sound angry and undiplomatic," he said. "But I'm angry and you should be, too."[56]

Stewart sat at the hearing room table beside Luis Alvarez, the former New York City police officer who testified about enduring 68 rounds of che-motherapy for cancer (and who would enter end-of-life hospice care just days later and die within three weeks).[57] Stewart referred to the lengths to which the gravely ill Alvarez had gone to testify for the bill that would sup-port his fellow victims. "Lou doesn't want to be here," Stewart said. "None of these people want to be here. And they're not here for themselves."[58]

Stewart's words seemed motivated to rectify several of Gert's moral harms—death, pain, disability, loss of freedom and loss of pleasure—that faced Alvarez and thousands of first responders or their families. Stewart's words powerfully reminded the public and politicians of our loyalties to one another. As political analyst Peter Wehner points out, "Words are not simply descriptive; they can be *aspirational*. But even more than that, words can help us better understand ourselves. They bind us together. In politics they articulate for us what goals we are trying to reach, so that there is more than just a struggle for power. We reach higher truths through words."[59]

> "At some point, we have to stand up for the people who have always stood up for us."

The 9/11 victims' compensation funding bill progressed through Con-gress that summer, quickly being passed by the U.S. House of Representa-tives in June and then being stalled for a time before ultimately being passed by the U.S. Senate at the end of July. Along the way, headlines offered Stewart credit for his advocacy. Stewart did not take credit, however. He disappeared between bursts of advocacy that were tied to the bill's progress, or lack of it. When first responder advocates felt stymied by Senate Majority Leader Mitch McConnell's delay in putting the bill before the Senate, Stewart gave inter-views and appeared on late night television to goad McConnell into action. (See Chapter 2 for a detailed analysis for that episode.) A few days later, Stew-art was photographed outside the Queens, New York, parish church where funeral services were held for Luis Alvarez, but Stewart declined to speak to reporters and referred them instead to the Alvarez family.[60]

When McConnell did bring the bill to the Senate in July, his fellow Kentucky senator, Rand Paul, challenged its cost and further stalled its pas-sage. Stewart stepped back into the public conversation, joining John Feal to give television interviews to draw attention to what Stewart called Paul's "fiscal responsibility virtue signaling" on the bill. Stewart found Paul's objection to the cost of the bill hypocritical because Paul some 18 months before had voted for a trillion-dollar tax cut that benefited wealthy Americans. Stewart called Paul "a guy that puts us in hundreds of billions of dollars of debt" and then "stands up at the last minute after 15 years of blood, sweat and tears from the 9/11 community to say that it's all over now." Stewart went on to say, "At some point, we have to stand up for the people who have always stood up for us, and at this moment in time, maybe cannot stand up for themselves due to their illnesses and their injuries."[61] In return, Paul called Stewart a "guttersnipe."[62]

When the bill eventually was put to a vote in the Senate, Stewart joined Feal and other 9/11 community members in the Senate Gallery to watch. In a news conference and interviews afterward, Stewart and Feal made a point of crediting Senate Majority Leader McConnell for ensuring the bill passed, despite Paul's objections.[63]

A CNN interviewer asked afterward why Stewart kept speaking out about the first responders' bill. He pointed to his experience as a lower Manhattan resident on 9/11, and said, "Having lived down there, having seen what the first responder community, what the survivor community, what the volunteer community, what they gave to the city during that incredibly chaotic and—and frightening time was irreplaceable."[64]

Then, as if his work was done, Stewart disappeared from public view. Feal, 9/11 community members and their families attended the White House bill signing ceremony a few days later without Stewart, whose absence was noted by many journalists covering the event. Stewart apparently was content to let the result of his transition from on-camera satirist to public advocate stand on its own, leaving others to assign merit to his motive for speaking out. Media and politics scholar Allaina Kilby was among those who did so, writing, "What Stewart has shown us is that comedy and satire have limited capabilities. They can draw our attention to a problem, but the ability to create real political change is dependent on passion, tenacity and sustained engagement in the democratic process."[65]

Examining the evidence gleaned from Stewart's sustained episodes of speaking out about 9/11 first responders' benefits allows us to conclude that Stewart acted from ethically justifiable motivations to use his citizen free speech rights to engage in the democratic process, to tell the truth about a significant public issue, to call the attention of lawmakers to that issue, and to help rectify previous harm and prevent future harm to vulnerable people. The next chapter examines the ethical harms that may arise when famous public figures speak out, even if they are strongly connected to their subjects and demonstrate seemingly justifiable motives.

6

What Is the Nature
of Any Harm Created?

Late in her career, as she attempted the nearly impossible feat of winning more Grand Slam titles than anyone in professional tennis history, Serena Williams faced intense scrutiny. The sports world wondered if Williams, whose body was battered from two decades of playing tennis at the highest levels, could break the Grand Slam record while competing against talented young players who grew up idolizing her but now seemed fearless when facing her across the net. Headlines like this one from *The Washington Post*—"A 37-year-old Williams pursuing a major record while biology sustains its everlasting rudeness"—were typical every time she stepped onto a major tournament court.[1] Such public scrutiny was not new to Williams. She had been the focus of television programs, magazine covers and news headlines for years, and had overcome many challenges in what the *Post* called her "hustles toward all-time greatness."[2]

Stories of Williams' remarkable accomplishments often note she began learning tennis at age three, when she was handed an adult-sized racquet by her parents. They taught themselves enough about the sport to give their daughters daily lessons on litter-strewn, cracked cement-courts in public parks after her father decided tennis could be his daughters' "ticket up and out" of Compton, California.[3] When Venus and Serena Williams entered competitive tennis, the African American sisters stood out from the mostly white, private club-trained players against whom they soon were winning tournaments.[4]

For years, as her powerful serve helped her claim women's titles, Serena Williams faced body-shaming from tennis players, coaches, sports reporters and commentators, and the sport's fans,[5] whom *The New Yorker* said repeatedly criticized the "size of her butt, her thighs ... and toned arms" or suggested she looked "more like a male boxer or linebacker than a women's tennis player."[6] It was not unusual for Williams to be described by tennis fans and commentators with such bigoted terms as "animal" or "gorilla."[7] Rather than admire the achievements of a pair of home-taught sisters who attained the top of the women's tennis rankings, the tennis world "worked overtime" to maintain its emphasis on "whiteness and blondness," according to *The New York Times*.[8] Williams said she felt such hurtful racial hostility as a 19-year-old "outsider" playing in the finals of a 2001 Indian Wells, California, tournament that she then boycotted the event for 13 years.[9]

After winning several Grand Slam titles, Williams skipped some events on the women's tour to pursue business ventures in fashion and acting instead, saying she wanted to lay the foundation for career success after tennis. She was labeled "frivolous," "self-indulgent" and "arrogant" by tennis commentators and former champions who apparently couldn't imagine how important planning for long-term career success might be to a Black woman who grew up in a city widely regarded as a ghetto.[10]

In 2003, Williams was away from the tennis tour recovering from a knee injury when her eldest sister, Yetunde Price, was killed in a shooting in their home town of Compton, California.[11] When Williams returned to competition, sports journalists and commentators described her absence not as a period of recovery from both a physical injury and a shattering trauma to her close-knit family, but as "disrespect" and "indifference" toward the tennis tour and her corporate sponsors.[12]

> *"There was a time when Williams was a somewhat facetious interview. Not anymore."*

Despite facing such prejudices as she competed, by 2017 Williams had won 23 Grand Slam singles titles, 14 Grand Slam doubles titles and four Olympic gold medals, which for many sports historians made her the greatest tennis player of all time.[13] When she won her 23rd Grand Slam singles title at the 2017 Australian Open, Williams was in the early stages of pregnancy. Her daughter was born via Caesarean section in September 2017, and shortly after the birth, Williams experienced near-fatal blood clots in her lungs. She spent months recovering, and yet she returned to professional tennis before her daughter's first birthday. In July 2018, she reached the Wimbledon final, displaying what one sports writer called an "out-of-category strength … to return to the top of her profession at 36 years old with a baby on her shoulder and scars on her belly and in her lungs from the childbirth ordeal that almost killed her."[14]

Williams also returned to tennis with a passion for speaking out about life-threatening maternal health issues that disproportionately affect Black women and racist violence that disproportionately kills Black people. "There was a time when Williams was a somewhat facetious interview. Not anymore," observed a sports columnist.[15]

Now, Williams was both a legendary athlete chasing a history-making record and a confident business entrepreneur and venture capitalist who spoke with authority about the connections of racial bias to such topics as gun violence, the criminal justice system, health care and women's pay. This chapter uses examples of Williams speaking out to examine the nature of harms that must be considered if celebrity athletes and entertainers are to speak out with ethical justification.

Examining the possibility of harm created by speaking out is the third element of the justification test celebrity athletes and entertainers can use to justify transcending role-related expectations and speaking out. The four-part test asks speakers to consider their relationship to the topic they are speaking out about, their motivation for speaking, the nature of any harm created by speaking, and the tendency of speaking out to promote dialogue about the topic.[16] (See chapters 4 and 5 for analysis of the first two parts of the test.) This third element of the test—the nature of possible harm—requires a famous speaker to reasonably anticipate consequences that could occur from speaking out. If the potential consequences of the speech would cause harm to the speaker or to others, the speaker should consider how to avoid or mitigate the harm before speaking.[17]

The Harm Principle

The 19th century British philosopher John Stuart Mill receives credit for introducing the harm principle to philosophical thinking. The harm principle is the idea that moral agents are free to act however they think best, unless their actions harm other people. Mill's emphasis on moral agents' individual liberty is a "bedrock" influence on views about citizen speech.[18] Author Adam Gopnik notes, "When it comes to free speech, Mill wants us to ask something simple: Is this practice causing me any real harm? Not potential harm to my feelings, not social harm to my idea of right, not damage to the great precepts of religion or to my stuffy uncle's sense of propriety or to my inner sense of safety. Unless the speaker is actually about to cut your throat, you have to let him work his jaw."[19]

Mill does allow that moral agents' freedom justifiably can be curtailed if the agents' actions would inflict harm. Philosophers Lawrence Becker and Charlotte Becker define harm as "an adverse effect on someone's interests" and interests as "the distinguishable components of a person's good or well-being."[20] These interests, or components of well-being, might be such goods as a person's health, safety and privacy. Naturally, these interests will conflict with one another from time to time, and when they do, philosopher Bernard Gert suggests moral agents should engage in "a comparative evaluation of conflicting interests"[21] as they decide which interests they should avoid harming when they decide how to behave.

Moral agents considering whether speaking out is ethical should anticipate how to prevent or rectify harmful consequences to others' interests as a result of their proposed speech. For instance, after experiencing the trauma of her 31-year-old sister's murder by a reported gang member in 2003, and upon observing the continuing occurrence of gun violence in Black communities, a public figure such as Serena Williams might be motivated to transcend her role as a top athlete and speak out to her legions of fans about gun violence. Perhaps a comment on the subject from an athlete of Williams' stature might help create urgency for public discussions of how to reduce gun violence and prevent harm to future victims. But in speaking out to share her family's traumatic loss of her sister in a drive-by shooting, Williams would need to proceed with delicacy and consider the privacy and vulnerability of her mourning family members, especially the three minor children her sister left behind. As a moral agent concerned with harm, she would need to balance the potential harm of invasion of privacy against the potential good of creating public awareness about shooting deaths.

When confronting the harms that could occur from speaking out, moral agents can find guidance in Gert's system of "common morality." Gert contends that whether we act to maximize our freedom, as Mill would have us do, or we act to uphold our intentions, as philosopher Immanuel Kant would have us do, all of us as moral agents want to prevent harm to ourselves and others. Thus, Gert's system of common morality identifies 10 harms—which he calls "evils"—we must avoid inflicting on ourselves or others: killing, causing pain, disabling or depriving of ability, depriving of freedom, depriving of pleasure, deceiving, breaking promises, cheating, disobeying the law, and failing to exercise one's duty.[22] If Williams spoke out about the effects of gun violence in a compelling way, while protecting her family's privacy, her comments would be justifiable as an attempt to prevent or mitigate Gert's harms of killing, causing pain, and depriving of ability, freedom and pleasure for gun violence victims, their families and their communities.

Distinguishing Harm and Offense

In evaluating possible harms to prevent or rectify when speaking out, moral agents also must distinguish between harm and offense. "Not everything that we dislike or resent, and wish to avoid, is harmful to us," Becker and Becker point out. "These experiences can distress, offend, irritate, disappoint, or bore us, without harming any of our interests. They come to us, are suffered for a time, and then go, leaving us as whole and undamaged as before. Offended states, in this broad sense, are diverse, having little in common except that they are generally disliked. They include affronts to sense or sensibility, disgust, shock, shame, fear, and even minor pains and discomforts."[23]

Harm that occurs as a result of speech affects us adversely and is hard to justify ethically, although it might be done. Offense that occurs as a result of speech typically affects us less negatively and sometimes may be ethically justifiable, especially if it achieves a greater good of directing our attention to serious issues of shared public concern. For instance, some audience members could be offended—that is, irritated or resentful—if Serena Williams spoke out about gun violence and its particular effects on Black people. Perhaps audience members could be irritated because they think Williams should stick to tennis and stay out of conversations about crime, or perhaps audience members could be resentful because they think gun violence experienced in Black communities is no more important than other types of violence affecting other communities. But any offense those audience members felt would not harm their physical or intellectual well-being, and so Williams would be ethically justified in speaking out about gun violence if she were motivated to prevent for others the harm her family suffered. Because Williams would not be causing harm to people offended by her speech, Mill's harm principle would allow her the freedom as a moral agent to speak out.

Of course, the line between harm and offense created by speaking out is not always bright. Offensive speech sometimes may harm a person's well-being. No doubt Serena Williams herself, as a target of hateful racist and sexist speech for most of the two decades she has spent in the public spotlight, understands the power of offensive words to wound. Gopnik contends that offensive speech's wounding power reveals the limits of relying on Mill's preference for moral agents' individual liberty. "The liberal assertion of free speech must never be seen as a value outside the larger context of power: who gets to speak, and how speech is heard, and how pained or threatened the listeners of that speech may feel. Mill's idea of free speech is what we now call elitist or class-bound. He assumes a pleasant argument among gentlemen, or at most gentlemen and gentlewomen. … He does not know what it really feels like to hear hatred directed at your person or your group. Free speech is fine; freed people are better."[24] In considering instances when offensive speech could become harmful speech, Gopnik asserts that moral agents "have to distinguish between insulting someone's beliefs—something none of us enjoy but which all of us have to endure—and threatening someone's safety."[25]

When Mill advanced his principle emphasizing moral agents' individual liberty unless they caused harm, he could not have imagined the environment in which public figures now are free to speak. Today, when celebrity athletes and entertainers speak out about topics of shared public concern they often do so through digital media channels. In fact, the rise of social media seems related to an increased volume of these public figures' speech, and speaking out through social media can complicate the potential harms of speech public figures must consider.

> *"It can reach so many people and impact so many lives by just taking 10 seconds."*

With 12.5 million Instagram followers,[26] 10.8 million Twitter followers,[27] and 5.3 million Facebook followers,[28] Serena Williams is among the most prolific of athletes communicating via social media. "Now you just open up your phone and you can say something or you can post something, you can shoot a video," Williams said when asked about her social media use. "It can reach so many people and impact so many lives by just taking 10 seconds. I think that's really awesome. I think having that opportunity and that platform that we have, to be able to say things that we feel and speak up for social issues or things that aren't right, or things that are right, good things and bad things, I think is really important."[29]

The motive Williams expresses for speaking out is ethically justifiable, with its focus on drawing attention to "social issues or things that aren't right, or things that are right," but her enthusiasm for using social media tools for speaking focuses on the speed and reach of those tools. "However, social media blur boundaries between presence and absence, time and space, control and freedom, personal and mass communication, private and public, and virtual and real, affecting how old patterns should be understood and raising new challenges and opportunities for people engaging others through new technologies," note digital media scholars Nancy Baym and danah boyd.[30] These characteristics of social media should give a speaker pause.

Social media messages are more persistent, visible, spreadable and searchable than were previous types of media messages, according to boyd.[31] Thus, the comments Williams posts on social media channels will persist much longer than her comments did in the days when a tennis star spoke to sports journalists who gathered in a pre- or post-tennis match interview room and then reported a few quotations in a newspaper sports story or on the sports segment of the late television news. Williams' social media comments also will be visible immediately to her millions of followers and will spread quickly, thanks to the ease with which followers can share social media content in their own circles. Ultimately, because users find it easy to search for social media content after it has been posted and shared, Williams' comments will persist. Years ago, a potentially harmful or offensive remark might have been uttered casually before fading away, but today, such a comment will not vanish. Rather, it will be resurrected time after time, when the topic of the remark or the speaker who made it are noticed by audiences, including the many journalists who follow public figures' social media channels.

Therefore, when Williams considers transcending role-related expectations that apply to her as an athlete and speaking out through social media channels about a topic of public concern such as racial injustice, her ethical analysis should consider the persistence, visibility, spreadability and searchability of her words, as well as how those particular characteristics might complicate other harms related to speaking out.

Williams' engagement on issues of racial bias can be traced to her early years on the professional tennis tour. In 2000, when she was an 18 year old ranked sixth in the world and the first African American woman to win a Grand Slam title in 40 years, she made headlines for withdrawing from a South Carolina tournament to support a boycott of events there because the Confederate flag flew over the state capitol.[32] In 2006 and 2008, Williams visited Africa to better understand the history of the slave trade, and while there gave tennis clinics and established schools for young people.[33] Williams' commitment to issues of racial justice intensified by 2015. That year, she achieved impressive professional success, winning 53 of 56 matches she played on the tour, advancing to the finals of all four Grand Slam tournaments and winning three of them. Even skeptics began to agree that breaking the career Grand Slams record would not be unreasonable for Williams. *Sports Illustrated* named Williams its Sportsperson of the Year, making her only the ninth woman in the award's 60-year history to receive it. Six of those nine women, however, had shared the honor with men, and none of them had been Black.[34]

In honoring Williams, the magazine's managing editor noted her "stranglehold" on the No. 1 ranking in tennis that year, during which she "built the most yawning ranking points gap between her and her closest competitor in tennis history," and added, "But we are honoring Serena Williams too for reasons that hang in the grayer, less comfortable ether, where issues such as race and femininity collide with the games."[35] Among those reasons, the editor said, was the way Williams "brushed aside justifiable rage and fear of public humiliation—not to mention a point of family honor—to address the darkest chapter of her career."[36]

"I needed to go back there and speak out against racism."

Early in 2015, Williams addressed that dark chapter with a *Time* magazine essay in which she explained her surprising decision to return to the Indian Wells, California, tournament she had vowed for years never again to play. At Indian Wells in 2001, Venus and Serena Williams were scheduled to face each other in a highly anticipated semifinal match, but Venus withdrew because she was suffering from tendinitis, and Serena thus advanced to the final match. By the time Serena Williams entered the stadium to play the final, "unfounded rumors of a Williams family match fix sparked unprecedented ugliness," *Sports Illustrated* reported.[37] Some observers reported spectators uttered "explicit racial slurs and threats of bodily harm,"[38] both to Williams and to her family in the stands. In her 2015 essay, Williams recalled "jeering and booing" spectators who created "an undercurrent of racism" throughout the match that "was painful, confusing and unfair" to her as a 19 year old. She wrote that although she won the tournament, she left Indian Wells "feeling as if I had lost the biggest game ever— not a mere tennis game but a bigger fight for equality." Yet 13 years later, Williams said she had "a new understanding of the true meaning of forgiveness," rooted in her religious faith. She wrote, "I was raised by my mom to love and forgive freely. 'When you stand praying, forgive whatever you have against anyone, so that your Father who is in the heavens may also forgive you' (Mark 11:25). I have faith that fans at Indian Wells have grown with the game and know me better than they did in 2001. Indian Wells was a pivotal moment of my story, and I am a part of the tournament's story as well. Together we have a chance to write a different ending."[39]

Tennis fans and sports commentators found Williams' change of heart remarkable. Known as a ruthless competitor, Williams had been considered incapable of forgiving tournament officials who made no attempt to quiet the booing crowd that day in 2001. Williams' own mother said she was surprised at her daughter's "big step," telling *Sports Illustrated*, "To learn to forgive: She has a big problem with that."[40]

Williams, however, had been deeply affected by the killing of Michael Brown, an unarmed Black teenager in Ferguson, Missouri, who was shot six times by a white police officer in August 2014. In November, when that officer was not indicted for murder, Williams tweeted, "Shameful. What will it take???"[41] A few weeks later, when she revealed her return to Indian Wells, Williams publicly connected the "narrative of her own racial reconciliation" to "a broader anti-racist struggle."[42] She said, "I had been a teenager at Indian Wells, and that was hard for me to go through…. Now fast-forward to 2015, and we still have young black men being killed. Someone needed to do something. And I thought then that there was something greater than me and tennis. I needed to go back there and speak out against racism."[43] The media-savvy Williams knew news coverage of her Indian Wells decision would be "enormous,"[44] and she took advantage of that attention. She arranged a raffle in which fans could buy a $10 ticket for the chance of VIP treatment at the tournament.[45] Raffle ticket sales and additional donations raised $200,000 for the Equal Justice Initiative, a Montgomery, Alabama, organization that "provides legal representation for prisoners, mostly black and poor, who might have been wrongly convicted."[46]

For Williams to speak out in a spirit of racial reconciliation about Indian Wells was sufficient for many observers who praised her forgiveness. *Sports Illustrated*, for instance, called Williams "a conciliator seeking to raise the level of discourse about hard questions, the hardest ones, really."[47] Williams' added advocacy for the Equal Justice Initiative provided other observers evidence of her motivation to mitigate the harm of racism not just to herself but to some of society's most disadvantaged people. "It was quite the rare sight seeing a notable figure, celebrity or celebrity athlete, highlight a criminal justice organization," said one sports writer. "Her going back to the tournament was one thing. But her support for a criminal justice law firm located in the Deep Southern town of Montgomery, with its racist past and systematic racist present, was staggeringly tremendous."[48]

> "Yeah, my husband looks just like this in a dress. You're an idiot."

After winning the U.S. Open in September 2014, the Australian Open in January 2015 and the French Open in June 2015, Williams won Wimbledon for a sixth time in July 2015, achieving a second career "Serena Slam," a term coined in tennis to describe consecutively winning all four Grand Slam titles (as opposed to winning the four Grand Slam titles in one season).[49]

Williams' accomplishment was marred, however, by the sorts of hateful sexist and racist remarks that had been directed at her for years. *Sports Illustrated* reported that "there was endless chatter and scrutiny across various media platforms about her physique," and noted the scrutiny "centered on why her body doesn't fit into society's idea of femininity and beauty; on why she isn't skinny and white and blonde."[50] Surprisingly, the topic was not fomented only on unruly social media; it was magnified by a usually thoughtful source of sports journalism. *The New York Times* published a story suggesting women competitors on the tennis tour took great pains to appear more "feminine" than Williams. Those "rivals could try to emulate her physique, but most of them choose not to," *The Times* reported.[51] When criticized for the story, the newspaper's sports editor defended it by saying three of the story's four editors were women—as if women could not employ sexist stereotypes about other women. The editor's response didn't appease critics who pointed out the racism and sexism embedded in reporting that asked only Williams' white rivals on the tour to comment on her physique.[52]

Some 65 years before Williams achieved her second career "Serena Slam" that summer, American athlete Althea Gibson broke the color barrier in professional tennis, but only after she was forced to submit to a chromosome test that proved to tennis officials harboring "supremacist beliefs about the unwomanly nature" of Black female athletes that she was a woman.[53] For Williams to endure similar racist and sexist attitudes about her body must have been painful, but as she almost always had during her career, she publicly ignored hateful social media comments calling her "manly" and a "gorilla." On the day Williams won Wimbledon, a Twitter user wrote that it was "ironic then that the main reason for her success is that she is built like a man." When social media disagreement erupted, British author J.K. Rowling "joined a chorus of angry responses, only she didn't indulge in anger herself," *Time* magazine reported.[54] Setting aside her role as author of the internationally best-selling Harry Potter novels, Rowling pulled no punches when she spoke out to defend Williams. Posting two photos of Williams in a high-fashion, body-hugging red dress, Rowling wrote directly to the Twitter user, "Yeah, my husband looks just like this in a dress. You're an idiot."[55] Rowling's act of speaking out about sexist and racist treatment of Williams attracted news headlines worldwide, and it was an ethically justifiable instance of a powerful voice disputing a painful harm all too frequently inflicted on Williams.

"Keep it up. Don't let those trolls stop you."

Williams herself did not speak out about the racist and sexist treatment she had faced that summer until October 2015, when she guest-edited a special issue of *WIRED* magazine on the topic of "race, gender, and equality in the digital age."[56] In an essay introducing the issue, Williams explained that she collaborated with the magazine to encourage "more women and people of different colors and nationalities in tech." She continued, "I'm a black woman, and I am in a sport that wasn't really meant for black people. And while tennis isn't really about the future, Silicon Valley sure is. I want young people to … become trailblazers themselves. Together we can change the future."[57] Then, she addressed racial justice advocacy efforts that were gaining attention across the United States: "So to those of you involved in equality movements like Black Lives Matter, I say this: Keep it up. Don't let those trolls stop you. We've been through so much for so many centuries, and we shall overcome this too…. To other people, I say: When someone's harassing someone else, speak up! J.K. Rowling spoke up for me this summer, and it was an amazing feeling—I thought, well, 'I can speak up too.'"[58]

"If one person hears me, maybe that person can speak out and help. I embrace that."

At the end of 2015, in naming Williams sportsperson of the year, *Sports Illustrated*'s managing editor wrote that both Williams' tennis prowess and her public speaking earned her the magazine's award. "She is not perfect, and assorted confrontations with, and perceived slights of, tournament officials, opponents and the public at large will find their way into her narrative, this one included. But as a performer, as a doer, as a symbol, no one extended themselves and embraced the best (and worst) the sports world has to offer quite like Serena Williams, champion, 2015 Sportsperson of the Year."[59] Williams told the magazine, "I've been a little more vocal, but I want to do more" as an advocate for racial justice and the Black Lives Matter movement that emerged after shootings of African American men across the country. She said, "there are a lot of other athletes, actors, politicians who are speaking out—of all colors, by the way. They're not sitting back. They're calling for justice straight away. It makes me look at myself and say, like, What am I doing? I have a platform. I can speak out, too. If one person hears me, maybe that person can speak out and help. I embrace that."[60]

The Symbolic Volume of the Celebrity Voice

When celebrity athletes and entertainers such as Williams embrace the opportunity to speak out about issues the public may not regard as clearly related to the roles that made them famous, the symbolic volume of their voices is one of the potential harms they must consider, whatever channels they use to speak. Sometimes, these famous figures' powerful voices may pose a harm to public discourse about a topic of serious public concern by drowning out less powerful voices of other speakers, some of whom might be better qualified to speak on the topic. Powerful celebrity speakers certainly enjoy the same First Amendment free speech rights as do other citizens, and thus are entitled to express their views, but they ought to employ those free speech rights wisely, taking care not to quash the qualified voices of experts or the engaged voices of citizens with long-term commitments to an issue.

In *The Death of Expertise*, author Tom Nichols warns of the harm that may occur if celebrities who are expert in one field cross into another field and speak out as if they are experts in that field as well. He writes, "Activism is the right of every person in an open and democratic society. There is a fundamental difference, however, between activism and a celebrity abusing his or her fame. Activism among laypeople requires taking sides among experts, and advocating for preferred policies. When celebrities substitute their own judgment for that of experts, however ... they are no better than a microbiologist weighing in on modern art, or an economist arguing about pharmacology."[61] Drowning others' voices out of the public discourse may result in Gert's harm of depriving others of freedom.

In other instances, celebrities' influential voices could divert public attention from topics of serious public concern to other, potentially less important or perhaps more fashionable, topics. Advocacy for racial justice in the wake of police shootings of Black people played a growing role in American public discourse in 2015. Imagine that Serena Williams decided not to use her powerful speaking platform to amplify that discourse. Affordable health care, the economy, future terrorist attacks, hunger and homelessness, and Social Security reform also were issues on Americans' minds that year.[62] If Williams spoke out about those issues, might her powerful voice have, even inadvertently, diverted attention from the urgent questions of injustice being raised by movements such as Black Lives Matter? Concern about race relations rose 11 percentage points in a survey of Americans' concerns in 2015,[63] and it is likely that speaking out by superstar Black athletes such as Serena Williams and the National Basketball Association's LeBron James, with their millions of social media followers, helped elevate attention to issues of racial injustice. For instance, a 2019 study found superstar athletes "act as mediators and effective promoters of social justice in particular" among millions of sports fans who may not share the athletes' political views but who are devoted to following the athletes on social media.[64]

Celebrity athletes and entertainers who consider speaking out also must weigh possible harms stemming from power differentials between the potentially influential famous figures and their audiences. Famous figures should speak from a motivation to foster discourse and respect, not to coerce potentially impressionable fans into particular points of view. In some cases, fans' identification with athletes or entertainers is so strong the celebrities' influence could be disproportionate. Abusing the power differential of the celebrity-fan relationship by seeking to impose viewpoints through speech—"in effect, demanding to be trusted merely by the fact of their own fame," as Nichols puts it[65]—is not ethical; it's a kind of misguided paternalism.

The Need for a Sustained Commitment to a Topic

Too, celebrities must consider whether they are capable of sustaining a deep and ongoing interest in the topic of their speech. To be taken seriously as advocates for a serious public issue such as racial injustice requires consistent, well-informed advocacy for it. In their professional lives, actors and athletes often focus on short-term goals—winning this game or playing this part—for a few months, and then enjoy an "off season." Athletes in particular often are celebrated for their ability to rebound and start anew after suffering defeat, but a public issue such as racial injustice may require years of advocacy before even the smallest victory occurs. Because these famous athletes and entertainers possess platforms sometimes so powerful their remarks can edge other issues off the public radar,[66] they should not harm even incremental progress on the serious issues to which they've committed as advocates by abandoning those issues.

"How many hashtags now?"

Williams has evinced a long-term commitment to speaking out about racial injustice. In August 2015, a few months before being named *Sports Illustrated*'s sportsperson of the year for both her tennis accomplishments and her advocacy for justice, she used Twitter to protest the Texas killing of Christian Taylor, a Black football player shot by a white police officer. She wrote, "Really??????!!!!!!!!!!!? are we all sleeping and this is one gigantic bad nightmare? #ChristianTaylor how many hashtags now?"[67] In wondering "how many hashtags," Williams apparently referred to police killings of Black men that had become the focus of social media campaigns such as Black Lives Matter. Williams' Twitter followers quickly retweeted or discussed her post about Taylor's killing, and many of them pointed out her failure to note that although Taylor was unarmed, he was shot when police found him inside a car dealership late at night.[68] When she voluntarily assumed the role of speaking out about racial injustice, Williams accepted a duty to play that role with care. In 2015's racially charged climate, Williams owed her social media followers a check of the facts before posting a judgment about Taylor's killing. Williams' failure to provide context about the circumstances of Taylor's killing may have committed Gert's harm of deception by leading her audience to an inaccurate understanding of the case. Williams was not required to defend the police who killed Taylor. But a more careful tweet could have noted the uncertain context of his killing and urged police to find ways to detain without shooting an unarmed man suspected of a crime.

*"He was black. Shot 4 times. When will something be done—
no REALLY be done?!?!"*

Over the next several months, Williams ethically exercised her responsibility for speaking with care about issues of racial injustice, sharing her own reactions in compelling fashion. With her social media posts, Williams offered her followers "a reminder that African American athletes who have reached the pinnacles of their sports still exist in a world that at least overlaps with the one filled with everyday struggles and injustices," noted one journalist.[69]

For instance, mere hours after she qualified for her sixth Wimbledon final, Williams used Twitter to speak out about another police killing of an African American man. In Minnesota, Philando Castile was shot in his car during a traffic stop, and his girlfriend used her phone to livestream the bloody aftermath. Castile's was the second police shooting of a Black man in the United States in two days, and video of both killings went viral. Williams tweeted about Castile's death, "In London I have to wake up to this. He was black. Shot 4 times. When will something be done—no REALLY be done?!?!"[70]

Longtime ESPN host and sports analysts Michael Wilbon found power in Williams' tweet, saying, "When athletes like … Serena take those stances, they are taking it for all of the people who don't have the power to bring racism to the forefront."[71]

> *"'There comes a time when silence is betrayal.' I Won't Be Silent."*

Back home in Florida after the tennis season ended, Williams again spoke out about shootings of Black men. In a Facebook post a sports writer called "palpable and poignant,"[72] Williams worried about her family's safety. She wrote that she had asked her 18-year-old nephew to drive her to meetings while she worked in the car, but when she noticed a police car beside the road, she immediately remembered the "horrible video" of Castile's killing and worried about what would happen if her nephew were stopped by police. "All of this went through my mind in a matter of seconds. I even regretted not driving myself. I would never forgive myself if something happened to my nephew. He's so innocent. So were all 'the others.'"[73] She went on to write about police, "I am a total believer that not 'everyone' is bad. It is just the ones that are ignorant, afraid, uneducated and insensitive that is affecting millions and millions of lives."[74]

She wondered, "Why did I have to think about this in 2016? Have we not gone through enough, opened so many doors, impacted billions of lives? But I realized we must stride on—for it's not how far we have come but how much further still we have to go."[75] She finished the post with a promise to speak out about racial injustice more frequently, writing, "As Dr. Martin Luther King said, 'There comes a time when silence is betrayal.' I Won't Be Silent."[76]

Moral Courage and Moral Consistency

Over the years, in consistently speaking out about racial injustice, Williams displayed moral courage. She willingly risked inflicting harm to her own mental and emotional health by repeatedly speaking out to express the pain, anger, fear and exhaustion Black people experience when yet another Black person is killed through police brutality. She must have known doing so would expose her to the kind of racist hatred she had endured for years.

As a tennis player, Williams achieved greatness in a sport in which she never publicly was defended from the racist attacks of her competitors and their coaches, of sports columnists and commentators, and of fans by either the sport's governing board or corporate sponsors for whom her endorsements helped generate healthy profits.[77] As a *Forbes* columnist pointed out, "No matter what athletes like Venus and Serena Williams, Simone Biles, Allyson Felix, Lisa Leslie, Florence Griffith-Joyner, Wilma Rudolph, Althea Gibson and others contribute to the fields of play and American society, it's never been enough to shake off the unmerited hate that America's government, fans, leagues and companies have perpetuated on and allowed against black women."[78]

"I'm with a heavy heart. I'm lost for words."

Still, in the face of hate, Williams displayed the moral consistency to speak out, risking possible harm to her own wellbeing even while giving raw voice to the experiences of Black people who lacked her powerful platform. In 2020, when outrage erupted around the world over the Minnesota police killing of a Black man named George Floyd and set off a summer of Black Lives Matter protests, Williams joined scores of famous athletes who quickly spoke out. Her initial attention-getting Instagram post didn't express outrage. Rather, Williams generated headlines when she wrote candidly, "I can't and still can't find the words to say or express how sad I feel. A lot of us are numb ... lost for words. I know I am." She concluded, "I'm with a heavy heart. I'm lost for words."[79]

Despite that loss of words, Williams continued finding ways to speak out. The next chapter examines her speech about Black maternal health disparities to consider whether public figures' speaking out on behalf of less powerful people is an ethical act of fostering public discourse or an unjustifiable act that eliminates the voices of the less privileged.

7

Does Speaking
Out Promote Dialogue?

"I want to be remembered for things I do off the court."

In summer 2019, tennis champion Serena Williams chased sports history, as she attempted a record-tying 24th Grand Slam singles title, and made business history, as she became the first athlete named to *Forbes* magazine's annual list of "America's richest self-made women." With a net worth estimated at $225 million, Williams' inclusion on the list vaulted her into the company of 80 of "the country's most successful self-made women entrepreneurs and executives as measured by their net worths."[1]

Describing Williams as the "most famous woman athlete in the world,"[2] the *Forbes* article about Williams noted her history-making tennis accomplishments, but it emphasized her business successes, which included funding and designing her own women's clothing line, owning stakes in the National Football League's Miami Dolphins and the mixed martial arts promoter United Fighting Championship, and investing in nearly three dozen ventures launched by women and minority entrepreneurs.[3] About her business strategy, Williams told the magazine that as her tennis career wound down, she wanted to own and invest in companies rather than sign deals to endorse their products. "I want to be the brand instead of being the face," she said. As a trailblazing African American athlete devoted to issues of gender and racial equity, Williams said she wanted to support startup companies headed by women and minorities. "What better way to preach that message?" she asked. *Forbes* concluded Williams knew "how to handle the star power" that came with 20 years of winning Grand Slam titles, and, more importantly, "how to harness it."[4]

Indeed, Williams increasingly wanted to use her place in the public spotlight to speak out about equity and justice. "A lot of people say what I do on the court is amazing, but I feel like that's just the beginning," she told *Forbes*. "I want to be remembered for things I do off the court; lives I've been able to impact and voices that have been heard."[5]

With the ability to give headline-making magazine and television interviews, and with social media accounts followed by millions of people, Williams could make audiences aware of the topics she wanted to discuss outside tennis. Her social media posts about police shootings, starting after the 2014 killing of an unarmed African American teenager in Ferguson, Missouri, had the power to draw attention to racial injustice. Her television and magazine interviews about her near-fatal experience giving birth in 2017 had the power to draw attention to disproportionate health risks facing Black mothers. Her social media posts and pre- and post-tennis match interviews about how difficult she found balancing tennis and motherhood had the power to draw attention to challenges confronting working women.

Williams' interviews and social media posts exemplified ethically justifiable and powerful messages that attracted attention to issues worth discussing publicly. Yet that kind of speaking out by Williams and other superstar athletes and entertainers often is one-way communication from the powerful famous speakers to their less powerful followers. Famous speakers who are fully attuned to the ethical nuances of speaking out might accept an ethical duty to foster a more reciprocal kind of communication—say, a dialogue, as opposed to a monologue—about important issues of shared public concern. In this chapter, examples of Williams speaking out about serious issues of gender and racial equity will be used to explore when speaking out promotes dialogue among speakers and listeners.

Dialogue as a Form of Understanding

Exploring whether speaking out promotes dialogue is the final element of Wyatt's and Bunton's four-part test to ethically justify speaking out. The test asks famous speakers to consider whether they have a sustained and informed relationship with the topic of their speech, why they are motivated to speak out about the topic, whether their speech will create unjustifiable harm to the topic or other stakeholders, and whether they can use speaking out to promote dialogue about the topic.[6] This fourth element of the test specifically uses the word "dialogue." Although words such as "dialogue," "discussion," "discourse" and "debate" often are used interchangeably by laypeople and scholars alike,[7] here "dialogue is a form of discourse that reveals the interests, concerns, and values" shared by speakers and listeners, as philosophy professor Lauren Swayne Barthold explains.[8] She writes, "Unlike debate, dialogue does not utilize the techniques of argumentation to win. Dialogue aims at mutual understanding, which is achieved when a space has been created in which each person can truly listen and be listened to in such a way that a common humanity is revealed."[9]

This emphasis on dialogue requires famous speakers to pause and assess the potentially powerful volume of their voices as they consider transcending their typical roles as athletes and entertainers to speak out about public issues unrelated to those roles. In the United States, free expression is a fundamental legal principle because the Constitution's framers believed representative democracy would succeed best if citizens were free to speak, listen and respond to one another and to their government about issues of shared concern without worrying that government would retaliate against citizens' viewpoints. Popular public figures are as much U.S. citizens with guaranteed First Amendment rights to free expression as is anyone, so they are of course *legally* free to speak out. The fourth part of Wyatt's and Bunton's speaking-out test asks when public figures are *ethically* free to exercise their First Amendment rights, especially if their speech might inhibit dialogue or impinge on other voices' ability to be heard in that dialogue.

The Persistence of the Marketplace of Ideas Metaphor

The premise that democracy flourishes in a robust culture of speech free of government censorship has been described for a century with the marketplace of ideas metaphor. Scholars trace widespread use of the metaphor to a 1919 U.S. Supreme Court case in which Justice Oliver Wendell Holmes wrote "that the ultimate good desired is better reached by free trade in ideas—that the best test of truth is the power of the thought to get itself accepted in the competition of the market."[10] Legal scholar Jared Schroeder notes, "The much-discussed passage in which these words were written includes no footnotes or other attributions that indicate the influences Justice Holmes drew from in bringing the ideas together,"[11] but lack of attribution has not stopped scholars from finding sources for Holmes' use of the marketplace of ideas metaphor. Often, scholars suggest that Holmes, like other well-educated thinkers of his era, was influenced by the works of the 17th century British poet and philosopher John Milton or the 19th century British philosopher John Stuart Mill, both of whom scholars credit with advancing the proposition that truth emerges when rational people free of censorship debate competing ideas.[12]

The powerful metaphor of a marketplace of ideas in which citizens are free to speak out persists in contemporary law and philosophy. Yet despite its status as the "longest-standing and most commonly used articulation" of a rationale for free speech,[13] the marketplace metaphor always has been and remains a metaphor. Political scholar Danielle Allen observes that a metaphor is imperfect, highlighting some aspects of an idea while obscuring others.[14] She notes, "Were it otherwise, we would have not a metaphor but a definition."[15] Schroeder explains the difficulty of applying the market-place metaphor to today's digital world: "The word 'metaphor,' translated from Greek, means 'transference.' Such a process of transference can be complicated by a variety of factors, particularly in regard to the inherent variables that come with using a communication tool, such as a metaphor, for conveying understanding not only to similar others but, in the case of the marketplace concept, across a century of substantial social and technological change."[16]

Among the complications of the marketplace of ideas metaphor is its origin in the economic concept of a market.[17] Theoretically, rational con-sumers are free to choose from a market's many competing products and, after thoughtful evaluation, will buy only products deemed best suited to consumers' needs and purchasing power. Products that fail to satisfy con-sumers' criteria will find no buyers and fade from the market. However, as philosophy scholar Jill Gordon points out, every consumer in a market does not possess the same power. Consumers with the most individual or collective buying power prevail in making products they prefer the most popular. Just as an economic market responds to more powerful buyers, "[i]n the marketplace of ideas, the ideas that survive or prevail will be those espoused either by the most powerful or the most numerous in the society," Gordon writes.[18] Therefore, "the ideas that would prevail would be popular ones, which are not necessarily the true ones."[19]

A lesson drawn from Gordon's analysis is that public figures who command powerful platforms for speaking out sometimes bear an ethical obligation not to speak out. They must avoid the harm of depriving other speakers—especially less powerful speakers or speakers who possess less popular ideas—of the opportunity to participate and be heard in the pub-lic conversation. Gordon points out that John Stuart Mill, the utilitarian philosopher and bedrock influence on the marketplace of ideas metaphor, warned that minority opinions were "not merely to be tolerated, but to be encouraged and countenanced," and that the "social tyranny" of the most powerful people and their opinions was to be avoided.[20]

The Complications of Networked Public and Social Media Channels

Another complication of the marketplace of ideas metaphor for free speech is its failure to reflect the nature of today's networked publics and the social media channels those publics so frequently use.[21]

"Networked publics are publics both in the spatial sense and in the sense of an imagined community," according to digital media scholar danah boyd. "They are built on and through social media and other emergent technologies. As spaces, the networked publics that exist because of social media allow people to gather and connect, hang out, and joke around."[22]

An optimistic view suggests anyone with access to a digital device—smart phone, tablet or computer—and an internet connection can participate in a networked public.[23] This ease of participation in public conversation theoretically offers citizens more agency in what social media scholars call a culture of "mass self-communication," in which "self-directed communication by individuals using their chosen online channels" can reach "potentially global audiences of other individuals who self-select such content—outside the institutional gatekeeping of the traditional mass media."

Social media scholars suggest the resulting "blurring or merging of the roles of producer and user" of content means potentially everyone can be a "produser" and join the culture of "participatory media."[24] Statistics about social media use suggest most people have done just that. At the beginning of 2020, almost half—49 percent, or 3.8 billion people—of the world's population was classified as active social media users.[25] In the United States, about 70 percent of people were considered active social media users.[26]

This increasingly ubiquitous participatory media culture suggests a global marketplace of ideas could thrive in a way that would have been impossible before networked publics existed. All sorts of citizens could join the dialogue from wherever they are physically located, using digital devices to offer ideas about shared issues of public concern, to listen to others' ideas, to question and discuss them, and ultimately to agree on which ideas are best.

This optimistic view fails to recognize the constraints of the internet, where popular channels such as Facebook, Twitter and Instagram are privately owned. The First Amendment to the U.S. Constitution does not constrain private owners from censoring citizens' expression; it constrains government from censorship. Therefore, Schroeder points out, "the marketplace of ideas, in the instance of social media, can be compared to trying to conduct discourse in a Wal-Mart. The property owner is generally happy for you to frequent the establishment, but might remove you if your ideas are unpopular or potentially damaging to their business enterprise."[27] Social media thus may be what Schroeder labels a "faux public forum,"[28] appearing freely open to all but actually "raising concerns about the future of discourse in a democratic society."[29]

Issues of Bots, Echo Chambers and Filter Bubbles

Other characteristics of social media and networked publics also complicate the metaphor of a marketplace of ideas as the standard for public dialogue. Whether the metaphor is credited to John Milton in the 18th century, John Stuart Mill in the 19th century or Oliver Wendell Holmes in the 20th century, none of these thinkers imagined a world in which artificially intelligent communicators enter and influence public dialogue. These "new, non-human communicators, including 'chat bots' or 'bots,' which perform a variety of communicative tasks in virtual spaces, have already begun to fundamentally alter the twenty-first-century marketplace," Schroeder points out.[30] Social media channels are filled with bots that "rely only on biased information and produce a stream of fake news"[31]—and that often produce "combinations of ideas that can lead to misleading, defamatory, confusing, or otherwise problematic communication" with people who receive those ideas in their social media feeds, Schroeder warns.[32] The potentially deceptive participation of non-human artificially intelligent communicators in public dialogue seems entirely antithetical to the notion of an authentic marketplace of ideas.

A further complication for the marketplace of ideas metaphor as the ideal for public dialogue is the fact that both human and non-human communicators participating in social media and networked publics are not participating in a single marketplace. Rather, they are participating in what Schroeder calls "a multiverse of marketplaces within smaller, self-selected virtual communities."[33]

Instead of using digital media to create a "decentralized and democratic meeting place," people have tended to "cluster together into tribes that comfort us with reaffirmation and protect us from disagreement," which create "echo chambers" that confirm our biases and previous perspectives, according to sociologist Petter Tornberg.[34] Echo chambers—or "polarized communities that tend to consume the same types of information"[35]—can become "capable green-houses for the seedling of rumors and misinformation," Tornberg notes.[36]

The echo chamber problem is aggravated by predictive algorithms that tailor digital content searches for users, who then unknowingly consume information in what social media scholars label "filter bubbles"[37] that can reinforce existing perspectives. The filter bubble concept describes a result of digital content searching, but the concept obviously relates to longer-known behavioral concepts, including selective exposure and confirmation bias, which describe how people tend to seek out and process information. Selective exposure and confirmation bias "make us more likely to interact with content which confirms our pre-existing views"[38] and less likely to "proactively discuss ideas with people or groups of a different opinion," according to digital media scholar Dominic Spohr.[39]

These tendencies of people clustering inside social media's echo chambers and filter bubbles to selectively expose themselves to information confirming their biases may combine with additional characteristics of social media messages. For instance, social media messages are more persistent, visible, spreadable and searchable than were previous types of media messages,[40] and their long-term searchability means a message's original audience and context may become invisible, creating what boyd terms a "context collapse" of misunderstanding.[41]

In her book *Dare to Speak,* free speech advocate Suzanne Nossel observes that when we use social media we often fail to note the context in which words were spoken. "To understand a word's meaning, you need to know who is saying it and what the intended message is," she writes. "In the digital arena, where nearly all speech can be cut, pasted, screenshot, re-posted, and otherwise transmitted without regard to how the speaker had situated the remarks, context disappears."[42]

At worst, the combination of all these factors—echo chambers, filter bubbles, context collapses—can create damaging viral "cascades" of information,[43] in which "damaging and misleading information spreads rapidly, often further boosted by the Internet reputation of some commentator or self-proclaimed authority," according to philosopher Martha Nussbaum.[44]

A Discursive Marketplace of Ideas

Well before the ubiquity of networked publics and social media, and the challenges they present to the marketplace of ideas metaphor, legal scholar Stephen Carter suggested the metaphor no longer applied in an increasingly digital culture with tendencies that foster audience members' selective exposure and confirmation bias. Carter wrote in 1998, "[N]ow you can skip all that held us together and create a world in which the only facts that matter are the ones you yourself choose to know. So not only do we no longer share experience, we do not even share information: I have mine and you have yours, and each of us is equally entitled to our facts." He continued, "The metaphor of a marketplace of ideas collapses against this postmodern onslaught. John Milton's romantic paean to freedom to publish, the *Aeropagitica,* presents a vision of truth as somehow rising from the cacophony of public speech by virtue of its own shining nobility. Civil libertarians have long proclaimed that the cure for bad speech is good speech. As the Supreme Court wrote in 1974, 'However pernicious an opinion may seem, we depend for its correction not on the conscience of judges and juries but on the competition of other ideas.' What speech breaks, in other words, speech can fix. This theory is at the heart of freedom of speech. But the theory presupposes the existence of a conversation somewhere, with willing speaker meeting willing listener, because truth will out only if we hear it alongside falsehood."[45]

Because the traditional understanding of the marketplace of ideas metaphor inadequately reflects how public discourse occurs in today's networked publics and social media, Schroeder suggests replacement with a "discursive marketplace of ideas."[46] Schroeder situates his discursive marketplace in the work of democratic theorists John Dewey and Jurgen Habermas, and suggests their advocacy for citizen engagement and collective action through public discourse applies to the "inherently collective, community-based tools" of the digital environment.[47]

Democracy's Need for Public Discourse

Both Dewey, "the foremost American philosopher of democracy"[48] in the 19th and 20th centuries, and Habermas, the German philosopher born 70 years after him, suggest people fundamentally are expressive, social beings whose ability to communicate without restriction by government and other powerful forces is the essence of democracy.[49] Dewey and Habermas agree democracy depends on skilled public discourse.[50]

Dewey focuses on discourse as "social intelligence," a process of "disciplined" and "honest, intelligent, and creative communication" in which citizens possess a duty to conduct thoughtful inquiry into shared public concerns, identify and discuss multiple views about concerns, and propose possible solutions, according to Dewey scholar James Gouinlock.[51] "This is not a power struggle or an adversarial situation. It is a common effort," Gouinlock writes. "The discourse that typifies such a process would presumably resemble the sort that Mill speaks of at the conclusion of chapter II of *On Liberty*. It would not be rude, abusive, deceptive, uninformed, or dogmatic; it would welcome contributions from all concerned, and it would consider them conscientiously."[52]

From Dewey, ethical parameters emerge for speaking out in ways essential to democratic life. Prime among them is free and respectful engagement in the communal process of social intelligence. Dewey contends, "Intolerance, abuse, calling of names because of differences of opinion about religion or politics or business, as well as because of differences of race, color, wealth, or degree of culture, are treason to the democratic way of life. ... Merely legal guarantees of the civil liberties of free belief, free expression, free assembly are of little avail if in daily life freedom of communication, the give and take of ideas, facts, experiences, is choked by mutual suspicion, by abuse, by fear and hatred."[53]

In contrast to Dewey's view of discourse as social intelligence,

Habermas views discourse as social critique. Habermas criticizes official discourse for too often upholding views of the powerful and excluding voices of the less powerful. Free expression scholar David Allen suggests "Habermas forces us to investigate systematic abuses of power that might hinder the realization of democratic life."[54] His ethic of discourse widens the public sphere and includes everyone who is capable of participating in public conversation, because "the value of the expression is not simply what is said, but the fact that citizens are engaging in discourse,"[55] Allen explains. "Habermas, then, teaches us not only what discourse is for, but also how to critique what passes for discourse in our society. Habermas's ethics leads us to question power, influence, and the proper role for institutions to play in society."[56]

Like Dewey, Habermas "finds a model for public discourse … in which communication is mutual, open, and free of distortion," according to moral philosopher Thomas McCullough.[57] Dewey and Habermas also suggest effective public discourse is a values-based skill to be learned from social institutions and role models. "Public discourse, as a conceptually distinct communicative space, entails certain values: tolerance—both a tolerance of individual differences and a tolerance for frustration and ambiguity—in the search for the common good, diversity, community, reason, and critique," according to scholar Peggy Ruth Geren.[58] These values embedded in public discourse, as articulated by Dewey and Habermas, offer guidance for public figures who consider transcending role-related expectations and speaking out in a discursive marketplace of ideas.

Celebrity Speakers as Intermediaries in a Discursive Marketplace of Ideas

The discursive marketplace of ideas metaphor offers further guidance for public figures. Schroeder suggests the process of securing acceptance by citizens for the best approaches to shared public concerns differs in the discursive marketplace from the traditional marketplace of ideas view that truths emerge fully formed and appear directly to citizens. He writes, "The process now requires the additional step of coalition building among different but interconnected virtual communities. Thus, non-government organizations, individuals, and other groups with large social media or other network-based followings can leverage such tools in order to act as intermediaries in a coalition-building process."[59]

Famous athletes and entertainers who transcend role-related expectations and speak out to their large social media audiences about matters of shared public concern may function as those intermediaries who help build coalitions in the discursive marketplace of ideas. Political scholar Danielle Allen contends public discourse operates as both "influential" and "expressive," with influential discourse tending toward deliberative and authoritative decision-making channels and expressive discourse tending toward less formal channels in which people's identities are formed, expressed and cemented. Allen suggests expressive discourse may be as important in the digital world as influential discourse because expressive discourse may include places where "voice becomes influence" on public issues of shared concerns. "We must consider not merely the deliberative but also the adversarial, the playful, and the prophetic" forms of expressive discourse,[60] Allen suggests. These are the forms of social media discourse that many celebrity entertainers and athletes use to speak out to huge audiences, and thus these famous people should recognize how their speech can contribute toward the "essential need" Dewey sees for "the improvement of the methods and conditions of debate, discussion, and persuasion," which he identifies as "*the* problem of the public."[61]

> "We had a lot of complications, but look who we got. We got a baby girl."

Tennis legend Serena Williams' acts of speaking out about Black women's maternal health disparities provide a compelling example of speaking out that promotes public dialogue about an important issue.

In January 2017, Williams won her 23rd Grand Slam tennis title, defeating her sister Venus in the Australian Open final. Sports commentators marveled at the 36- and 35-year-old sisters' ability to continue competing at the highest levels of professional tennis and noted Serena Williams' win placed her second on the list of most Grand Slam titles ever earned.[62] Although the Australian Open victory returned her to the No. 1 ranking on the women's professional circuit, Williams did not compete in subsequent tournaments, announcing her withdrawal from both the Indian Wells and Miami Open events in March.[63] In April, tennis fans learned why. *The Washington Post* reported that the prolific social media user "revealed her pregnancy by accident … on Snapchat when she posted a picture of her baby bump with the text '20 weeks.' Williams quickly deleted the post, but by then it was too late. Not only were her fans excited about the news of an impending little one, but they were left astonished to learn she won the Australian Open while pregnant."[64]

Williams gave several interviews during her pregnancy, including an August *Vanity Fair* article accompanied by a nearly nude cover photo of her very pregnant figure.[65] A Florida television station broke the news that Williams gave birth September 1 at a Palm Beach hospital near her home, reporting "both mother and baby are said to be healthy."[66] Two weeks later,

Williams' fiancé Alexis Ohanian announced their daughter's name by posting on several social media channels a video montage about the pregnancy and the family's departure from the hospital after the birth. As the video showed the infant cradled on her lap, Williams could be heard saying to Ohanian, "So we're leaving the hospital after six, six, seven days, six days? It's been a long time, but we had a lot of complications, but look who we got. We got a baby girl."[67]

> *"Every mother, everywhere ... deserves to have a healthy pregnancy and birth."*

Less than six months later, Williams began to speak out about her experience giving birth—and what she revealed was not the healthy, uncomplicated experience observers might have assumed she'd share when they saw a vibrant *Vogue* magazine cover photo of Williams balancing her daughter in one hand, with a headline that read "Serena Williams on Motherhood, Marriage, and Making Her Comeback." The article reported, "Though she had an enviably easy pregnancy, what followed was the greatest medical ordeal of a life that has been punctuated by them."[68]

In the *Vogue* interview, a Facebook post and a first-person essay published on CNN.com a few weeks later, Williams said her daughter was born by emergency Caesarean section surgery. "The surgery went smoothly. Before I knew it, Olympia was in my arms," Williams wrote. "It was the most amazing feeling I've ever experienced in my life. But what followed just 24 hours after giving birth were six days of uncertainty." She continued, "It began with a pulmonary embolism, which is a condition in which one or more arteries in the lungs becomes blocked by a blood clot. Because of my medical history with this problem, I live in fear of this situation. So, when I fell short of breath, I didn't wait a second to alert the nurses. This sparked a slew of health complications that I am lucky to have survived." Williams reported undergoing two surgical procedures to treat the blood clots, and wrote, "When I finally made it home to my family, I had to spend the first six weeks of motherhood in bed."

Williams said that while she was privileged to be treated by "an incredible team of doctors and nurses at a hospital with state-of-the-art equipment," many Black women do not share that privilege. She wrote, "According to the Centers for Disease Control and Prevention, Black women in the United States are over three times more likely to die from pregnancy or childbirth-related causes." She concluded her CNN essay by speaking directly to her readers with a call to action addressing them as potential participants in a dialogue about the issue: "Every mother, everywhere, regardless of race or background deserves to have a healthy pregnancy and birth. And you can help make this a reality. How? You can demand governments, business and health care providers do more to save these precious lives. You can donate to UNICEF and other organizations around the world working to make a difference for mothers and babies in need. In doing so, you become part of this narrative—making sure that one day, who you are or where you are from does not decide whether your baby gets to live or to die. Together, we can make this change. Together, we can be the change."[69]

Within hours of *Vogue*'s publication of its cover story about Williams' maternal health crisis, the topic was featured by news outlets worldwide and shared widely on social media channels. For instance, *The New York Times* quickly reported Williams' experience in the context of health risks to all mothers. The *Times* reported that pregnancy-related deaths in the United States rose steadily from 7.2 deaths per 100,000 live births to 17.8 deaths per 100,000 live births between 1987 and 2011. The *Times* article verified Williams' facts about maternal health risks that disproportionately face Black women, reporting that the chance of pregnancy-related death is three to four times greater for Black women than for white women in the United States. The article also reported Williams' initial difficulty getting her medical team to take her complications seriously.[70] The *Times* then reported on studies that tried to explain why Black women face maternal health risks and how often the complications these new mothers suffer can be traced to such factors as "[p]overty, access to care, culture, communication and decision-making" during birth. The *Times* quoted a New York doctor whose research found that health care providers too often don't listen to Black and Hispanic female patients, that college-educated Black mothers receive lower-quality care than less-educated white mothers, and that racial "bias shapes the way we hear our patients." Finally, the article noted that Rutgers University's medical school and a private foundation had created a "Stop. Look. Listen!" campaign to better train medical professionals to listen to new mothers such as Williams—and the many other women who might lack her power to get lifesaving attention.[71]

Meanwhile, in London, *The Guardian* connected Williams' CNN essay with maternal health in the United Kingdom. The newspaper reported that the United Kingdom did not compile "official figures around maternal death and race," but at least one study found that medical care in the UK for "women from ethnic minority backgrounds, especially asylum seekers and newly arrived refugees, is substandard." The newspaper also reported that "women in the UK are more than twice as likely to die in pregnancy and childbirth as those in Poland, Austria or Belarus ... with the UK ranked 30th out of 1709 countries on maternal health."[72]

Clearly, Williams' acts of speaking out about her health crisis generated worldwide attention to the topic of maternal health issues facing Black

women. Audiences for her story included fashion magazine readers of
Vogue, news readers of *The New York* Times and *The Guardian,* and cable
television news watchers of CNN, not to mention all the audiences of the
myriad other news, sports and entertainment information channels that
picked up the story. That Black women suffer health crises or die giving
birth in the United States and United Kingdom, two of the world's most
developed nations, obviously is a concern worth public consideration, and
multiple audiences learned about the issue through Williams' story.

A few weeks after her CNN essay appeared, Williams drew the attention of another audience to the maternal mortality topic when she appeared
in a five-episode documentary series for the HBO cable television network.
The second episode of *Being Serena* depicted an "unguarded and emotional" Williams inviting viewers "into a surprisingly raw experience of her
life." The episode used hospital room video to show that "despite Williams's
fame and fortune, her testimony of her own experience was greeted with
skepticism" by nurses and that "even a woman as affluent as Williams may
have struggled to be heard by her doctors."[73] Multiple news outlets and digital media sites used the *Being Serena* episode to address the issue of Black
maternal mortality. For instance, the website Yahoo! Lifestyle described
Williams' near-fatal birth experience and related statistics about maternal health disparities, noting a "groundbreaking" University of Michigan
study that found racism contributes to "health deterioration" among African American women.[74]

> *"I didn't expect that sharing ... would start such an outpour-
> ing of discussion from women."*

With these acts of speaking out about her maternal health crisis, Williams generated worldwide attention, much of it through news and entertainment coverage, to the topic of maternal health issues facing many Black
women. This outcome alone would seem an ethical consequence of speaking out by a public figure whose role-related expertise primarily stems
from her accomplishments as an athlete. Another ethical consequence
came through the dialogue created when other women began sharing
their maternal health care stories through social media channels. The website BuzzFeed reported that Williams' story of her health crisis "ignited a
conversation" among Black women on social media within hours of her
disclosure.[75]

Williams also fostered dialogue in ways evoking Dewey's and Habermas's concerns about respecting multiple voices and including the less
powerful in public dialogue. After she disclosed her health crisis, Williams
spoke candidly with her Facebook followers: "I didn't expect that sharing
our family's story of Olympia's birth and all of complications after giving

birth would start such an outpouring of discussion from women—especially black women—who have faced similar complications and women whose problems go unaddressed." She noted her experience was just one of many women's maternal crises. "These aren't just stories: according to the CDC, (Center for Disease Control) black women are over 3 times more likely than White women to die from pregnancy- or childbirth-related causes. We have a lot of work to do as a nation and I hope my story can inspire a conversation that gets us to close this gap." She concluded, "I want to thank all of you have opened up through online comments and other platforms to tell your story. I encourage you to continue to tell those stories. This helps. We can help others. Our voices are our power."[76]

> "It is important that black women start having dialogues about these negative experiences."

As she returned to competition on the tennis circuit later in 2018, Williams continued speaking out about maternal health issues and "continued to be open about her struggles as a mother," sharing on social media her concerns about juggling her tennis career with parenting her daughter.[77] Her voice was magnified in August, when music superstar Beyonce gave her own *Vogue* interview, revealing that as an African American mother she, too, had suffered a health crisis after giving birth to twins the year before. "By publicly sharing the darker, and often traumatic, sides of their pregnancies, the women have reignited concerns surrounding maternal mortality rates, a trend that is especially high among black mothers," *The Washington Post* reported. "Beyonce and Serena Williams help to put a very well-known face to these risks."[78] In the *Post*'s "On Parenting" column the next day, journalist Rochaun Meadows-Fernandez shared her own distressing account of "giving birth while black in America," and praised Beyonce and Serena Williams for speaking out. "Black women deserve to have medical experiences free of racial bias," Meadows-Fernandez wrote. "I hope black women with platforms and power such as Williams and Beyonce bring awareness to these types of issues. They are spreading information to an audience that does not spend its time researching medical and peer-reviewed journals. While we bring awareness to these issues and do our best to change the culture of racism and bias in the United States, it is important that black women start having dialogues about these negative experiences. We have many paths to trailblaze and successes to forge."[79]

Philosophy professor Lauren Swayne Barthold suggests first-person accounts such as Williams' story of her maternal health crisis play a powerful role in stimulating public dialogue about issues. "The sharing of personal experiences serves as an antidote against harmful stereotyping and generalizations that frequently prevent the openness required to truly listen to the other. In a dialogue, without the need to prove one's own rightness and the other's wrongness, the particularity of first person experience can actually help others connect as humans. Dialogue not only allows one to see the other through new eyes, it also allows one to confront one's own (often hidden) assumptions and prejudices. It utilizes subjective experiences and narratives to arrive at mutual understanding in which the other's claim of humanity is acknowledged."[80]

"It's about speaking up and saying, 'You know what? You belong here, too.'"

In 2019, Williams took her concerns about maternal health disparities further, announcing that her venture capital firm had joined others to invest $3 million in a start-up company called Mahmee that was developing digital media applications for maternal health practitioners and their patients to use in monitoring their health. "Given the bleak data surrounding maternal death and injury rates, I believe that it is absolutely critical right now to invest in solutions that help protect the lives of moms and babies," Williams said.[81] Soon afterward, she told *Essence* magazine that speaking up for Black women and participating in dialogue with them was particularly important to her: "Freedom means standing up and not being afraid to say, 'I'm here' or 'Hear my voice' or 'This isn't what I agreed to' or 'This isn't fair and that isn't right.' That's freedom for me. I've done it my whole career. It's knowing where I've come from, knowing my history. In particular, the sport that I'm in. When I first started, there weren't a lot of people who looked like me. So it was really important to always help other people feel as if this is something they could also be a part of. This is something they could be into. It's about speaking up and saying, 'You know what? You belong here, too.' This is freedom."[82]

As both athlete and speaker, Williams has achieved significant success in disproving gender and racial stereotypes, and generating dialogue about equity. The next two chapters of this book further examine the ethical contexts and consequences that confront athletes like Williams who parlay their athletic success into speaking out and questioning injustice.

PART III

Ethical Actors and Topics to Evaluate

8

Shut Up and Play?

*Athletes Speaking Out
About Inequality*

Sports provide as close to a universal experience as anything people share. We play sports. We watch sports. We talk sports. Even if we're not sports fans, we fluently speak the language of sports, understanding when people call a surprise a "curveball" or a success a "grand slam." In fact, one study finds 1,700 commonly used sports metaphors in the English language. These metaphors play a powerful role in "framing how the world is seen, not least in the sense that life itself is a kind of 'game,'" according to sports scholar Michael Serazio,[1] who notes how we apply sports metaphors to serious topics. For instance, we accept journalistic descriptions of electoral campaigns as "horse races" that reduce us as citizens to spectators in the democratic process designed to depend on us as participants.[2] For generations, we have used sports language to describe our values about societal inequality. Sports journalist Howard Bryant observes that "when America needed to extol its promise, sports would be its bullhorn, and its scoreboard-meritocracy metaphors would be so appealing that they would become baked into the language. Eradicating inequality was a concept now literally part of the American language. Society's goal was to *level the playing field*."[3]

This chapter examines linkages between cultural and economic values in sports that may create ethical concerns for athletes who speak out. The chapter also examines consequences that may face athletes when they summon the moral courage to speak out in politically fraught environments about issues of inequality and injustice, and find their messages rejected by fans, sports executives and politicians who demand athletes "shut up and play"—or, as became the case in 2020, evince a new willingness to hear athletes' messages about inequality and injustice.

People always have cared about sports. "Sports are, after all, timeless as a cultural practice: No society in human history has ever existed without them in some form," Serazio observes.[4] Yet the game is "the least interesting thing" about sports today, he contends: "For in and of itself, the game is, of course, totally meaningless; but ironically, it is *because* of its meaninglessness that it can serve such an important function for meaning-making. *Because* of the cultural fragmentation and political polarization that otherwise alienates postmodern lives, sport is more important than ever as a site of social debate and intellectual exploration. By looking at sports, we can see and critique issues and trends far from the field of play, relating to religion, journalism, digitalization, commerce, celebrity, feminism, masculinity, violence, labor, inequality, militarism, activism, and, of course, identity and community. This is sports' not-so-hidden power."[5]

This power creates high stakes for athletes who speak out. Sports, like religion, provide deeply personal and communal meanings for people who may come together only because of their love of a specific sport, team or athlete, and who may not want their experience interrupted by controversial speech.

Many of us cherish our sports affiliations. We pick favorite college and professional teams as children, and we remain loyal to those teams for life. We dress in team colors not just to attend games, but to watch on television in homes we decorate with team memorabilia. We plan parties and weddings around our team's schedule so we won't miss a game. Some of us even permanently tattoo team symbols on our bodies or etch those symbols onto our tombstones.[6] We affiliate so strongly with our favorite teams that we possess a feeling of ownership in these businesses owned by billionaires,[7] and Serazio points out that our "merging of personal identity with team identity" is so thorough that we talk about "our" team and how "we" are faring, as if "we" are members of the team.[8] In an era of divisiveness, Serazio argues, there remains "something uniquely, deep, tribal, and even existential in sport's capacity to unify."[9]

Sports as Teacher of Moral Values

These intense affiliations allow sports to function as "unique cultural carriers of our values," according to *Washington Post* sports columnist Sally Jenkins.[10] We may think we're just playing or watching games, but sports convey values. Sports scholars Robert Simon, Cesar Torres and Peter Hager find "an unusually intimate relationship between participation in athletics and ethics."[11] They suggest this relationship exists because the "inner morality" of sports presents "such values as dedication, concern for excellence, and fair play" through the performance of athletes.[12]

For example, in October 2019, shortly after baseball's Nationals won a dramatic do-or-die game that brought Washington, D.C., its first World Series title in 95 years, *Washington Post* sports columnist Barry Svrulga found moral values in the team's performance, encouraging Nationals' fans to "remember not just *that* they won but *how* they won," and proclaiming the under-dog team "taught us all lessons—about patience and belief, about faith and fortitude, about finding life where none seemed to exist."[13] A day before, longtime *Washington Post* political columnist and diehard baseball fan George Will scolded players for "preening" over their World Series home runs, accusing the athletes of flouting the sport's long-held values of civility and grace.[14]

Baseball fans and newspaper readers took little issue with these columnists casting the World Series as a teacher of moral values, making it more than a sports event. Yet three days later, fans and readers took issue with pitcher Sean Doolittle's expression of values. Doolittle declined an invitation to join Nationals teammates for a celebratory White House visit because he could not support President Donald Trump's record on race relations or his treatment of people with disabilities. The pitcher reported receiving myriad social media messages excoriating him for speaking out about his values.[15]

Even casual fans who follow sports easily understand values conveyed by sports as an institution, such as obeying rules, respecting officials, persisting individually and working as a team, but those same fans often display less tolerance for values conveyed by individual athletes who speak out about what fans regard as "political" issues.

Values conveyed by sports as an institution can be more accessible and understandable to lay people than the values of more abstract institutions such as science, medicine, fine arts or religion, which can require education or training of audiences if they are to appreciate excellence in these disciplines.[16] Sports values—the kind of values Simon, Torres and Hager note are conveyed by athletes, teams, journalists and commentators to "large and diverse portions of the population"[17]—portray athletic success as the outcome of "the blood, sweat, and tears that *anyone* could have committed themselves to, if only they had enough gumption," Serazio observes.[18] Further, he observes, this emphasis on hard work makes athletes some of the few famous people who earn their celebrity, as compared to, say, a reality television personality who is "discovered."[19] Simon, Torres and Hager write, "Arguably, because of the special connection between competitive sport and the quest for excellence as well as the broad accessibility of sport it is not unreasonable for many segments of the population, particularly children and young people, to hold athletes in high regard and seek to emulate them."[20] Simon, Torres and Hager go so far as to assign athletes an ethical duty for upholding values, arguing "the role of athletes in illustrating and expressing important values through their play suggests that sport tends to thrust them into the spotlight in a way that carries some moral obligation."[21]

> *"When they don't agree with you, then you hear, 'Shut up and play and just do your job.'"*

Over the years, a conundrum often has existed for athletes who want to exercise that moral obligation. Sports leagues and team executives, and the journalists and commentators who analyze sports—such as those columnists writing about the World Series—have seemed free to convey shared values with little objection, but athletes who wished to speak out about their own understandings of societal values, norms and power—such as Nationals pitcher Sean Doolittle—needed to exercise great care in the intensely charged landscape of affiliation with sports.

Fans want to believe "we" possess the same values as "our" team's athletes, so, as former professional basketball player Etan Thomas puts it, "when people agree with you, they praise you for speaking out, but when they don't agree with you, then you hear, 'Shut up and play and just do your job.'"[22] Thomas experienced that response as a member of the Washington Wizards, when he spoke out and opposed U.S. president George W. Bush's 2003 invasion of Iraq.[23]

The athlete who speaks out also must understand the overwhelming profit motive of sports. Thomas, for instance, played basketball in the late 1990s and early 2000s, when "an exponential rise in the financial incentives of professional sports" made athletes skittish about expressing their views. "Owners, league executives, media members covering the games, and advertisers all had a vested interest in keeping their sports entertainment products politically neutral, and star players were compensated handsomely for it," noted one sportswriter.[24]

The Financial Stakes Connected to Speaking Out in Sports

The financial stakes in sports indeed are high. The World Economic Forum estimated the global sports industry's value in 2018 was $471 billion, a 45 percent increase in value since 2011.[25] The sports industry's revenues were significantly affected by the 2020 coronavirus pandemic that shut down professional and college sports for months, keeping athletes off playing fields and courts, and keeping fans out of stadium and arena seats. Before the pandemic shutdown, the sports industry provided at least 456,000 U.S. jobs annually.[26] Some 25 percent of Americans said they spent money at least once a month on sports,[27] which produced almost $70 billion worth of revenue from tickets, clothing, television subscriptions and such—an amount that was expected to increase by $10 billion within five years.[28]

In an increasingly fragmented media landscape of tailoring content to audience members' individual interests, rather than offering content that appeals to mass audiences, media companies depended on millions of Americans—some 60 percent of whom describe themselves as sports fans[29]—to devote significant amounts of time to watching sports. U.S. television provided more sports content in 2017 than at any time in the previous 15 years, and 86 of the top 100 most-watched live television programs in the United States were sports events.[30] During the pandemic shutdown, sports leagues and television networks such as ESPN scrambled to air reruns of "classic" games that sports fans who were stuck at home in self-isolation to avoid contracting the virus happily would watch on TV until live sporting events returned to their screens.[31]

Although sports organizations braced for losses in 2020, nothing signaled that their attention to profitability would be any less important after the pandemic. Rather, sports were likely to continue striving to be a global economic force that "absolutely overpowers film and everything else in the entertainment genre,"[32] as well as a powerhouse that focuses relentlessly on profitability and shuns controversy. "Sports and sports media have so seamlessly aligned with commercial objectives, there has been simultaneous pushback—from fans, brands, players, and journalists alike—that sports and politics shouldn't mix," Serazio notes.[33]

Ethically Salient Issues for Athletes Who Speak Out

Athletes who speak out in this complicated intersection of fans' adherence to what they believe are sports values and organizations' adherence to what they believe will make money would do well to understand the ethically salient characteristics of speaking out that suggest a need for ethical care.

> "I want people to know that I put thought into this, and at the end of the day, I just can't go."

The speaker's role is the first ethically salient characteristic of speaking out. Fans expect athletes' primary—perhaps only—role is to perform skillfully on the court or the field. Athletes who upend that expectation need to understand and justify the possible upset of fans' expectations that speaking out may cause. Professional baseball pitcher Sean Doolittle appears to have done so. Many Washington baseball fans knew that Doolittle previously transcended his role as an Oakland A's pitcher into the role of public speaker, addressing issues such as health care and housing for U.S. military veterans or immigration policies for refugees.[34] Doolittle was careful about expressing himself when he was traded from Oakland to Washington in July 2017. He said he "intentionally kept a super low profile" about speaking out so he first could send the message his primary goal was helping the Nationals win.[35] However, in August 2017, when a counter-protester was killed at a white nationalist rally in Charlottesville, Virginia, where Doolittle attended college, he felt compelled to begin speaking out again, posting social media messages advocating for "a patriotic obligation to condemn racism and domestic terrorism by white supremacists."[36] Doolittle often used Twitter to express his views, but when he decided in November 2019 to skip the White House World Series celebration, he did not tweet about it. Instead, he gave *The Washington Post* an extended interview to explain his decision to Nationals fans. "It starts with not compromising his beliefs and an aversion to President Donald's Trump's actions, despite wanting to celebrate with teammates as much as possible," the newspaper reported, quoting Doolittle as saying, "I want people to know that I put thought into this, and at the end of the day, I just can't go."[37]

"I can't get past that stuff."

The speech's subject is the second ethically salient characteristic of speaking out. As are all citizens, athletes are philosophically and legally free to speak out about issues of shared public concern. However, depending on the topic's gravity, and the related possible harms of misrepresenting the topic's complexity or misinforming the audience, high-profile athletes should speak with factual and contextual accuracy. Baseball remains among the most socially and politically conservative of professional sports, and Doolittle developed a reputation for carefully gathering facts on issues and speaking judiciously about them. For instance, in 2016, Doolittle called himself a life-long Republican who needed to watch numerous political debates to select a presidential candidate to support.[38] Before he spoke out about mental health resources for military veterans, he arranged 10 briefings to learn about the topic from experts and advocacy groups.[39] When he spoke out about declining to join President Trump in celebrating the World Series victory, the pitcher named specific concerns about the president's stances. "'I feel very strongly about his issues on race relations,' Doolittle said, and he listed the Fair Housing Act, the Central Park Five and Trump's comments following a white supremacist rally in 2017." Doolittle also identified concerns about the president's treatment of vulnerable people, saying, "I have a brother-in-law who has autism, and [Trump] is a guy that mocked a disabled reporter. How would I explain that to him that I hung out with somebody who mocked the way that he talked, or the way that he moves his hands? I can't get past that stuff."[40] Then, after participating exuberantly in the city's victory parade—and sharing his exuberance with a social media stream of photos and comments to teammates and fans—Doolittle stopped speaking out about his objections to President Trump.

"We can't worry about what endorsements we gonna lose."

The speaker's intent is the third ethically salient characteristic of speaking out. Athletes who speak out do not do so accidentally. They intend to join public conversation about a serious topic, and as autonomous moral agents, they understand the choice to speak out may pose risks to reputation or livelihood. Professional basketball star Carmelo Anthony has urged fellow athletes not to let their own incomes matter more than their moral obligations to speak out and confront injustice. In 2015, Anthony joined citizens for protest marches in his hometown of Baltimore, where a young Black man named Freddie Gray died of spinal cord injuries suffered while he was in police custody.[41] By 2016, prosecutors had failed for a fourth time to convict police officers on charges related to Gray's death and a "summer of horrific gun violence … from Orlando to Milwaukee"[42] had galvanized many people, including Anthony. In a July Instagram post he implored athletes "to step up and take charge."[43] "There's NO more sitting back and being afraid of tackling and addressing political issues anymore," Anthony wrote. "We can't worry about what endorsements we gonna lose or whose [sic] going to look at us crazy. I need your voices to be heard."[44] He also exchanged text messages with fellow NBA stars LeBron James, Chris Paul and Dwyane Wade about how they could speak out after a "gruesome" week of police killings of Black men in Minnesota and Louisiana, and of citizen killings of police officers in Texas and Louisiana. Anthony, James, Paul and Wade leveraged their status to command the stage of "ESPN's annual glamourfest award show,"[45] the ESPYS, and speak to hundreds of sports luminaries in the auditorium—and to an audience of 5.6 million live television viewers.[46] As the athletes condemned gun violence and social injustice, a sportswriter suggested they represented "a combined $632 million in career earnings on the stage."[47] Sports journalist Howard Bryant suggests Black athletes who achieve a level of "ubiquitous" prominence like Anthony, James, Paul and Wade, thanks to their huge contracts and endorsement deals, become "a privileged, corporate bridge between the races."[48] If so, their unique role gives these "super" athletes a particularly weighty responsibility for speaking out with ethical care.

"Congress, do something now. End gun violence. Let's go!"

The speaker's platform is the fourth and final ethically salient characteristic of speaking out. If athletes speak out using a platform or venue intended for something other than serious public topics, the athletes may complicate the audience's role-related expectations for the venue. For instance, in August 2019, after Alejandro Bedoya scored a goal in a professional soccer match, he ran to the sideline, picked up a microphone used for television broadcast and shouted, "Congress, do something now. End gun violence. Let's go!" Bedoya's outburst came just hours after mass shootings killed 31 people in Ohio and Texas. Bedoya had advocated for gun control legislation since 2018, when a shooter killed 17 people at a Florida high school near his hometown,[49] and he had posted social media messages about gun control on the day of the match, but his on-field advocacy was unusual.[50] Although fans in the soccer stadium could not hear Bedoya's shout, it was transmitted via the microphone to television viewers, who may have been confused about what he was shouting during the match. Afterward, Bedoya told sports reporters, "I'm not going to sit idly and watch this stuff happen and not say something. Before I'm an athlete, a soccer player, I'm a human being first."[51] That's certainly true, and speaking out about the issue of gun violence is worthwhile, although it might require more context than television viewers received through nine words shouted into a microphone during a match.

Applying the Justification Test to Speaking Out About Sports

To ensure moral agents consider each of these four ethically salient characteristics of speaking out, Wyatt and Bunton proposed a specific test of moral justification for speaking out. Using the test, athletes who want to speak out should consider their relationship to the issue they are speaking out about, their motivation for speaking out, the nature of any harm they would create by speaking out, and whether speaking out would promote dialogue.[52]

The relationship between athletes and the topic of racial and social injustice is among the most immutable, given the topic's link to athletes' identities and lived experiences. "Historically, in professional sports, and in almost no other arena to the same extent, athletes and sports stars have publicly broken racial and gender barriers, at times simply by being in the game. As long as sports have been played, issues of discrimination and inequality have played a part and the athlete has found him- or herself in a public position to take a stand (or not) and start a discourse about inclusion and equality," writes former professional tennis player James Blake.[53] Jackie Robinson, who in 1947 became the first Black man to play major league baseball, is a prime example. Robinson's presence on the baseball diamond by itself spoke out symbolically for equality, but he also amplified his relationship to the topic with words. Using his experiences with segregation, Robinson spoke out for years about baseball's and America's failures to fully integrate, and his example "increased the importance of the black athlete to adopt a voice of influence, to be heard as well as seen," Bryant observes.[54]

> "Seeing Black athletes in support of Ali inspired others to speak out."

Basketball Hall of Famer Kareem Abdul-Jabbar traces "the modern era of athletes speaking out" about injustice to 1967, when boxer Muhammad Ali refused to serve in the U.S. military.[55] As a Black man, Ali said he could not fight brown people in Vietnam on behalf of the United States while it condoned segregation of Black citizens.[56] Convicted of draft evasion, sentenced to five years in prison, and banned from boxing for three years in the prime of his career, Ali appealed his sentence, which ultimately was overturned by the U.S. Supreme Court.[57] Shortly after his ban from boxing, prominent athletes met with Ali to gauge the seriousness of his protest. When he attended the meeting, Abdul-Jabbar was a college basketball star so dominant that his sport changed its rules to ban him from dunking the ball. Some 50 years later, Abdul-Jabbar wrote of the meeting, "I don't know how much we were able to accomplish on a practical level, but seeing Black athletes in support of Ali inspired others to speak out."[58] Abdul-Jabbar was inspired to boycott the 1968 Olympics because he "recognized that while he was fortunate because of his basketball ability, he couldn't celebrate his privileged status as long as racial inequality persisted," according to sportswriter Johnny Smith.[59] The young basketball star generated heated criticism when he spoke out to say as much in media interviews about his boycott.[60]

U.S. track and field champions Tommie Smith and John Carlos also were influenced by Ali. Unlike Abdul-Jabbar, they participated in the 1968 Olympics in Mexico City, and in a moment of silent protest atop the medal stand, destroyed their athletic careers to advocate for civil rights. In what sportswriter Jerry Bembry calls "one of the most iconic acts of defiance in American sports history," the runners "stood silently on the medal stand in bare feet, each hoisting a gloved fist above his head."[61] Smith and Carlos suffered threats and harassment, lost running sponsorships and commercial endorsements, and never again competed internationally. Blake contends "the fact that they made such a life-changing decision during what could be seen as one of the most important moments in their lives represents a monumental sacrifice."[62] (For a more detailed analysis of their symbolic gesture as an act of speaking out, see Chapter 9.)

"What I'm not willing to accept is the enduring status quo around maternity."

In addition to establishing justifiable relationships with their topics, athletes who want to speak out should establish justifiable motivations for speaking out. Runner Allyson Felix did so when she spoke out about pregnancy and Black maternal health. Felix was such an outstanding high school athlete she eschewed college scholarships for an Adidas sponsorship that paid her tuition.[63] Later, for a decade, Felix ran under a Nike sponsorship. "Obsessive focus helped make her the most decorated American woman in Olympic history. By age 30, she won nine Olympic medals—six gold, three silver—and 11 world championships. She ran for an apparel company and endorsed products and stayed silent on issues outside of her performance. The thought of using her platform for other purposes scared her. She viewed herself, first and only, as an athlete," according to sports writer Adam Kilgore.[64] Her view changed in May 2019, when Felix saw fellow female runners "heroically" risk their financial livelihoods to publicize their pregnancy and motherhood experiences, and felt compelled to share her own.[65] Unlike in other sports, track and field track athletes aren't paid by a league. They support themselves with sponsorship agreements to compete under the name of athletic companies like Nike, whose apparel they wear exclusively.[66] Multiple runners and their agents told *The New York Times* that Nike's contracts reduced or eliminated runners' sponsorship payments if they could not compete and remain highly ranked in track during pregnancy and the early stages of motherhood. Women described risking physical health and suffering injuries to honor their contracts. "When Alysia Montaño ran in the 2014 United States Championships while eight months pregnant, she was celebrated as 'the pregnant runner.' Privately, she had to fight with her sponsor to keep her paycheck," *The New York Times* reported. Another runner said, "Getting pregnant is the kiss of death for a female athlete."[67]

Felix decided she could help other women by sharing her story.[68] In a *New York Times* opinion piece, she said, "I felt pressure to return to form as soon as possible after the birth of my daughter in November 2018, even though I ultimately had to undergo an emergency C-section at 32 weeks because of severe pre-eclampsia that threatened the lives of me and my baby." She added that her contract renewal negotiation was unsuccessful: "Despite all my victories, Nike wanted to pay me 70 percent less than before. If that's what they think I'm worth now, I accept that. What I'm not willing to accept is the enduring status quo around maternity."[69] Unable to come to terms with Nike, Felix returned to competition and raced without sponsorship for the first time in her professional career at the July 2019 U.S. outdoor track and field championships. A few days afterward, Felix said she had signed with Athleta to become the apparel company's first sponsored athlete in a deal "supporting me as an athlete, but also as a mom and activist." Meanwhile, as a likely result of "major public backlash" from people who heard the stories of Felix and her fellow runners, Nike announced it no longer would financially penalize pregnant athletes for 18 consecutive months starting a month into their pregnancies; other athletic companies also announced new sponsorship protections for pregnant athletes.[70]

"Athletes are told to shut up and play," Felix said. "We are told that no one cares about our politics. We are told that we're just entertainers, so run fast, jump high, and throw far. And don't mess up. But pregnancy is not messing up; for women it can and should be able to be part of a thriving professional athletic career, as my teammates have shown and I hope to show too. And I dream of a day when we don't have to fight in order to try." She continued, "Protection during maternity isn't just limited to Olympians; working women all over the U.S. deserve protection when they have children. We shouldn't have to rely on companies to do the right thing. Our families depend on it."[71]

"I do not feel that I am a piece of property to be bought and sold irrespective of my wishes."

After justifying relationships to their topics and motivations for speaking out, athletes must consider harms that may result from speaking. When athletes challenge inequity and question power structures, harm to the athletes themselves can be immediate and significant. They risk the ire of fans, team executives, league officials and politicians who suggest outspoken athletes are ungrateful for wealth and celebrity.[72] Black athletes who speak out about racial injustice commonly have received fans' and commentators' attempts to deflect the athletes' speech from an examination of racism into a "public discourse of ingratitude" that suggests "speaking out should be accompanied with a loss of athletic playing opportunity."[73] In 1969, for instance, center fielder Curt Flood effectively ended his athletic career when he "led a charge for free agency in baseball, where teams had been able to control the fate of a player for an entire career."[74] Challenging his trade from the St. Louis Cardinals to the Philadelphia Phillies, Flood sent baseball's commissioner a letter sports writer William Rhoden calls "one of the most significant communications in sports labor history," in which Flood wrote that "after twelve years in the major leagues, I do not feel that I am a piece of property to be bought and sold irrespective of my wishes."[75] Flood then sat out the 1970 baseball season while suing the league—and losing. Having described himself as "a well-paid slave"[76] and as "cattle" on baseball's "ranch,"[77] Flood destroyed any chance to resume a meaningful baseball career, even though he had earned seven Gold Gloves, been named an all-star three times and achieved a .293 batting average.[78] "Flood's critics, echoing today's 'shut up and play' chorus targeting outspoken black athletes, said ballplayers were wealthy and should not complain about limits to their autonomy," reported sportswriter Kurt Streeter.[79]

Over the years, athletes understandably have worried that speaking out could harm their financial positions. After the experiences of Ali, Smith, Carlos and Flood, all of whom paid dearly for speaking out, Black athletes who began to earn fortunes from lucrative playing contracts and commercial endorsements were criticized for "the strengthening of the *shut up and play* code," in which "*stick to sports* quickly became the default" and "'activism' was a hostile word," Bryant contends.[80] Perhaps more than any other Black athlete, Chicago Bulls basketball superstar Michael Jordan—and the "Republicans buy sneakers, too" remark he may or may not have uttered to explain why he wouldn't speak out in a 1990 political campaign in his home state[81]—served "as a notable exemplar of athletes" who possessed "a fear of financial consequences caused by speaking out on polarizing topics," according to one study.[82]

Although not speaking out may preserve athletes' ability to earn millions of dollars from endorsements, as Jordan's record-setting deals with Nike did, silence may harm athletes' sense of self. The "shut up and play" and "stick to sports" codes erase essential aspects of Black athletes' identity, Bryant argues. "Why was it so necessary for the black athlete's skin to be erased? Why was it that the only way he could be enjoyed by the white public was for him to not be seen for what he was at all, in full dimension? Why was the public asking him to make this deal? And what were the future effects constant erasure might have on the black player himself charged with the responsibility of making race irrelevant, on his wife, his children, and his life beyond the zeroes on his paycheck?"[83]

> "*Leadership in America is the athletes.... That's why I feel I have to start speaking out.*"

In 1992, Chicago Bulls player Craig Hodges spoke out to criticize his far more famous teammate for silence during six days of rioting in Los Angeles, after a jury failed to convict four police officers of brutally beating Black truck driver Rodney King. "Hodges, the Bulls' 3-point shooting specialist and one of the league's best, chided Jordan and other National Basketball Association players for failing to use their visibility to call attention to pressing social and political issues, from the deepening plight of inner-city youth to the failure of owners to hire more black head coaches," Rhoden reported in *The New York Times*.[84] After a post-season game, Hodges told Rhoden the Los Angeles riots were "war" and urban poverty was "hellish," and asked, "Then you have us playing in here—how much money did we make here last night? How many lives will it change?" He continued, "Leadership in America is the athletes and entertainers. That's why I feel I have to start speaking out. I don't like to, I don't like to step on toes. I don't feel like somebody should tell you what you should be doing. On one hand, being in this league, you have a right to make as much as you can make, but you have a responsibility. A lot of us don't look at the responsibility end of it as much as we do our right to ask for as much as we can get."[85] Subsequently, Hodges attended the Bulls' NBA championship celebration at the White House and handed President George W. Bush a letter outlining failures to help America's Black citizens. With that, Hodges apparently had terminated his career by speaking out. The 32 year old never again played in the NBA, although he had won three consecutive all-star weekend 3-point shooting contests and contributed to two league championships. "Whether Hodges was blacklisted or not remains a mystery, but his situation was always going to be precarious. It's certainly likely that teams weighed his fiery outspokenness against a potentially diminishing skill set," notes *New Yorker* writer Hua Hsu.[86]

Sometimes, potential harm from speaking out is to athletes' wellbeing. Receiving vile racial insults and threats, as many athletes do when they share views about injustice, may harm their mental and emotional health. Racism also may harm physical health; studies conclude coping with life in a world of almost constant racial bias negatively affects the physical health of African American people.[87]

Sometimes, potential harm from speaking out is to athletes' safety. In the racially charged atmosphere of 1968—a violent year that included the assassination of civil rights leader the Rev. Dr. Martin Luther King, Jr., and, just days before the Mexico City Olympics began, the killing of hundreds of student protesters there—runners John Carlos and Tommie Smith acknowledged to one another before ascending the medal stand to raise their fists that they could be targeted by a shooter hiding in the stadium's crowd.[88]

> *"My hope is that by sharing my experience with you it will continue a conversation."*

After justifying a relationship to a topic, examining a motivation for speaking about the topic and considering harms that could occur from speaking, athlete speakers must consider whether speaking out promotes dialogue. The goal of promoting dialogue is understanding one another's issues and values, even if agreement does not result. Because of their accessibility to broad swaths of people, sports may lend themselves to dialogue more than other institutions, creating opportunities for people to discuss such issues as racism, sexism and inequality.[89] Promoting dialogue about these difficult issues often involves athletes calling for systemic change, which is rarely comfortable for speaker or listener, suggests former athlete James Blake. However, he writes, "It is this discomfort that creates a discourse and enables people with different points of view to come together to discuss it and hopefully create change, or at the very least shine a light on the issues we are passionate about, that we think are unjust."[90]

In 2019, runner Allyson Felix shone a light on the issue of Black maternal health, as had tennis legend Serena Williams before her. (See Chapter 7 for an analysis of Williams speaking out.) Felix testified at a U.S. House of Representatives Ways and Means Committee hearing on maternal health and mortality, and said when she underwent emergency C-section surgery to deliver her daughter two months prematurely, she didn't understand how close she was to dying. "Mothers don't die from childbirth, right?" she said. "Not in 2019, not professional athletes, not at one of the best hospitals in the country, and certainly not to women who have a birthing plan and a birthing suite lined up. I thought maternal health was solely about fitness, resources and care. If that was true, then why was this happening to me?" While her daughter spent a month in an intensive care unit and Felix spent eight weeks on bed rest, she learned the shocking statistics that confront Black mothers. She told the congressional hearing, "I learned that black women are upwards of three times more likely to die from childbirth than white mothers are in the United States and that we suffer severe complications twice as often." She urged lawmakers to help Black mothers. "My hope is that by sharing my experience with you it will continue a conversation that needs much more attention and support," she said.[91]

Near the end of 2019, Felix attracted attention for winning her 12th and 13th world championship gold medals, breaking the record for number of world championships, which had been held by a male runner. Breaking the record hadn't been on her mind. "For me, this year was really about overcoming, and that's what was on my mind," she told CBS News. Part of her overcoming was returning to world competition after giving birth, and part was learning to speak out about women's health and careers. "This is an issue that everyone is affected by," she said. "And I tackled it in my industry, but I think that's just really the starting point. That's what I want to leave behind: changes for the next generation and for my daughter."[92]

Felix could not have known that less than a year later, she and athletes all over the world would speak out like never before to urge change for the next generation as a viral pandemic and the virus of racism collided.

Speaking Out About Racial Injustice During a Pandemic

In spring 2020, a coronavirus pandemic forced authorities to shut down schools, workplaces, houses of worship and sports venues so

Americans could avoid contracting the virus and over-burdening inundated hospitals and health care resources. By the last week of May 2020, three months after the United States documented its first coronavirus death, more than 100,000 coronavirus deaths had been reported.[93] By the same date, evidence showed that Black Americans were significantly more likely than white Americans to experience serious complications or death from the virus.[94] Evidence also showed that Black Americans were more likely to experience the crippling economic effects of the pandemic shutdown. As unemployment claimed 21 million Americans' jobs by May, 16.8 percent of Black workers were unemployed, as compared to 12.4 percent of white workers.[95]

At the end of May, an act of police brutality in Minnesota compounded these racial disparities. Americans became outraged after bystanders' video showed a white Minneapolis police officer killing a Black man named George Floyd by kneeling on his neck for almost nine minutes on Memorial Day.[96] The video of Floyd's death quickly dominated news reports and social media channels, which soon overflowed with messages opposing racism. For instance, in the 10 days after Floyd's death, Twitter users mentioned the #BlackLivesMatter hashtag 47.8 million times, or an average of 3.7 million times per day, according to the Pew Research Center.[97]

"We have a lot on our minds, and a lot that we want to say."

Many social media messages came from athletes, whose voices were among some of the most prominent speaking out to oppose the racism represented by Floyd's death. Athletes from sports' highest ranks—whether they were the National Basketball Association's current stars or its legends such as Michael Jordan, many of the National Football League's current quarterbacks, or some of Major League Baseball's elite pitchers—took to social media platforms and news outlets to condemn injustice. For instance, runner Allyson Felix posted Instagram messages that supported Black Lives Matter demonstrations and remembered additional Black people killed by police. As a six-time Olympic champion, Felix was able to amplify her social media anti-racism messages on mainstream television news shows when they sought her reaction to the 2020 Tokyo Olympics' postponement to 2021 because of the coronavirus pandemic. She told CNN her 2019 acts of speaking out about disparities in Black maternal health care "really pushed me to have the courage to stand up and fight for the voiceless and to come out against things that I don't think are right." Felix said seeing video of Floyd crying out for his mother as he lay dying galvanized her as a mother and athlete to speak out. "I feel a lot of times the Black community does not feel heard," she said. "People are crying out and we want to be heard, we want to be seen, and we want change to happen." Felix vowed she and her fellow athletes would continue speaking out. "We have a lot on our minds, and a lot that we want to say," she said.[98]

"By sports standards this is an avalanche."

What was remarkable about the post–Floyd speaking out by athletes such as Felix was not that it occurred, but that it involved so many athletes at all levels—and without apparent concern for the "shut up and play" culture of old, suggested columnist Thomas Boswell, who has covered sports for *The Washington Post* for some 50 years. "For at least the past half-century, with a few conspicuous exceptions, prominent athletes either have stayed close to the political mainstream or avoided controversial social issues almost entirely," he observed. During summer 2020, however, "more well-known athletes, sports executives and even commissioners" had "taken strong public stands on societal-political issues than I have ever seen," Boswell wrote. "And by a big margin." This volume of speaking out by athletes represented "something more than a trend," he suggested. "By sports standards this is an avalanche."[99]

Time magazine reporter Sean Gregory echoed Boswell's assessment, writing, "The days of keeping a social conscience off the field seem gone forever." Gregory reported that prominent athletes at both the professional and college levels seemed newly emboldened to fight for justice with words and actions. Summer 2020 was, according to Gregory's sources, "a moment where the outrage of players is stronger than their fear of speaking out."[100]

The next chapter examines athletes who set aside any fear of speaking out to use powerful symbols to advocate for social and political change. The chapter asks what ethical care may be required when athletes speak out without words, especially when their symbolic speaking questions systems of power and privilege.

9

Raise a Fist or Take a Knee?

*Athletes Speaking Out
Symbolically About Injustice*

"They were pariahs."

At the 1968 Olympics in Mexico City, U.S. track and field champions Tommie Smith and John Carlos produced "the most enduring, riveting image in the history of either sports or protest"[1] when they ascended the medal stand and spoke out symbolically against injustice. Historian Ted Widmer described the "endlessly reproduced" image they created: "As the tinny sound of 'The Star-Spangled Banner' began to fill the Estadio Olimpico, Smith and Carlos looked at the ground, and raised their right and left arms, respectively, in the air. Each was wearing a single black glove, covering a clenched fist: the black power salute."

Almost as quickly as they raised their fists, Carlos and Smith were depicted as dangerous radicals and dismissed from the Olympics. "But in fact, Smith and Carlos were more moderate than their gesture suggested. They were trying to raise awareness of suffering," Widmer recounted. The athletes' symbolic act protested such injustices as the paucity of Black coaches in sports, the dearth of affordable housing for Blacks, and the failure of prominent colleges to welcome Black students. "That was not exactly the stuff of revolution," Widmer noted. "But they were important causes in a country that seemed to have forgotten how to take care of the poor, particularly the black urban poor."[2]

After their protest, Smith and Carlos endured racial slurs, death threats and years of FBI surveillance.[3] Neither competed internationally again. "They were pariahs," sports columnist Jerry Brewer observed.[4]

"I love America. ... That's why I'm doing this. I want to help make America better."

As the 2016–2017 National Football League season began, San Francisco 49ers quarterback Colin Kaepernick started symbolically speaking out against injustice. First, he sat on the football field sidelines while "The Star-Spangled Banner" played. The 49ers played several games before sportswriters noticed Kaepernick sitting. "When they asked the young quarterback about it, he talked about police brutality and too many dead black Americans: 'To me this is bigger than football, and it would be selfish on my part to look the other way,'" *The New York Times* reported.[5]

A military veteran and former NFL player soon suggested to Kaepernick his protest would better respect the U.S. flag if he knelt rather than sat,[6] so Kaepernick began kneeling on one knee during the national anthem in what he explained "as a non-violent form of expression designed to raise awareness of social and racial injustices."[7]

Despite reiterating respect for the flag and the anthem, the symbolic speech Kaepernick intended to "protest police brutality and social injustice had careened into a national debate on everything but that," *The New York Times* observed. Fans, commentators and politicians argued about whether Kaepernick was unpatriotic, and crowds booed him repeatedly.

After he first knelt during the anthem, Kaepernick attempted to "redirect the narrative" with a news conference. He told reporters, "I love America. I love people. That's why I'm doing this. I want to help make America better."[8] His attempt didn't work. As Kaepernick continued kneeling throughout the season, he received racial slurs and death threats. He also attracted "sprays of vitriol" from candidate and then U.S. president Donald Trump, who regularly blasted Kaepernick.

By season's end, when Kaepernick became a free agent, no other NFL team offered him a contract. Nor would any team sign him in the next three seasons. Kaepernick filed a grievance against NFL owners for colluding to ban him from football. Ultimately, he reached a non-disclosure agreement in which the NFL reportedly paid him several million dollars but restricted him from discussing what *The New York Times* described as an "apparent blackballing by the most powerful sports league in North America."[9]

Some 50 years apart, Smith and Carlos raised their fists, and Kaepernick took a knee. The men uttered no words, but their gestures spoke so powerfully they polarized sports fans, team executives, media sponsors and politicians who argued for years afterward about the athletes' patriotic duties and free expression rights. Although the athletes steadfastly maintained their gestures were protests against injustice and not disrespect for the U.S. flag and the national anthem, these two episodes remain among the most controversial acts of speaking out symbolically by athletes in U.S. history.

This chapter explores the dramatic power of symbolic speech acts. The chapter considers the ethical heritage established by athletes like Smith, Carlos and Kaepernick who spoke out symbolically to oppose injustice, and discusses the harmful consequences they faced afterward. Based on racial injustice protests in 2020, the chapter also examines the emerging ethical landscape facing athletes who speak out symbolically.

Symbolic Speech as Mind to Mind Communication

"Symbolic speech as a form of protest, like taking a knee at a football game while others stand for the National Anthem, enjoys a long history in America," according to historian Stephen Solomon. "The founding generation did not have Twitter, Facebook, blogs, or broadcasting, but they did understand the power of symbolic expression to command attention and rally supporters."[10]

Patriots seeking American independence astutely realized that symbols, such as "liberty trees" from which protesters hung effigies of influential British loyalists, instantly communicated the revolutionary movement's goals to people who couldn't read or easily understand the ideals of democracy being expressed in the pamphlets and public speeches of the day.[11] "In that way, the symbols could drive home complex arguments in a simple, unified way," Solomon notes.[12]

The American patriots also realized symbolic expression's power to create dialogue. When crowds gathered in town squares to gape at shocking effigies hung in liberty trees, they "couldn't help but talk with those around them about what they saw and what it meant for the future."[13] The symbolic expression often became "an impromptu town meeting with vast participation" when effigies were cut down from liberty trees and paraded through other parts of town, where even more people—including women who typically were excluded from political communication because they did not have the right to vote[14]—saw the symbols and talked about what they meant with fellow townspeople.[15] "Much of this symbolic expression was controversial and even offensive but a powerful form of protest then and now," Solomon observes.[16]

The First Amendment to the U.S. Constitution, enacted after the American revolution, ensures citizens' legal freedom to speak symbolically. Although not specifically mentioned in the First Amendment, symbolic speech—"wordless acts that are said to communicate messages," according to legal scholar Terry Eastland[17]—is protected from government infringement unless the wordless acts pose a threat to specific people or the public good.[18]

In interpreting limits to First Amendment free expression, the U.S. Supreme Court long has recognized the power of symbolic speech, or expressive conduct, as it sometimes is called. A 1940s Supreme Court ruling upheld school children's legal right not to stand to salute the American flag and recite the pledge of allegiance for religious reasons. The court called symbolic expression, such as saluting the flag, "a primitive but effective way of communicating ideas" that "is a short cut from mind to mind."[19]

"We had no guide, no blueprint."

U.S. runners Smith and Carlos no doubt understood the "mind to mind" power of communicating with symbols when they planned their Olympic medal stand protest. They deliberately selected each element of their appearance. "We had no guide, no blueprint. No one had ever turned the medal stand into a festival of visual symbols to express our feelings," Carlos remembered. "We decided that we would wear black gloves to represent strength and unity. We would have beads hanging from our neck, which would represent the history of lynching. We wouldn't wear shoes to symbolize the poverty that still plagued so much of black America. On the medal stand, all we would wear on our feet would be black socks."[20]

Likewise, Kaepernick must have understood the "mind to mind" power of speaking out about injustice with symbols. As his season of kneeling on football field sidelines progressed, he began letting it speak for itself, even as public ire built. After he was dropped from the NFL and could no longer kneel publicly during the national anthem, he adroitly leaned on symbolic images—and few words—in social media messages intended to question injustice, becoming "one of the most prominent, and influential, public figures in American culture,"[21] at least in part through what *The New York Times* called his "canny use" of videos posted on social channels.[22]

However, the sustained public fury over these athletes' protests shows speaking out symbolically may be rapidly and significantly misunderstood, even as it may immediately and powerfully draw attention to a speaker's cause. Therefore, athletes who speak out through a symbolic act must understand the legal principles and ethical responsibilities involved in symbolic expression.

Legal Controversies Over Symbolic Speech

Legally, symbolic speech resides on a spectrum between what courts call "pure speech" and "pure conduct." Symbolic speech sometimes is called "speech plus," meaning "speech plus conduct."[23] Because it involves conduct, symbolic speech receives less First Amendment protection than pure speech does, but because it includes speech intended to make a point, symbolic speech receives more legal protection than pure conduct does.

In 1968, the same year Smith and Carlos spoke out symbolically on the Olympic medal stand, the Supreme Court acknowledged David O'Brien was speaking out symbolically to protest the Vietnam war when he burned his draft card while he stood on the steps of a courthouse. However, the court did not uphold a legal right for O'Brien to speak symbolically by burning his draft card, instead ruling that the government's duty to induct draftees into the military meant draft cards were official records not to be destroyed. The government's interest in maintaining order outweighed O'Brien's right to speak out symbolically.[24]

The next year, the Supreme Court did protect symbolic speech against the Vietnam war, ruling John and Mary Beth Tinker and Christopher Eckhardt had a legal right to wear black armbands to their public school to protest the war. As long as the teens' armbands did not disrupt the school, the "unpopular viewpoint" they represented could not be squelched simply because some teachers and students found the symbolic act uncomfortable.[25]

The Supreme Court again protected symbolic speech against the war in 1971. In that case, Paul Cohen spoke out symbolically by walking through a courthouse while wearing a jacket stenciled with the words "Fuck the Draft." The profanity's use may have been offensive or immature, but the court upheld Cohen's right to communicate in a way that spoke to observers' cognitive and emotional understandings of the war.[26]

Most controversial among the symbolic speech protections upheld by the Supreme Court have been those involving desecration of the U.S. flag. In 1974, the court upheld Harold Spence's right to protest the Vietnam war by taping peace symbols to the flag and hanging it upside down from his college dormitory window. The court protected Spence's expressive conduct because it included an "intent to convey a particularized message" and a great likelihood "that the message would be understood by those who viewed it."[27]

Desecrating the flag by burning it is especially contentious symbolic speech. Flag burning is powerful because it can "grab our attention like few other things can,"[28] according to legal scholar James McGoldrick. Flags are not burned publicly for any reason except to create a shocking protest statement. "Burning a flag in a public place is nothing short of play acting, pretending that one is so upset at the evils of government that only the cathartic act of ritualistic destruction by fire can communicate the depth of despair," McGoldrick contends.[29]

Flag burning as symbolic speech has been protected by the Supreme Court since its 1989 ruling upholding Gregory Johnson's right to burn a flag in front of a city hall to protest President Ronald Reagan's policies. As long as Johnson did not harm the public or city hall, government could not restrict his symbolic speech just because people were upset by the act that expressed his view.[30]

Ethical Principles Suggested by Legal Rulings on Symbolic Speech

These First Amendment rulings provide principles for speaking out symbolically that amplify the four-part Wyatt and Bunton test for ethical justification of speaking out.[31] The test suggests speakers first consider relationships to speech acts' topics. The legal rulings offer the principle that speakers using symbolic acts have ethical duties to ascertain the acts are capable of communicating views speakers are known to hold. For instance, black armbands could be worn to protest war or to express bereavement. Students who wear armbands to school have to be known by teachers and other students for opposing war if the armbands are to effectively communicate an anti-war message, rather than communicating about a family member's death.

Second, the test asks speakers to consider motivations for speaking. The legal rulings suggest the principle that speakers using symbolic acts have ethical duties to demonstrate clear intentions to communicate via action. For example, wearing a profanity-stenciled jacket through a courthouse might be an anti-war protest or might be a fashion choice. People who see the jacket don't easily know which. A citizen who wants to use the jacket to oppose war needs to wear it in a way that conveys the profanity is protest rather than fashion.

Third, the test asks speakers to consider harms created by speaking. The legal rulings offer the principle that speakers using symbolic acts have ethical duties not to pose harm to public safety and wellbeing with their acts. The courts long have said citizens' protests may be regulated for time, place and manner concerns. This means, for example, that a symbolic speaker burning a draft card on the courthouse steps cannot impede people's entrances and exits from the building, and certainly cannot spark a fire that would imperil people or damage the building.

Finally, the test asks speakers to consider whether speaking out promotes dialogue. The legal rulings suggest the principle that speakers using symbolic acts have ethical duties to recognize audiences' shock and offense at powerful symbolic acts may overshadow the views speakers seek to communicate. People may be so appalled to see a flag flying upside down, for instance, that they may not recognize the anti-war view it represents or they may conclude all anti-war protesters disrespect the flag. Dialogue resulting from the symbolic act thus may focus on patriotism and respect for the flag, and not on the morality of war, as the symbolic speaker intended.

Athletes' Use of Symbolic Speech to Protest Injustice

For years, athletes, especially Black athletes, have spoken out with powerful American symbols to protest social and racial injustice. (See Chapter 8 for analysis of athletes speaking out with words.) Smith and Carlos on the 1968 Olympic medal podium are perhaps the best-known example of athletes symbolically speaking out, probably because of the outrage they created—and probably because journalists gave "scant media attention" to "female athletes, particularly Black female athletes" who also spoke out symbolically, *The Washington Post* noted many years later.[32]

At the 1959 Pan American games, for example, U.S. high jumper Eroseanna Robinson refused to stand for the national anthem, "making her one of the earliest American athletes to do so."[33] Robinson was both an athlete and a community activist who organized civil rights protests and hunger strikes,[34] so when she sat during the anthem, she possessed an ethically defensible relationship between her activism against injustice and her symbolic speech protesting it. At the 1968 Olympics, sprinter Wyomia Tyus wore black shorts, rather than the official white shorts of the U.S. uniform, to protest the treatment of Blacks. "'I was wearing the shorts long before Tommie and Carlos did their victory stand protest,' she said. 'But women were not heard or spoke to, and Black women definitely were not.'" When she publicly dedicated one of her two gold medals to Smith and Carlos, who had been dismissed from the Olympics by then, no journalists reported her comments (or reported that she had just become the first athlete to win the 100 meters at consecutive Olympics).[35]

As the tumultuous 1960s and 1970s civil rights and anti–Vietnam war protests receded, sports became bigger business, and fewer athletes symbolically spoke out against injustice. "Right around the time that revenues began to flood the coffers of the sports industry—namely, TV money and endorsement deals—the iconic activist athlete receded from view, leaving a 'chasmic' gap between the 1960s and today, filled in by a 'Nike culture that told athletes there was no higher calling than becoming a brand,'"[36] observes sports scholar Michael Serazio. In the 1980s and 1990s, basketball superstar Michael Jordan, with his lucrative Nike endorsement deals, represented the "apolitical ideal" athlete.[37]

"A symbol of oppression, of tyranny."

His fellow professional basketball player, Mahmoud Abdul-Rauf, did not. In 1996, Abdul-Rauf became the first athlete sanctioned for conduct during the national anthem since Smith and Carlos were dismissed from the Olympics nearly 30 years before. While playing for the Denver Nuggets, Abdul-Rauf avoided standing for the national anthem, stretching on the sidelines while it played or, for at least 60 games, waiting in the locker room until it ended. When sports reporters finally noticed what he was doing, "Abdul-Rauf explained his long-standing protest as an act of his Muslim conscience, describing the U.S. flag as 'a symbol of oppression, of tyranny,'" according to historian Zareena Grewal.[38] The National Basketball Association rapidly imposed a policy requiring players to "line up in a dignified posture" during the anthem.

After serving a one-game suspension, Abdul-Rauf stood during the anthem with his head bowed and his hands raised in a prayerful position. Fans, sportswriters, politicians and fellow players condemned him. Many focused on what they perceived as Abdul-Rauf's ingratitude. For instance, New Jersey Nets player Jayson Williams said, "I'm no politician, but the man has to remember he's made a lot of money in this country." Abdul-Rauf said he endured racial slurs and death threats for his stance, and a fellow Nuggets player called him "a dead man walking as far as playing in the NBA again." Indeed, by season's end the Nuggets traded their highest-scoring player, and before long, he was out of the NBA entirely.[39]

"Hands up, don't shoot."

Some 15 years passed before professional athletes began more often speaking out symbolically, especially to protest injustice after the killings of Black people. In 2012, for instance, basketball superstar LeBron James tweeted a photo of his fellow Miami Heat players wearing hooded sweatshirts to protest the killing of Trayvon Martin, an unarmed Florida teen shot while he walked home wearing a hoodie.

In 2014, several NBA players wore "I can't breathe" T-shirts during pre-game warm-up sessions to protest the police killing of Eric Garner, a New York man who repeatedly uttered the phrase as he died while locked in a chokehold. In 2014, five St. Louis Rams players walked onto their football field with arms raised in a "hands up, don't shoot" gesture to protest the killing of Michael Brown, an unarmed teen shot by a police officer in Ferguson, Missouri, just miles away from the Rams' stadium.

In July 2016, several Minnesota Lynx players appeared on their Women's National Basketball Association court wearing T-shirts featuring the phrases "Change starts with us, justice and accountability" and Black Lives Matter both to show respect for five Dallas police officers shot and killed while on duty, and to protest the killing of Philando Castile, an unarmed driver shot by police during a traffic stop near the basketball arena.[40]

"Boycott the Rams"

In each instance, fans, politicians, police and media commentators objected to the views athletes sought to communicate symbolically. Minneapolis police officers who worked off-duty providing security for the Lynx said they would no longer work for the team.[41] St. Louis fans launched "boycott the Rams" campaigns on social media, suggesting players who made the "hands up, don't shoot" gesture should be punished—and sometimes using racist language to make that suggestion.[42]

Potential Harms to Athletes Who Speak Symbolically

As moral agents who intend to speak out symbolically about injustice, athletes must accept the risk of some harm. Sometimes, the harm from speaking out threatens the athlete's mental or emotional wellbeing and physical safety. Both Abdul-Rauf and Kaepernick received death threats when they communicated symbolically as the national anthem played.

"Even if I had only coins jingling in my pocket, I was honored to have the platform."

Sometimes, the harm from speaking out threatens athletes' financial wellbeing. After their Olympic protest, Smith and Carlos earned a little money with "bare-bones, do-it-yourself speaking" engagements at historically Black colleges, where "they would pass the hat around and see what they would collect." It wasn't enough income to support their families, Carlos said. "But when we would do an event and even if I had only coins jingling in my pocket, I was honored to have the platform, to take a deep breath, and to express why we did what we did."[43]

When Kaepernick spoke out symbolically by kneeling during the national anthem, he accepted harm in a much different financial context. He lost his NFL salary, which reportedly was $14.3 million in 2016.[44] As a mid-career quarterback with a limited number of years during which his body could withstand football's battering, he accepted future loss of income from a league that pays top quarterbacks as much as $30 million a year.[45] In early 2019, Kaepernick reportedly received less than $10 million in his grievance against the NFL for colluding to ban him from the league.[46] In 2018, the athletic products giant Nike made Kaepernick the face of its 30th anniversary "Just Do It" advertising campaign. Known for signing elite athletes to contracts worth tens of millions of dollars, Nike likely compensated

Kaepernick handsomely as well, banking on the controversy surrounding the "famously quiet activist" quarterback to generate widespread attention for the company.[47] Indeed, both Kaepernick's endorsement deal with Nike and his grievance settlement with the NFL generated more uproar over his patriotism. President Donald Trump repeatedly demonized Kaepernick on Twitter and at political rallies, and sports fans raged about boycotting Nike's products.[48]

More harmful than the financial risks of symbolic speaking out, however, were the potential harms to Kaepernick's mental and emotional wellbeing that happened each time outraged fans, politicians and commentators compared him to the 9/11 hijackers who attacked the United States, demanded he renounce his U.S. citizenship, or threatened to kill him.[49] Psychiatrist J. Corey Williams points out that when Kaepernick knelt, he joined "an entire history of blacks stepping outside of the social order—or protesting it—only to be told they can't" and therefore faced with chronic mental health stress as a result.[50]

Applying the Justification Test to Symbolic Speech

Having accepted these harms created by symbolically speaking out, Kaepernick survives scrutiny under the ethical justification test for speaking out, as do Smith and Carlos before him.

The test requires a relationship between speaker and topic. Athletes who transcend the public's role-related expectations for athletes to "shut up and play" by speaking out about public issues should evince an ethically justifiable relationship to those issues. Given the historical and cultural significance of symbols such as the U.S. flag or the national anthem, demonstrating a relationship to a topic is especially important if athletes seek to speak out by using one of those symbols, rather than words, to convey their views.

Both the 1968 and 2016 acts of symbolic speaking out occurred during periods of public debate about Black citizens' treatment in the United States. Smith and Carlos participated in Olympic Project for Human Rights conversations about boycotting the 1968 games to advocate for civil rights, and Smith in particular was identified as a public face of the conversation, perhaps because he ranked first in the world in his sport.[51] Likewise, in the year before he began kneeling during the national anthem, Kaepernick actively posted social media messages to protest racial injustice, publicly affiliating with the ideas of Black activists such as Malcolm X. "Kaepernick's social media posts flared with urgent intensity" in July 2016, "when black men were killed by police on back-to-back days," *The New York Times* reported.[52]

Second, the test requires justifiable motivation for speaking out. Athletes who transcend role-related expectations must demonstrate ethically defensible motivations such as creating awareness and understanding of a public issue, serving the common good, or supporting less-privileged people whose voices go unheard.

Certainly, Smith, Carlos and Kaepernick each was motivated to raise awareness of the ways America treats its Black citizens. Kaepernick also could afford to advance his speaking out beyond raising awareness to creating change. He gave $1 million to various charities during the season he knelt during the national anthem, and he funded "Know Your Rights" camps to teach children about Black history, physical and mental health, higher education and civil rights.[53]

When speaking out with symbols as powerful as the U.S. flag or the national anthem, athletes bear extra responsibility to address serious public concerns instead of something frivolous. Athletes must intend to convey worthwhile messages through symbolic acts and intend for audiences to understand the acts represent those messages.[54] "Conduct is more likely to be perceived as intentionally communicative if it is done in close physical or temporal proximity to an event or condition to which its message relates, particularly if the event or condition is in the public eye," suggests legal scholar Peter Tiersma.[55]

In 1968, when Smith and Carlos spoke out symbolically, the United States had been roiled by civil rights protests and the assassination of the Rev. Dr. Martin Luther King, Jr., and an Olympic boycott had been discussed publicly for some time. Those events provided temporal context for Smith and Carlos, who obviously intended to convey a message as they added symbolic elements so their uniforms communicated their message. "A speaker may also show that conduct is intended to communicate by doing an act for a prolonged period of time, and in any event, longer than the act is done naturally," Tiersma contends.[56] Kaepernick accomplished that, sitting and then kneeling during the national anthem for some 20 NFL games. Audiences couldn't help but recognize what he was doing, especially as his symbolic act increasingly attracted news coverage.

Next, the justification test requires considering potential harms created by speaking out. When speaking out symbolically, especially in a public place such as a crowded sports stadium, athletes must attempt to protect the security of those present. The symbolic act is not ethically justifiable if it poses a risk to public safety. "It is acceptable if the idea creates chaos, but not if the method of communicating does," McGoldrick warns.[57] Smith, Carlos and Kaepernick certainly created uproar, but their symbolic acts were themselves peaceful. No one in attendance was harmed physically by a raised fist or a bowed knee.

Furthermore, when speaking out with symbols as open to multiple interpretations as the U.S. flag or the national anthem, athletes must attempt to prevent the harm of misunderstanding. Athletes must examine the likelihood their symbolic speech will be understood. "While the ritual of the anthem in sports culture usually (if superficially) unifies sports fans before dividing the arena into two competing sides, such protests reveal the much more complex and divisive racial and political fractures in the ways we see the flag," Grewal observes. Certainly, that was the case for Smith, Carlos and Kaepernick. "One of the reasons the flag can be a polarizing national symbol is because, as with all symbols, its meaning is in the eye of the beholder," Grewal notes. "To those offended by Kaepernick's protest, the flag represents the best of our American values and ideals. In contrast, Kaepernick sees the flag as a symbol of the U.S. government that he faults for being inactive and callous to the extrajudicial killings of Black people by the police. Again, this is the very nature of symbols: What the flag stands for is *not* self-evident in its Stars and Stripes."[58]

Therefore, athletes may bear ethical duties to amplify symbolic gestures with explanation. Smith, Carlos and Kaepernick were not responsible for audiences who continued to misunderstand the symbolic speech acts, once the athletes had fulfilled their ethical duties by explaining the acts through news conferences, interviews and public talks. Nor were the athletes responsible for journalists' ethical failure for labeling the symbolic acts "national anthem protests" rather than "civil rights protests."

"The larger conversation is what he was protesting about."

Finally, the justification test requires considering whether speaking out about a public issue promotes dialogue. When speaking out symbolically with powerful yet ambiguous symbols such as the U.S. flag and the national anthem, Smith, Carlos and Kaepernick risked the possibility that audience dialogue would focus on patriotism and respect for these national symbols, or on the limits to free expression, rather than focusing on the topic of injustice the athletes intended. That does not mean the athletes did not attempt to promote dialogue. Kaepernick's "actual point of protest" was questioning the status quo in a country in which Black people are killed too often, notes former NFL player and activist Wade Davis. "Whether you agree with his tactics or not is one type of conversation. The larger conversation is what he was protesting about," Davis observes. "The fact that so many don't want to have that specific conversation speaks to the fact that they know what is happening in America is beyond tragic."[59]

Fifty years after their act, when Smith and Carlos found themselves treated as "icons," rather than "pariahs" on the world stage, they provided "living examples that athlete protesters, no matter how vilified in the moment, grow in reverence as they persist," according to Brewer.[60] Carlos said he believed Kaepernick eventually would be revered, too. Carlos suggested history would celebrate Kaepernick "as righteous and courageous for calling attention to income equality and policy brutality."[61]

For several years, however, Kaepernick's name still sparked strong views. A 2019 survey found 57 percent of Americans knew who he was and many regarded him negatively.[62] Other people regarded Kaepernick more positively and claimed his "calibrated gesture—meant to call attention to racism, social injustice and police brutality against people of color" to use as "a broader distress signal" around the world, *The New York Times* reported.[63] Sociologist Brian Foster said the signal provided moral agency for Black people in particular "to take a stance about an injustice that they think should be different or is unfair."[64] In that way, Kaepernick's act of symbolic speech fostered further symbolic dialogue, as athletes at all levels of amateur and professional sports "took a knee" on occasion.

Symbolic Speech After George Floyd's Killing and During the Coronavirus Pandemic

Within a year of that survey's negative reflection on Kaepernick, "taking a knee" became common—and led to historic acts of speaking out symbolically in sports. Playing the national anthem before games, which "for decades had been a passive show of patriotism," in 2020 "turned into a roll call of demonstration," Brewer noted.[65]

"Two unexpected events catalyzed this moment," reported *The Washington Post.* "The coronavirus pandemic has disproportionately killed black Americans and exposed a broader range of inequalities that persist in black communities; the recession that accompanied the pandemic has highlighted similar inequities. And the brutal killing of George Floyd by police in Minneapolis has prompted many white Americans to acknowledge that their lives are profoundly different from those of black Americans—and that racism is part of that lived experience."[66]

After Floyd's killing, millions of Americans poured out of their home quarantines to take to the streets in protest. Scholars counted at least 5,000 distinct U.S. protests against racism and police brutality between the end of May and early July 2020, labeling them "the largest sustained mobilization in the United States in our lifetimes."[67] Athletes from all around the sports world who normally avoid hazards to their physical health "jumped off the sidelines to join the sprawling protests," risking exposure to the coronavirus or to the violence that occurred at some demonstrations, *The New York Times* reported.[68] Protesters linked Floyd's death to recent unprosecuted deaths of other Black people, including Ahmaud Arbury, who was chased and fatally shot in February 2020 by two white men while he jogged through a Georgia neighborhood,[69] and Breonna Taylor, who died after being shot eight times in March 2020 when police seeking her ex-boyfriend burst into her Louisville, Kentucky, apartment while she slept.[70]

"Say Her Name."

In July, when the first professional sports teams returned to competition after the pandemic shutdown, many athletes worked with team owners and sports leagues to find newly sanctioned ways to speak out symbolically about racial injustice and to say the names of Floyd, Arbury and Taylor, among other victims of injustice.

At players' behest, the NBA offered social justice messages for the backs of players' jerseys, with "Equality" and Black Lives Matter the two messages players chose most frequently,[71] while the WNBA offered Black Lives Matter or "Say Her Name" for the backs of its players' jerseys.[72] Basketball created "bubbles" to protect players from coronavirus by quarantining them for weeks near arenas where games were played without fans attending. Players who had spoken out symbolically with their presence at protests across the country ensured the basketball leagues, long the most socially conscious of the major U.S. sports, emblazoned the "bubble" arenas with Black Lives Matter messages that were highly visible on television, where fans saw games begin with almost all players kneeling during the national anthem.

"Today, athletes may have to explain why they chose to stand, not kneel."

Evidence of new tolerance for athletes symbolically speaking out appeared when other, more conservative professional leagues resumed their seasons. When the National Women's Soccer League returned, players wore Black Lives Matter warm-up shirts, and as the national anthem played, nearly every player knelt. Four years before, when soccer star Megan Rapinoe followed Kaepernick and knelt alone on the field, NWSL officials enacted a rule requiring players to stand during the anthem. In 2020, soccer quickly repealed the rule.[73] Rapinoe did not play in the tournament that re-started soccer, but she tweeted her support of the many players who knelt for the anthem. "You love to see these women using their voice, demanding better for America, and for black people and people of color," she wrote.[74]

Afterward, sportswriter John Branch observed the "stand-or-kneel debate" ignited by Kaepernick was "reignited—bigger than before, and this time with an unexpected twist." Branch wrote, "Today, athletes may have to explain why they chose to stand, not kneel, during 'The Star-Spangled Banner.'" He mentioned one of the few soccer players who did not kneel during the anthem but placed her hand on the shoulder of a teammate who did. Her gesture, which Branch suggested just a year before would have been "hailed for her understated support in fighting racial equality," in 2020 met "a barrage of online criticism and debate" compelling her to issue a public explanation.[75]

> "I kneel because I'm unhappy with the injustice in our country."

When Major League Baseball resumed play, significant change marked this most conservative of sports. "Taking a stand, or a knee, or refusing to play because of racial injustice in M.L.B.—a sport saturated with tradition and unwritten rules of conduct where the majority of players, coaches, executives and owners are white is different than doing so in the N.B.A., W.N.B.A. or N.F.L., leagues where most of the players are Black," *The New York Times* noted.[76] Black athletes accounted for just 8 percent of baseball's players, and in 2016, when other athletes echoed Kaepernick's gesture, the lone baseball player who knelt said he felt ostracized. Yet in 2020, as baseball opened its season, the league let players wear Black Lives Matter warm-up shirts and write social justice messages on their cleats. Players' uniforms featured social justice sleeve patches, and on the field, Black Lives Matter was stenciled in the dirt behind the pitcher's mound.[77]

Baseball's new recognition of players' desire to speak out symbolically about injustice extended further. The season's exhibition games opened with first-year San Francisco Giants manager Gabe Kapler kneeling during the national anthem, as did several Giants players, who were followed by players in other games. The symbolic message made Kapler "the first manager or head coach in any of the four major North American pro leagues to protest in such a way," *The Washington Post* reported.[78]

Not surprisingly, President Trump opposed Kapler's message just as he had Kaepernick's. The president tweeted he was "looking forward to live sports" returning from the pandemic shutdown, "but any time I witness a player kneeling during the National Anthem, a sign of great disrespect for our Country and our Flag, the game is over for me!"[79] *The Post* reported a #boycottMLB hashtag trended briefly on Twitter, "with fans saying they were done with the sport." Remarkably, MLB tweeted support for Kapler and players "using their platforms to peacefully protest" and added, "Supporting human rights is not political."[80] For his part, Kapler tweeted, "I kneel because I'm unhappy with the injustice in our country."[81]

Athletes shared his view. "The overwhelming majority of people who actually play these games, regardless of their race and life experiences, want racial equality and demand their leagues join them," Brewer suggested. "In the fight to make black lives matter, it seems players have had an epiphany about how much they themselves matter. For now, there's enough public agreement that it empowers athletes in team sports to speak or protest openly without fear of becoming the next Kaepernick or Mahmoud Abdul-Rauf."[82]

Speaking Out Symbolically by Stopping Play

Then, a month after 2020 sports seasons resumed—and exactly four years from the 2016 day Kaepernick began protesting[83]—athletes' power to speak out symbolically about racial injustice reached a historic crescendo. Kenosha, Wisconsin, police shot a Black man named Jacob Blake seven times in the back as he tried to get into a car that held his children. Within days, athletes who saw video of Blake's shooting joined across sports to speak out symbolically with the strongest message they could send: They refused to play. Athletes said they would not entertain fans when they instead could draw fans' attention to persistent police brutality and racial injustice.[84]

> "It is the most powerful thing they can do to express the seriousness of the problem."

Milwaukee Bucks players, whose home arena is less than an hour's drive from Kenosha, sent the initial symbolic message by refusing to play. Their message set off player-driven cancellations over three days that included nearly all professional sports. Six NBA games, three WNBA games, 10 baseball games, five soccer matches, four men's hockey playoff games and nine NFL practices were cancelled.[85] Black athletes in particular "stopped playing because it is the most powerful thing they can do to express the seriousness of the problem," Brewer observed. "It should not be their burden. They have no power to change laws. ... But they do have the ability to get the attention of millions. Even if it means hurting the game they love and possibly triggering a catastrophe of financial and public support, they are willing to assume the risks. Why? Because human ingenuity can insulate them from a virus that has killed nearly 180,000 Americans. But there is not enough human decency to create a bubble effective against racism."[86]

The New York Times called the athletes' cancellations "one of the broadest political statements across sports leagues that the United States had ever seen,"[87] while sports biographer Jonathan Eig called the cancellations "perhaps the sporting world's boldest move for racial justice since two black-gloved fists were raised in the Mexico City Olympics."[88]

"We don't need another publicity parade, so we'll just stay inside until it's time to play."

After the bold move of athlete-orchestrated cancellations, the sports world waited to see what players would do in the National Football League, where Kaepernick's symbolic act of speaking out still hovered. Three weeks after the other sports' cancellations, the NFL was set to open its season in Kansas City, where the 2020 Super Bowl champions would face the Houston Texans on Thursday night, before other teams took to football fields on the weekend.

The NFL echoed other sports leagues. It emblazoned racial justice messages in football stadiums, painting "End Racism" and "It Takes All of Us" messages on the football fields' end zones, playing both the national anthem and "Lift Every Voice and Sing" (which is often considered the "Black national anthem") before the games, and allowing players to wear Black Lives Matter warmup shirts and to place names of Black victims of injustice on their helmets.[89]

Unlike the other sports leagues, however, the NFL opened its season with limited numbers of fans in some football stadiums, and many observers wondered whether the presence of fans would change athletes' plans to speak out symbolically during the national anthem. Observing physical distancing practices designed to minimize coronavirus transmission, the opening game between Kansas City and Houston included about 17,000 fans in a stadium that usually seated at least 75,000 people.

Houston team members chose to remain in their locker room during the national anthem and "Lift Every Voice and Sing." When Houston players emerged, both teams' players "linked arms on the field in a moment of silence for racial justice and a smattering of boos could be heard from the crowd," *The New York Times* reported.[90] At the league's other opening games that weekend, some players knelt during the national anthem, some teammates stood and linked their arms during the anthem, and at least four teams besides Houston opted to stay in their locker rooms during the anthem. Miami Dolphins players, for instance, released a video statement saying, "We don't need another publicity parade, so we'll just stay inside until it's time to play the game."[91]

Like the "smattering of boos" heard in Kansas City, fans' reactions to the "new, wider wave of protests" that enjoyed "the explicit blessing of the N.F.L." were mild, *USA Today* reported. The newspaper also reported that the five most-watched live television shows during football's opening week were NFL games, that the NFL signed four new corporate sponsors and retained all of the previous year's sponsors, despite the economic downturn of the pandemic, and that sales of NFL merchandise increased by 35 percent over the previous year. "But the figure that perhaps best explains why protests this season won't pose a threat to the NFL is 56. That's the percentage of Americans who now believe it's appropriate for athletes to kneel during the national anthem in protest of police brutality, according to a Washington Post poll last week," *USA Today* noted. "That result is similar to a Yahoo News/YouGov poll earlier this summer, which found 52% supported athlete protests. … Unlike four years ago, when irate fans accused the NFL of 'changing,' there's a recognition now that it's the country that is different, and the protests, demonstrations and calls to action by players, coaches and even the league are a reflection of that."[92]

The next chapter examines another type of speaking out in a country facing great change. Specifically, the chapter considers how celebrities spoke out ethically about health issues during 2020's coronavirus pandemic.

10

Who's an Expert?

*Celebrities Speaking Out
During a Pandemic*

A confusing new reality faced Americans in the first days of March 2020, as a deadly coronavirus infected the country. People were uncertain about terms popping up in increasingly frequent news reports about the virus. What was the difference between "coronavirus" and "COVID-19," "pandemic" and "epidemic," or "quarantine" and "isolation"? People were stunned by how quickly authorities began closing offices, factories, government agencies, colleges, schools, houses of worship, stores and restaurants to try to slow coronavirus transmission. What exactly did officials mean when they asked people stay home to "flatten the curve" of rising infection rates? People who lived in communities that hadn't yet reported any cases wondered if coronavirus was a hoax, or if shutting down the economy was an excessive response to the virus, especially as workers were laid off. When venturing out to stock up on supplies to tide them over while hunkering down at home, why did people find store shelves bare of staples such as toilet paper? Could the virus really be slowed if people stayed six feet away from one another and wore face masks?

Then came March 11. Three events that day required little understanding of infectious disease, public health policy or economics, but the events made the coronavirus pandemic real to many Americans, according to both *The Atlantic* and *The Washington Post*.[1] President Donald Trump gave a rare televised prime-time speech from the White House, calling coronavirus a "foreign virus" and saying travel into the United States from other countries was banned.[2] The National Basketball Association abruptly suspended its season, even as that night's games were being played.[3] And superstar actor Tom Hanks announced he and his wife, actress and singer Rita Wilson, had tested positive for the coronavirus. To many people, when the actor often called "America's Dad" spoke out about his COVID-19 diagnosis, the pandemic became concrete. *The Atlantic* suggested the announcement from Hanks seemed "in some ways, like the most seismic news the U.S. has received since the pandemic reached our shores." The magazine further argued Hanks provided calm, solid information, communicating more effectively about the pandemic than the president. "Whether because of sheer star power or the straightforward, fact-based nature of the post, the actor's words carried more weight and solemnity" than the president's speech, the magazine contended.[4]

Over his decades-long movie career, the two-time Oscar-winning Hanks became "America's Mr. Nice Guy" playing such roles as "Forrest Gump," "Woody" the *Toy Story* cowboy, astronaut Jim Lovell, the wise World War II captain in *Saving Private Ryan*, airline pilot Captain "Sully" Sullenberger, and most recently, the beloved Mr. Rogers of children's television fame. When Hanks tweeted he and Wilson tested positive for coronavirus while he was in Australia filming a movie and she was giving concerts, Hanks found himself playing a new role: celebrity face of the pandemic, *Time* magazine suggested.

As they were treated for COVID-19, Hanks used social media to discuss his and Wilson's symptoms, and as he and she recovered, he used media interviews to urge others to practice behaviors public health officials said would help prevent coronavirus spread, such as wearing face coverings, washing hands and maintaining distance from other people. "As with all his other roles, Hanks handled it with grace, sincerity, and honesty," *Time* concluded. "He shared his experience and the world got to learn a little bit more about the virus when the growing health threat was first making headlines."[5]

Like Hanks, celebrities who speak out about their health can raise awareness of medical conditions in powerful ways that physicians, scientists and politicians may not. "Celebrities might not be medical experts, but often they have had personal experiences that make them qualified to advise ordinary people, in lay terms, to take action to protect themselves or those they care about in relation to health matters," notes media scholar Barrie Gunter.[6] Almost certainly, celebrities speak out about their health because they hope to raise awareness and prevent harm to others. But if celebrities' personal stories contravene established health advice, or are inaccurate or misleading, those stories inadvertently may create, rather than prevent, harm as they influence people's attitudes and behaviors about their own health care. Because potentially serious consequences may result both for individuals and the health care system, speaking out about health requires ethical scrutiny.

This chapter examines the ethical responsibilities confronting celebrities such as Hanks when they speak out with powerful personal stories about health issues. The chapter presents documented effects of celebrities' health stories on audience members' cancer treatment choices to illustrate the need for ethical care in speaking out about health issues. The chapter then contends these effects mean speaking out during a historic global public health emergency requires extra ethical care for the damages that careless or misinformed speaking could contribute to the information climate during that emergency.

Ethically Salient Characteristics of Speaking Out About Health

Understanding the ethically salient characteristics of speaking out clarifies why celebrities' speech about health issues requires ethical justification. The speaker's role is the first ethically salient characteristic that distinguishes speaking out from more casual speaking. Speaking out requires ethical analysis when it upends the expectations of audiences, who often expect celebrities to play one role, such as favorite actor or star athlete, and may be surprised or annoyed when celebrities speak out and assume the role of health advocate. Celebrities who step outside audiences' role-related expectations must use ethical care in communicating as people adjust to celebrities' new roles as "expert" speakers about health topics.

The topic is the second ethically salient characteristic that distinguishes speaking out from more casual speaking. Speaking out requires ethical analysis because celebrity entertainers and athletes are not discussing award-winning movie roles or sports championships but are discussing serious topics of shared public concern, such as cancer treatment and research. For instance, multiple studies over the years have documented effects on people's behaviors—such as searching online for cancer information, seeking cancer detection tests, or asking doctors about celebrities' treatments—when celebrities speak out about cancer.[7] These findings suggest ethical caution applies when celebrities speak out about a health topic.

The speaker's intent is the third ethically salient characteristic that distinguishes speaking out from more casual speaking. Speaking out is not accidental. Speaking out is a deliberate interjection into public discourse about serious topics. Thus, celebrity entertainers and athletes must possess an ethically defensible motive for speaking out. Often, celebrities who are known for one role—such as movie acting success or professional football prowess—and who speak out about unrelated issues—such as cancer or coronavirus—do so because they want to help prevent others from enduring the pain they have experienced.

The speaker's platform is the fourth ethically salient characteristic that distinguishes speaking out from more casual speaking. When celebrity entertainers and athletes use a public venue or occasion not typically used for serious public speech, such as a concert stage or a football field, they must justify departing from the recognized purpose of the platform to use it for speaking out. Celebrity speakers also must be aware that because of their fame, they may be afforded platforms more powerful than other people possess. When they use social media to discuss their health, for instance, celebrities must realize their messages will capture public attention and may silence other voices or topics.

The Powerful Impact of Personal Health Stories

Once celebrities' speech has been identified as ethically salient, celebrities as moral agents who are transcending role-related expectations to speak out about health issues should justify that speaking. Wyatt's and Bunton's four-part test for ethical justification of speaking out can be applied. The test asks celebrity speakers to consider their relationship to the topic of the speech, their motivation for speaking, the nature of any harms speaking may create, and the possibility speaking will promote public dialogue.[8]

When celebrities speak out about health issues, their relationship to the topic typically derives from lived experience. In this way, speaking out about health differs from speaking out about other topics. When the Dixie Chicks trio opposed American involvement in Iraq (as discussed in this book's Introduction), or when basketball player Stephen Curry objected to President Donald Trump's policies (as discussed in Chapter 2), or when television satirist Jon Stewart advocated for government benefits for 9/11 first responders (as discussed in Chapter 4), these celebrities demonstrated ethically defensible relationships to the issues they were speaking about, but they were not living in the issues quite like celebrities may be when speaking about health issues.

By contrast, consider that when tennis star Serena Williams (as discussed in Chapter 7) and world-class runner Allyson Felix (as discussed in Chapter 8) spoke out about Black maternal health disparities, each had survived a harrowing childbirth experience.

Personal experience with the health topic can strengthen the relationship between speaker and topic, making speaking out potentially more compelling for listeners. "We are, all of us, compelled by story," points out Paul Offitt, a pediatrician and infectious disease scientist whose book *Bad Advice: Or Why Celebrities, Politicians, and Activists Aren't Your Best Source of Health Information* cautions audiences to carefully evaluate celebrities' health stories.[9] When celebrities we respect or admire tell a personal story, we pay attention, especially if the story suggests celebrities struggle just as we do. We also make health decisions based on the believability and attractiveness of the storyteller,[10] a finding famously confirmed after actress Angelina Jolie spoke out with her health story.

> *"I am writing about it now because I hope that other women can benefit from my experience."*

In 2013, the Academy Award winner spoke out about her preventive double mastectomy. Jolie explained that her risk of hereditary cancer derived from a mutation in a gene named BRCA and that her doctors used genetic testing to estimate she possessed an 87 percent chance of developing breast cancer and a 50 percent chance of developing ovarian cancer. "I am writing about it now because I hope that other women can benefit from my experience," she stated in a *New York Times* essay. "Cancer is still a word that strikes fear into people's hearts, producing a deep sense of powerlessness. But today it is possible to find out through a blood test whether you are highly susceptible to breast and ovarian cancer, and then take action."[11]

Within days of her essay's publication, Jolie's image was splashed across magazine covers worldwide, including a *Time* magazine cover heralding "The Angelina Effect." *Time*'s cover story noted the powerful effect when issues of breast cancer, genetic testing and preventive surgery were raised by "a megawatt star" considered "the most beautiful woman in the world." The magazine suggested that "when a woman whose very name signals beauty and whose profession depends on it" disclosed "a dramatic choice" to have both breasts removed after genetic testing, thousands of women who might not be at risk for hereditary breast cancer would insist on genetic testing. "Jolie, to all appearances, made a sober and well-thought-through choice," *Time* reported. "But every patient is different, and the gravitational pull of a superstar role model has a way of distorting what needs to be a highly individual decision."[12]

Indeed, over the next several years, cancer researchers verified evidence of the "Angelina effect." One study examined genetic testing and mastectomy rates starting years before Jolie spoke out and continuing for years afterward, and concluded the "Angelina effect" produced "a long-lasting impact of celebrity on public health awareness with significant increases in genetic testing and mastectomy rates, which were measurable and sustained."[13]

The Issues of Cross-Expertise Violations and Deception

Because they may influence people's attitudes and behaviors about health care, celebrity speakers must avoid the ethical problem of cross-expertise violations.[14] These violations occur when celebrities who are skilled in one field—such as Jolie, whose skill as an actress earned awards for performance—venture into a field with little relationship to their skill—such as cancer treatment. When they do venture across the boundaries of expertise, celebrities who speak out about health should take care to be well-informed, as Jolie apparently was.

Celebrities who appear to voluntarily speak out about health issues, when they actually are paid to speak out, commit both cross-expertise violation and deception. For instance, when an actor appears in a prescription drug advertisement, viewers logically assume the actor is paid to endorse a product, but when an actor appears on a morning news show to discuss a disease, viewers logically assume the actor is being interviewed because of a newsworthy relationship to the disease. Viewers potentially are deceived into thinking the actor is speaking out authentically to create awareness of a disease or a treatment. In fact, discussing a treatable condition without mentioning a specific drug by name is a strategy pharmaceutical companies use to skirt legal restrictions on drug advertising.[15]

An agent who arranges celebrities' paid work as spokespeople for health care and pharmaceutical companies says the "sense of urgency" that can occur when celebrities speak about a health issue they have experienced "often results in a new dialogue between doctor and patient and can sometimes make a significant impact on a patient's quality of life," according to the newsletter *Drugwatch*.[16] Nevertheless, failure to fully disclose a paid relationship remains deceptive on the part of the celebrities, drug companies and news programs that treat celebrities' comments as news rather than advertising.[17]

This kind of paid relationship is complicated further by social media use. "When a celebrity promotes a drug in a commercial, it's usually easy for consumers to tell that they're being paid to do it. When they promote drugs on talk shows, the transparency isn't as clear. But when celebrities promote products on social media, it can be almost impossible to tell if the endorsement is unsolicited or paid," *Drugwatch* contends.[18] This confusion indicates an ethical obligation for celebrities to affirmatively disclose in any setting whether they are being paid or are speaking voluntarily through a defensible relationship to a health topic.

Defensible Motivations for Speaking Out About Health

After demonstrating a defensible relationship to a health topic, celebrities next must demonstrate a defensible motivation for speaking out, under the justification test. Philosopher Bernard Gert calls preventing harm a "basic reason for acting morally."[19] Preventing any of several harms Gert suggests all moral agents should seek to prevent—killing, causing pain, disabling or depriving of ability, depriving of freedom, and depriving of pleasure[20]—is a defensible motivation for speaking about health issues. For example, when Jolie spoke out, she used words suggesting motivation to create cancer awareness and prevent the death, pain and loss of ability or autonomy that can accompany cancer.

This motivation is common among celebrities who speak out about health. A study of celebrity health disclosures found most celebrities spoke out because they were motivated by "the potential of educating others about misconceptions, symptoms, and the benefits of early detection," especially if their diseases were rare or misunderstood. "Notably, disclosures about disease, in general, and 'unacceptable' ones, in particular, can alter previous opinions about individuals and reframe relationships and roles," the study concluded.[21]

A more personal motivation exists for celebrities to speak out about health. Celebrities may attempt to prevent for themselves Gert's harms of loss of ability, freedom and pleasure by controlling public disclosures, especially by using their own social media platforms. The celebrity health disclosure study found many celebrities needed to "confront the pressure of a seemingly ever-present press and the physical realities of their respective, ever-progressing medical situations."[22]

"1 in 8 women get breast cancer. Today, I'm the one."

A cancer announcement by actress Julia Louis-Dreyfus is illustrative. Louis-Dreyfus made headlines in 2017 by winning a record-breaking sixth consecutive Emmy Award for her leading role on the television series *Veep*. The next day, she was diagnosed with breast cancer. Louis-Dreyfus was both star and executive producer of *Veep*, and after consulting oncologists, she realized she could not work for several months while undergoing treatment. "I had 200 people waiting to go back to work in three weeks, and I get this diagnosis," she said. "I knew we had to shut down, and I needed to manage that and make it public."[23] Louis-Dreyfus also was motivated to use her diagnosis to speak out about the politics of health care, so her nearly 1 million Twitter followers found an announcement saying, "1 in 8 women get breast cancer. Today, I'm the one. The good news is that I have the most glorious group of supportive and caring family and friends, and fantastic insurance through my union. The bad news is that not all women are so lucky, so let's fight all cancers and make universal health care a reality."[24]

Social media let Louis-Dreyfus "somewhat control the messaging and use her bully pulpit to talk about the inequities of our current health care system," *Vanity Fair* reported.[25] Her post quickly was commented on and re-tweeted by tens of thousands of people. As did Louis-Dreyfus, many celebrities find "a 'silver lining' in these difficult personal situations involves the potential educational impact of 'going public,'" researchers noted.[26]

Possible Harms Created by Speaking Out About Health

After celebrities demonstrate both a defensible relationship to the health topic and a defensible motivation for speaking about it, the justification test asks celebrities to consider harms speaking out could cause. Celebrities, like all moral agents, are not ethically responsible for harms no reasonable person could anticipate, but all moral agents, including celebrities, are responsible for failing to prevent or mitigate harms to self or other stakeholders that can be anticipated.

Because much speaking out about health issues starts with a personal disclosure, the possibility exists that celebrity speakers will be harmed by invasions of privacy or negative reactions when revealing one of life's most personal experiences. For instance, Louis-Dreyfus said she didn't expect the "intense" public reaction her cancer disclosure created. "In many ways it was very nice to get the support from the outside world," she said. "Having said that, I didn't consider that it would've taken on a life of its own, which it did."[27] When Louis-Dreyfus spoke about her cancer, she needed to consider how much she wanted to share while she was ill. Social media platforms allow followers to alter celebrities' stories in ways both positive and negative.

"I think I kind of burst the bubble on a lot of it because of my social-media presence."

Celebrities who are fully candid about cancer diagnosis and treatment may find their decisions second-guessed and even vilified by those who think they know more than celebrities about treatment options. News coverage of social media disclosures amplify them, perhaps exposing celebrities and their families to loss of privacy at a vulnerable time. Louis-Dreyfus said she repeatedly discussed her cancer on social media to subvert photographers "trying to get pictures of me looking ill, and I think I kind of burst the bubble on a lot of it because of my social-media presence."[28] As she tried to control her own story, Louis-Dreyfus also needed to consider how closely she wanted to link her cancer to the need for universal health care, which was a controversial political issue that could generate negative attitudes and behaviors toward her.

Another possible harm to celebrity speakers is the expectation that after celebrities share their experience with a health issue, they ought to continue speaking about it. For example, some celebrities become what researchers call "ambassadors of cancer care" who "destigmatize the diagnosis, promote self-empowerment, and help people find support in common experiences."[29] Of course that is a positive outcome of speaking out. Because Louis-Dreyfus as a cancer patient spoke out about other cancer patients' need for health care coverage, may the public expect her to champion the issue for decades? A public expectation that Louis-Dreyfus should be a permanent "ambassador of cancer care" might foist onto her Gert's harm of depriving a moral agent of freedom. If she disengaged from the issue, she also might risk harm to her reputation, if a career-damaging perception suggested she no longer cared about less powerful cancer patients.

Celebrity speakers also must consider potential harms to other stakeholders. Prime among those harms is the potential abuse of power differentials between famous people and ordinary people, especially those who are ardent fans. Celebrities whose careers depend on visibility and positive reputations may "strategically capitalize" on social media's abilities to offer fans "what appears to be backstage access: revealing information, creating a sense of intimacy, acknowledging fans, and using pop culture references to engage followers," according to researchers.[30] As a result, parasocial relationships with fans may develop. "Although celebrities' social ties to most people are weak, their newsworthiness and star quality—and the intense unidirectional interactions super fans have with them, known as parasocial relationships—allow them to feature prominently within social networks and achieve great influence as medical advisers to the masses," a study of celebrity health advice found.[31]

A parasocial relationship may be harmless in many circumstances, but choosing cancer tests or treatments based on the disclosure of a favorite actress differs significantly from choosing a hairstyle based on her photos. One study found women who had parasocial relationships with Jolie, as well as a cancer diagnosis in their families, were more likely than other women to seek genetic testing for breast cancer after learning Jolie's genetic test results led her to undergo a preventive mastectomy.[32] The genetic mutation Jolie carried "is present in only 0.24% of the population and accounts for no more than 10% of all cases of breast cancer," yet many women with no family history of breast cancer also sought genetic testing or requested unnecessary mastectomies after hearing about Jolie's situation, another study found.[33] That such testing saved some women's lives is a welcome result of Jolie's act of speaking out. It is not a cost-free result, however. Obviously, Jolie could afford genetic testing and surgery, but some women influenced by her story might not have been able to afford a test that can cost as much as $3,500, depending on a patient's health insurance coverage. Nor could some women who sought preventive mastectomy afford the cost of major surgery.[34] Too, women influenced by Jolie's story might have paid mental and emotional costs, experiencing fear and stress about genetic testing and surgery.[35]

Another potential harm from speaking out about health issues exists because celebrity narratives now matter more to people seeking information online than medical research.[36] Celebrity stories typically are shorter, more anecdotal, easier to understand, more compelling—and potentially less accurate than meticulous evidence-based medical studies.

While Jolie "tried to empower women at risk of breast cancer," medical ethicists concluded many women not at risk for hereditary cancer misunderstood how their situations differed from Jolie's. "This misunderstanding of medical facts in many cases leads women to pursue unnecessarily aggressive surgical options when they might otherwise pursue less invasive and less morbid preventative and treatment options," researchers concluded.[37] Perhaps inadvertently, then, Jolie's act of speaking out about her risk of hereditary breast cancer created some harm for doctors who faced the challenge of "trying to guide patients through their choices" when their cancer-screening results, unlike Jolie's, did "not yield clear treatment options," *Time* magazine reported.[38]

Yet another harm celebrities should consider is how their health stories story may affect the larger system of health care and research. Drawing attention to a cancer type affecting a fraction of breast cancer patients, as Jolie did, may create new awareness of cancer's complexities. It also may deflect attention from breast cancer types affecting far more women—or deflect attention from other conditions, such as heart disease. Celebrities' voices may be so compelling they influence public policy and funding for research and treatment, which ultimately affects who lives and dies.[39]

Because these potentially serious harms may arise from speaking out about health issues, celebrities as moral agents must proceed carefully, recognizing that no mechanisms exist to hold them accountable except perhaps themselves. "They are not physicians, and the general public is not their collective patient. They have a right to express their experience of care and how it impacts their lives in the way they choose," a research team suggests. "Technically, they owe nothing more than any other cancer patient owes in the public domain."[40] Ethically, however, celebrities owe multiple stakeholders consideration of possible harms before speaking out.

Health Stories' Promotion of Dialogue

Once celebrity speakers demonstrate a justifiable relationship to a health topic, a defensible motivation for speaking about it, and a careful consideration of possible harms, the justification test requires considering whether speaking out may promote dialogue about the topic. Here, celebrities' lived experience can be a bonus. Their stories may promote public dialogue about issues because "the particularity of first person experience can actually help others connect as humans" and discuss difficult issues, according to philosophy professor Lauren Swayne Barthold.[41] For instance, studies of celebrity cancer disclosures on social media find the disclosures at least temporarily get social media followers to digitally discuss celebrities' experiences and then to discuss their own or their families' and friends' experiences with cancer,[42] including cancer prevention, detection or treatment.[43]

> "The most important thing is to ... choose what is right for you personally."

Jolie's disclosure appeared to serve that purpose. Two years after she spoke out, Jolie wrote a second *New York Times* essay. In it, she reminded readers she had "promised to follow up with any information that could be useful, including about my next preventive surgery, the removal of my ovaries and fallopian tubes."[44]

Jolie seemed to speak out even more carefully than she had initially, perhaps because she now understood the "Angelina effect" led many women to seek genetic testing and preventive mastectomy. Jolie clarified that not all women carried a genetic mutation as she did and that not all women who did carry the mutation should make the choices she did. "There is more than one way to deal with any health issue," she wrote. "The most important thing is to learn about the options and choose what is right for you personally."[45]

Jolie's new essay quickly made headlines and occupied social media users, who shared and commented on it. Among the commenters was a cancer physician who lauded Jolie's disclosure, saying, "Her courage pushed a deeply sensitive issue into the spotlight."[46]

Speaking Out About COVID-19

In 2020, however, cancer and all other public health issues were shoved from the spotlight by the coronavirus pandemic. No public issue was more serious that year. "A year that started out normal—with packed sports arenas, busy airports and handshake-heavy political campaigning—quickly became defined by the pandemic," *The New York Times* observed.[47]

The World Health Organization declared coronavirus a "public health emergency of international concern" at the end of January 2020, after coronavirus cases reported in China in late 2019 began to spread around the globe. By mid–February, the WHO devised the COVID-19 acronym from "coronavirus disease 2019" and clarified that COVID-19 was the illness resulting from coronavirus. Soon, coronavirus had spread to 177 countries. In the United States, the first COVID-19 death was reported at the end of February,[48] and within seven months, more than 193,000 people in the United States had died from COVID-19 and at least 6.5 million people had tested positive for coronavirus.[49]

Concurrently, health researchers learned that coronavirus discriminated along racial lines, with Black and Latino people in the United States three times more likely to contract COVID-19 and two times more likely to die from it than white people.[50] The pandemic's effects spread beyond public health as the historic economic shutdown intended to slow viral spread devastated people's finances.[51] By mid–August, 29 million Americans were jobless and depending on unemployment benefits,[52] and a September survey found nearly half, or 46 percent, of American households—especially Black and Latino households—reporting "serious financial pain during the pandemic."[53]

"Facebook is making it harder for us to do our jobs."

In the pandemic's early months, Americans were "swimming—and sometimes drowning—in an ocean of information that, paradoxically" was "also a desert of clarity and consensus" because public health officials did not provide "consistent, authoritative advice" about how to minimize coronavirus transmission or how to treat COVID-19 cases, *The Washington Post* reported. Many people felt "left to figure out for themselves how to live safely" and came to rely on, among others, "self-appointed experts" whose social media posts confirmed audiences' biases, the newspaper contended.[54]

In a *New York Times* essay, two doctors cautioned readers about "medical myths and health hoaxes" burgeoning during the pandemic. The doctors said a nonprofit group found 460 million views of health hoax information posted on Facebook in April 2020. "We see the consequences in the clinic and the emergency room. Patients question our evidence-based medical guidance, refuse safe treatments and vaccines, and cite Facebook posts as 'proof' that Covid-19 is not real," the doctors wrote. "While we try, each day, to counter these dangerous falsehoods that circulate among our patients and our peers, our ability to counsel and provide care is diminished by a social network that bolsters distrust in science and medicine. Facebook is making it harder for us to do our jobs."[55]

"We are all in the same boat."

In this climate of inaccurate or inappropriate information, celebrities who spoke out about coronavirus on social media platforms needed to exercise ethical care. Unfortunately, in the pandemic shutdown's early weeks, several celebrity speakers conveyed questionable messages that were publicly perceived as frivolous, even if the celebrities intended to offer optimism. Television talk show host Ellen DeGeneres said she wanted to provide "words of encouragement" and posted a video in which she said quarantining in the sumptuous home viewers could see around her was "like being in jail ... mostly because I've been wearing the same clothes for 10 days." Social media users quickly called her language inexcusable given conditions in U.S. jails, which one prison physician called a "public health disaster" of coronavirus infections.[56] Other celebrities—actor Ryan Reynolds, singer Katy Perry, and actress Jennifer Lopez and her fiancé, the former baseball star Alex Rodriguez, for instance—were berated for tone-deaf messages encouraging social media followers to remember "we're all in this together," to "stay positive" or to "work together to flatten the curve"—while the messages featured images of palatial homes where these celebrities quarantined far from pandemic job losses and food shortages.[57]

Singer and actress Madonna seemed particularly tone deaf, apparently violating distancing protocols to employ a crew to record a video showing her bathing in an elaborate tub as she told viewers the pandemic "made us all equal" and "we are all in the same boat." Perhaps that message was more tasteless than unethical. Others of her messages were potentially harmful. *The Washington Post* reported Madonna shared videos claiming that wearing face masks did not stop viral transmission and asserting that potentially lethal substances cured COVID-19. In one post, she wrote that a coronavirus vaccine "has been available for months" but not distributed because authorities preferred to let "the poor get poorer and sick get sicker." Instagram soon branded the post false, and Madonna deleted it.[58]

Celebrity Health Capital

Other celebrities spoke out with ethical care, however. For instance, many celebrities used their social media channels to reinforce the importance of wearing face masks, as recommended by health experts before many states enacted mask-wearing orders. Actresses Jennifer Aniston, Kerry Washington and Reese Witherspoon, as well as singers Lady Gaga, Lizzo and Katy Perry, posted similar messages emphasizing the importance of wearing masks. Including photos of themselves wearing masks undoubtedly helped legitimize the practice among some of their fans.[59]

Celebrities also joined a "pass the mic" initiative in which they used their powerful social media platforms to interview global health experts about the pandemic's effects on public health and poverty. Superstar actress Julia Roberts kicked off the initiative by interviewing the nation's leading infectious disease expert, Dr. Anthony Fauci.[60] Their Instagram Live session attracted more than 350,000 views.[61] When actor Matthew McConaughey interviewed Fauci, their conversation attracted 1.2 million Instagram Live views.[62] The celebrities' interviews of health experts undoubtedly helped convey credible information to social media users who were not receiving it through other media outlets.

Culturally, celebrities possess several kinds of value, or capital, including social, political or economic capital, media scholar Barrie Gunter notes. Another type of celebrity capital is health capital, which can be used effectively to draw attention to public health issues and health campaigns aimed at changing people's attitudes or behaviors.[63] The celebrities who encouraged social media followers to wear face masks or who interviewed health experts on social media platforms ethically used their health capital to draw attention to public health issues and recommended behaviors during the pandemic.

So did Tom Hanks. Gunter suggests "if a celebrity has a very high profile and has previously apparently enjoyed good health, the fact that even those who are rich and famous have become seriously unwell might convey the message to others that a particular health condition is something that could happen to anyone."[64]

> *"Not much more to it than a one-day-at-a-time-approach, no?"*

In the early days of the pandemic, Tom Hanks spent a significant amount of health capital, speaking out about his COVID-19 diagnosis, symptoms and adherence to public health advisories. Because using his powerful social media platform could affect his followers' health care attitudes and behaviors, Hanks needed to use his platform ethically, speaking from an intent to help inform people about coronavirus and to foster calm about an illness they hadn't experienced.

Indeed, Hanks seemed to understand that need as he spoke out clearly and authentically. Hanks used simple terms to describe symptoms he and his wife, Rita Wilson, experienced. "We felt a bit tired, like we had colds, and some body aches. Rita had some chills that came and went. Slight fevers too," he wrote. Then, he encouraged audiences to follow public health protocols, writing, "To play things right, as is needed in the world right now, we were tested for the Coronavirus, and were found to be positive." He added, "We Hanks will be tested, observed, and isolated for as long as public health and safety requires. Not much more to it than a one-day-at-a-time-approach, no?"

His post was "liked" 2.9 million times and commented on by more than 175,000 Instagram users.[65] *The Atlantic* said the post "had the soothing cadence of a vacation email update from your parents" that was "typical of his online persona."[66]

While Hanks and Wilson were hospitalized for a few days, he continued speaking out with what CNN called the "palpable sense of decency, self-deprecating humor and personal honor" audiences expected from him, based on his movie roles.[67] In a second social media post, Hanks offered thanks for "everyone here Down Under who are taking such good care of us" and noted the importance of isolating to minimize viral transmission to those "for whom it could lead to a very serious illness." His post was liked 3.2 million times and commented on by nearly 120,000 Instagram users. *Vogue* magazine called his update "the calm and reassurance" American public health authorities and elected officials had "thus far failed to impart."[68]

> "Like the rest of America, we carry on with sheltering in place and social distancing."

As he recovered, Hanks posted occasional updates, often injecting a bit of quirkiness. In a post a week after his diagnosis, for example, he wrote that he and Wilson continued in isolation and no longer had fevers, but they felt "the blahs" and were tired. "I travelled here with a typewriter, one I used to love," he wrote. Careful viewers of the photo beside the post could see that his typewriter bore the name of its manufacturer, which, of course, was "Smith Corona." The most devoted Hanks fans among the 1.67 million Instagram users who saw the photo knew Hanks as a fanatical collector of vintage typewriters and author of a short story collection titled *Uncommon Type* in which every story features a typewriter.[69]

Whether they got his jokes, the actor's social media followers consistently heard from him about best practices for dealing with coronavirus. Some 10 days after his diagnosis Hanks wrote, "Hey, folks. Two weeks after our first symptoms and we feel better. Sheltering in place works like this: You don't give it to anyone—You don't get it from anyone. Common sense, no? Going to take awhile, but if we take care of each other, help where we can, and give up some comforts … this, too, shall pass. We can figure this out."[70]

Hanks and Wilson returned from Australia 17 days after he revealed their COVID-19 diagnosis, and he continued to remind social media followers about recommended public health behaviors. "We're home now, and like the rest of America, we carry on with sheltering in place and social distancing," he wrote on Instagram.[71] In reiterating this message, Hanks spoke out with moral consistency.

"We have said, do you want our blood? Can we give plasma?"

In mid–April, Hanks used National Public Radio's *Wait Wait ... Don't Tell Me!* current events quiz show to speak out about an opportunity for recovered COVID-19 patients to help find coronavirus treatments. "We have said, do you want our blood? Can we give plasma? And, in fact, we will be giving it now to the places that hope to work on what I would like to call the Hank-ccine," he quipped.[72] Subsequently, Hanks posted Instagram photos of bags filled with plasma he donated to contribute to coronavirus vaccine research. "Plasmatic!" he exclaimed online.[73]

Soon, Hanks was joking about himself as "the celebrity canary in the coal mine for the coronavirus"[74] and using media interviews scheduled to publicize a new movie to continue speaking out about coronavirus. He reminded audiences of recommended health practices to reduce their chances of contracting the virus or passing it to others. Hanks drew on his public persona as "America's Dad" to gently scold the public, telling *The Guardian*, for instance, "There's really only three things everyone needs to do: wear a mask, social distance, wash your hands. I know societally it's been politicized, but I don't get it, man. I don't understand how anyone can put their foot down and say: 'I don't have to do my part.'"[75]

Doing his part appeared to matter to Hanks in speaking out about coronavirus. As the pandemic continued throughout 2020, it would become less important for a celebrity to reveal his COVID-19 diagnosis. After all, as thousands of Americans contracted coronavirus, the experience would become common. *Time* magazine suggested that by then, celebrities or other people would have to ask what could be achieved by sharing their diagnoses.

But in announcing his diagnosis and symptoms in simple terms in the confusing days of early March, Hanks likely helped people understand the pandemic in several ways. First, "he helped make the threat real by sending a message that even the richest, best-loved among us are not immune," *Time* observed. Second, Hanks repeatedly "used his clout to help spread the instructions of public health officials," and third, he helped discount early stigmas suggesting a COVID-19 diagnosis was something to be ashamed about.[76] "If 'America's Dad' could get it, so could anyone," the Associated Press suggested.[77]

Hanks shrugged off the impact of his speaking out on attitudes about coronavirus by simply saying he couldn't change the facts of his diagnosis, so he wouldn't hide them.[78] But his decision to speak out clearly and authentically can be seen as evidence of what one global health analyst said was a crucial task during a pandemic: setting the tone of narrative about it. "With pandemics, the timing, content and manner in which information is narrated is of key importance. Information needs to be timely and precise but also comprehensive enough to satisfy public curiosity," analyst Ayesha Jacub asserted. People faced with "the magnitude of the consequences, the disruption to the status quo, the rapidity and the limited control" they can exert over a pandemic "try to make sense of such events by narratives: telling stories—to ourselves and to others."[79]

> *"You know, you are the only person I've ever known to have the name Corona."*

As "America's Dad," Hanks shared one more story about coronavirus that conveyed the ethical values of listening after speaking out and behaving with respect for others in a time of uncertainty. Upon receiving a letter from an eight-year-old Australian boy named Corona De Vries, who said he loved his name and was "sad and angry" schoolmates called him the coronavirus, Hanks replied. "You know, you are the only person I've ever known to have the name Corona—like the ring around the sun, a crown," Hanks wrote. Then he included a gift, writing, "I thought this typewriter would suit you. I had taken it to [Australia], and now, it is back—with you. Ask a grown up how it works. And use it to write me back." Of course, the gift was the Corona typewriter Hanks pictured on social media while he recovered from the virus.[80]

The next chapter presents celebrity entertainers and athletes who, like Hanks, listen and respond ethically after they speak out. The chapter also examines ethical responses to speaking out from journalists who report on it and audiences who hear it.

11

Shut Up and Listen?

Ethical Responses to Speaking Out

"Well, 'what was the message that you got?' was more the question."

As a professional tennis player, Naomi Osaka won her first Grand Slam title in September 2018 by defeating superstar Serena Williams at the U.S. Open. The contentious nature of their match, in which Williams repeatedly was penalized by and clashed with the umpire, meant the shy 20-year-old Osaka cried, rather than smiled, after defeating her childhood idol to claim the title in the country's premier tennis tournament. Because the match was so controversial, public attention afterward focused on Williams, rather than on the newly crowned champion.[1]

When Osaka claimed the U.S. Open title a second time in September 2020, she came from behind to win a hard-fought match with Victoria Azarenka.[2] This time, public attention focused directly on the champion Osaka, who during her run to the title repeatedly had used words and symbolic acts to speak out about issues of racial injustice.

To each of her matches, Osaka walked to the tennis court wearing a face mask, as necessitated by public health advisories during the coronavirus pandemic. Each of her masks featured the name of a Black person who was a victim of racial injustice. Before and after each match she played during the two-week tournament, Osaka answered questions about what she wanted to achieve with the masks. She consistently offered one answer, saying she wanted "to bring awareness about racial and social injustice in the United States and overseas."[3]

In an on-court interview immediately after winning the title, Osaka was asked by a reporter for ESPN, which was televising the event, "You had seven matches, seven masks, seven names. What was the message you wanted to send?"[4] This time, instead of saying she wanted to create awareness of injustice, Osaka quickly pivoted the question back to the reporter.

"Well, 'what was the message that you got?' was more the question," she said. "I feel like the point is to make people start talking."[5]

In the weeks leading to her second U.S. Open title, Osaka displayed both moral consistency and moral courage in speaking out with words and symbols to confront racial stereotypes and injustice. Hers were ethically justifiable acts of speaking out, according to the criteria presented throughout this book. She transcended traditional role-related expectations for athletes to "shut up and play." As a biracial person, she displayed a strong relationship to the topic of speaking out about injustice. She expressed a motivation to inform listeners about racially motivated violence, and she displayed an intent to foster public conversation about unjustified killings of Black people in the United States.

Osaka's behavior in the run-up to her second U.S. Open title also can be seen both as an ethical response to listening to the country's turmoil over injustice and police brutality during the summer of 2020 and as an ethical response to hearing those who responded to her acts of speaking out. Using her example, this chapter examines listening as an ethical response to speaking out, with attention to three types of stakeholders: famous figures who speak out, as did Osaka, and bear a corresponding ethical duty to listen to responses to their speech; audience members to whom speaking out is directed and who may or may not choose to engage ethically with the speech; and journalists whose news coverage of speaking out may enhance or impede listening and dialogue about the public issue the speech is intended to address.

Listening as a Central Element of Communication

Frankly, most of us think more about speaking than listening. Yet we actually spend more time listening than speaking, even if our listening is distracted and rarely "truly engaged" in an era of "private listening" that involves "pods, pads, tablets, or cell phones while walking, running, or driving," according to communication scholar Lisbeth Lipari.[6] Because listening "is so commonplace in our lives," and because we value speaking more than listening, "listening is often taken for granted," suggests communication scholar Elizabeth Parks.[7] Lipari points out that "the dominant emphasis in U.S. culture—in education, politics, law, or religion—is on speech and speaking rather than listening." Lipari notes that our schools field debate teams and require public speaking courses but rarely teach listening skills, and that many of our political events and television programs feature "verbal wrestling matches" in which "listening occurs only, if at all, as a means of preparing one's next move in the spectacle."[8]

In her 1998 book *The Argument Culture,* published well before the rise of social media channels with their emphasis on competing bursts of opinion, linguist Deborah Tannen criticized American political, judicial, educational and media institutions for inciting polarizing debates instead of modeling thoughtful discourse about serious public issues. Although her analysis pointed out the harms of a cultural "war of words" and suggested alternative methods of resolving conflicts in public discourse, Tannen paid scant attention to listening as a key element of discourse.[9]

Our neglect of listening as a crucial element of communication "is a curious oversight, given the centrality of listening to communicative, experiential and public life,"[10] according to communication scholar Kate Lacey. After all, speakers need listeners, especially if speaking out is intended to raise attention to serious issues of public concern and contribute to dialogue about those issues. "To start simply—without a listener, speech is nothing but noise in the ether," Lacey writes. "More to the point, without a listener there would be no reason, no *calling,* to speak. And if the speaker is not also at turns a listener, only a perverted version of communication remains."[11] In other words, "having a voice and speaking out is nullified if nobody listens," observe communication ethicists Stephen Ward and Herman Wasserman.[12]

An Ethical Duty for Speakers to Listen

We bear an ethical duty to listen, Parks insists. "Listening, as an active communication process that shares our individual and collective identities, is one process that impacts ethical discourse," she writes. "Listening gives shape to speaking, inviting other people into a dialogue that impacts the discursive environments that then impact us."[13]

As a foundation for democratic discourse, the marketplace of ideas metaphor (examined in Chapter 7) relies on citizens discussing multiple competing ideas until a true idea emerges. Uses of the marketplace metaphor rarely invoke the idea of listening, but the metaphor's premise that democracy will flourish in a culture of ideas competing robustly with one another necessarily must involve listeners. In *On Liberty,* the 19th century British philosopher John Stuart Mill said ideas should compete in the marketplace whether they seemed false, partly true or wholly true. Ideas that seemed false should not be silenced before citizens could decide if they were true or if they contained a grain of truth necessary to find a whole truth, and ideas that seemed true should be debated by citizens so the ideas became stronger.[14]

What Mill didn't explicitly state, but what seems obvious, is that citizens engaged in the marketplace of ideas must be both speakers and listeners. "We normally think about agency in the public sphere as speaking up, or as finding a voice; in other words, to be listened to, rather than to listen," Lacey contends. "And it goes 'without saying' that one of the central tenets of modern democratic theory is the freedom of speech; and yet what really goes unsaid is that speech requires a listener. What is actually at stake here is the freedom of *shared* speech or, to put it another way, the freedom to be heard. But this formulation still puts the speaker centre stage; it is still formulated as the politics of *voice*. The presence of a listening public is simply assumed, and no special freedoms or protections are afforded to the act of listening. But inasmuch as there is a mutual responsibility (or *response-ability*) in any communicative exchange between speaker and listener, the question arises whether there is not also another freedom implicit in the proper functioning of democracy, the freedom of *listening*."[15]

From Lacey's work, we can derive an ethical obligation for public figures who speak out about shared public issues to listen *to* citizens and a corresponding ethical obligation for people in the audience to listen *as* citizens.[16] In his history of American citizenship, Michael Schudson points out the traditional ideal of the fully engaged, "informed citizen" who could listen to all public discourse unrealistically requires "omnicompetence and omniscience" of citizens.[17] He proposes replacing that ideal with the concept of the "monitorial citizen," who "is not an absentee citizen but watchful" and engaged in "environmental surveillance" of what is occurring in our shared public spheres, "poised for action if action is required."[18] Schudson's monitorial citizen likely would devote more attention to listening than to speaking, and thus would reflect Parks' exhortation that we must both prize all people's rights to speak out freely and "seriously consider people's ethical responsibilities to listen to those voices."[19]

What, then, might ethical listening responsibilities require of us as citizens? First, we would recognize that listening and hearing are not precisely the same concept, and second, we would make listening our ethical goal. "Etymologically, 'listening' comes from a root that emphasizes attention and giving to others, while 'hearing' comes from a root that emphasizes perception and receiving from others,"[20] Lipari explains.

Ethical Responsibilities to Listen Out and Listen Otherwise

Ethical listeners actively give their attention to others, rather than passively receive others' attention. Lipari calls this "listening otherwise,"[21] while Lacey calls it "listening out."[22]

To "listen otherwise" or "listen out" requires ethical listeners to cultivate the moral virtues of respect and humility. This kind of listening may be hard work, especially if we are used to hearing just long enough to be ready to talk back. Parks explains: "Listening is difficult as it mandates that we open ourselves to new ideas, new people, new ways of being, and choose to embrace the role of learners, rather than pretending that we are experts who know everything."[23]

Legal scholar Stephen Carter also advocates respect and humility in listening. He writes, "Confrontational listening signals others that they are, in your opinion, not worthy of respect. True listening—what we might usefully call *civil listening*—signals your belief in the equality of all people, because it treats them as equal, even if you dislike their views. 'What my opponent has to say,' the civil listener implies, 'is as important as what I have to say. If you would listen to me, listen to my opponent with the same courtesy and the same care. I will do the same.'"[24]

Listening with respect for others' ideas—and with recognition of the fallibility of our own ideas—helps foster the kinds of public discourse and dialogue essential to the ethical justification of speaking out. "Dialogue esteems listening" and is rooted in philosopher John Dewey's principle of fallibilism, according to philosophy professor Lauren Swayne Barthold, who writes: "No matter how strongly one believes or feels, no matter how many facts are on one's side, no single human knows everything, there is always more to learn, more to consider, new perspectives to take seriously. Specifically, one can always learn more about the 'desires, interests and purposes' of the other and thus learn better how to acknowledge their humanity. An openness to the other, a willingness to listen, and the humility to consider anew one's long held beliefs and assumptions all underlie the dialogic process."[25]

Certainly, this kind of listening is harder work than mere hearing. "True listening requires courage and constraint to allow significant differences," Barthold suggests.[26] Communication scholar Tanya Dreher uses the term "difficult listening" to describe our ethical obligation to listen in particular to the voices of less powerful people whose perspectives have been overlooked or discounted by more powerful public figures and institutions.[27] The ethical duty of "difficult listening" requires those of us who "enjoy the prerogative of not listening" to less powerful people or perspectives must surrender our privilege and listen. "Listening across difference is open to learning and joy and play but also to being challenged," Dreher contends. "This entails not merely polite conversation or consensus but also risk and conflict, the possibility of discomfort and difficulty rather than absolute safety and security."[28] Similarly, Lipari urges us to listen with an understanding of the "politics of listening," which "relates to who speaks, and who doesn't, what is and is not said, how what is said is said, as well as, of course, to whom it is said and what is and what is not heard, and *how* what is heard is heard."[29]

Listening to Address Ethical Loneliness

Lipari's idea of "listening out," Lipari's idea of "listening otherwise" and Dreher's idea of "difficult listening" would seem to have in common a goal for listeners to help eliminate the condition human rights philosopher Jill Stauffer calls "ethical loneliness." Stauffer explains that ethical loneliness occurs when the isolation felt by a person who has been treated unjustly is "compounded by the experience of not being heard."[30] When someone speaks out about injustice, a moral agent who hopes to prevent the harm of ethical loneliness to that speaker should therefore try to listen out and listen otherwise, no matter how difficult the message being conveyed. "If hearing is meaningful, it has to be embedded in an openness where what is said might be heard even if it threatens to break the order of the known world for those who listen," Stauffer asserts.[31]

Responding "shut up and sing" or "shut up and play" when entertainers and athletes speak out to challenge societal ills such as racism therefore seems a less-than-virtuous attempt at ethical "listening out" or "listening otherwise." Rather than demanding LeBron James "shut up and play" basketball instead of speaking out about racial injustice, or insisting Colin Kaepernick "shut up and play" football instead of kneeling during the national anthem to protest injustice (see chapters 9 and 10), ethical listeners would listen beyond the athletes' words and gestures to hear the lived experiences of the Black community members James or Kaepernick intend their speech to represent.

Of course, ethical listening works more than one way. Before and after expressing themselves, these powerful speakers bear a "response-ability," to use Lacey's term,[32] to consider who else's voices and perspectives merit attention. In other words, both stakeholder parties—audience members and famous speakers—are ethically obliged to "shut up and listen" as part of public discourse.

Listening in a Digital Culture

Ethical listening is complicated by the reality that much of today's speaking out occurs via digital media platforms, which appear to enhance speakers' and listeners' engagement with one another but which in reality often default to one-way communication from speaker to listener.[33] Many analyses overstate digital media's ability to foster reciprocal "conversations" among active users who post and comment, and many of those same analyses neglect digital listeners' ability to foster engagement. "'Lurking' is a common pejorative term for those who are present in public spaces but do not prominently speak up,"[34] observes communication scholar Kate Crawford. She suggests reducing listeners to lurkers disregards the value of stakeholders who listen online.

Speakers need listeners, and listeners' presence online can foster discourse by providing a receptive audience that encourages others to make public posts, Crawford contends.[35] Treating listening as a form of digital participation as important as contributing posts and making comments on others' posts would recognize "the deep sense of connection that listening participants can feel"[36] in the digital spaces where listeners perform the important role of bearing witness to others' identities and perspectives, Crawford suggests.

Listening and bearing witness to one another is an expression of respect—a way to affirm other moral agents as human persons worth the dignity of being heard. "Listening well is often silent but never passive," suggests psychologist Michael Nichols.[37] Listening online can be an ethically receptive, reciprocal role that serves as a corollary to speaking out.

Journalism's Ability to Amplify Speaking for Listeners

Ethical listening also is complicated by the ways in which journalists report on speaking out. Some of us directly receive tweets or Instagram posts from the celebrity entertainers and athletes whose social media platforms we follow, but many more of us learn those celebrities have spoken out when news media cover the celebrities' speech. "Thus, the power of a tweet is not derived from the number of followers who receive it but the number of media gatekeepers (traditional and new) embracing it in some ancillary format," communication scholar Andrew Billings points out. "The nexus of power is the reverberation of a tweet, not the initial tweet rendered to a comparatively small number of followers."[38]

This role of journalism in amplifying public figures' social media speech involves the agenda setting and framing functions of news. Simply put, agenda setting is the power to put a topic on the public's radar. "The agenda-setting influence of the press operates at two sequential levels in the communication process: attention and comprehension," according to media scholar Maxwell McCombs.[39] For example, we might not have watched a televised U.S. Open tennis match to which Naomi Osaka wore face masks displaying the names of Black people killed through injustice, but when various national news outlets chose to report on the masks she wore during her run to the tournament title, instead of other happenings in the sports world, the media coverage drew Osaka's symbolic speech to our attention and made it seem worthy of our attention. Then, after drawing our attention, the headlines and descriptions news outlets used to present Osaka's act affected how we comprehended it.

Agenda setting overlaps with framing, which "is the process by which journalists give interpretation or definition to an event or development in order to provide an explanation or judgement about it," according to media scholars Thomas Patterson and Philip Seib.[40] A news story with the headline "Naomi Osaka, While Rallying for Social Justice, Wins U.S. Open Title,"[41] frames the topic of Osaka's symbolic speaking and tournament victory slightly differently than does the headline "Naomi Osaka Cements Her Status as Leader On and Off the Court with 2020 US Open Run"[42] or "Naomi Osaka's U.S. Open Masks Showcase One of an Athlete's Most Powerful Tools for Protest."[43] As these headlines show, "it is the frame, as much as the event or development itself, which affects how the citizen will interpret and respond to news events."[44] If we receive Osaka's symbolic speech as an act of protest, we may listen and respond differently than if we receive her act as evidence of leadership.

The Need for Precision in News Coverage of Speaking Out

Agenda setting and framing functions can be complicated further by journalists' ethical failure to use words precisely and report facts accurately when they cover acts of speaking out. For instance, when quarterback Colin Kaepernick began to kneel during "The Star-Spangled Banner" before NFL games, his symbolic speech quickly and frequently was reported as a "national anthem protest." But Kaepernick did not protest the national anthem. He said he knelt during the national anthem to protest racial injustices in the United States.[45] Journalists' failure to report precisely what Kaepernick was protesting had the unfortunate effect of framing the story in a way that led NFL fans and other audiences to hear Kaepernick's act as a challenge to patriotism, rather than to listen to Kaepernick's words and intent when he explained, "I love America. I love people. That's why I'm doing this. I want to help make America better."[46] Nor were many audiences seemingly able to "listen out" or "listen otherwise" to the lived experiences of the Black Americans that Kaepernick was trying to champion.

Asking journalists to report more precisely on this kind of speaking out that challenges societal institutions "shifts some of the focus and responsibility for change from marginalized voices and on to the conventions, institutions and privileges which shape who and what can be heard in the media," Dreher suggests.[47] Communication scholar Penny O'Donnell finds an ethical role for journalists "to 'help' people to hear each other through the media and journalism" especially when it comes to marginalized citizens.[48]

For years, journalists and the scholars who study them have suggested journalism has an ethical duty to give "voice to the voiceless," often by reporting on untold stories of society's less privileged people.[49] O'Donnell, however, reminds us that rarely is anyone voiceless; rather, she suggests, their voices simply have not been listened to.[50] Journalists might help foster those "voiceless" voices not by reporting on them, but by opening news media channels to them in ways that would let people who have been marginalized or overlooked speak out to wider audiences.

"Women have been speaking loudly and clearly. The problem is that men aren't listening."

The New York Times tried a project along these lines in early 2019, after a reader named Kimberly Probolus wrote *The Times* observing how frequently women's voices were not heard in the newspaper's letters columns, where any reader is invited to speak out. *Times* editors launched the "Women's Project," which tried "to correct that imbalance and better reflect the diversity in society" and "work toward a goal of gender parity" in the letters columns within a year. When letters section editors reported their results early in 2020, they admitted, "We haven't reached the goal line yet." The editors noted "far more" women's letters had been published than in past years, but at the end of the year during which women's voices were actively recruited, male writers still accounted for 57 percent of published letters. On some subjects, letters section editors said they found themselves "struggling" to find women's voices to include in the letters column. "At the project's one-year mark, we're reaffirming our commitment to working to reach gender parity," the editors wrote. "But what was reinforced by this project is that our letters pages are richer for this new collection of voices—and it compels us to broaden our efforts further, to ensure that we are publishing a range of letters from an even more diverse pool of writers going forward."[51] Kimberly Probolus responded to the results her letter had inspired. She suggested the underlying issue was not that women didn't speak out; the issue was that others didn't listen to women. She wrote, "I hope that women will continue to write. But it's not enough to ask women to speak up: to write more letters, to raise our voices, to 'lean in.' The problem is not that women aren't speaking up. As far back as Ancient Greece—when

Cassandra warned the Trojans about that giant wooden horse—women have been speaking loudly and clearly. The problem is that men aren't listening." In essence, Probolus suggested the ethical duty of listening is equally as important as the duty of speaking out. "This ask may seem small, but listening must be the first step toward systemic change," she wrote. "Listening will not solve inequality. But progress is impossible if men can't hear women."[52]

"Women have a right, though, to speak out against injustice."

After their controversial U.S. Open match in 2018, Osaka and Williams undoubtedly understood what women feel when men seem unable to hear them. "What was supposed to be a memorable moment for tennis, with Serena Williams, perhaps the greatest player of all time, facing off against Naomi Osaka, the future of our sport, turned into another example of people in positions of power abusing that power," tennis legend Billie Jean King recounted in a *Washington Post* essay. "Lost in the craziness of the evening was the fact that Osaka played excellent tennis and won her first major title. Competing against her childhood idol, she summoned her A game and earned her championship—no need for any asterisk in the record book. She was the best player on the court Saturday. But that's not what many will remember." King said what people would remember was that Williams "was penalized for standing up for herself" to a male umpire who was treating her unfairly. "Women have a right, though, to speak out against injustice," King admonished. "Nothing will ever change if they don't."[53]

Two years later, King and many others praised the formerly shy Osaka for speaking out against injustice. Osaka, who is Black and Asian, was raised in the United States by her Haitian father and Japanese mother. In 2020 she was playing on the professional women's tennis tour and preparing to compete for Japan in the Tokyo Olympics, where she "was going to be one of the most high-profile athletes competing for the host nation."[54] Then, abruptly, the coronavirus pandemic postponed the summer Olympics until 2021 and shut down the tennis tour.

"I decided it was time to speak up about systemic racism and police brutality."

In a magazine essay she titled "I Never Would've Imagined Writing This Two Years Ago," Osaka explained how she spent the shutdown. She wrote of initially reflecting on how she had spent the two years since she won the 2018 U.S. Open "and my life changed overnight." She said, "In the past few months, I've re-evaluated what's actually important in my life. It's a reset that perhaps I greatly needed. I asked myself, 'If I couldn't play tennis, what could I be doing to make a difference?' I decided it was time to speak up." Osaka said after she saw video of George Floyd's killing in Minneapolis, "I felt a call to action. Enough was finally enough. I flew to Minneapolis with my boyfriend days after the murder to pay our respects and have our voices heard on the streets. We grieved with the people of St. Paul and protested peacefully. We visited the George Floyd Memorial and connected with those who came together to mourn yet another senseless act and life lost without reason. Being on the ground in Minneapolis was what felt right at that moment."[55] Her visit to Minnesota offered Osaka the opportunity to practice difficult listening, as she heard citizens anguish over police brutality and racial violence.

Upon return to her California home, Osaka was motivated to share what she had heard. In her magazine essay, she wrote, "When I came back to Los Angeles, I signed petitions, I protested, and I donated, like many of us. But I kept asking myself what can I do to make this world a better place for my children? I decided it was time to speak up about systemic racism and police brutality."[56]

"What gives you more right to speak than me?"

As she did, Osaka faced criticism. When she encouraged Twitter followers to join a Black Lives Matter march in Japan, for example, she was blasted online by people who said racism didn't exist in Japan and she should stick to sports. One commenter called her "a terrorist" for speaking out. Osaka replied to her critics by pointing out she had been a victim of racism in Japan the year before, when a pair of comedians had to apologize after saying her skin's color "needed some bleach" because it was "too sunburned," *The Washington Post* reported. Furthermore, she responded via Twitter, "I hate when random people say athletes shouldn't get involved with politics and just entertain. Firstly, this is a human rights issue. Secondly, what gives you more right to speak than me? By that logic if you work at Ikea you are only allowed to talk about the [store's products]?"[57]

In August, when Osaka heard the news that Kenosha, Wisconsin, police shot a Black man named Jacob Blake, she was about to play a semifinal match in a warm-up tournament before the U.S. Open. She quickly joined other athletes in speaking out symbolically by refusing to play sports that day.[58] (See Chapter 9 for discussion of those athletes' symbolic speech.)

Several morally particular differences faced Osaka as she decided to withdraw from the tournament. Unlike the professional basketball, baseball, hockey and soccer players who spoke out symbolically by refusing to play, Osaka competed in an individual sport and could not rely on support for her decision from teammates or present the decision as a joint effort with teammates. Osaka "stood tall, and alone" when she refused to play, *The Los Angeles Times* observed.[59]

Osaka also could not rely on the security of a contract with a team or a league; tennis players fund their own expenses to train and play internationally, typically through endorsement deals. In 2019, *Forbes* named Osaka the highest-paid female athlete in the world, largely because of the $37 million worth of endorsements she landed to represent popular brands in Japan, where the dearth of other sports stars with global appeal made her attractive to Japanese corporations. In deciding to withdraw from the tournament, Osaka risked those endorsements.

> *"Japan is a very homogenous country, so tackling racism has been challenging for me."*

"Though white America has come a long way in understanding why Black athletes are compelled to protest social injustice and police violence, Osaka assumed a not small amount of risk by leaning all the way into these issues," *USA Today* columnist Dan Wolken pointed out. "In other words, from purely a corporate standpoint, Osaka has far more to worry about than how her public profile resonates with an American audience. There's a lot of upside for Osaka to put the focus on issues like racism that are viewed differently in other countries, other cultures. But there's also potential downside, too."[60] Competing as a representative of a country with conservative attitudes about speaking out, especially about racism, Osaka risked the popularity with Japanese people that earned her those endorsement deals. "Negative outbursts against people who stand out can be common in Japan, where conformity and teamwork are valued, and individualism is often seen as selfish and unbecoming," the Associated Press noted.[61]

Osaka knew contravening traditional Japanese values posed a risk for her, but it was one she seemed willing to take. "Japan is a very homogenous country, so tackling racism has been challenging for me," she had written in her magazine essay about deciding to speak out. "I have received racist comments online and even on TV. But that's the minority. In reality, biracial people—especially biracial athletes—are the future of Japan. ... We can't let the ignorance of a few hold back the progressiveness of the masses."[62]

> *"Before I am an athlete, I am a black woman."*

As she announced her decision to withdraw from the warm-up tournament, Osaka was resolute. "Hello, as many of you are aware I was scheduled to play my semifinals match," she tweeted. "However, before I am an athlete, I am a black woman. And as a black woman I feel as though there are much more important matters at hand that need immediate attention, rather than watching me play tennis. I don't expect anything drastic to happen with me not playing, but if I can get a conversation started in a majority white sport I consider that a step in the right direction."[63]

Yet something drastic did occur. Shortly after Osaka's tweet, "the entire tournament postponed itself for the day, signaling not just the moment in sports, but Osaka's clout within her game," *The Wall Street Journal* reported. "She had literally shut tennis down" to protest racial injustice.[64] Several leaders in tennis, including the legend, Billie Jean King, praised Osaka's act of symbolic speech. King called it "a brave & impactful move" in a tweet to Osaka that concluded, "Don't remain silent."[65]

When the tournament resumed, Osaka continued speaking out symbolically, wearing a Black Lives Matter shirt onto the court for her semifinal match. After that match, she told reporters she was surprised her withdrawal had influenced tennis officials to stop the warm-up tournament and she had not assumed they would invite her to rejoin the tournament once she officially withdrew. She also acknowledged that withdrawing was not an entirely easy decision. After the pandemic shutdown of tennis, the warm-up tournament provided competition that would help her prepare to contend for the U.S. Open title. But, she said, "If withdrawing from a tournament would cause the most stir, then that was something I needed to do. I don't feel like I am being brave, I just feel like I am doing what I should be doing."[66]

A week later, as she began competing in the U.S. Open, Osaka displayed another means of speaking out symbolically while observing the regulations of tennis during the coronavirus pandemic. Each day, she walked onto the court wearing a black face mask emblazoned with the name of a Black victim of racial injustice. Because she wore each day's mask during her pre-match television interviews on the court, the name of a victim was front and center on screens around the world. Osaka indicated to reporters she wanted to strategically use that visibility.[67] "It was a small gesture, more personal than the well-intentioned but clunky demonstrations happening in other sports," *The Wall Street Journal* observed. "And Osaka's masks grew more powerful as the tournament went on, because she kept winning."[68]

> *"I feel like I'm a vessel at this point in order to spread awareness."*

After winning her quarterfinal match, Osaka sat for a live interview, during which ESPN aired a video featuring families of some of the victims whose names were featured on her face masks. The mother of Trayvon Martin, a Florida teen killed in 2012 while walking home from a convenience store in his neighborhood, thanked Osaka for representing him on one of her masks. So did the father of Ahmad Arbery, who was killed in 2020 while jogging through his Georgia neighborhood. "Naomi, I just want to tell you thank you for the support of my family. God bless you for what you're doing," Arbery's father said. "My family really, really appreciates that." Osaka listened quietly and appeared near tears as the families' thanks aired. "I feel like they're so strong. I'm not sure what I would be able to do if I was in their position. I feel like I'm a vessel at this point in order to spread awareness," she said.[69]

In speaking out symbolically by halting play in the warm-up tournament and by strategically wearing face masks in the U.S. Open, Osaka seemed motivated to listen with humility and respect for victims of racial injustice, and to respond with symbolic speech acts that would foster discourse. But it was her on-court interview after winning the U.S. Open that best showcased her ethical listening and responding skills. By the time an ESPN reporter asked the victorious Osaka what message she wanted to send with the masks she wore during the tournament, she had heard and "patiently answered upwards of 100 English and Japanese questions about her reasons for doing so," *The Guardian* estimated. "She [was] consistent and clear throughout, yet still, standing in Arthur Ashe Stadium as the newly crowned US Open champion, she was asked to explain her message once more. Her response: 'Well, what was the message you got?'"[70]

With her question to ESPN's Tom Rinaldi, Osaka quietly challenged the way reporters had been hearing, framing and amplifying her symbolic speech throughout the tournament. "Corporate sports media entities have been in contact with athletes making demonstrations for racial justice for long enough that they've learned a variety of tactics for politely disarming those demonstrations. Rinaldi was using one of the more tried-and-true methods, which is to ask the person doing the demonstrating to explain the validity and importance of their act," observed Tom Ley, editor of the sports journalism site *Defector Media*. "It's a neat trick, in that it saves the questioner from having to do anything other than nod along with whichever answer they get. It also lays a trap for the person doing the answering. Refuse to engage the question, and bad-faith critics can immediately begin arguing that there are no actual ideas behind the gesture in question, that the person doing it is childish and clearly hasn't thought things through, and that the whole thing should be ignored. Answer the question, though, and those same critics will find a way to reach the same set of conclusions by poking holes in any part of the answer that isn't expressed with perfect clarity and nuance. Perhaps Osaka has seen this happen enough times to know better than to play the game. By answering Rinaldi's question with one of her own, she reminded everyone watching that it is not incumbent on the demonstrator to defend the rationality or reasonableness of their act. An expression of anguish at the continued brutalization of black people in America is not a policy position. It is not something that requires explaining or debating in the marketplace of ideas."[71]

The Guardian called Osaka's response to Rinaldi "a fitting end" to her summer of speaking out. "Before the event, Osaka was unsure of what the outcome of her amplifying police violence and anti–Black killings would be, yet her actions have challenged journalists to cover anti–Black racism in the same breath they cover her relatively unimportant matches."[72]

> *"You better believe I'm gonna try to be on your tv for as long as possible."*

Two weeks later, one of Japan's leading newspapers amplified Osaka's message. *The Mainichi* sought out young people in a central Tokyo business district, asking them to answer Osaka's "What was the message you got?" question. They replied "equality," "diversity" and "speak up without fear of criticism." One of the young people the newspaper quoted said Osaka should "stick to sports," but others seemed more supportive of her speaking out. "It can't be easy as a top athlete to champion political messages opposing racism, but I think she's really amazing," said one 20 year old. "In the future, if I'm in a position to make a statement, I want to try to do the same thing." The newspaper concluded, "Naomi Osaka has sent a powerful serve to the world. Young people in Japan, too, are responding to her challenge."[73]

After her victory, Osaka continued listening and responding to social media followers who objected to her symbolic speech during the tournament. She reminded people who were "telling me to 'keep politics out of sports'" that she viewed racial injustice as a human rights issue, not as a political one, and said their opposition inspired her to keep trying to win tennis matches so she could use her visibility to speak out. "You better believe I'm gonna try to be on your tv for as long as possible," she tweeted.[74]

In the concluding chapter, we reflect on examples presented throughout this book, such as Osaka's, and consider what they show those of us who are not famous about speaking out and responding ethically.

Conclusion

How Do We Speak Out Ethically
When We're Not Famous?

Speaking out matters. Just ask the Dixie Chicks how speaking out can change careers. In March 2003, just before the U.S. invasion of Iraq, the trio's lead singer Natalie Maines, a Texas native, told a concert audience, "We do not want this war, this violence, and we're ashamed that the president of the United States is from Texas."[75] How did that change the musicians' careers? "What happened next was ugly: their record sales plunged, their radio airplay dried up, and the biggest female group in the world was in effect cancelled."[76]

Speaking out matters. Just ask the Dixie Chicks how one person's words can change relationships. Years after Maines spoke out to oppose President George W. Bush and the Iraq war, and the country music world's response crushed the three musicians' careers and subjected them to death threats, Maines stood by her words. How did those words change the women? Maines said speaking out was "a freedom" for her, but she also told an interviewer, "I *need* these two," and "I hated that I was dragging two people through" the controversy. Her bandmate Emily Strayer responded, "No, 'dragging' isn't the word. We were all in the middle of it."[77]

Speaking out matters. Just ask the Dixie Chicks how long an act of speaking out can persist. In March 2020, the trio released the title track from their first studio album in 14 years.[78] How did many news outlets frame stories about their new music? By quoting the text of Maines' words or embedding video of her speaking from that concert stage almost exactly 17 years before.[79]

Speaking out matters. Just ask the Dixie Chicks about the importance of moral consistency and moral voicing after speaking out. In June 2020, the United States roiled with protest over police killings of Black citizens. What did that require of the trio if they were to continue being opponents of injustice? Dropping "Dixie" and its "romanticization of the

Confederacy" from their longtime name. "We want to meet this moment," the Chicks simply said in a social media post.[80]

Speaking Out in Our Own Spheres of Influence

Most of us are not famous, and we never will be. But we always will be speakers and listeners. When we speak out, the words we use matter. Our words affect our lives and careers. Our words can do good or harm to ourselves and to others. And in the digital age, our words persist. Therefore, this book ends with an exhortation: Speaking out ethically and responding ethically to speaking out are acts of everyday moral courage that each of us can perform with integrity, even though we're not famous. We can speak out about shared issues of public concern, we can listen attentively to what others are saying about those issues, and we can respectfully question or amplify what we are hearing, even in our ordinary circles. "We all have a sphere of influence," observes psychologist Beverly Daniel Tatum. "Each of us needs to find our own sources of courage so that we will begin to speak. There are many problems to address, and we cannot avoid them indefinitely. We cannot continue to be silent. We must begin to speak."[81]

Too often, when we think about summoning up our courage to speak out or to respond to speaking out, we think courage means impressive acts performed by specifically gifted or trained people. We think of firefighters, who knew that running into the World Trade Center towers after the September 2001 terrorist attacks would endanger their own lives but still ran into those burning buildings, because they were courageous enough to try to save victims' lives. We think of astronauts, who knew that attempting the first human landing on the moon in 1969 was risky but still boarded the Apollo 11 spacecraft, because they were courageous enough to advance the exploration of our solar system. We think of the Rev. Dr. Martin Luther King, Jr., who knew would-be assassins were escalating death threats against him in 1968 but still crusaded for Black Americans' civil rights, because he was courageous enough to challenge human oppression.

Moral Courage, Moral Competence and Ethical Fitness

These acts of courage certainly deserve our admiration, and we can and should learn from the examples of these moral agents. Yet we should not think that if we are untested by burning buildings, space travel or death threats we cannot be courageous. We can. "[M]oral courage is the everyday enactment of principles such as integrity, honesty, compassion, service, generosity, caring, fairness, and respect,"[82] explains ethics scholar Judith White. If we think of moral courage not as an extraordinary feat but as an everyday act, we can think of ourselves as capable of acting courageously. "One of the first and most important lessons" we may learn "from the stories of voicing values is that the way we frame our ethical challenges has a great deal to do with how we perceive our ability and confidence and willingness to act on them," observes ethics scholar Mary Gentile. If we think we can be ethical, we likely can. "That is, if we believe that we have the skills and the arguments or scripts to voice and act upon our values, the quest for Herculean stores of courage becomes less relevant."[83]

Gentile suggests the concept of moral competence is the key to moral courage.[84] Similarly, ethicist Rushworth Kidder suggests the concept of ethical fitness is the key to moral courage. Kidder defines ethical fitness as "a capacity to recognize the nature of moral challenges and respond with a well-tuned conscience, a lively perception of the difference between right and wrong, and an ability to choose the right and live by it."[85]

Whether we call it moral competence or ethical fitness, both Gentile and Kidder suggest we can learn skills for using the concept. Both also suggest that as we learn, we should focus less on the flaws of ethical wrongdoers and more on the successes of ethical right doers. "So once we have released ourselves from the assumption that ethical ... conduct requires a superhuman level of courage, and once we have recognized that it is about training and preparation for all of us, rather than about some sort of ethical radar that enables us to detect and eject the dangerous few, then we can turn to naming, developing, and practicing the perspectives, frames, and skills we will need," Gentile contends.[86]

Moral Consistency and Moral Voicing

As we attempt the goal of ethical fitness, we can learn from the moral consistency and moral voicing of famous figures who transcended their audiences' role-related expectations to speak out about issues of shared public concern. Moral consistency, discussed in Chapter 5, is the idea that as moral agents, we should act the same ways in both our public and private lives, exhibiting congruence between what we do and what we value.[87] Moral voicing, also discussed in Chapter 5, is the idea that as moral agents, we should be neither morally blind nor morally deaf to ethical issues but speak out when we see them.[88]

Consider television satirist Jon Stewart as an example of moral consistency and moral voicing. (See chapters 4 and 5.) He spoke out for nearly 20 years in support of the health issues faced by firefighters, paramedics and police officers who responded to the September 2001 terrorist attacks in New York. As a resident of lower Manhattan, Stewart lived through the devastation caused by the attacks. As a citizen, Stewart publicly parlayed his celebrity into advocacy for government funds to compensate 9/11 first responders' medical and burial expenses or lost wages.

Or consider runners Tommie Smith and John Carlos as an example of moral consistency and moral voicing. (See chapters 8 and 9.) They spoke out symbolically to oppose racism with raised fists as they stood atop the medal stand at the 1968 Olympics—and continued to stand up for civil rights for the next 50 years. As Black Americans, Smith and Carlos lived through the kinds of racial discrimination they were protesting at the Olympics. As citizens, they risked both public condemnation, and their safety and livelihoods, to protest inequality on the day they received Olympic medals and for years afterward.

These examples show us that moral consistency and moral voicing link the values we choose in our private and public lives with one another, and urge us to behave with the same integrity in both. The "unity between conduct and fundamental moral values" is a fundamental aspect of moral decency, ethics scholar Mike Martin reminds us. "Persons of integrity are reliable in meeting their responsibilities and commitments. They are decent, honest, and fair."[89]

Respect for Human Dignity

To speak out with integrity requires attention to two additional moral values: respect for human dignity and respect for the power of communication.

The late 18th century philosopher Immanuel Kant is undoubtedly philosophy's foremost advocate for the principle that all human beings possess human dignity. Kant stipulates that the intrinsic dignity and worth of every person means each of us has the ability to act morally—an ability that sets us apart from other creatures. Furthermore, the human dignity we intrinsically possess means we cannot use one another as means to our own ends. The Kantian principle of respect for human dignity has come to represent the belief that our moral worth as humans cannot be assigned on the basis of our race, gender, intelligence, skills, talents or other characteristics.[90] We are simply worth dignity, no matter our social stations.

Consider the examples of speaking out to express respect for human dignity provided by tennis star Serena Williams and world champion runner Allyson Felix. (See chapters 7 and 8.) After both survived serious complications in giving birth to their daughters, they learned about the disproportionate health risks that face all Black mothers, who are three to four times more likely to die from pregnancy in the United States than are white women. Williams and Felix began speaking out about the crisis of Black maternal mortality, demonstrating a fundamental respect for Black women and children. In several venues, Williams and Felix acknowledged that many Black mothers possess far less power than elite athletes to seek the best health care and to bring the issue of maternal mortality to the attention of powerful figures. Williams and Felix used the power their status afforded them to advocate that all Black women deserve adequate health care.

Or consider again the many examples of Black athletes who have spoken out to challenge racial injustice, in the wake of police shootings of Black Americans. (See chapters 8, 9 and 11.) Just as the Rev. Dr. Martin Luther King, Jr., had done long before most of them were born, these athletes spoke out forcefully to insist that all human people, including Black citizens, deserve justice. Many of these athletes—basketball star LeBron James, football quarterback Colin Kaepernick and tennis champion Naomi Osaka, just to name three—used their social media platforms and the knowledge that journalists would amplify the athletes' social messages to shine a light on the goals of the Black Lives Matter movement for racial justice.

Respect for the Power of Communication

The power of communication today is staggering, thanks to digital media, and we should respect that power and use it thoughtfully. "We are living in the middle of the largest increase in expressive capability in the history of the human race," contends internet scholar Clay Shirky. "More people can communicate more things to more people than has ever been possible in the past, and the size and speed of this increase, from under one million participants to over one billion in a generation, makes the change unprecedented, even considered against the background of previous revolutions in communications tools."[91]

The digital tools most of us have at our disposal mean we can "publish" our words nearly anywhere, anytime. "In a world where publishing is effortless, the decision to publish something isn't terribly momentous,"[92] Shirky points out. But maybe it should be. When we are freed from the filtering of our words provided by editors and gatekeepers of old, the duty to respect the potential power or harm of our words devolves to us individually. Maybe, instead of saying "shut up and play" or "shut up and sing" to others, we should more often say "shut up and think" or "shut up and listen" to ourselves before we speak—especially because, as Shirky reminds us, in the digital world, "the default mode for many forms of communication is instant, global, and nearly permanent."[93]

Consider the example singer Taylor Swift provides here. (See the Introduction.) She demonstrated a respect for the potential power of her own communication platform by declining to answer journalists' questions about which candidate she supported in the first two presidential elections in which she was old enough to vote. "I don't think that I know enough yet in life to be telling people who to vote for," she said at one point.[94] After she was criticized for failing to endorse Hillary Clinton in the 2016 presidential election, Swift again appeared to respect the power of her communication status, saying she thought Republican candidate Donald Trump would "weaponize" celebrity endorsements of his opponent, so Swift remained silent rather than contribute to backlash for Clinton.

Six years later, Swift appeared to engage in thoughtful deliberation about whether to make an Instagram post with her first-ever endorsement of candidates in the 2018 midterm elections. The singer said she considered the career disaster that befell the Chicks when they spoke out politically in 2003, and she also consulted with her parents and other advisors before making the post. She further displayed respect for the power of communication in the way her Instagram message accurately conveyed information about registering to vote that she offered to her more youthful followers. Then, building on the enormous number of young voters she apparently had motivated to register in 2018, she displayed moral consistency and continued speaking out about the importance of voting. As the 2020 presidential campaign unfolded, for example, she encouraged her social media followers to vote by mail if necessary to make their votes count.[95]

Communication, including that which uses digital venues, can be a force for human good. Consider here the example of actor Tom Hanks. (See Chapter 10.) In speaking out about his experience during the once-in-a-lifetime coronavirus pandemic that confused and scared many people in 2020, he used simple, direct language, never purporting to be an expert but clearly conveying the advice recommended by public health authorities. His calm and kind "America's Dad" demeanor no doubt settled the fears of many people and encouraged them to emulate the "wash your hands, wear a mask and keep your distance" behaviors he endorsed in frequent social media posts and news interviews.

Choosing Digital Outrage or Forgiveness

Sadly, however, our digital communication too frequently disrespects our own and others' human dignity. Liking, disliking, flaming, trolling, canceling: Whatever you call these sometimes mean-spirited tactics, many of us too often use them without thinking about how they may inflict harm on ourselves and on others.

In her book *Outraged: Why Everyone Is Shouting and No One Is Talking*, radio host Ashley Charles observes that the ease with which we now can express our outrage online is, in fact, "diluting our moral expression and weakening our moral leverage."[96] We don't have to instantly agree or disagree with every act of speaking out we hear. In fact, belief in the moral worth of human dignity gives us an ethical obligation to challenge falsity, to resist hate and to be willing to voice unpopular views. "So by all means get angry" at offensive, uninformed or hateful speech, Charles suggests. "But do it with an ambition that extends beyond social media kudos" and aims toward actions that will help end injustice.[97]

Similarly, author Tom Nichols worries "the Internet is making us meaner, shorter-fused, and incapable of conducting discussions where anyone learns anything." He writes, "While the Internet enables more people to talk to each other than ever before—a distinctly new historical condition—everyone talking immediately to everyone else might not always be such a good idea. Sometimes, human beings need to pause and to reflect, to give themselves time to absorb information and to digest it."[98]

As we observe our ethical obligation to pause and reflect, we may also bear an ethical obligation to forgive offensive speech. We are all fallible. We have each spoken and responded in error. For our discursive marketplace of ideas to function, we must consider when and if it is appropriate to forgive what free speech advocate Suzanne Nossel calls "speech-related transgressions." Nossel writes, "To keep speech free in our cacophonous modern public square, we need the capacity to forgive those who antagonize and offend. Otherwise, there can be little incentive to apologize for an offense or to try to mitigate its harm."[99] To qualify for forgiveness, rather than censure, a speaker who has committed a transgression must express authentic contrition, evince a history of otherwise good character, and attempt to earn absolution, rather than expect mercy, from the target of the inappropriate or hurtful speech, Nossel suggests.[100]

Consider here the example of a former Chicks fan. In 2006, the singers remained so upset by the death threats they received in response to their 2003 opposition to U.S. involvement in Iraq that they referred to those threats in a song titled "Not Ready to Make Nice" on an album titled "Taking the Long Way." The message they sent, obviously, was that they weren't yet up to forgiving fans who had threatened them. Years later, however, a woman who had protested outside one of their concerts, encouraging her young child to scream "Screw 'em!"—which had been seen on the documentary "Shut Up and Sing"—sent the trio a letter of apology, saying she had learned new attitudes since her hurtful behavior. Chicks' lead singer Natalie Maines received the belated apology as "amazing."[101]

Shut Up and Think? Shut Up and Listen?

Even when speaking out and responses to speaking out occur many years after an injustice, as with the apology years after death threats to the Chicks, these acts of ethical communication indeed can be amazing ways to question, challenge and protest issues of public concern. For instance, the line of Black athletes stretching more than 50 years from Tommie Smith and John Carlos to Colin Kaepernick and Naomi Osaka, each speaking out with words and symbols, contributed to changes in attitudes about racial injustice in the United States. Like the many high school athletes who have followed the professionals' examples and amplified their speech, those of us who are not famous can speak out and respond ethically in our own circles of influence. As we do, we may all benefit if we "shut up and think" and "shut up and listen" so we can subsequently speak out and respond to speaking out in ways that minimize harm to ourselves and others, and that foster meaningful conversations with one another about the public concerns we share. Thoughtful speaking and listening can change our world, if we do so with ethical care in our own roles as moral agents.

Chapter Notes

Introduction

1. Bryson, Donna. "Taylor Swift Was Groped by Radio Host, Jury Finds." *The New York Times*, August 14, 2017, nytimes.com/2017/08/14/arts/music/taylor-swift-trial-jury-verdict.html. Accessed February 21, 2020.

2. Swift, Taylor. "I'm writing this post about the upcoming midterm elections …" *Instagram*, October 7, 2018, instagram.com/p/BopoXpYnCes/?hl=en. Accessed November 28, 2018.

3. Haag, Matthew. "Voter Registrations Spike as Deadlines Loom. Taylor Swift Had Something to Do with It." *The New York Times*, October 9, 2018, nytimes.com/2018/10/09/us/politics/taylor-swift-voter-registration.html. Accessed November 28, 2018.

4. Finan, Eileen. "Taylor Swift Votes for First Time 'With My Gut.'" *People*, October 31, 2008, people.com/celebrity/taylor-swift-votes-for-first-time-with-my-gut/. Accessed November 28, 2018.

5. Macsai, Dan. "Taylor Swift on Going Pop, Ignoring the Gossip and the Best (Worst) Nickname She's Ever Had." *Time*, October 19, 2012, entertainment.time.com/2012/10/19/taylor-swift-on-going-pop-ignoring-the-gossip-and-the-best-worst-nickname-shes-ever-had/. Accessed November 28, 2018.

6. Farzan, Antonia Noori. "'I Just Knew I Wasn't Going to Help': Taylor Swift Finally Explains Why She Didn't Endorse Hillary Clinton." *The Washington Post*, August 9, 2019, washingtonpost.com/nation/2019/08/09/taylor-swift-hillary-clinton-trump-vogue-interview/. Accessed February 21, 2020.

7. Farzan.

8. Yahr, Emily. "After the Trump-Putin News Conference, Here's Why People Are Talking about the Dixie Chicks." *The Washington Post*, July 17, 2018, washingtonpost.com/news/arts-and-entertainment/wp/2018/07/17/after-the-trump-putin-news-conference-heres-why-people-are-talking-about-the-dixie-chicks/. Accessed November 28, 2018.

9. Pareles, Jon. "The Dixie Chicks: America Catches Up with Them." *The New York Times*, May 21, 2006, nytimes.com/2006/05/21/arts/music/21pare.html. Accessed February 23, 2020.

10. Smith, Grady. "Is Country Music Ready to Forgive the Dixie Chicks?" *The Guardian*, November 19, 2015, theguardian.com/music/2015/nov/19/the-dixie-chicks-tour-is-country-music-ready-to-forgive. Accessed February 23, 2020.

11. Williamson, Nigel. "Free the Dixie Three." *The Guardian*, August 21, 2003, theguardian.com/music/2003/aug/22/1. Accessed February 23, 2020.

12. Pareles.

13. Smith.

14. Smith.

15. Smith.

16. Williamson.

17. Pareles.

18. Smith.

19. Williamson.

20. Bryant, Howard. *The Heritage: Black Athletes, a Divided America, and the Politics of Patriotism*. Beacon Press, 2018, p. 117.

21. Holden, Stephen. "In an Instant, Country Stars Became Political Casualties." *The New York Times*, October 27, 2006, nytimes.com/2006/10/27/movies/

in-an-instant-country-stars-became-politi
cal-casualties.html. Accessed February 23,
2020.

22. Leeds, Jeff. "Grammy Sweep by Dixie
Chicks Is Seen as a Vindication." *The New
York Times*, February 13, 2007, nytimes.
com/2007/02/13/arts/music/13gram.html.
Accessed February 23, 2020.

23. Sanneh, Kelefa. "It's Dixie Chicks vs.
Country Fans, but Who's Dissing Whom?"
The New York Times, May 25, 2006, nytimes.
com/2006/05/25/arts/music/25sann.html.
Accessed November 28, 2018.

24. Holden.

25. Sanneh.

26. Williamson.

27. Pareles.

28. Willman, Chris. "Taylor Swift: No
Longer 'Polite at All Costs.'" *Variety*, January
21, 2020, variety.com/2020/music/features/
taylor-swift-politics-sundance-doc
umentary-miss-americana-1203471910/.
Accessed February 23, 2020.

29. Willman.

30. Willman.

31. Willman.

32. "Full Text of Brokaw's Interview
with Bush." *The New York Times*, April 25,
2003, nytimes.com/2003/04/25/interna-
tional/world special/full-text-of-brokaws-
interview-with-bush.html. Accessed July
20, 2020.

33. Hill, Evan, et al. "How George Floyd
Was Killed in Police Custody." *The New
York Times*, May 31, 2020, Updated July 28,
2020, nytimes.com/2020/05/31/us/George-
Floyd-investigation.html. Accessed August
7, 2020.

34. After George Floyd's killing and
weeks of racial injustice protests around
the world, several prominent national news
organizations in the United States decided
they would capitalize Black when reporting about Black people. The decision was
intended to recognize shared Black culture
and identity that includes a history of racial
discrimination. Most of those same news
organizations decided not to capitalize
white when reporting about white people.
That decision was intended to recognize
that the term "white" does not reflect a
shared culture and identity, let alone a
shared history of discrimination, and to
avoid the capitalized use of white that often
has been employed by racist groups to promote hate of Black people. See, for example:

Coleman, Nancy. "Why We're Capitalizing
Black." *The New York Times*, July 5, 2020,
nytimes.com/2020/07/05/insider/capital
ized-black.html. Accessed July 6, 2020.
Daniszewski, John. "Why We Will Lowercase White." The Associated Press, July 20,
2020, blog.ap.org/announcements/why-
we-will-lowercase-white?utm_campaign.
Accessed July 20, 2020. This book will follow the practice of these news organizations
in capitalizing Black and lowercasing white,
unless directly quoted source material does
not capitalize Black.

35. Boswell, Thomas. "It's Not Which
Sports Figures Are Speaking Out That's
Telling. It's How Many." *The Washington
Post*, June 10, 2020, washingtonpost.com/
sports/2020/06/10/its-not-which-sports-
figures-are-speaking-out-thats-telling-its-
how-many/. Accessed June 10, 2020.

36. Gunter, Barrie. *Celebrity Capital:
Assessing the Value of Fame*. Bloomsbury,
2014, pp. 15–16.

37. See, for example, these four
well-researched titles: Caulfield, Tim-
othy. *Is Gwyneth Paltrow Wrong about
Everything? How the Famous Sell Us Elix-
irs of Health, Beauty and Happiness*. Bea-
con Press, 2015; Hotez, Peter J. *Vaccines Did
Not Cause Rachel's Autism: My Journey as a
Vaccine Scientist, Pediatrician, and Autism
Dad*. Johns Hopkins University Press, 2018;
Mnookin, Seth. *The Panic Virus: A True
Story of Medicine, Science, and Fear*. Simon
& Schuster, 2011; Offit, Paul A. *Bad Advice:
Or Why Celebrities, Politicians, and Activists
Aren't Your Best Source of Health Informa-
tion*. Columbia University Press, 2018.

Chapter 1

1. van Elteren, Mel. "Celebrity Culture,
Performative Politics, and the Spectacle of
'Democracy' in America." *The Journal of
American Culture*, vol. 36, no. 4, December
21, 2013, pp. 263–283, doi: 10.1111/jacc.
12049.

2. Rabidoux, Greg R. *Hollywood Politicos, Then and Now: Who They Are, What
They Want, Why It Matters*. University Press
of America, 2009, pp. 71–90.

3. Wheeler, Mark. *Celebrity Politics:
Image and Identity in Contemporary Political Communications*. Polity Press, 2013,
pp. 42–44.

4. Raymond, Emilie. *Stars for Freedom: Hollywood, Black Celebrities, and the Civil Rights Movement.* University of Washington Press, 2015, pp. 87–88.

5. Wheeler, p. 46.

6. Wheeler, pp. 46–49.

7. Rabidoux, pp. 117–125.

8. "Forbes Most Powerful Women in the World in 2016." *Telegraph,* June 13, 2016, telegraph.co.uk/business/2016/06/06/the-most-powerful-women-in-the-world/oprah-winfrey/. Accessed February 9, 2019.

9. Baum, Matthew A., and Angela S. Jamison. "The Oprah Effect: How Soft News Helps Inattentive Citizens Vote Consistently." *The Journal of Politics,* vol. 68, no. 4, November 2006, pp. 946–959, doi: 10.1111/j.1468–2508.2006.00482.x.

10. Puente, Maria. "The 'Oprah Effect': Does Everything She Touch Turn to Gold?" *USA Today,* October 19, 2015, usatoday.com/story/life/tv/2015/10/19/oprah-effect-does-everything-she-touches-turn-gold/74211636/. Accessed February 9, 2019.

11. Zeleny, Jeff. "Oprah Endorses Obama." *The New York Times,* May 3, 2007, thecaucusblogs.nytimes.com/2007/05/03/oprah-endorses-Obama-2/. Accessed February 9, 2019.

12. Garthwaite, Craig, and Timothy J. Moore. "Can Celebrity Endorsements Affect Political Outcomes? Evidence from the 2008 U.S. Democratic Presidential Primary." *The Journal of Law, Economics, and Organization,* vol. 29, no. 2, February 10, 2012, pp. 355–384, doi: 10.1093/jleo/ewr031.

13. "Celebrity Endorsement Tracker." *Los Angeles Times,* April 12, 2016, graphics.latimes.com/celebrity-presidential-endorsements/. Accessed February 8, 2019.

14. Zubcevic-Basic, Nives. "U.S. Election: What Impact Do Celebrity Endorsements Really Have?" *The Conversation,* October 4, 2016, theconversation.com/us-election-what-impact-do-celebrity-endorsements-really-have-66204. Accessed February 9, 2019.

15. Raymond, p. ix.

16. Raymond, p. ix.

17. Rabidoux, p. 135.

18. *Academy Awards Acceptance Speech Database.* aaspeechesdb.oscars.org/link/044–3/. Accessed February 8, 2019.

19. *Academy Awards Acceptance Speech Database.* aaspeechesdb.oscars.org/link/045–1/. Accessed February 8, 2019.

20. Associated Press. "Political Oscars Speeches Started with Marlon Brando." *Page Six,* February 27, 2018, pagesix.com/2018/02/27/political-oscar-speeches-started-with-marlon-brando/. Accessed February 8, 2019.

21. Rabidoux, p. 109.

22. Associated Press.

23. *Academy Awards Acceptance Speech Database.* aaspeechesdb.oscars.org/link/035–1/. Accessed February 9, 2019.

24. Associated Press. "Political Oscars Speeches Started with Marlon Brando."

25. "Politics at the Oscars." *The New York Times,* March 1, 2014, nytimes.com/2014/03/01/us/politics/politics-at-the-oscars.html. Accessed February 15, 2019.

26. "Politics at the Oscars."

27. Victor, Daniel, and Giovanni Russonello. "Meryl Streep's Golden Globes Speech." *The New York Times,* January 8, 2017, nytimes.com/2017/01/08/arts/television/meryl-streep-golden-globes-speech.html. Accessed February 16, 2019.

28. Deb, Sopan. "Robert De Niro's Anti-Trump Screed and Meryl Streep's Ode to Men." *The New York Times,* January 10, 2018, nytimes.com/2018/01/10/arts/robert-de-niro-meryl-streep-national-board-of-review.html. Accessed February 16, 2019.

29. Russonello, Giovanni. "Read Oprah Winfrey's Golden Globes Speech." *The New York Times,* January 7, 2018. nytimes.com/2018/01/07/movies/oprah-winfrey-golden-globes-speech-transcript.html. Accessed February 16, 2019.

30. Ugwu, Reggie. "President Oprah? After the Golden Globes, Some Have a 2020 Vision." *The New York Times,* January 8, 2018, nytimes.com/2018/01/08/movies/oprah-winfrey-lifetime-achievement-golden-globes.html. Accessed February 16, 2019.

31. La Ferla, Ruth. "The Land of the Oscars, the Home of the Dove." *The New York Times,* March 25, 2003, nytimes.com/2003/03/25/us/the-land-of-the-oscars-the-home-of-the-dove.html. Accessed February 15, 2019.

32. Tamblyn, Amber. "Amber Tamblyn: Redefining the Red Carpet." *The New York Times,* January 7, 2018, nytimes.com/2018/01/07/opinion/sunday/amber-

tamblyn-golden-globes-metoo.html. Accessed February 15, 2019.

33. Ember, Sydney, and Lisa Lerer. "Julia Louis-Dreyfus Caps a Week of Starring Roles for 4 Actresses." *The New York Times*, August 20, 2020, nytimes.com/2020/08/20/us/politics/julia-louis-dreyfus-dnc.html. Accessed August 20, 2020.

34. Deb, Sopan. "Stephen and Ayesha Curry Endorse Biden at Democratic National Convention." *The New York Times*, August 20, 2020, nytimes.com/2020/08/20/us/politics/Stephen-Ayesha-curry-endorse-Biden.html. Accessed August 21, 2020.

35. Bradner, Eric. "Top Takeaways from the Democratic National Convention." *CNN Politics*, August 21, 2020, cnn.com/2020/08/21/politics/dnc-2020-takeaways/index.html. Accessed August 23, 2020.

36. Bonesteel, Matt. "Stephen Curry's Endorsement of Joe Biden a Natural Step in NBA Star's Political Progression." *The Washington Post*, August 21, 2020, washingtonpost.com/sports/2020/08/21/stephen-Curry's-endorsement-joe-biden-natural-step-nba-stars-political-progression/. Accessed August 21, 2020.

37. Scribner, Herb. "Twitter Goes Wild for Steph and Ayesha Curry During the Democratic National Convention." *MSN*, August 21, 2020, msn.com/en-us/sports/nba/twitter-goes-wild-for-steph-and-ayesha-curry-during-the-democratic-national-convention/at-BB18di6g?. Accessed August 22, 2020.

38. Rabidoux, p. 90.

39. Rabidoux, p. 78.

40. Jones, Jeffrey M. "As Industry Grows, Percentage of U.S. Sports Fans Steady." *Gallup*, June 17, 2015, news.gallup.com/poll/183689/industry-grows-percentage-sports-fans-steady.aspx. Accessed June 24, 2019.

41. "Year in Sports Media Report, U.S. 2017." *Nielsen*, nielsen.com/us/en/insights/report/2018/2017-year-in-sports-media/. Accessed June 24, 2019.

42. Norman, Jim. "Football Still Americans' Favorite Sport to Watch." *Gallup*, January 4, 2018, news.gallup.com/poll/224864/football-americans-favorite-sport-watch.aspx. Accessed June 24, 2019.

43. Rhoden, William C. *Forty Million Dollar Slaves: The Rise, Fall, and Redemption of the Black Athlete.* Three Rivers Press, 2006.

44. Hsu, Hua. "The Political Athlete: Then and Now." *The New Yorker*, March 22, 2017, newyorker.com/culture/cultural-commenht/the-political-athlete-then-and-now. Accessed June 24, 2019.

45. Hsu.

46. Bembry, Jerry. "Athletes Getting Back in the Protest Game." *The Undefeated*, August 25, 2016, theundefeated.com/features/athletes-getting-back-in-the-protest-game. Accessed March 2, 2019.

47. Bembry.

48. Hill, Evan, et al. "How George Floyd Was Killed in Police Custody." *The New York Times*, May 31, 2020, Updated July 28, 2020, nytimes.com/2020/05/31/us/George-Floyd-investigation.html. Accessed August 7, 2020.

49. Buchanan, Larry, Quoctrung Bui and Jugal K. Patel. "Black Lives Matter May Be the Largest Movement in U.S. History." *The New York Times*, July 3, 2020, nytimes.com/interactive/2020/07/03/us/george-floyd-protests-crowd-size.html. Accessed August 7, 2020.

50. Buchanan, Bui and Patel.

51. Anderson, Joel. "Why the NFL Is Suddenly Standing Up for Black Lives." *Slate*, June 7, 2020, slate.com/culture/2020/06/nfl-roger-goodell-black-lives-matter-players-video-kaepernick.html. Accessed July 21, 2020.

52. Hedges, Chris. *Empire of Illusion: The End of Literacy and the Triumph of Spectacle.* Nation Books, 2009, p. 17.

53. Hedges, p. 45.

54. Boorstin, Daniel. *The Image: A Guide to Pseudo-Events in America.* Harper & Row, Harper Colophon edition, 1961.

55. Furedi, Frank. "Celebrity Culture." *Society*, vol. 47, 2010, pp. 493–497, doi: 10.1007/s12115–010–9367–6, p. 493.

56. Furedi, p. 496.

57. Furedi, p. 496.

58. Choi, Chong Ju, and Ron Berger. "Ethics of Celebrities and Their Increasing Influence in 21st Century Society." *Journal of Business Ethics*, vol. 91, 2010, pp. 313–318, doi: 10.1007/s10551–009–0090–4, p. 313.

59. Boren, Cindy. "LeBron James on Ahmaud Arbery Shooting: 'We're Literally Hunted Everyday.'" *The Washington Post*, May 7, 2020, washingtonpost.com/

sports/2020/05/07/lebron-james-ahmaud-arbery-shooting-were-literally-hunted-everyday/. Accessed June 2, 2020.

60. Goldsmith, Reid. "Stephen Curry, Chris Paul, Other NBA Stars React to Ahmaud Arbery Killing." *ClutchPoints*, May 7, 2020, clutchpoints.com/nba-news-stephen-curry-chris-paul-other-nba-stars-react-to-ahmaud-arbery-killing/. Accessed August 19, 2020.

61. Boren.

62. Goldsmith.

63. "Instagram Accounts with the Most Followers Worldwide as of February 2020 (in Millions)." *Statista*, statista.com/statistics/421169/most-followers-instagram/. Accessed August 18, 2020.

64. "Twitter Accounts with the Most Followers Worldwide as of May 2020 (in Millions)." *Statista,* statista.com/statistics/273172/twitter-accounts-with-the-most-followers-worldwide. Accessed August 18, 2020.

65. "Number of Monthly Active Facebook Users Worldwide as of 2nd Quarter 2020 (in Millions)." *Statista,* statista.com/statistics/264810/number-of-monthly-active-facebook-users-worldwide/. Accessed August 18, 2020.

66. "Most Popular Facebook Fan Pages as of June 2020, Based on Number of Fans (in Millions)." *Statista*, statista.com/statistics/269304/international-brands-on-facebook-by-number-of-fans/. Accessed August 18, 2020.

67. Couldry, Nick, and Tim Markham. "Celebrity Culture and Public Connection: Bridge or Chasm?" *International Journal of Cultural Studies,* vol. 10, no. 4, 2007, pp. 403–421, doi: 10.1177/1367877907083077.

68. van Elteren, p. 266.

69. Couldry and Markham, p. 404.

70. Andrews, David L., and Steven J. Jackson. "Introduction: Sports Celebrities, Public Culture, and Private Experience." *Sports Stars: The Cultural Politics of Sporting Celebrity*, edited by David L. Andrews and Steven J. Jackson. Routledge, 2001, p. 8.

71. Couldry and Markham, p. 405.

72. Marshall, P. David. *Celebrity and Power: Fame in Contemporary Culture.* 1997. University of Minnesota Press, 2014, p. xlviii.

73. Wyatt, Wendy N., and Kristie Bunton. "The Ethics of Speaking Out." *Ethics in Entertainment: Essays on Media Culture and Media Morality,* edited by Howard Good and Sandra L. Borden. McFarland, 2010, pp. 9–22.

74. May, William F. *Beleaguered Rulers: The Public Obligation of the Professional.* Westminster John Knox Press, 2001, p. 193.

75. Couldry and Markham, p. 404.

76. Wanshel, Elyse. "John Legend Becomes First Black Man to Reach EGOT Status." *HuffPost*, September 10, 2018, huffpost.com/entry/john-legend-first-black-man-with-egot_n_5b9693fce4b0511db3e4ce6d. Accessed August 18, 2020.

77. Cheong, Wayne. "A Special Interview and Shoot with John Legend in These COVID Times." *Esquire,* June 19, 2020, esquiresg.com/features/john-legend-interview-chrissy-teigen-lockdown-a-special-interview-and-shoot-in-these-covid-times/. Accessed August 18, 2020.

78. Harrington, Jim. "Should Artists Speak Out on Politics? John Legend Weighs In on Subject." *Marin Independent Journal,* July 14, 2020. marinij.com/2020/07/14/should-artists-speak-out-on-politics-john-legend-weighs-in-on-subject/. Accessed July 15, 2020.

Chapter 2

1. Curry, Stephen. "Underrated." *The Players Tribune*, January 2, 2019, theplayerstribune.com/en-us/articles/stephen-curry-underrated. Accessed February 25, 2019.

2. Curry.

3. Kroichick, Ron. "Stephen Curry at 30: From Baby-Faced Warriors Guard to Basketball Revolutionary and Beyond." *San Francisco Chronicle*, March 8, 2018, sfchronicle.com/warriors/article/Stephen-Curry-at-30-From-baby-faced-Warriors-12736239.php. Accessed February 23, 2019.

4. Kroichick.

5. "Warriors' Stephen Curry Wins 2015–16 Kia NBA Most Valuable Player Award." *NBA Communications*, May 10, 2016, pr.nba.com/stephen-curry-2015-16-kia-nba-mvp-award-warriors/. Accessed February 23, 2019.

6. "NBA MVP Award Winners." *NBA. com,* nba.com/history/awards/mvp. Accessed February 23, 2019.

7. Golliver, Ben. "Grades: Warriors

Lavish Stephen Curry with Record-Setting $201 Million Max Deal." *Sports Illustrated*, June 30, 2017, si.com/nba/2017/07/01/warriors-stephen-curry-contract-nba-free-agency-signing-kevin-durant. Accessed February 23, 2019.

8. Shekhar, Rishabh. "NBA: 10 Most Popular Current Players on Social Media." *Sportskeeda*, December 20, 2019, sportskeeda.com/basketball/10-most-popular-current-players-on-social-media/5. Accessed March 3, 2020.

9. @StephenCurry30. "Twitter Profile: @StephenCurry30." *Twitter*, mobile.twitter.com/stephencurry30. Accessed February 22, 2019.

10. Shipnuck, Alan. "Exclusive: Stephen Curry and Wife Ayesha on Marriage, Kids and Their Matching Tattoos." *Parents*, June 2016, parents.com/parenting/celebrity-parents-moms-dads/exclusive-stephen-curry-and-wife-ayesha-on-marriage-kids-and/. Accessed February 23, 2019.

11. Barker, Jeff. "Under Armour Has Stories to Tell about Its Celebrity Athletes." *Baltimore Sun*, November 13, 2015, baltimoresun.com/business/bs-by/under-armour-athletes-20151113-story.html. Accessed February 23, 2019.

12. Barker.

13. DePaula, Nick. "Decoding the Sneaker Scribbles of NBA Stars." *ESPN*, March 22, 2018, espn.com/nba/story/_/id/22835960/decoding-sneaker-scribbles-nba-stars. Accessed February 23, 2019.

14. DePaula.

15. Bontemps, Tim. "Stephen Curry Has Long Been Reluctant to Speak Out. Then Along Came Donald Trump." *The Washington Post*, September 22, 2017, washingtonpost.com/news/sports/wp/2017/09/22/stephen-curry-has-long-been-reluctant-to-speak-out-then-along-came-donald-trump/. Accessed February 23, 2019.

16. Thompson, Marcus. "Warriors' Stephen Curry Talks North Carolina Transgender Law, But He Answered Already without Words." *Mercury News*, April 5, 2016, blogs.mercurynews.com/thompson/2016/04/05/warriors-stephen-curry-talks-north-carolina-transgender-law-answered-already-without-words/. Accessed February 23, 2019.

17. Simmons, Rusty. "Curry's Good Deeds Earn Visit with President Obama." *SFGate*, February 25, 2015, sfgate.com/warriors/article/Curry-meets-Obama-tours-White-House-6101475.php. Accessed February 23, 2019.

18. "What Is Malaria?" *Nothing But Nets*, nothingbutnets.net/about-malaria/. Accessed February 23, 2019.

19. "Ambassadors: Stephen Curry," *Nothing But Nets*, nothingbutnets.net/about/. Accessed February 23, 2019.

20. "Why Stephen Curry's Latest Shoe Release Is Designed to Save Souls." *Nothing But Nets*, December 27, 2017, nothingbutnets.net/press-releases/stephen-curry-latest-shoe-release-is-designed-save-souls. Accessed February 23, 2019.

21. Becker, Jon. "Is Steph Curry the Most Likable Star in Bay Area Sports History?" *The Mercury News*, March 15, 2018, mercurynews.com/2018/03/15/is-steph-curry-the-most-likable-star-in-bay-area-pro-sports-history-2/. Accessed February 23, 2019.

22. Glidden, Paige. "3 Facts About Steph Curry After His 3rd Championship Win." *Nothing But Nets*, June 12, 2018, nothingbutnets.net/press-release/3-facts-about-steph-curry. Accessed February 23, 2019.

23. Glidden.

24. Simmons.

25. Letourneau, Connor. "Stephen Curry, Barack Obama Discuss Trials of Their Youth at Oakland Event." *San Francisco Chronicle*, February 19, 2019, sfchronicle.com/warriors/article/Stephen-Curry-Barack-Obama-discuss-trials-of-13629222.php. Accessed February 23, 2019.

26. Martin, Nick. "President Obama Helps Curry Out with His Jumpshot in 'The Mentorship.'" *The Washington Post*, April 16, 2016 washingtonpost.com/news/early-lead/wp/2016/04/16/president-obama-helps-curry-out-with-his-jumpshot-in-the-mentorship/?utm_term=.30c4b2f88e65. Accessed February 28, 2019.

27. Martin.

28. "Remarks by the President at Visit of the 2015 NBA Champion Golden State Warriors." *White House Office of the Press Secretary*, February 4, 2016, obamawhitehouse.archives.gov/the-press-office/2016/02/04/remarks-president-visit. Accessed March 2, 2019.

29. Nakamura, David, and Cindy Boren. "Warriors Visit White House to See Steph Curry's Friend President Obama." *The Washington Post*, February 4, 2016, washingtonpost.com/news/early-lead/wp/2016/02/04/watch-live-as-warriors-visit-white-house-a-place-stephen-curry-knows-well/. Accessed February 23, 2019.

30. Disbrow, Bill. "Warriors MVP Stephen Curry Says He'll Take Clinton over Trump." *SFGate*, September 14, 2016, sfgate.com/politics/article/Warriors-MVP-Stephen-Curry-says-he-ll-take-9222970.php. Accessed March 2, 2019.

31. Disbrow.

32. Andrews, Travis M. "'How Do I Explain This to My Children?': Van Jones Gives Voice to the 'Nightmare' Some Are Feeling." *The Washington Post*, November 9, 2016, washingtonpost.com/news/morning-mix/wp/2016/11/09/how-do-i-explain-this. Accessed March 3, 2019.

33. Dowd, Katie. "After Years of Silence, Steph Curry Is Finally Getting Political." *SFGate*, November 9, 2016, sfgate.com/elections/article/After-years-of-silence-Steph-Curry-gets-political-10604186.php. Accessed February 22, 2019.

34. Zillgitt, Jeff. "Openly Gay NBA Executive Decides to Participate in All-Star Weekend in Charlotte." *USA Today*, February 17, 2019, usatoday.com/story/sports/nba/allstar/2019/02/17/openly-gay-nba-executive-attend-all-star-weekend-charlotte/2898930002/. Accessed February 23, 2019.

35. Zillgitt.

36. Associated Press. "Steph Curry Hopes for Changes to LGBT Law in North Carolina." *USA Today*, September 15, 2016, usatoday.com/story/sports/nba/2016/09/15/steph-curry-hopes-for-changes-to-lgbt-law-in-north-carolina/90438676/. Accessed February 23, 2019.

37. Associated Press. "Steph Curry Hopes for Changes to LGBT Law in North Carolina."

38. Associated Press. "Steph Curry Hopes for Changes to LGBT Law in North Carolina."

39. Aliko, Carter. "Stephen Curry Church Realization Should Signal Public Endorsement of LGBT Rights." *Forbes*, March 31, 2016, forbes.com/sites/alikocarter/2016/03/31/stephen-curry-church-realization-should-signal-public-endorsement-of-lgbt-rights/#6a43084419b0. Accessed February 23, 2019.

40. Carter.

41. Heath, Thomas. "Under Armour, Stephen Curry and the Risk of Celebrity Endorsements." *The Washington Post*, February 13, 2017, washingtonpost.com/business/economy/under-armour-steph-curry-and-the-risk-of-celebrity-endorsements/2017/02/13/d418dbea-f208-11e6-b9c9-e83fce42fb61_story.html. Accessed March 2, 2019.

42. Heath.

43. Heath.

44. Heath.

45. Bontemps. "Stephen Curry Has Long Been Reluctant to Speak Out. Then Along Came Donald Trump."

46. Thrush, Glenn. "New Outcry as Trump Rebukes Charlottesville Racists 2 Days Later." *The New York Times*, August 14, 2017, nytimes.com/2017/08/14/us/politics/trump-charlottesville-protest.html. Accessed March 5, 2019.

47. Associated Press. "Steph Curry Doesn't Want to Visit the White House, and Trump, in a Tweet, Withdraws the Invitation." *Los Angeles Times*, September 23, 2017 latimes.com/sports/sportsnow/la-sp-curry-trump-20170923-story.html. Accessed March 5, 2019.

48. Associated Press. "Steph Curry Doesn't Want to Visit the White House, and Trump, in a Tweet, Withdraws the Invitation."

49. Bontemps. "Stephen Curry Has Long Been Reluctant to Speak Out. Then Along Came Donald Trump."

50. Associated Press. "Steph Curry Doesn't Want to Visit the White House, and Trump, in a Tweet, Withdraws the Invitation."

51. Medina, Mark. "Stephen Curry's Mother Proud of How He Has Handled White House Controversy." *The Mercury News*, October 12, 2017, mercurynews.com/2017/10/12/stephen-currys-mother-proud-of-how-he-has-handled-white-house-controversy/. Accessed February 23, 2019.

52. Bontemps, Tim. "'It's Surreal, to Be Honest,' Stephen Curry Says of President Trump Uninviting Warriors to the White House." *The Washington Post*, September 23, 2017, washingtonpost.com/news/

sports/wp/2017/09/23/stephen-curry-steve-kerr-and-the-warriors-respond-to-president-trump/. Accessed February 22, 2019.

53. Medina.

54. Medina.

55. Hoffman, Benjamin. "LeBron James and Stephen Curry Unite Against White House Visits." *The New York Times,* June 5, 2018, nytimes.com/2018/06/05/sports/lebron-james-stephen-curry-trump.html. Accessed March 9, 2019.

56. Bontemps. "It's Surreal, to Be Honest,' Stephen Curry Says of President Trump Uninviting Warriors to the White House."

57. Bontemps. "It's Surreal, to Be Honest,' Stephen Curry Says of President Trump Uninviting Warriors to the White House."

58. Bonesteel, Matt. "Warriors Skip the White House, Meet with Former President Barack Obama Instead." *The Washington Post,* January 25, 2019, washingtonpost.com/sports/2019/01/25/warriors-skip-white-house-meet-with-former-president-barack-obama-instead/. Accessed March 9, 2019.

59. Strauss, Ben. "'This Era of Athlete Is Unafraid': Stephen Curry Speaks Up in D.C., Again without White House Trip." *The Washington Post,* January 24, 2019, washingtonpost.com/sports/2019/01/24/this-era-athlete-is-unafraid-stephen-curry-speaks-up-dc-again-without-white-house-trip/. Accessed February 22, 2019.

60. Strauss.

61. Strauss.

62. Strauss.

63. Plaisance, Patrick Lee. *Media Ethics: Key Principles for Responsible Practice.* Sage, 2009, p. 3.

Chapter 3

1. Wootson, Cleve R., Jr. "Stephen Curry Says the U.S. Never Landed on the Moon. NASA Cries Foul." *The Washington Post,* December 11, 2018, washingtonpost.com/sports/2018/12/11/stephen-curry-says-us-never-landed-moon-nasa-cries-foul/. Accessed February 22, 2019.

2. Friedell, Nick. "Stephen Curry Never Lost Sight of His Charlotte Roots." *ESPN,* February 25, 2019, espn.com/nba/story/_/id/26057432/stephen-curry-never-lost-sight-charlotte-roots. Accessed March 16, 2019.

3. Curry, Stephen. "The Noise," *The Players' Tribune,* November 11, 2017, the playerstribune.com/en-us/articles/stephen-curry-veterans-day. Accessed February 22, 2019.

4. Wootson Jr.

5. *New York Times Co. v. Sullivan,* 376 U.S. 254 (1964).

6. Lawrence, Andrew. "Fake Moon Landings and a Flat Earth: Why Do Athletes Love Conspiracy Theories?" *The Guardian,* December 27, 2018, theguardian.com/sport/2018/dec/27/stephen-curry-kyrie-irving-conspiracy-theories-nba. Accessed March 16, 2019.

7. Bogage, Jacob. "Steph Curry Says He Was Joking about Not Believing in the Moon Landing and Everything Is Fine." *The Washington Post,* December 12, 2018, washingtonpost.com/sports/2018/12/12/steph-curry-says-he-was-joking-about-not-believing-moon-landing-everything-is-fine/. Accessed March 16, 2019.

8. Hoffman, Benjamin. "Stephen Curry Doubts Moon Landings. NASA Offers to Show Him the Rocks." *The New York Times,* December 10, 2018, nytimes.com/2018/12/10/sports/stephen-curry-moon-landing.html. Accessed February 22, 2019.

9. Lawrence.

10. Wootson Jr.

11. Bogage, "Steph Curry Says He Was Joking about Not Believing in the Moon Landing and Everything Is Fine."

12. Davis, Scott. "ESPN's Michael Wilbon and Tony Kornheiser Blast Stephen Curry for Saying the Moon Landing Was Fake: 'Does That Mean You Don't Believe in Slavery?'" *Business Insider,* December 12, 2018. businessinsider.com/steph-curry-moon-landing-comments-blasted-espn-pardon-the-interruption-2018–12. Accessed February 22, 2019.

13. Davis.

14. Russell, Jake. "Kyrie Irving Believes the Earth Is Flat. It Is Not." *The Washington Post,* February 17, 2017, washingtonpost.com/news/early-lead/wp/2017/02/17/kyrie-irving-believes-the-earth-is-flat-it-is-not/?smid=nytcore-ios-share. Accessed March 23, 2019.

15. Joseph, Andrew. "Kyrie Irving Apologized for Saying Earth Is Flat." *USA*

Today, October 1, 2018, usatoday.com/
story/sports/ftw/2018/10/01/kyrie-irving-
apologized-for-saying-the-earth-is-flat-
i-was-huge-into-conspiracies/38012367/.
Accessed March 23, 2019.

16. Bieler, Des. "Kyrie Irving Sorry for
Saying Earth Is Flat, Blames it on a You-
Tube 'Rabbit Hole.'" *The Washington Post*,
October 1, 2018, washingtonpost.com/
sports/2018/10/02/kyrie-irving-sorry-
saying-earth-is-flat-blames-it-youtube-
rabbit-hole/?noredirect=on. Accessed
March 23, 2019.

17. Bogage, Jacob. "Stephen Curry, Now
Very Sure of the Moon Landing, Interviews
Astronaut Scott Kelly." *The Washington
Post*, December 15, 2018, washingtonpost.
com/sports/2018/12/15/stephen-curry-
now-very-sure-moon-landing-interviews-
astronaut-scott-kelly/. Accessed March 16,
2019.

18. Joseph, Andrew. "How the Science
Community Reacted to Steph Curry's
Moon-Landing Conspiracy." *USA Today*,
December 11, 2018 ftw.usatoday.com/
2018/12012/stephen-curry-moon-landin
g-fake-conspiracy-nasa-scien. Accessed
March 25, 2019.

19. Joseph. "How the Science Community Reacted to Steph Curry's Moon-
Landing Conspiracy."

20. Joseph. "How the Science Community Reacted to Steph Curry's Moon-
Landing Conspiracy."

21. Lawrence.

22. May, William F. *Beleaguered Rulers:
The Public Obligation of the Professional.*
Westminster John Knox Press, p. 193.

23. May, p. 196.

24. Hoffman.

25. "NASA Head Claps Back at Steph
Curry, We Went to Moon Six Times!"
TMZSports, December 11, 2018, tmz.
com/2018/12/11/jim-bridenstine-nasa-
steph-curry-moon-landing-nba. Accessed
March 25, 2019.

26. Jaramillo, Antonia. "NASA, Boeing
and Others Pounce on Stephen Curry after
He Said Moon Landing Was a Hoax." *Florida Today*, December 12, 2018, floridatoday.
com/story/tech/science/space/2018/12/12/
nasa-boeing-and-others-pounce-step.
Accessed March 25, 2019.

27. Bogage. "Stephen Curry, Now Very
Sure of the Moon Landing, Interviews
Astronaut Scott Kelly."

28. Wall, Mike. "Steph Curry Tells Former Astronaut Scott Kelly Moon-Landing
Comment Was 'Made in Jest.'" *Space*,
December 17, 2018, space.com/42763-
steph-curry-moon-landing-scott-kelly.
html. Accessed March 16, 2019.

29. Bogage. "Stephen Curry, Now Very
Sure of the Moon Landing, Interviews
Astronaut Scott Kelly."

30. Bogage. "Stephen Curry, Now Very
Sure of the Moon Landing, Interviews
Astronaut Scott Kelly."

31. Bogage. "Stephen Curry, Now Very
Sure of the Moon Landing, Interviews
Astronaut Scott Kelly."

32. Wolfman-Arent, Avi. "The Ongoing Battle between Science Teachers and Fake News." National Public
Radio, July 28, 2017, npr.org/sections/
ed/2017/07/28/537907951/the-ongoing-
battle-between-science-teachers-and-fake-
news?smid=nytcore-ios-share. Accessed
March 23, 2019.

33. Tavag, Yasmin. "Steph Curry Called
Out by Educators for Spreading Moon
Landing Conspiracy." *Inverse*, December
11, 2018, inverse.com/article/51671-steph-
curry-the-moon-landing-is-real. Accessed
March 25, 2019.

34. Lawrence.

35. Friedell, Nick. "Warriors' Stephen
Curry Says He Was Joking About Moon
Landing, Will Visit NASA." *ESPN*, December 18, 2018 espn.com/nba/story/_/id/
25518468/stephen-curry-golden-state-war
riors-says-joking-moon-landing-accept-na
sa-invitation. Accessed March 16, 2019.

36. Friedell. "Warriors' Stephen Curry
Says He Was Joking About Moon Landing,
Will Visit NASA."

37. The Observer Editorial Board,
"Did Stephen Curry Really Say the Moon
Landings Were Fake? We Hope Not." *The
Charlotte Observer*, December 10, 2018,
charlotteobserver.com/opinion/arti-
cle222902600.html. Accessed March 31,
2019.

38. Bunnin, Nicholas, and Jiyuan Yu.
*The Blackwell Dictionary of Western Philos-
ophy*. John Wiley & Sons, 2004, p. 443.

39. Bok, Sissela Bok. *Lying: Moral Choice
in Public and Private Life*. Vintage Books,
1989, p. 91.

40. Wyatt, Wendy N., and Kristie Bunton. "The Ethics of Speaking Out." *Ethics in
Entertainment: Essays on Media Culture and*

Media Morality, edited by Howard Good and Sandra L. Borden. McFarland, 2010, p. 15.

41. Sprung, Schlomo. "Vince Carter, Kent Bazemore Discuss Winging It Podcast, Steph Curry Moon Landing Incident." *Forbes,* January 25, 2019, forbes.com/sites/shlomosprung/2019/01/25/vince-carter-kent-bazemore-discuss-popular-winging-it-podcast-steph-curry-moon-landing-incident/#20339e0d20a3. Accessed March 25, 2019.

42. McIntyre, Lee. *Post-Truth.* The MIT Press, 2018, p. 7.

43. McIntyre, p. 8.

44. McIntyre, p. 13.

45. McIntyre, p. 15.

46. Usher, Nikki, and Janel S. Schuh. "'I'm Sorry, oh, So Sorry': Celebrity Apologies and Public Ethics." *Ethics in Entertainment: Essays on Media Culture and Media Morality,* edited by Howard Good and Sandra L. Borden. McFarland, 2010, p. 26.

47. Hearit, Keith, and Sandra Borden. "Apologetic Ethics." *Crisis Management by Apology: Corporate Response to Allegations of Wrongdoing,* edited by Keith Hearit. Lawrence Earlbaum, 2006, pp. 58–78.

48. Bunnin and Yu.

49. Friedell. "Warriors' Stephen Curry Says He Was Joking About Moon Landing, Will Visit NASA."

50. Kleinschmidt, Jessica. "Warriors' Stephen Curry 'Moon Landing' Shoes Auctioned Off for $58,000." *NBC Sports,* January 14, 2019, nbcsports.com/bayarea/warriors/warriors-stephen-curry-moon-landing-shoes-auctioned-58000. Accessed March 31, 2019.

51. Medina, Mark. "Opinion: Stephen Curry's Coronavirus Interview with Dr. Anthony Fauci Is Most Significant Move of His Career." *USA Today,* March 26, 2020, usatoday.com/story/sports/nba/columnist/mark-Medina/2020/02/36/stephen-curry-coronavirus-interview-anthony-fauci-most-significant-move/2922652001/. Accessed July 4, 2020.

52. Taylor, Derrick Bryson. "A Timeline of the Coronavirus Pandemic." *The New York Times,* August 6, 2020, nytimes.com/article/coronavirus-timeline.html. Accessed August 20, 2020.

53. Curry, Stephen. "Stephen Curry: Small Gestures Can Make All the Difference in Times of Crisis." *Time,* April 16, 2020,
https://time.com/collection/finding-hope-coronavirus-pandemic/5820660/steph-curry-helping-coronavirus/. Accessed July 4, 2020.

54. Curry. "Stephen Curry: Small Gestures Can Make All the Difference in Times of Crisis."

55. Curry. "Stephen Curry: Small Gestures Can Make All the Difference in Times of Crisis."

56. Wallace, Ava. "Stephen Curry and Anthony Fauci Chatted on Instagram. Thousands Watched, Including Barack Obama." *The Washington Post,* March 26, 2020, washingtonpost.com/sports/2020/03/26/stephen-curry-anthony-fauci-chatted-instagram-thousands-watched-including-barack-obama/. Accessed July 4, 2020.

57. Medina.

58. Medina.

59. Medina.

60. Wong, Wilson. "Latest to Interview Fauci on Coronavirus? NBA's Steph Curry, on Instagram." NBC News, March 26, 2020, nbcnews.com/news/nbcblk/latest-interview-fauci-coronavirus-nba-s-steph-curry-instagram-n1169746. Accessed June 2, 2020.

61. Curry. "Stephen Curry: Small Gestures Can Make All the Difference in Times of Crisis."

Chapter 4

1. Moore, Mark. "Read Jon Stewart's Full Testimony Supporting the 9/11 Victims Fund." *New York Post,* June 12, 2019, nypost.com/2019/06/12/read-jon-stewarts-full-testimony-supporting-the-9-11-victims-fund/. Accessed June 29, 2019.

2. Kilby, Allaina. "Jon Stewart: Journey from Satirist to Political Advocate Is No Laughing Matter." *The Conversation,* June 14, 2019, theconversation.com/jon-stewart-journey-from-satirist-to-political-advocate-is-no-laughing-matter-118784. Accessed June 22, 2019.

3. Serfaty, Sunlen, and Paul LeBlanc. "'We Pay for That Shit': 9/11 First Responder Goes Off on Congress after McConnell Commits to Vote on Victims Fund Extension." *CNN,* June 25, 2019, cnn.com/2019/06/25/politics/mitch-mcconnell-first-responders-meeting/index.html. Accessed June 27, 2019.

4. Compton, Josh. "Introduction:

Surveying Scholarship on The Daily Show and The Colbert Report." *The Stewart/Colbert Effect: Essays on the Real Impacts of Fake News,* edited by Amarnath Amarasingam. McFarland, 2011, p. 9.

5. Dowd, Maureen. "Jon Stewart and Stephen Colbert: America's Anchors." *Rolling Stone,* November 16, 2006, rollingstone.com/tv/tv-news/jon-stewart-and-stephen-colbert-americas-anchors-247689/. Accessed June 22, 2019.

6. Kakutani, Michiko. "Is Jon Stewart the Most Trusted Man in America?" *The New York Times,* August 15, 2008, nytimes.com/2008/08/17/arts/television/17kaku.html. Accessed June 22, 2019.

7. Kakutani.

8. Dowd.

9. Bunnin, Nicholas, and Jiyuan Yu. *The Blackwell Dictionary of Western Philosophy.* John Wiley & Sons, 2004, p. 612.

10. Bunnin and Yu, p. 612.

11. Bunnin and Yu, p. 443.

12. Blakemore, Erin. "9/11 Memorial Glade: A Monument to Responders, Survivors Who Paid for the Attacks with Their Health." *The Washington Post,* June 8, 2019, washingtonpost.com/health/911-memorial-glade-a-monument-to-responders-survivors-who-paid-for-the-attacks-with-their-health/2019/06/07/7f411d66-87b7-11e9-a870-b9c411dc4312_story.html?utm_term=.2db56a9ae945. Accessed June 16, 2019.

13. Barrett, Devlin. "After Emotional Testimony from 9/11 Responders, House Panel Votes to Replenish Victims Fund." *The Washington Post,* June 12, 2019, washingtonpost.com/world/national-security/after-emotional-testimony-from-911-responders-house-panel-votes-to-replenish-victim-fund/2019/06/12/826ffa1e-8d27-11e9-8f69-a2795fca3343_story.html?utm_term=.4669d265c146. Accessed June 16, 2019.

14. Bunnin and Yu, p. 444.

15. Wyatt, Wendy N., and Kristie Bunton. "The Ethics of Speaking Out." *Ethics in Entertainment: Essays on Media Culture and Media Morality,* edited by Howard Good and Sandra L. Borden. McFarland, 2010, p. 15.

16. Wyatt and Bunton, p. 15.

17. Smith, Chris. *The Daily Show (The Book): An Oral History.* Grand Central Publishing, 2016, p. 69.

18. Smith, p. 71.

19. Smith, p. 72.

20. Smith, pp. 72–74.

21. Smith, p. 75.

22. Smith, p. 76.

23. Berenson, Tessa. "Watch Jon Stewart's 5 Greatest Daily Show Moments." *Time,* August 4, 2015, time.com/3704285/the-daily-show-finale-jon-stewart-best-moments/; Egner, Jeremy. "Jon Stewart's Notable Moments on 'The Daily Show.'" *The New York Times,* February 11, 2015 artsbeat.blogs.nytimes.com/2015/02/11/jon-stewarts-notable-moments-on-the-daily-show/; Heritage, Stuart. "Jon Stewart's 10 Best Moments." *The Guardian,* February 11, 2015, theguardian.com/tv-and-radio/2015/feb/11/jon-stewarts-10-best-moments; VanMetre, Elizabeth. "Jon Stewart's Most Memorable Moments on 'The Daily Show.'" *New York Daily News,* Feb. 10, 2015, nydailynews.com/entertainment/tv/jon-stewart-top-10-daily-show-moments-article-1.2110423. Accessed June 29, 2019.

24. Smith, p. 76.

25. Smith, p. 77.

26. Stelter, Brian. "Jon Stewart, the Advocate, on the 9/11 Health Bill." *The New York Times,* December 17, 2010, mediadecoder.blogs.nytimes.com. Accessed June 16, 2019.

27. Smith, p. 275.

28. Stelter.

29. Stelter.

30. Associated Press. "Obama Signs Sept. 11 First Responders Bill." *NBC News,* January 2, 2011, nbcnews.com/id/40879753/ns/politics-white-house/t/obama-signs-sept-first-responders-bill/#.XRkM-0MpOmhA. Accessed June 30, 2019.

31. Adams, Guy. "The Serious Side of Jon Stewart: The Man Who Is Famous for Lampooning Politicians Is Now Forging a Reputation as a Political Campaigner Himself." *The Independent,* December 30, 2010, independent.co.uk/news/people/news/the-serious-side-of-jon-stewart-2171794.html. Accessed June 22, 2019.

32. Carter, Bill, and Brian Stelter. "In 'Daily Show' Role on 9/11 Bill, Echoes of Murrow." *The New York Times,* December 26, 2010, nytimes.com/2010/12/27/business/media/27stewart.html. Accessed June 16, 2019.

33. Carter and Stelter.

34. Adams.

35. Andrews-Dyer, Helena. "'No Self-ies If You're Not on the Bill': Jon Stewart's Day on the Hill." *The Washington Post*, September 16, 2015, washingtonpost.com/news/reliable-source-wp/2015/09/16/no-selfies-if-youre-not-on-the-bill-jon-stewarts-day-on-the-hill/?utm_term=.fe9c4dcbaaeb. Accessed June 30, 2019.

36. McAuliff, Michael. "Jon Stewart and 9/11 Responders Walk the Halls of Congress." *HuffPost*, September 16, 2015, huffpost.com/entry/jon-stewart-911-responders_n_55f950bce4b0b48f67014d60. Accessed June 30, 2019.

37. Samuelsohn, Darren. "Jon Stewart's Next Act: Lobbyist?" *Politico*, July 31, 2015, politico.com/agenda/story/2015/07/jon-stewarts-next-act-lobbyist-000179. Accessed June 22, 2019.

38. Samuelsohn.

39. McAuliff.

40. Smith, p. 406.

41. Smith, p. 409.

42. Butler, Bethonie. "Jon Stewart's 'Daily Show' Changed How We Consume News. His Political Influence Still Endures." *The Washington Post*, June 19, 2019, washingtonpost.com/arts-entertainment/2019/06/19/jon-stewarts-daily-show-changed-how-we-consume-news-his-political-influence-still-endures/?utem_term=.e2d27a4cd5e9. Accessed June 20, 2019.

43. Pallotta, Frank. "Stephen Colbert 'Trumps Up' Jon Stewart on 'Late Show.'" *CNN Money*, December 11, 2015, money.cnn.com/2014/12/11/media/stephen-colbert-jon-stewart-donald-trump/index.html. Accessed July 1, 2019.

44. Smith, p. 411.

45. Smith, p. 411.

46. Smith, p. 411.

47. Rogak, Lisa. *Angry Optimist: The Life and Times of Jon Stewart*. Thomas Dunne Books, 2015, p. 113.

48. Boyle, Brian. "Jon Stewart Just Reminded Us How Outrage Is Supposed to Work." *Los Angeles Times*, June 11, 2019, latimes.com/opinion/enterthefray/la-ol-jon-stewart-911-outrage-congress-20190611-story.html. Accessed June 21, 2019.

49. Boyle.

50. Sonmez, Felicia. "McConnell: I Don't Know Why Jon Stewart Is 'All Bent Out of Shape' on 9/11 Victims Fund." *The Washington Post*, June 14, 2019, washingtonpost.com/politics/mcconnell-i-dont-know-why-jon-stewart-is-all-bent-out-of-shape-on-911-victims-fund/2019/06/17/193143bc-913e-11e9-b570-6416efdc0803_story.html?utm_term=.6bf06320e648. Accessed June 18, 2019.

51. Chiu, Allyson. "'I'm Bent Out of Shape for Them': Jon Stewart Roasts Mitch McConnell over 9/11 Victims Fund." *The Washington Post*, June 18, 2019, washingtonpost.com/nation/2019/06/18/jon-stewart-mitch-mcconnell-stephen-colbert-funding/?utm_term=.5ee6e-5a7d5e0. Accessed June 18, 2019.

52. Chiu.

53. Chiu.

54. Daugherty, Owen. "McConnell Says Senate Will Vote on 9/11 Responders Bill after Jon Stewart Criticism." *The Hill.com*, June 25, 2019, thehill.com/homenews/senate/45039-mcconnell-says-senate-will-vote-on-9-11-compensation-fund-after-criticism. Accessed June 27, 2019.

55. "House Panel Approves Funds for Sept. 11 First Responders." *National Public Radio*, June 13, 2019, npr.org/2019/06/13/732270815/house-panel-approves-funds-for-sept-11-first-responders. Accessed July 1, 2019.

56. Daugherty.

57. Bowers, Peggy. "Charles Taylor's Practical Reason." *Moral Engagement in Public Life*, edited by Sharon Bracci and Clifford Christians, Peter Lang, 2002, p. 37.

58. Bowers, p. 40.

59. Kilby.

60. McCullough, Thomas E. *The Moral Imagination and Public Life: Raising the Ethical Question*. Chatham House Publishers, Inc., 1991, p. 5.

Chapter 5

1. "Remarks by President Trump at Signing of H.R. 1327, an Act to Permanently Authorize the September 11th Victim Compensation Fund." *White House Briefings and Statements*, July 29, 2019, whitehouse.gov/briefings-statements/remarks-president-trump-signing-h-r-1327-act-permanently-authorize-september-11th-victim-compensation-fund/. Accessed July 29, 2019.

2. Hernandez, Raymond. "Senate Passes 9/11 Health Bill as Republicans Back Down." *The New York Times,* December 22, 2010, nytimes.com/2010/12/23/nyregion/23health.html. Accessed September 6, 2019.

3. Stieglitz, Brian. "Zadroga Act Renamed to Honor Pfeifer, Alvarez." *Long Island Herald,* July 12, 2019, liherald.com/stories/zadroga-act-renamed-to-honor-pfeifer-alvarez. Accessed September 6, 2019.

4. Aguilera, Jasmine, and Tara Law. "9/11 First Responder Luis Alvarez Has Died, 18 Days After Testifying Before Congress With Jon Stewart." *Time,* June 29, 2019, time.com/5613357/9-11-first-responder-luis-alvarez-dies-jon-stewart/. Accessed June 29, 2019.

5. Pierce, Charles P. "Jon Stewart's Outrage Forced Washington to Actually Do Something Good." *Esquire,* July 23, 2019, esquire.com/news-politics/politics/a28485934/9-11-first-responders-bill-jon-stewart-rand-paul/. Accessed Aug. 2, 2019.

6. Salant, Jonathan D. "Trump Signs 9/11 First Responders Bill Championed by Jon Stewart." *NJ.com,* July 29, 2019, nj.com/politics/2019/07/trump-signs-911-first-responders-bill-championed-by-jon-stewart.html. Accessed July 29, 2019.

7. Jackson, Hallie. "'This One's for Them': 9/11 First Responder Dedicates Funding Bill to Memory of Those Who Died." *MSNBC,* July 29, 2019, msnbc.com/hallie-jackson/watch/-this-one-s-for-them-9-11-first-responder-dedicates-funding-bill-to-memory-of-those-who-died-64800837639. Accessed July 29, 2019.

8. Edelman, Adam. "Trump Signs Bill Ensuring 9/11 Victims Fund Will Never Run Out of Money." *NBC News,* July 29, 2019, nbcnews.com/politics/white-house/trump-signs-bill-ensuring-9-11-victims-fund-will-never-n1035656. Accessed July 29, 2019. McGraw, Meridith. "Trump Signs 9/11 Victim Compensation Fund Bill for First Responders." *ABC News,* July 29, 2019, abcnews.go.com/Politics/trump-signs-911-victim-compensation-fund-bill-responders/story?id=64630468. Accessed July 29, 2019.

9. Wyatt, Wendy N., and Kristie Bunton. "The Ethics of Speaking Out." *Ethics in Entertainment: Essays on Media Culture and Media Morality,* edited by Howard Good and Sandra L. Borden. McFarland, 2010, p. 15.

10. Becker, Lawrence C., and Charlotte B. Becker, editors. *Encyclopedia of Ethics.* Garland Publishing, 2nd ed., 2001, p. 1185.

11. Kant, Immanuel. *Groundwork on the Metaphysic of Morals.* Translated by H.J. Patton. Harper Torchbooks, 1964, p. 62.

12. Kant, p. 61.

13. Kant, p. 62.

14. Becker and Becker, p. 1186.

15. Hyde, Marina. *Celebrity: How Entertainers Took Over the World and Why We Need an Exit Strategy.* Vintage Books, 2010, p. 94.

16. Rabidoux, Greg R. *Hollywood Politicos, Then and Now: Who They Are, What They Want, Why It Matters.* University Press of America, 2009, p. 78.

17. Nichols, Tom. *The Death of Expertise: The Campaign Against Established Knowledge and Why It Matters.* Oxford University Press, 2017, p. 3.

18. Nichols, p. 189.

19. Nichols, p. 190.

20. boyd, danah. *It's Complicated: The Social Lives of Networked Teens.* Yale University Press, 2014, p. 149.

21. Bird, Frederick Bruce. *The Muted Conscience: Moral Silence and the Practice of Ethics in Business.* Quorum Books, 1996, p. 4.

22. Bird, pp. 1–4.

23. Drumwright, Minette E., and Patrick E. Murphy. "How Advertising Practitioners View Ethics: Moral Muteness, Moral Myopia, and Moral Imagination." *Journal of Advertising,* vol. 33, no. 2, 2004, pp. 7–24, doi: 10.1080/00913367.2004.10639158.

24. Kidder, Rushworth M. *How Good People Make Tough Choices: Resolving the Dilemmas of Ethical Living.* HarperCollins, 2003, p. 48.

25. Bok, Sissela. *Lying: Moral Choice in Public and Private Life.* Vintage Books Edition, 1989, p. 18.

26. Bok, pp. 18–19.

27. Gert, Bernard. *Common Morality: Deciding What to Do.* Oxford University Press, 2007, p. 133.

28. Gert, pp. 20–53.

29. Gert, p. 12.

30. Royce, Josiah. *The Philosophy of Loyalty.* Macmillan, 1914, p. 15.

31. Royce, p. 15.

32. Royce, pp. 16–17.

33. Royce, p. 17.

34. Royce, p. 19.

35. Royce, p. 20.

36. Kidder, p. 192.

37. Nichols, p. 191.

38. Editorial Board. "Give Sept. 11 Survivors the Help They Deserve." *The New York Times*, Feb. 28, 2019 nytimes.com/2019/02/28/opinion/9-11-first-responders-fund.html. Accessed June 16, 2019.

39. Flynn, Meagan. "Again, 9/11 First Responders Are Pleading with Congress to Fund Their Health Care. Again, Jon Stewart Is Joining Them." *The Washington Post*, February 26, 2019, washingtonpost.com/nation/2019/02/26/again-first-responders-are-pleading-with-congress-fund-their-health-care-again-jon-stewart-is-joining-them/?utm_term=.c9a2e1b3203d. Accessed June 16, 2019.

40. Stewart, Jon. "Jon Stewart: What 9/11 Heroes Need from Congress. Make the Victim Compensation Fund Permanent, and Fund It." *New York Daily News*, February 25, 2019, nydailynews.com/opinion/ny-oped-what-911-heroes-need-from-congress-20190222-story.html. Accessed September 6, 2019.

41. "House Panel Approves Funds for Sept. 11 First Responders." National Public Radio, June 13, 2019, npr.org/2019/06/13/732270815/house-panel-approves-funds-for-sept-11-first-responders. Accessed July 1, 2019.

42. Flynn.

43. McAuliff, Michael. "Jon Stewart Sticks By Praise for Trump Administration's Handling of 9/11 Fund." *New York Daily News*, March 3, 2019, nydailynews.com/new-york/ny-pol-stewart-trump-praise-20190303-story.html. Accessed September 10, 2019.

44. Lim, Naomi. "Jon Stewart: Trump's Justice Department 'Doing an Excellent Job' on 9/11 Fund." *Washington Examiner*, February 25, 2019, washingtonexaminer.com/news/jon-stewart-trumps-justice-department-doing-an-excellent-job-on-9-11-fund. Accessed August 30, 2019.

45. McAuliff, "Jon Stewart Sticks By Praise for Trump Administration's Handling of 9/11 Fund."

46. Pierce.

47. McAuliff, Michael. "The Inside Story of How a 9/11 First Responder Pounded McConnell into Action." *The Daily Beast*, July 23, 2019, thedailybeast.com/the-inside-story-of-how-911-first-responder-john-feal-pounded-mitch-mcconnell-into-action. Accessed September 6, 2019.

48. McAuliff, "The Inside Story of How a 9/11 First Responder Pounded McConnell into Action."

49. McAuliff, "The Inside Story of How a 9/11 First Responder Pounded McConnell into Action."

50. McAuliff, "The Inside Story of How a 9/11 First Responder Pounded McConnell into Action."

51. Gallucci, Nicole. "Watch a Tearful Jon Stewart Receive a Touching Gift from 9/11 First Responders." *Mashable*, June 14, 2019, mashable.com/video/jon-stewart-cries-september-11-first-responders-friend-bunker-coat/. Accessed September 6, 2019.

52. McAuliff, "The Inside Story of How a 9/11 First Responder Pounded McConnell into Action."

53. McAuliff, "The Inside Story of How a 9/11 First Responder Pounded McConnell into Action."

54. "House Panel Approves Funds for Sept. 11 First Responders."

55. "House Panel Approves Funds for Sept. 11 First Responders."

56. Iati, Marisa. "'You Should Be Ashamed of Yourselves': Watch Jon Stewart Tear into Congress Over 9/11 Victims Fund." *The Washington Post*, June 12, 2019, washingtonpost.com/politics/2019/06/11/jon-stewart-blasts-congress-first-responders-fund/. Accessed June 16, 2019.

57. Aguilera and Law.

58. Barrett, Devlin. "Tears, Anger at Congressional Hearing Seeking Extension of Victim Fund for 9/11 Responders." *The Washington Post*, June 11, 2019, washingtonpost.com/world/national-security/tears-anger-at-congressional-hearing-seeking-extension-of-victim-fund-for-911-responders/2019/06/11/20d7c254–8c51–11e9-adf3-f70f78c156e8_story.html. Accessed June 22, 2019.

59. Wehner, Peter. *The Death of Politics: How to Heal Our Frayed Republic After Trump*. HarperCollins, 2019, p. 104.

60. Mongolian, Lorena, and Jackie Salo. "Hundreds Pay Respects at Funeral of 9/11 Hero Luis Alvarez," *New York Post*, July 3, 2019, nypost.com/2019/03/03/

hundreds-pay-respects-at-funeral-of-9–11 hero-luis-alvarez/. Accessed July 29, 2019.

61. Chiu, Allyson. "Jon Stewart Accuses Rand Paul of 'Fiscal Responsibility Virtue Signaling' in Stalling 9/11 Victims Funding." *The Washington Post,* July 18, 2019, washingtonpost.com/nation/2019/07/18/jon-stewart-rand-paul-mike-lee-victims-fund-delay/. Accessed July 18, 2019.

62. Sonmez, Felicia. "Jon Stewart Calls Rand Paul a 'Scalawag' and 'Ragamuffin' Amid Feud over 9/11 Bill." *The Washington Post,* July 24, 2019, washingtonpost.com/politics/jon-stewart-calls-rand-paul-a-scalawag-and-ragamuffin-amid-feud-over-911-bill/2019/07/24/6f2e56e6-ae2c-11e9-bc5c-e73b603e7f38_story.html. Accessed July 24, 2019.

63. Cole, Devan. "Jon Stewart Says 9/11 First Responders Fund Is the 'Least' Lawmakers Can Do 'for the Best of Us' after Bill's Passage." *CNN Wire,* July 24, 2019, cnn.com/2019/07/24/politics/john-feal-jon-stewart-9-11-fund-cnntv/index.html. Accessed July 24, 2019.

64. Cole.

65. Kilby, Allaina. "Jon Stewart: Journey from Satirist to Political Advocate Is No Laughing Matter." *The Conversation,* June 14, 2019, theconversation.com/jon-stewart-journey-from-satirist-to-political-advocate-is-no-laughing-matter-118784. Accessed June 22, 2019.

Chapter 6

1. Culpepper, Chuck. "At the U.S. Open, Serena Williams's Story Line Eclipses All Others." *The Washington Post,* August 25, 2019, washingtonpost.com/sports/tennis/at-the-us-open-serena-williams-story-line-eclipses-all-others/2019/08/23/9333d37c-c5b5-11e9-9986-1fb3e4397be4_story.html. Accessed August 26, 2019.

2. Jenkins, Sally. "Serena Williams Finds Her Path to History Narrowing to a Tightrope." *The Washington Post,* July 13, 2019, washingtonpost.com/sports/tennis/serena-williams-finds-her-path-to-history-narrowing-to-a-tightrope/2019/07/13/c18df4ac-a5ab-11e9-b732-41a79c2551bf_story.html. Accessed July 15, 2019.

3. Williams, Serena, with Daniel Paisner. *On The Line.* Grand Central Publishing, 2009, pp. 9–14.

4. Williams, with Paisner, p. 21.

5. Thomas, Etan. *We Matter: Athletes and Activism.* Edge of Sports/Akashic Books, 2018, pp. 260–264.

6. Crouch, Ian. "Serena Williams Is America's Greatest Athlete." *The New Yorker,* September 9, 2014, newyorker.com/sports/sporting-scene/serena-williams-americas-greatest-athlete. Accessed June 22, 2019.

7. Desmond-Harris, Jenee. "Despite Decades of Racist and Sexist Attacks, Serena Williams Keeps Winning." *Vox,* January 28, 2017, vox.com/2017/1/28/14424624/serena-williams-wins-australian-open-venus-record-sexist-attacks. Accessed September 17, 2019.

8. Rankine, Claudia. "The Meaning of Serena Williams." *The New York Times,* August 25, 2015, nytimes.com/2015/08/30/magazine/the-meaning-of-serenawilliams.html. Accessed June 20, 2019.

9. Williams, Serena. "Serena Williams: I'm Going Back to Indian Wells." *Time,* February 4, 2015, time.com/3694659/serena-williams-indian-wells/. Accessed June 21, 2019.

10. Douglas, Delia D. "Venus, Serena, and the Inconspicuous Consumption of Blackness: A Commentary on Surveillance, Race Talk, and New Racism(s)." *Journal of Black Studies,* vol. 43, no. 2, 2012, pp. 127–145, doi: 10.1177/0021934711410880.

11. Williams, with Paisner, p. 156.

12. Douglas.

13. Crouch; Tignor, Steve. "The 50 Greatest Players of the Open Era (W): No. 1, Serena Williams." *Tennis,* tennis.com/pro-game/2018/03/50-greatest-players-open-era-w-no-1-serena-williams/72477/. Accessed June 22, 2019.

14. Jenkins, Sally. "Serena Williams Has Her Greatest, Most Hard-Won Title: Champion of Women." *The Washington Post,* July 14, 2018, washingtonpost.com/sports/tennis/serena-williams-has-her-greatest-most-hard-won-title-champion-of-women/2018/07/14/a14ea062-8796-11e8-8553-a3ce89036c78_story.html. Accessed June 20, 2019.

15. Jenkins, "Serena Williams Has Her Greatest, Most Hard-Won Title: Champion of Women."

16. Wyatt, Wendy N., and Kristie Bunton. "The Ethics of Speaking Out." *Ethics in Entertainment: Essays on Media Culture and*

Media Morality, edited by Howard Good and Sandra L. Borden. McFarland, 2010, p. 15.

17. Wyatt and Bunton, p. 17.

18. Gopnik, Adam. *A Thousand Small Sanities: The Moral Adventure of Liberalism.* Basic Books, 2019, p. 184.

19. Gopnik, p. 184.

20. Becker, Lawrence C., and Charlotte B. Becker, editors. *Encyclopedia of Ethics.* Garland Publishing, 1992, 2nd ed. 2001, p. 652.

21. Becker and Becker, p. 653.

22. Gert, Bernard. *Common Morality: Deciding What to Do.* Oxford University Press, 2007.

23. Becker and Becker, p. 654.

24. Gopnik, p. 185.

25. Gopnik, p. 189.

26. @serenawilliams. *Instagram.* instagram.com/serenawilliams/?hl=en. Accessed August 23, 2020.

27. @serenawilliams. *Twitter.* twitter.com/serenawilliams. Accessed August 23, 2020.

28. @SerenaWilliams. *Facebook.* facebook.com/SerenaWilliams/. Accessed August 23, 2020.

29. Harwitt, Sandra. "Serena Williams on Why Social Media Matters." *USA Today,* January 19, 2017, usatoday.com/story/sports/tennis/aus/2017/01/19/serena-williams-caroline-wozniacki-social-media/96765240/. Accessed September 12, 2019.

30. Baym, Nancy K., and danah boyd. "Socially Mediated Publicness: An Introduction." *Journal of Broadcasting & Electronic Media,* vol. 56, no. 3, 2012, pp. 320–329, doi: 10.1080/08838151.2012.075200, p. 320.

31. boyd, danah. *It's Complicated: The Social Lives of Networked Teens.* Yale University Press, 2014, p. 9.

32. Associated Press. "Serena Williams Withdraws From S.C. Event." *The Washington Post,* April 13, 2000, washingtonpost.com/archive/sports/2000/04/13/citing-flag-serena-williams-withdraws-from-sc-event/a4967b46–4831–488f-b7bb-1f870de3dd55/. Accessed September 20, 2019.

33. Williams, with Paisner, pp. 178–195.

34. Soong, Kalyn. "Here's Just How Rare Serena Williams's SI's Sportsperson of the Year Award Is." *The Washington Post,* December 14, 2015, washingtonpost.com/news/early-lead/wp/2015/12/14/heres-just-how-rare-serena-williamsssis-sportsperson-of-the-year-award-is/. Accessed June 20, 2019.

35. Stone, Christian. "Why Serena Williams Is SI's 2015 Sportsperson of the Year." *Sports Illustrated,* December 14, 2015, si.com/sportsperson/2015/12/14/why-serena-williams-is-sportsperson-of-theyear. Accessed September 16, 2019.

36. Price, S.L. "Serena Williams Is Sports Illustrated's 2015 Sportsperson of the Year." December 14, 2015, si.com/sportsperson/2015/12/14/serena-williams-si-sportsperson-year. Accessed June 21, 2019.

37. Price.

38. Desmond-Harris.

39. Williams, "Serena Williams: I'm Going Back to Indian Wells."

40. Price.

41. Price.

42. Zirin, Dave. "Serena Williams, Indian Wells and Rewriting the Future." *The Nation,* February 6, 2015, thenation.com/article/serena-williams-indian-wells and-rewriting-future/. Accessed September 20, 2019.

43. Price.

44. Price.

45. Zirin.

46. Price.

47. Stone.

48. Zirin.

49. Tognotti, Chris. "What Does 'Serena Slam' Mean? Serena Williams Just Notched Another One." *Bustle,* July 11, 2015, bustle.com/articles/96572-what-does-serena-slam-mean-serena-williams-just-notched-another-one. Accessed September 17, 2019.

50. Newman, Elizabeth. "No Room for Body Image Criticism in Serena Williams' Grand Slam Chase." *Sports Illustrated,* July 14, 2015, si.com/tennis/2015/07/14/serena-williams-body-image-wta-tennis. Accessed September 17, 2019.

51. Newman.

52. Newman.

53. Douglas, p. 129.

54. Kedmey, Dan. "J.K. Rowling Just Crafted the Perfect Response to a Serena Williams Hater." *Time,* July 11, 2015, time.com/3954611/jk-rowling-twitter-serena-williams/. Accessed September 17, 2019.

55. Kedmey.

56. Dadich, Scott. "The Battle for Equity is a WIRED Issue." *WIRED*, October 27, 2015, wired.com/2015/10/editor-letter-november-2015/. Accessed September 17, 2019.

57. Williams, Serena. "The Ball Is In Your Court," *WIRED*, November 2015, wired.com/2015/10/serena-williams-guest-editor-race-gender-equality/. Accessed September 17, 2019.

58. Williams, "The Ball Is In Your Court."

59. Stone.

60. Soong.

61. Nichols, Tom. *The Death of Expertise: The Campaign Against Established Knowledge and Why It Matters.* Oxford University Press, 2017, p. 191.

62. Feather, A.J. "Top 15 Issues That Have Americans Worried." *ABC News,* March 19, 2015, abcnews.go.com/Politics/top-15-issues-americans-worried-/story?id=29758744. Accessed September 20, 2019.

63. Feather.

64. Hayat, Tsahi, Yair Galily, and Tal Samuel-Azran. "Can Celebrity Athletes Burst the Echo Chamber Bubble? The Case of LeBron James and Lady Gaga." *International Review for the Sociology of Sport*, vol. 55, no. 7, June 2019, pp. 900–914, doi: 10.1177/1012690219855913, p. 12.

65. Nichols, p. 191.

66. Hyde, Marina. *Celebrity: How Entertainers Took Over the World and Why We Need an Exit Strategy.* Vintage Books, 2010, p. 119.

67. Boren, Cindy. "Serena Williams Reacts to Shooting of Unarmed College Football Player." *The Washington Post*, August 9, 2015, washingtonpost.com/news/early-lead/wp/2015/08/09/serena -williams-reacts-to-shooting-of-unarmed-college-football-player/. Accessed September 21, 2019.

68. Boren.

69. Bieler, Des. "'Silence Is Betrayal': Serena Williams Vows to Speak Out on Racial Injustice." *The Washington Post*, September 28, 2016, washingtonpost.com/news/early-lead/wp/2016/09/27/silence-is-betrayal-serena-williams -vows-to-speak-out-on-racial-injustice/. Accessed June 20, 2019.

70. Gibbs, Lindsay. "Serena Williams' First Tweet After Reaching Wimbledon Was On the Murder of Philando Castile."

ThinkProgress, July 7, 2016, thinkprogress.org/serena-williams-first-tweet-after-reaching-wimbledon-final-was-on-the-murder-of-philando-castile-c74b312f972.e. Accessed September 17, 2019.

71. Thomas, p. 186.

72. Yates, Clinton. "Serena Williams Breaks Her Silence: In Powerful Facebook Post, Williams Addresses Police Brutality." *The Undefeated*, September 27, 2016, theundefeated.com/whew/serena-williams-breaks-her -silence/. Accessed June 21, 2019.

73. Williams, Serena. "Today I Asked My 18 Year Old Nephew …" *Facebook,* September 27, 2016, facebook.com/SerenaWilliams/posts/10154607381941834. Accessed September 21, 2019.

74. Williams, "Today I Asked My 18 Year Old Nephew …"

75. Williams, "Today I Asked My 18 Year Old Nephew …"

76. Williams, "Today I Asked My 18 Year Old Nephew …"

77. Townes, Cecilia. "Dawn Staley, Natasha Cloud Reaction to George Floyd's Death Shows Women's Sports Link to Racial Inequality." *Forbes Sports-Money*, June 1, 2020, forbes.com/sites/ceceliatownes/2020/06/01/george-floyds-killing-has-everything-to-do-with-womens-sports/#11f1e2ca5b55. Accessed August 23, 2020.

78. Townes.

79. Proudfoot, Jenny. "Serena Williams' Heartbreaking Words on Inequality Are Going Viral." *Marie Claire*, June 5, 2020. marieclaire.co.uk/news/serena-williams-racial-injustice-message-700141. Accessed August 25, 2020.

Chapter 7

1. Kroll, Luisa, and Kerry A. Dolan. "America's Richest Self-Made Women." *Forbes*, June 4, 2019, forbes.com/self-made-women/#5677d3e16d96. Accessed June 20, 2019.

2. Badenhausen, Kurt. "Inside Serena Williams' Plan to Ace Venture Investing." *Forbes*, June 3, 2019, forbes.com/sites/kurtbadenhausen/2019/06/03/inside-serena-williams-plan-to-ace-venture-investing/#62c75d587787. Accessed June 20, 2019.

3. Cuccinello, Hayley C. "From

Taylor Swift to Katrina Lake, America's Richest Self-Made Women Under 40." *Forbes*, June 4, 2019, forbes.com/sites/hayleycuccinello/2019/06/04/from-taylor-swift-to-katrina-lake-americas-richest-self-made-women-under-40/#41f8acc5753a. Accessed June 22, 2019.

4. Badenhausen.

5. Badenhausen.

6. Wyatt, Wendy N., and Kristie Bunton. "The Ethics of Speaking Out." *Ethics in Entertainment: Essays on Media Culture and Media Morality*, edited by Howard Good and Sandra L. Borden. McFarland, 2010, p. 15.

7. Russmann, Uta, and Anne B. Lane. "Doing the Talk: Discussion, Dialogue, and Discourse in Action." *International Journal of Communication*, vol. 19, 2016, pp. 4034–4039.

8. Barthold, Lauren Swayne. "Giving Birth in the Public Square: The Political Relevance of Dialogue." *The Good Society*, vol. 26, nos. 2–3, 2017, pp. 290–304. *Project MUSE* muse.jhu.edu/article/702185, p. 292.

9. Barthold, p. 292.

10. *Abrams v. U.S.*, 250 U.S. 616 (1919).

11. Schroeder, Jared. "Toward a Discursive Marketplace of Ideas: Reimaging the Marketplace Metaphor in the Era of Social Media, Fake News, and Artificial Intelligence." *First Amendment Studies*, vol. 52, nos. 1–2, 2018, pp. 38–60, doi: 10.1080/21689725.2018.1460215.

12. Schroeder; Gordon, Jill. "John Stuart Mill and the 'Marketplace of Ideas.'" *Social Theory and Practice*, vol. 23, no. 2, Summer 1997, pp. 235–249; and Levy, Leonard W. *Emergence of a Free Press*. Oxford University Press, 1985.

13. Schroeder, p. 38.

14. Allen, Danielle. "Reconceiving Public Spheres: The Flow Dynamics Model." *From Voice to Influence: Understanding Citizenship in a Digital Age*, edited by Danielle Allen and Jennifer S. Light. University of Chicago Press, 2015, pp. 178–207.

15. Allen, Danielle, p. 183.

16. Schroeder, p. 39.

17. Gordon, p. 235.

18. Gordon, p. 240.

19. Gordon, p. 241.

20. Gordon, pp. 239–240.

21. Schroeder.

22. boyd, danah, *It's Complicated: The Social Lives of Networked Teens*. Yale University Press, 2014, p. 9.

23. Coombs, Danielle Sarver, and Simon Collister, editors. *Debates for the Digital Age: The Good, the Bad, and the Ugly of Our Online World*. Praeger, 2016, p. xi.

24. Chandler, Daniel, and Rod Munday. *A Dictionary of Social Media*. Oxford University Press, 2016, doi: 10.1093/acref/9780191803093.001.0001.

25. Kemp, Simon. "Digital 2020: Global Digital Overview." *DataReportal,* January 30, 2020, datareportal.com/reports/digital-2020-global-digital-overview. Accessed August 26, 2020.

26. Kemp, Simon. "Digital 2020: The United States of America." *DataReportal*, February 11, 2020, datareportal.com/reports/digital-2020-united-states-of-america. Accessed August 26, 2020.

27. Schroeder, Jared. "The Future of Discourse in Online Spaces." *Social Media and the Law: A Guidebook for Communication Students and Professionals*, edited by Daxton R. Stewart. Routledge, 2017, 2nd ed., p. 261.

28. Schroeder, "The Future of Discourse in Online Spaces," p. 257.

29. Schroeder, "The Future of Discourse in Online Spaces," p. 261.

30. Schroeder, "Toward a Discursive Marketplace of Ideas," p. 41.

31. Azzimonti, Marina, and Marcos Fernandes. "Social Media Networks, Fake News, and Polarization." *National Bureau of Economic Research Working Paper Series*, March 2018, nber/org/papers/w24462. Accessed September 28, 2019.

32. Schroeder, "Toward a Discursive Marketplace of Ideas," p. 41.

33. Schroeder, "Toward a Discursive Marketplace of Ideas," p. 43.

34. Tornberg, Petter. "Echo Chambers and Viral Misinformation: Modeling Fake News as Complex Contagion." *PLoS ONE*, vol. 13., no. 9, September 20, 2018, e0203956, doi.org/10.1371/journal.pone.0203958. Accessed September 28, 2019.

35. Harvey, Chelsea. "Here's How Scientific Misinformation, Such as Climate Doubt, Spreads through Social Media." *Washington Post*, January 4, 2016, washingtonpost.com/news/energy-environment/wp/2016/01/04/heres-how-scientific-misinformation-such-as-climate-doubt-spreads-through-social-media/. Accessed September 28, 2019.

36. Tornberg.

37. Chandler and Munday.

38. Spohr, Dominic. "Fake News and Ideological Polarization: Filter Bubbles and selective Exposure on Social Media." *Business Information Review*, vol. 34, no. 3, 2017, pp. 150–160, doi: 10.1177/0266382117722446, p. 150.

39. Spohr, p. 151.

40. boyd, p. 9.

41. boyd, pp. 31–33.

42. Nossel, Suzanne. *Dare to Speak: Defending Free Speech for All.* HarperCollins, 2020, p. 73.

43. Nussbaum, Martha C. *The Monarchy of Fear: A Philosopher Looks at our Political Crisis.* Simon & Schuster, 2018, pp. 48–49.

44. Nussbaum, p. 53.

45. Carter, Stephen L. *Civility: Manners, Morals, and the Etiquette of Democracy.* Basic Books, 1998, p. 195.

46. Schroeder, "Toward a Discursive Marketplace of Ideas," p. 43.

47. Schroeder, "Toward a Discursive Marketplace of Ideas," p. 47.

48. Gouinlock, James. *Excellence in Public Discourse: John Stuart Mill, John Dewey, and Social Intelligence.* Teachers College Press, 1986, p. 1.

49. Antonio, Robert J., and Douglas Kellner. "Communication, Modernity, and Democracy in Habermas and Dewey." *Symbolic Interaction*, vol. 15, no. 3, Fall 1992, pp. 277–297, doi: 10.1525/si.1992.15.3.277, p. 277.

50. Gouinlock, *Excellence in Public Discourse*, p. 68.

51. Gouinlock, *Excellence in Public Discourse*, pp. 57–62.

52. Gouinlock, *Excellence in Public Discourse*, p. 62.

53. Gouinlock, James, editor. *The Moral Writings of John Dewey.* Prometheus Books, 1994, pp. 269–270.

54. Allen, David S. "Jurgen Habermas and the Search for Democratic Principles." *Moral Engagement in Public Life,* edited by Sharon Bracci and Clifford Christians. Peter Lang, 2002, p. 117.

55. Allen, David S., p. 112.

56. Allen, David S., p. 117.

57. McCullough, Thomas E. *The Moral Imagination and Public Life: Raising the Ethical Question.* Chatham House Publishers, 1991, p. 77.

58. Geren, Peggy Ruth. "Public Discourse: Creating the Conditions for Dialogue Concerning the Common Good in a Postmodern Heterogeneous Democracy." *Studies in Philosophy and Education,* vol. 20, 2001, pp. 191–199, doi: 1023/A:10103676511519.

59. Schroeder, "Toward a Discursive Marketplace of Ideas," p. 43.

60. Allen, Danielle, pp. 203–204.

61. Dewey, John Dewey. *The Public and its Problems: An Essay in Political Inquiry.* Edited by Melvin L. Rogers. Swallow Press, 2016, p. 225.

62. Culpepper, Chuck. "Serena Williams Stands Alone Atop Modern Tennis After Winning Australian Open." *The Washington Post,* January 28, 2019, washingtonpost.com/sports/tennis/serena-williams-stands-alone-atop-modern-tennis-after-beating-sister-to-win-australian-open/2017/01/28/b4422ed4-e542-11e6-a453-19ec4b3d-09ba_story.html. Accessed October 9, 2019.

63. Associated Press. "Serena Williams Withdraws at Indian Wells and Will Lose No. 1 Ranking." *The New York* Times, March 8, 2017, nytimes.com/2017/03/08/sports/tennis/serena-williiams-indian-wells-withdrawal.html. Accessed October 14, 2019.

64. Payne, Marissa. "It's a Girl: Serena Williams Reportedly Gives Birth to Her First Child." *The Washington Post,* September 1, 2017, washingtonpost.com/news/early-lead/wp/2017/09/01/its-a-girl-serena-williams-reportedly-gives-birth-to-her-first-child/. Accessed October 9, 2019.

65. Bissinger, Buzz. "Serena Williams's Love Match." *Vanity Fair,* August 2017, vanityfair.com/style/2017/06/serena-williams-cover-story. Accessed June 22, 2019.

66. Payne.

67. Shamsian, Jacob. "Serena Williams and Her Husband Made a Video About Her Pregnancy and It'll Make You Cry." September 13, 2017, insider.com/serena-williams-baby-video-photo-alexis-olympia-ohanian-2017-9. Accessed October 12, 2019.

68. Haskell, Rob. "Serena Williams on Motherhood, Marriage, and Making Her Comeback." *Vogue,* January 2018, vogue.com/article/serena-williams-vogue-cover-interview-february-2018. Accessed June 21, 2019.

69. Williams, Serena. "Serena Williams: What My Life-Threatening Experience Taught Me About Giving Birth." *CNN.com,* February 20, 2018, cnn.com/2018/02/20/opinions/protect-mother-pregnancy-

williams-opinion-index.html. Accessed June 21, 2019.

70. Haskell.

71. Salam, Maya. "For Serena Williams, Childbirth Was a Harrowing Ordeal. She's Not Alone." *The New York Times*, January 11, 2018, nytimes.com/2018/01/11/sports/tennis/serena-williams-baby-vogue.html. Accessed June 15, 2019.

72. Philby, Charlotte. "Serena Williams and the Realities of the 'Maternal Mortality Crisis.'" *The Guardian*, February 21, 2018, theguardian.com/lifeandstyle/shortcuts/2018/feb/21/serena-williams-maternal-mortality-crisis. Accessed October 12, 2019.

73. Saraiya, Sonia. "We've Never Seen an Athlete's Story Quite Like Serena Williams's HBO Docuseries." *Vanity Fair*, May 2, 2018, vanityfair.com/hollywood/2018/05/serena-williams-hbo-review. Accessed October 13, 2019.

74. Haglage, Abby. "Serena Williams's HBO Series 'Being Serena' Is Shedding Light on the Crisis of Black Maternal Mortality." *Yahoo! Lifestyle*, May 10, 2018, yahoo.com/lifestyle/serena-williams-hbo-series-serena-shedding-light-crisis-black-maternal-mortality-110036121.html. Accessed October 13, 2019.

75. Reinstein, Julia. "Black Women Are Speaking Out After Serena Williams Revealed She Faced Life-Threatening Birth Complications." *BuzzFeed News*, January 11, 2018, buzzfeednews.com/article/juliareinstein/serena-williams-birth-complications. Accessed October 14, 2019.

76. Williams, Serena. "I Didn't Expect that Sharing …" *Facebook*, January 15, 2018, m.facebook.com/SerenaWilliams/videos/10156086135726834/. Accessed June 21, 2019.

77. Chiu, Allyson. "Beyonce, Serena Williams Open Up About Potentially Fatal Childbirths, A Problem Especially for Black Mothers." *The Washington Post*, August 7, 2018, washingtonpost.com/news/morning-mix/wp/2018/08/07/beyonce-serena-williams-open-up-about-potentially-fatal-childbirths-a-problem-especially-for-black-mothers/?utm_term=.796c08631822. Accessed June 21, 2019.

78. Chiu.

79. Meadows-Fernandez, Rochaun. "Beyonce and Serena Speaking Out About Their Birth Experiences Is Good For All Black Women." *The Washington Post*, August 8, 2018, washingtonpost.com/news/parenting/wp/2018/08/08/beyonce-and-serena-speaking-out-about-their-birth-experiences-is-good-for-all-black-women/. Accessed June 20, 2019.

80. Barthold, p. 292.

81. Toole, Tucker. "Serena Williams Invests in Project Aimed at Improving Women's Maternal Health." *The Undefeated*, July 18, 2019, theundefeated.com/features/serena-williams-invests-in-project-aimed-at-improving -womens-maternal-health/. Accessed September 13, 2019.

82. Murray, Cori. "The Future of Serena Williams: The Tennis Superstar and Designer Is Ready to Conquer More." *Essence*, August 8, 2019, essence.com/feature/serena-williams-essence-magazine-cover-story-September-2019/. Accessed September 13, 2019.

Chapter 8

1. Serazio, Michael. *The Power of Sports: Media and Spectacle in American Culture.* New York University Press, 2019, p. 25.

2. Serazio, p. 346.

3. Bryant, Howard. *The Heritage: Black Athletes, a Divided America, and the Politics of Patriotism.* Beacon Press, 2018, p. 39.

4. Serazio, p. 25.

5. Serazio, p. 36.

6. Luker, Rich. "Sports Spending Not on Pace with Economic Growth." *Sports Business Journal*, February 22, 2016, sportsbusinessdaily.com/Journal/Issues/2016/02/22/Research-and-Ratings/Up-Next-with-Rich-Luker.aspx?hl=rich+luker&sc=0. Accessed October 31, 2019.

7. Jenkins, Sally. "China Is Getting Exactly What It Wants from LeBron James and the NBA: Capitulation." *The Washington Post*, October 16, 2019, washingtonpost.com/sports/nba/china-is-getting-exactly-what-it-wants-from-lebron-james-and-the-nba-capitulation/2019/10/16/364df696-efa5-11e9-b648-76bcf86eb67e_story.html. Accessed October 21, 2019.

8. Serazio, p. 28.

9. Serazio, p. 27.

10. Jenkins.

11. Simon, Robert L., et al. *Fair Play: The Ethics of Sport.* Westview Press, 2015, 4th ed., p. 235.

12. Simon, et al, pp. 235–236.

13. Svrulga, Barry. "For World Series Champion Nats, the Team That Wouldn't Die, There Was No Doubt, Just Hope." *The Washington Post*, October 30, 2019, washingtonpost.com/sports/nationals/for-world-champion-nats-the-team-that-wouldnt-die-there-was-no-doubt-just-hope/2019/10/31/6a758d56-fb4b-11e9-8906-ab6b60de9124_story.html. Accessed October 31, 2019.

14. Will, George F. "Poor Bat Behavior Is a Stain on Baseball's Unwritten Standards." *The Washington Post*, October 30, 2019, washingtonpost.com/opinions/poor-bat-behavior-is-a-stain-on-baseballs-unwritten-standards/2019/10/30/8ff1d55c-fb42-11e9-8190-6be4deb56e01_story.html. Accessed November 4, 2019.

15. Dougherty, Jesse. "Sean Doolittle on Declining White House Invite: 'I Don't Want to Hang Out with Somebody Who Talks Like That." *The Washington Post*, November 2, 2019, washingtonpost.com/sports/2019/11/01/sean-doolittle-declining-white-house-invite-i-dont-want-hang-out-with-somebody-who-talks-like-that/. Accessed November 4, 2019.

16. Simon, et al., p. 235.

17. Simon, et al., p. 235.

18. Serazio, pp. 242–243.

19. Serazio, pp. 131.

20. Simon, et al., p. 235.

21. Simon, et al., p. 236.

22. Thomas, Etan. *We Matter: Athletes and Activism*. Akashic Books, 2018, p. 76.

23. Kidwai, Aman. "Etan Thomas Addressed Social Issues Before It Was the Popular Thing to Do." *Washington City Paper*, December 26, 2018, washingtoncitypaper.com/sports/article/21038546/etan-thomas-addressed-social-issues-before-it-was-the-popular-thing-to-do. Accessed January 2, 2020.

24. Kidwai.

25. Hall, Stefan. "This Is How COVID-19 Is Affecting the World of Sports." *World Economic Forum Agenda*, April 9, 2020, weforum.org/agenda/2020/04/sports-covid19-coronavirus-excersise-specators-media-coverage/. Accessed August 30, 2020.

26. Burrow, Gwen. "Not Just a Game: The Impact of Sports on U.S. Economy." *Economic Modeling*, July 9, 2013, economicmodeling.com/2013/07/09/not-just-a-game-the-impact-of-sports-on-u-s-economy/. Accessed October 31, 2019.

27. Luker.

28. Serazio, p. 6.

29. Jones, Jeffrey M. "As Industry Grows, Percentage of U.S. Sports Fans Steady." *Gallup*, June 17, 2015, news.gallup.com/poll/183689/industry-grows-percentage-sports-fans-steady.aspx. Accessed June 24, 2019.

30. "Year in Sports Media, U.S." *Nielsen*, nielsen.com/us/en/insights/report/2018/2017-year-in-sports-media/. Accessed June 24, 2019.

31. Hall.

32. Serazio, p. 6.

33. Serazio, p. 225.

34. Janes, Chelsea. "Sean Doolittle and Eireann Dolan May Be Baseball's Most 'Woke' Couple." *The Washington Post*, March 27, 2018, washingtonpost.com/sports/nationals/sean-doolittle-and-eireann-dolan-may-be-baseballs-most-woke-couple/2018/03/27/646b32ca-2dda-11e8-8688-e053ba58f1e4_story.html. Accessed January 1, 2020; Kepner, Tyler. "Off the Mound, Sean Doolittle Brings Relief to the Ostracized." *The New York Times*, March 12, 2016, nytimes.com/2016/03/13/sports/baseball/off-the-mound-sean-doolittle-brings-relief-to-the-ostracized.html. Accessed January 1, 2020.

35. Frank, Noah. "Nats' Sean Doolittle and Wife, Eireann Dolan, Defy Baseball Convention." *WTOP*, April 5, 2018, wtop.com/washington-nationals/2018/04/eireann-dolan-sean-doolittle-defy-baseball-convention/. Accessed January 1, 2020.

36. Freed, Benjamin. "Nationals Pitcher Speaks Out Against Charlottesville Rally and Trump's Response." *The Washingtonian*, August 14, 2017, washingtonian.com/2017/08/14/washington-nationals-sean-doolittle-charlottesville-trump/. Accessed January 1, 2020.

37. Dougherty.

38. Kepner.

39. Janes.

40. Dougherty.

41. Spears, Marc J. "Carmelo Anthony: 'The System Is Broken. It Takes a Lot to Fix It." *The Undefeated*, July 19, 2016, theundefeated.com/features/carmelo-anthony-the-system-is-broken-it-takes-a-lot-to-fix-it/. Accessed January 6, 2020.

42. Bembry, Jerry. "Athletes Getting Back in the Protest Game." *The Undefeated*, August 25, 2016, theundefeated.com/features/athletes-getting-back-in-the-protest-game/. Accessed March 2, 2019.

43. Spears.

44. Vasilogambros, Matt. "When Athletes Take Political Stands." *The Atlantic*, July 12, 2016, theatlantic.com/news/archive/2016/07/when-athletes-take-political-stands/490967/. Accessed March 2, 2019.

45. Paulsen. "ESPY Awards a Mixed Bag." *Sports Media Watch*, July 12, 2019, sportsmediawatch.com/2019/07/espy-awards-ratings-viewership-abc/. Accessed January 6, 2020.

46. Bryant, p. 223.

47. Bembry.

48. Bryant, p. 224.

49. Feinstein, John. "'Sticking to Sports' Isn't Just Pointless. It's Inhuman." *The Washington Post*, August 7, 2019, washingtonpost.com/sports/sticking-to-sports-isnt-just-pointless-its-inhuman/2019/08/06/781ea97e-b88e-11e9-b3b4-2bb69e8c4e39_story.html. Accessed August 7, 2019.

50. Mather, Victor. "Alejandro Bedoya Spoke Out on Gun Violence. It Helped Make Him M.L.S.'s Player of the Week." *The New York Times*, August 7, 2019, nytimes.com/2019/08/05/sports/alejandro-bedoya-mls-gun-violence.html. Accessed January 1, 2020.

51. Mather.

52. Wyatt, Wendy N., and Kristie Bunton. "The Ethics of Speaking Out." *Ethics in Entertainment: Essays on Media Culture and Media Morality*, edited by Howard Good and Sandra L. Borden. McFarland, 2010, p. 15.

53. Blake, James, with Carol Taylor. *Ways of Grace: Stories of Activism, Adversity, and How Sports Can Bring Us Together*. HarperCollins, 2017, 28.

54. Bryant, p. 41.

55. Abdul-Jabbar, Kareem. "Abdul-Jabbar: Insulting Colin Kaepernick Says More About Our Patriotism Than His." *The Washington Post*, August 30, 2016, washingtonpost.com/posteverything/wp/2016/08/30/insulting-colin-kaepernick-says-more-about-our-patriotism-than-his/. Accessed January 2, 2020.

56. Pugmire, Lance. "Muhammad Ali Defied the Draft—and Polarized the Nation—49 Years Ago Today." *The Los Angeles Times*, April 28, 2016, latimes.com/sports/sportsnow/la-sp-sn-muhammad-ali-refused-draft-20160428-story.html. Accessed December 31, 2019.

57. Brown, DeNeen L. "'Shoot Them for What?' How Muhammad Ali Won His Greatest Fight." *The Washington Post*, June 16, 2018, washingtonpost.com/news/retropolis/wp/2018/06/15/shoot-them-for-what-how-muhammad-ali-won-his-greatest-fight/. Accessed December 29, 2019.

58. Abdul-Jabbar.

59. Smith, Johnny. "The Reign of Lew Alcindor in the Age of Revolt." *The Undefeated*, March 30, 2018, theundefeated.com/features/lew-alcindor-kareem-abdul-jabbar-ucla-boycot-1968-olympics/. Accessed January 4, 2020.

60. Smith; Bryant.

61. Bembry.

62. Blake, p. 43.

63. Shy, Leta. "Allyson Felix Wants to Save Black Mothers." *Self*, July 30, 2019, self.com/story/allyson-felix. Accessed January 6, 2020.

64. Kilgore, Adam. "As a Runner, Allyson Felix Didn't Want to Speak Out. As a Mom, She Felt She Had to." *The Washington Post*, July 31, 2019, washingtonpost.com/sports/2019/07/31/runner-allyson-felix-didnt-want-speak-out-mom-she-felt-she-had/. Accessed January 4, 2020.

65. Felix, Allyson, et al. "Allyson Felix: My Own Nike Pregnancy Story." *The New York Times*, May 22, 2019, nytimes.com/2019/05/22/opinion/allyson-felix-pregnancy-nike.html. Accessed January 4, 2020.

66. Montaño, Alysia, et al. "Nike Told Me to Dream Crazy, Until I Wanted a Baby." *The New York Times*, May 12, 2019, nytimes.com/2019/05/12/opinion/nike-maternity-leave.html. Accessed January 4, 2020.

67. Montaño, et al.

68. Shy.

69. Felix, et al.

70. Tsui, Bonnie. "Meet the Women Who Are Changing What It Means to Be a Mom and a Professional Athlete." *Sports Illustrated*, December 13, 2019, si.com/more-sports/2019/12/13/female-athlete-mothers-speaking-out-serena-felix-montano-goucher. Accessed January 6, 2020.

71. Felix, et al.

72. Bryant, p. 79.

73. Frederick, Evan L., et al. "Divided and United: Perceptions of Athlete Activism at the ESPYS." *Sport in Society*, November 2018, doi: 10.1080/17430437.2018.1530220.

74. Streeter, Kurt. "Is Slavery's Legacy in the Power Dynamics of Sports?" *The New York Times*, August 16, 2019, nytimes. com/2019/08/16/sports/basketball/slavery-anniversary-basketball-owners.html. Accessed October 21, 2019.

75. Rhoden, William C. *Forty Million Dollar Slaves: The Rise, Fall, and Redemption of the Black Athlete.* Three Rivers Press, p. 231.

76. Streeter.

77. Rhoden, *Forty Million Dollar Slaves*, p. 232.

78. Rhoden, *Forty Million Dollar Slaves*, pp. 231–234.

79. Streeter.

80. Bryant, pp. 80–82.

81. Wagner, Laura. "'Republicans Buy Sneakers, Too.' That Quote Has Haunted Michael Jordan for Decades. But Did He Really Say It?" *Slate*, July 28, 2016, slate. com/culture/2016/07/did-michael-jordan-really-say-republicans-buy-sneakers-too. html. Accessed November 21, 2018.

82. Frederick, et al.

83. Bryant, pp. 83–84.

84. Rhoden, William C. "Hodges Criticizes Jordan for His Silence on Issues." *The New York* Times, June 5, 1992, nytimes. com/1992/06/05/sports/basketball-hodges-criticizes-jordan-for-his-silence-on-issues. html. Accessed December 31, 2019.

85. Rhoden, "Hodges Criticizes Jordan for His Silence on Issues."

86. Hsu, Hua. "The Political Athlete Then and Now." *The New Yorker*, March 22, 2017, newyorker.com/culture/cultural-comment/the-political-athlete-then-and-now. Accessed March 2, 2019.

87. Villarosa, Linda. "Why America's Black Mothers and Babies Are in a Life-or-Death Crisis." *The New York Times Magazine*, April 11, 2018, nytimes. com/2018/04/11/magazine/black-mothers-babies-death-maternal-mortality.html. Accessed October 14, 2019.

88. Carlos, John, with Dave Zirin. *The John Carlos Story: The Sports Moment that Changed the World.* Haymarket Books, 2001, p. 121.

89. Trimbur, Lucia. "Taking a Knee, Making a Stand: Social Justice, Trump America, and the Politics of Sport." *Quest*, 2018, doi: 10.1080/00336297.2018.1551806.

90. Blake, p. 170.

91. O'Neal, Lonnae. "Olympic Champion Allyson Felix Tells Congress About the Black Maternal Health Crisis." *The Undefeated*, May 16, 2019, theundefeated.com/ whhw/olympic-medalist-allyson-felix-tells-congress-about-the-black-maternal-health-crisis/. Accessed January 7, 2020.

92. "Allyson Felix on Breaking Gold Medal Record 10 Months after Giving Birth." *CBS News*, October 9, 2019, cbsnews. com/news/allyson-felix-record-usain-bolt-winning-most-world-championship-gold-medals-10-months-after-giving-birth/. Accessed January 6, 2020.

93. Taylor, Derrick Bryson. "A Timeline of the Coronavirus Pandemic." *The New York Times*, August 6, 2020, nytimes. com/article/coronavirus-timeline.html. Accessed August 20, 2020.

94. Strings, Sabrina. "It's Not Obesity. It's Slavery. We Know Why Covid-19 Is Killing So Many Black People." *The New York Times*, May 25, 2020, nytimes. com/2020/05/25/opinion/coronavirus-race-obesity.html. Accessed August 31, 2020.

95. Cohen, Patricia and Ben Casselman. "Minority Workers Who Lagged in a Boom Are Hit Hard in a Bust." *The New York Times,* June 6, 2020, https://www.nytimes. com/2020/06/06/business/economy/jobs-report-minorities.html. Accessed August 31, 2020.

96. Hill, Evan, et al. "How George Floyd Was Killed in Police Custody." *The New York Times,* May 31, 2020, Updated July 28, 2020, nytimes.com/2020/05/31/us/George-Floyd-investigation.html. Accessed August 7, 2020.

97. Anderson, Monica, et al. "#BlackLivesMatter Surges on Twitter after George Floyd's Death." *Fact Tank: News in the Numbers*, June 10, 2020, pewresearch.org/fact-tank/2020/06/10/blacklivesmatter-surges-on-twitter-after-george-floyds-death/. Accessed July 6, 2020.

98. Trenaman, Calum, and Amanda Davies. "Becoming a Mother Inspired Allyxon Felix to Fight for 'Voiceless.'" *CNN*, June 15, 2020, cnn.com/2020/06/12/ sport/allyson-felix-race-protests-mother-

daughter-cmd-spt-intl/index.html. Accessed September 1, 2020.

99. Boswell, Thomas. "It's Not Which Sports Figures Are Speaking Out That's Telling. It's How Many." *The Washington Post*, June 10, 2020, washingtonpost.com/sports/2020/06/10/its-not-which-sports-figures-are-speaking-out-thats-telling-its-how-many/. Accessed June 10, 2020.

100. Gregory, Sean. "A New Era for Athletes." *Time*, June 25, 2020, time.com/5859194/athlete-activism/. Accessed July 19, 2020.

Chapter 9

1. Carlos, John, with Dave Zirin. *The John Carlos Story: The Sports Moment that Changed the World*. Haymarket Books, 2011, p. xi.

2. Widmer, Ted. "Why Two Black Athletes Raised Their Fists During the Anthem." *The New York Times*, October 16, 2018, nytimes.com/2018/10/16/opinion/why-smith-and-carlos-raised-their-fists.html. Accessed December 13, 2018.

3. Carlos with Zirin, pp. 106–132.

4. Brewer, Jerry. "Protesters Often Win History's Long Game. Ask Tommie Smith and John Carlos." *The Washington Post*, October 20, 2018, washingtonpost.com/sports/olympics/protesters-often-win-historys-long-game-ask-tommie-smith-and-john-carlos/2018/10/20/b4aef406-d48d-11e8-83d6-291fcead2ab1_story.html. Accessed December 13, 2018.

5. Powell, Michael. "Colin Kaepernick Is Silenced by a Settlement, but His Knee Spoke Volumes." *The New York Times*, February 15, 2019, nytimes.com/2019/02/15/sports/colin-kaepernick-nfl-human-rights.html. Accessed January 8, 2020.

6. Thomas, Etan. *We Matter: Athletes and Activism*. Akashic Books, 2018, p. 73.

7. McCann, Michael. "Colin Kaepernick and Eric Reid Settle Collusion Grievance with the NFL: What's the Significance?" *Sports Illustrated*, February 15, 2019, si.com/nfl/2019/02/15/colin-kaepernick-nfl-collusion-grievance-settlement-eric-reid. Accessed June 17, 2019.

8. Witz, Billy. "This Time, Colin Kaepernick Takes a Stand by Kneeling." *The New York Times*, September 1, 2016, nytimes.com/2016/09/02/sports/football/colin-kaepernick-kneels-national-anthem-protest.html. Accessed January 8, 2020.

9. Powell.

10. Solomon, Stephen. "From Liberty Tree to Taking a Knee: America's Founding Era Sheds Light on the NFL Controversy." *First Amendment Watch*, firstamendmentwatch.org/deep-dive/from-liberty-tree-to-taking-a-knee-americas-founding-era-sheds-light-on-the-nfl-controversy/. Accessed January 10, 2020.

11. Solomon, Stephen D. *Revolutionary Dissent: How the Founding Generation Created the Freedom of Speech*. St. Martin's Press, 2016, pp. 95–101.

12. Solomon, *Revolutionary Dissent*, p. 99.

13. Solomon, *Revolutionary Dissent*, p. 100.

14. Solomon, *Revolutionary Dissent*, p. 98.

15. Solomon, *Revolutionary Dissent*, p. 100.

16. Solomon, "From Liberty Tree to Taking a Knee."

17. Eastland, Terry, editor. *Freedom of Expression in the Supreme Court: The Defining Cases*. Rowman & Littlefield Publishers, 2000, p. ix.

18. Kahn, Ronald. "Symbolic Speech." *The First Amendment Encyclopedia*, 2009, mtsu.edu/First-amendment/article/1022/symbolic-speech. Accessed January 5, 2020.

19. Eastland, p. 57.

20. Carlos with Zirin, p. 110.

21. Shpigel, Ben. "Does Colin Kaepernick Still Need Football?" *The New York Times*, November 14, 2019, nytimes.com/2019/11/14/sports/football/colin-kaepernick-workout-nfl.html. Accessed November 18, 2019.

22. Rosen, Jody. "Who's Better at Image Management: Colin Kaepernick or the N.F.L.?" *The New York Times Magazine*, December 12, 2019, nytimes.com/2019/12/12/magazine/colin-kaepernick-nfl-video.html. Accessed December 20, 2019.

23. McGoldrick, James M., Jr. "Symbolic Speech: A Message from Mind to Mind," *Oklahoma Law Review*, vol. 61. No. 1, Spring 2008, pp. 2–3.

24. Eastland, pp. 173–177.

25. Eastland, pp. 186–190.

26. Eastland, pp. 196–197.

27. Tiersma, Peter Meijes. "Nonverbal Communication and the Freedom of 'Speech.'" *Wisconsin Law Review*, 1993, p. 1538.

28. McGoldrick, p. 6.

29. McGoldrick, p. 17.

30. Eastland, pp. 308–315.

31. Wyatt, Wendy N., and Kristie Bunton. "The Ethics of Speaking Out." *Ethics in Entertainment: Essays on Media Culture and Media Morality,* edited by Howard Good and Sandra L. Borden. McFarland, 2010, p. 15.

32. Wilson, Stephen. "Olympian Wyomia Tyus Sprinted to Gold and Spoke Out in Mexico City. America Forgot Her." *The Washington Post*, September 22, 2020, washingtonpost.com/sports/2020/09/22/wyomia-tyus-olympic-sprinter-gold-medals/. Accessed September 23, 2020.

33. Davis, Amira Rose. "Sixty Years Ago She Refused to Stand for the Anthem." *Zora,* September 26, 2019, zora.medium.com/sixty-years-ago-she-refused-to-stand-for-the-anthem-cf443b4e75c7. Accessed January 10, 2020.

34. Davis.

35. Wilson.

36. Serazio, Michael. *The Power of Sports: Media and Spectacle in American Culture.* New York University Press, 2019, p. 233.

37. Serazio, p. 230.

38. Grewal, Zareena. "Taking a Stand By Sitting Down: Kaepernick, Abdul-Rauf and the National Anthem." *The Undefeated,* August 30, 2016, theundefeated.com/features/taking-a-stand-by-sitting-down-kaepernick-abdul-rauf-and-the-national-anthem/. Accessed January 13, 2020.

39. Brockell, Gillian. "A National Anthem Protest Ruined His NBA Career. Now Abdul-Rauf Is Being Honored by LSU." *The Washington Post,* July 23, 2019, washingtonpost.com/history/2019/07/23/national-anthem-protest-ruined-his-nba-career-now-abdul-rauf-is-being-honored-by-lsu/. Accessed July 24, 2019.

40. Vasilogambros, Matt. "When Athletes Take Political Stands." *The Atlantic,* July 12, 2016, theatlantic.com/news/archive/2016/07/when-athletes-take-political-stands/490967/. Accessed March 2, 2019.

41. Vasilogambros.

42. Sanderson, et al. "When Athlete Activism Clashes with Group Values: Social Identity Threat Management via Social Media." *Mass Communication and Society,* vol. 19, 2016, pp. 301–322, doi: 10.1080/15205436.2015.1128549.

43. Carlos with Zirin, p. 133.

44. Belson, Ken. "N.F.L. Settlement with Kaepernick and Reid Is Said to Be Much Less than $10 Million." *The New York Times,* March 21, 2019, nytimes.com/2019/03/21/sports/colin-kaepernick-nfl-settlement.html. Accessed January 13, 2020.

45. McCann.

46. Belson.

47. Draper, Kevin, and Julie Creswell. "Colin Kaepernick 'Dream Crazy' Ad Wins Nike an Emmy." *The New York Times,* September 16, 2019, nytimes.com/2019/09/16/sports/football/colin-kaepernick-nike-emmy.html. Accessed January 13, 2020.

48. Draper and Creswell.

49. Grewal.

50. Williams, J. Corey. "The Oppressive Seeds of the Colin Kaepernick Backlash." *Protesting on Bended Knee: Race, Dissent, and Patriotism in 21st Century America,* edited by Eric Burn. The Digital Press at the University of North Dakota, 2018, p. 157.

51. Carlos with Zirin, p. 109.

52. Branch, John. "The Awakening of Colin Kaepernick." *The New York Times,* September 7, 2017, nytimes.com/2017/09/07/sports/colin-kaepernick-nfl-protests.html. Accessed January 9, 2020.

53. Branch.

54. Tiersma, p. 1561.

55. Tiersma, p. 1568.

56. Tiersma, p. 1565.

57. McGoldrick, p. 78.

58. Grewal.

59. Branch.

60. Brewer. "Protesters Often Win History's Long Game. Ask Tommie Smith and John Carlos."

61. Longman, Jere. "Kaepernick's Knee and Olympic Fists Are Linked by History." *The New York Times,* September 6, 2018, nytimes.com/2018/09/06/sports/kaepernick-nike-kneeling.html. Accessed January 10, 2020.

62. Shpigel.

63. Witz, Billy. "Kneeling During the Anthem at Ole Miss: 'I Needed to Stand Up for My Rights.'" *The New York Times,* February 27, 2019, nytimes.com/2019/02/27/sports/ole-miss-kneeling.html. Accessed March 2, 2019.

64. Witz, "Kneeling During the Anthem at Ole Miss."

65. Brewer, Jerry. "Sports Used to Be an Escape from the World. Now They're a Window into It." *The Washington Post,* August 5, 2020, washingtonpost.com/sports/2020/08/05/sports-used-be-an-escape-world-now-theyre-window-into-it/. Accessed August 6, 2020.

66. Balz, Dan. "The Politics of Race Are Shifting, and Politicians Are Struggling to Keep Pace." *The Washington Post,* July 5, 2020, washingtonpost.com/graphics/2020/politics/race-reckoning/. Accessed July 6, 2020.

67. Putnam, Lara, Jeremy Pressman and Erica Chenoweth. "Black Lives Matter Beyond America's Big Cities." *The Washington Post,* July 8, 2020, washingtonpost.com/politics/2020/07/08/black-lives-matter-beyond-americas-big-cities/. Accessed July 13, 2020.

68. Deb, Sopan. "As Protests Spur Posts from Athletes, N.B.A. Players Take to the Streets." *The New York Times,* June 1, 2020, nytimes.com/2020/06/01/sports/basketball/george-floyd-nba-protests.html. Accessed June 2, 2020.

69. Boren, Cindy. "LeBron James on Ahmaud Arbery Shooting: 'We're Literally Hunted Everyday.'" *The Washington Post,* May 7, 2020, washingtonpost.com/sports/2020/05/07/lebron-james-ahmaud-arbery-shooting-were-literally-hunted-everyday/. Accessed June 2, 2020.

70. Wood, Josh and Tim Craig. "As Breonna Taylor Protests Stretch into 12th Week, Calls for Officers' Arrests Intensify." *The Washington Post,* August 18, 2020, washingtonpost.com/national/as-breonna-taylor-protests-stretch-into-12th-week-calls-for-officers-arrests-intensify/2020/08/18/ce6f2b9a-d823–11ea-930e-d88518c57dcc_story.html. Accessed September 4, 2020.

71. Zillgitt, Jeff. "Full List of the Messages NBA Players Will Wear on Their Jerseys as Season Restarts." *USA Today,* July 30, 2020, usatoday.com/story/sports/nba/2020/07/30/what-message-nba-players-will-wear-on-back-of-jerseys/5536311002/. Accessed September 4, 2020.

72. Brewer, Jerry. "Taking a Stand Isn't New for the WNBA. It's a Way of Life." *The Washington Post,* August 7, 2020, washingtonpost.com/sports/2020/08/07/taking-stand-isnt-new-wnba-its-way-life/. Accessed August 7, 2020.

73. West, Jenna. "NWSL Challenge Cup Players Kneel in Mass During National Anthem." *Sports Illustrated,* June 27, 2020, si.com/soccer/2020/06/27/nwsl-players-kneeling-national-anthem-courage-thorns. Accessed September 5, 2020.

74. West.

75. Branch, John. "The Anthem Debate Is Back. But Now It's Standing That's Polarizing." *The New York Times,* July 4, 2020, nytimes.com/2020/07/04/sports/football/anthem-kneeling-sports.html. Accessed July 5, 2020.

76. Wagner, James. "After a Long Lull, Protesting Is Taking Hold Across Baseball." *The New York Times,* August 28, 2020, nytimes.com/2020/08/28/sports/baseball/mlb-protest-canceled-games.html. Accessed August 30, 2020.

77. Wagner.

78. Boren, Cindy. "Giants Manager Takes a Knee During Anthem and Trump Tweets 'The Game Is Over for Me.'" *The Washington Post,* July 21, 2020, washingtonpost.com/sports/2020/07/21/giants-manager-takes-knee-during-anthem-trump-tweets-game-is-over-me/. Accessed July 21, 2020.

79. Boren.

80. Boren.

81. Wagner.

82. Brewer, Jerry. "A New Day in Sports: Owners Don't Have to Agree with Players, But They Must Listen." *The Washington Post,* July 22, 2020, washingtonpost.com/sports/2020/07/22/new-day-sports-owners-dont-have-agree-with-players-they-must-listen/. Accessed July 22, 2020.

83. Mahoney, Brian and Tim Reynolds. "Boycott: NBA Playoff Games Called Off Amid Player Protest," *Associated Press,* August 26, 2020, apnews.com/313150f407d5d68eaa60f93554a5f43e. Accessed August 26, 2020.

84. Brewer, Jerry. "For Black Athletes, Social Unrest Is Not a Game, and This Historic Action Is an Urgent Plea." *The Washington Post,* August 26, 2020, washingtonpost.com/sports/2020/08/26/black-america-nba-strike/. Accessed August 28, 2020.

85. Waszak, Dennis, Jr. "9 NFL Teams Cancel Practice in Response

to Blake Shooting." *Associated Press*, August 27, 2020, apnews.com/6406e-0a34e55173e995885fea58a97f8. Accessed September 7, 2020; Wawrow, John. "NHL Players Use Pause to Focus on Racial Injustice Concerns." *Associated Press*, August 28, 2020, apnews.com/89370c875517020a4897 6f7a24547074. Accessed September 7, 2020.

86. Brewer, Jerry. "For Black Athletes, Social Unrest Is Not a Game, and This Historic Action Is an Urgent Plea."

87. Stein, Marc, Sopan Deb and Alan Blinder. "One N.B.A. Team Walked out. A Generation of Athletes Followed." *The New York Times*, August 27, 2020, nytimes. com/2020/08/27/sports/basketball/nba-resume.html. Accessed August 28, 2020.

88. Eig, Jonathan. "The NBA's Short Playoff Halt Was the Sports's World's Boldest Push for Racial Justice in Decades." *The New York Times*, August 27, 2020, washingtonpost.com/opinions/ 2020/08/27/nbas-short-playoff-halt-was-sp orts-worlds-boldest-push-racial-justice-de cades/. Accessed August 28, 2020.

89. Belson, Ken. "N.F.L. Kicks Off Season with Nods to Unrest and Focus on Anthem." *The New York Times*, September 13, 2020, nytimes.com/2020/09/13/sports/ football/nfl-protests.html. Accessed September 14, 2020.

90. Eligon, John. "Chiefs Fans, Used to Chops and Cheers, React to N.F.L.'s New Climate." *The New York Times*, September 11, 2020, nytimes.com/2020/09/11/sports/ football/nfl-chiefs-texans.html. Accessed September 11, 2020.

91. Belson.

92. Armour, Nancy. "Opinion: Truth Is, NFL Thriving While Players Take Action on Social Injustice." *USA Today*, September 17, 2020, https://www.usatoday. com/story/sports/columnist/nancy-armour/2020/09/17/protests-no-threat-nfls-status-americas-favorite-pastime/5811211002/. Accessed September 17, 2020.

Chapter 10

1. Sims, David. "The Strange Weight of Tom Hanks's Coronavirus Diagnosis." *The Atlantic*, March 12, 2020, theatlantic.com/ culture/archive/2020/03/tom-hanks-rita-wilson-coronavirus/607888/. Accessed September 14, 2020. Robinson, Eugene. "The Original Sin in the U.S. Response to Coronavirus Is Lack of Testing." *The Washington Post*, March 12, 2020, washingtonpost.com/opinions/the-original-sin-in-the-us-response-to-coronavirus-is-lack-of-testing/2020/03/12/ dff208c2–648a-11ea-acca-80c22bbee96f_ story.html. Accessed September 9, 2020.

2. Karni, Annie and Maggie Haberman. "In Rare Oval Office Speech, Trump Voices New Concerns and Old Themes." *The New York Times*, March 12, 2020, nytimes. com/2020/03/12/us/politics/trump-coronavirus-address.html. Accessed September 15, 2020.

3. Zillgitt, Jeff. "NBA Shuts Down after Rudy Gobert Tests Positive for Coronavirus." *USA Today*, March 11, 2020, usatoday.com/story/sports/nba/ 2020/03/11/coronavirus-nba-shuts-down-a fter-rudy-gobert-tests-positive/5028026002 /. Accessed September 15, 2020.

4. Sims.

5. Locker, Melissa. "Tom Hanks and Rita Wilson Had Very Different Reactions to COVID-19." *Time*, July 6, 2020, time. com/5863326/tom-hanks-coronavirus-reaction/. Accessed September 9, 2020.

6. Gunter, Barrie. *Celebrity Capital: Assessing the Value of Fame.* Bloomsbury, 2014, p. 172.

7. Hoffman, Steven J., and Charlie Tan. "Following Celebrities' Medical Advice: Meta-Narrative Analysis." *BMJ*, December 17, 2013, doi: 10.1136/bmj/f7151; Yerramilli, Divya, et al. "How Should Clinicians Respond When Patients Are Influenced by Celebrities' Cancer Stories?" *AMA Journal of Ethics*, vol. 20, no. 11, November 2018, doi: 10.1001/amajethics.2018.1075.

8. Wyatt, Wendy N., and Kristie Bunton. "The Ethics of Speaking Out." *Ethics in Entertainment: Essays on Media Culture and Media Morality,* edited by Howard Good and Sandra L. Borden. McFarland, 2010, p. 15.

9. Offit, Paul A. *Bad Advice: Or Why Celebrities, Politicians, and Activists Aren't Your Best Source of Health Information.* Columbia University Press, 2018, p. 20.

10. Offit, p. 7.

11. Jolie, Angelina. "My Medical Choice." *The New York Times*, May 14, 2013, nytimes. com/2013/05/14/opinion/my-medical-choice.html. Accessed January 18, 2020.

12. Kluger, Jeffrey, et al. "The Angelina Effect." *Time*, May 27, 2013, time.com/3450368/the-angelina-effect. Accessed January 18, 2020.

13. Liede, Alexander, et al. "Risk-Reducing Mastectomy Rates in the U.S.: A Closer Examination of the Angelina Jolie Effect." *Breast Cancer Research and Treatment*, vol. 171, 2018, pp. 435–442, doi: 10.1007/s10549-018-4824-9.

14. Nichols, Tom. *The Death of Expertise: The Campaign Against Established Knowledge and Why It Matters.* Oxford University Press, 2017, p. 189.

15. Elkins, Chris. "Celebrities Team with Big Pharma to Promote Drugs, Disease Awareness." *Drugwatch*, August 30, 2019, drugwatch.com/news/2015/11/09/celebrity-and-big-pharma-drug-promotion/. Accessed January 30, 2020.

16. Elkins.

17. Hamilton, David P. "Celebrities Help 'Educate' Public About the Virtues of New Drugs." *The Wall Street Journal*, April 22, 2002, wsj.com/articles/SB101943 3329579504640. Accessed January 28, 2020.

18. Elkins.

19. Gert, Bernard. *Common Morality: Deciding What to Do.* Oxford University Press, 2007, p. 133.

20. Gert, pp. 20–53.

21. Beck, Christina S., et al. "Blurring Personal Health and Public Priorities: An Analysis of Celebrity Health Narratives in the Public Sphere." *Health Communication,* vol. 29, 2014, pp. 244–256, doi: 10.1080/10410236.2012.741669.

22. Beck, et al.

23. Johnson, Sharilyn. "Julia Louis-Dreyfus Has 'Nothing But Regret' for Elaine's *Seinfeld* Fashion." *Vanity Fair*, December 8, 2019, vanityfair.com/hollywood/2019/12/julia-louis-dreyfus-stephen-colbert. Accessed January 19, 2020.

24. Salam, Maya. "Julia Louis-Dreyfus Shares Breast Cancer Diagnosis." *The New York Times*, September 28, 2017, nytimes.com/2017/09/28/arts/television/breast-cancer-julia-louis-dreyfus.html. Accessed January 19, 2020.

25. Sterling, Nicole. "Emmys Extra Cover: Julia Louis-Dreyfus, Out of Office." *Vanity Fair*, August 8, 2019, vanityfair.com/hollywood/2019/08/julia-louis-dreyfus-emmys-cover-story. Accessed January 19, 2020.

26. Beck, et al.

27. Sterling.

28. Levy, Ariel. "Julia Louis-Dreyfus Acts Out." *The New Yorker*, December 10, 2018, newyorker.com/magazine/2018/12/17/julia-louis-dreyfus-acts-out. Accessed January 19, 2020.

29. Yerramilli, et al.

30. Pavelko, Rachelle L., et al. "Public Reactions to Celebrity Cancer Disclosures via Social Media: Implications for Campaign Message Design and Strategy." *Higher Education Journal*, vol. 76, no. 4, 2017, doi: 10.1177/0017896917696122.

31. Hoffman and Tan.

32. Pavelko, et al.

33. Kluger, et al.

34. Paquette, Danielle. "The Angelina Jolie Effect: When a Sex Symbol Removes Her Ovaries to Prevent Cancer, Women More Likely to Follow." *The Washington Post*, March 24, 2015, washingtonpost.com/news/wonk/wp/2015/03/24/the-angelina-jolie-effect-when-a-sex-symbol-removes-her-ovaries-to-prevent-cancer-other-women-more-likely-to-follow/. Accessed January 23, 2020.

35. Yerramilli, et al.

36. Yerramilli, et al.

37. Yerramilli, et al.

38. Kluger, et al.

39. Beck, et al.

40. Yerramilli, et al.

41. Barthold, Lauren Swayne. "Giving Birth in the Public Square: The Political Relevance of Dialogue." *The Good Society*, vol. 26, nos. 2–3, 2017, pp. 290–304. *Project MUSE* muse.jhu.edu/article/702185, p. 292.

42. Vos, Sarah C., et al. "Celebrity Cancer on Twitter: Mapping a Novel Opportunity for Cancer Prevention." *Cancer Control*, vol. 26, 2019, pp. 1–8, doi: 10.1177/1073274819825826.

43. Pavelko, et al.

44. Pitt, Angelina Jolie. "Angelina Jolie Pitt: Diary of a Surgery," *The New York Times*, March 24, 2015, nytimes.com/2015/03/24/opinion/angelina-jolie-pitt-diary-of-a-surgery.html. Accessed January 18, 2020.

45. Pitt.

46. Paquette.

47. "Covid in the U.S.: Latest Map and Case Count." *The New York Times*, September 13, 2020, nytimes.com/interactive/

2020/us/coronavirus-us-cases.html. Accessed September 13, 2020.

48. Taylor, Derrick Bryson. "A Timeline of the Coronavirus Pandemic." *The New York* Times, August 6, 2020, nytimes. com/article/coronavirus-timeline.html. Accessed August 20, 2020.

49. "Covid in the U.S."

50. Oppel, Richard A., Jr., et al. "The Fullest Look Yet at the Racial Inequity of Coronavirus." *The New York Times*, July 5, 2020, nytimes.com/interactive/2020/07/05/us/coronavirus-latinos-african-americans-cdc-data.html. Accessed September 13, 2020.

51. Neel, Joe. "NPR Poll: Financial Pain from Coronavirus Pandemic 'Much, Much Worse' than Expected." National Public Radio, September 9, 2020, npr.org/sections/health-shots/2020/09/09/909669760/npr-poll-financial-pain-from-coronavirus-pandemic-much-much-worse-than-expected. Accessed September 9, 2020.

52. Cohen, Patricia, and Gillian Friedman. "Unemployment Claims Show Layoffs Continue to Batter Economy." *The New York Times*, September 3, 2020, nytimes. com/2020/09/03/business/economy/unemployment-claims.html. Accessed September 13, 2020.

53. Noguchi, Yuki. 'I Try So Hard Not to Cry': Nearly Half of U.S. Households Face a Financial Crisis." National Public Radio, September 10, 2020, npr.org/sections/health-shots/2020/09/10/910724801/overview-of-poll-data-on-pandemics-damage. Accessed September 13, 2020.

54. Fisher, Marc, and Rachel Weiner. "With Little Clarity on Coronavirus, Americans Crowdsource How to Live in a Pandemic." *The Washington Post*, July 20, 2020, washingtonpost.com/politics/with-little-clarity-on-coronavirus-americans-crowdsource-how-to-live-in-a-pandemic/2020/07/20/6abcb8ea-c5f6-11ea-b037-f9711f89ee46_story.html. Accessed July 21, 2020.

55. Yasmin, Seema, and Craig Spencer. "'But I Saw It on Facebook': Hoaxes Are Making Doctors' Jobs Harder." *The New York Times*, August 28, 2020, nytimes. com/2020/08/28/opinion/sunday/coronavirus-misinformation-faceboook. html. Accessed August 30, 2020.

56. Rao, Sonia. "Ellen DeGeneres Removes YouTube Video in Which She Compares Social Distancing to 'Being in Jail.'" *The Washington Post*, April 8, 2020, washingtonpost.com/arts-entertainment/2020/04/08/ellen-degeneres-jail-coronavirus-video-backlash/. Accessed June 2, 2020.

57. Hess, Amanda. "Celebrity Culture Is Burning." *The New York Times*, March 30, 2020, nytimes.com/2020/03/30/arts/virus-celebrities.html. Accessed June 2, 2020.

58. Andrews, Travis M. "Madonna Keeps Making Controversial Covid-19 Claims, Calling a Misinformation-Spreading Doctor Her 'Hero.'" *The Washington Post*, July 29, 2020, washingtonpost.com/technology/2020/07/29/madonna-instagram-covid-coronavirus-stella-immanuel-bath-tub/. Accessed July 29, 2020.

59. Trepany, Charles. "Jamie Foxx, Ellen Pompeo and Other Stars in Mask Up Campaign as More Celebs Encourage Face Masks." *USA Today*, July 16, 2020, usatoday.com/story/entertainment/celebrities/2020/07/16/what-tom-hanks-jamie-foxx-more-celebs-saying-face-masks/5456283002/. Accessed September 9, 2020.

60. Shaffer, Claire. "Penelope Cruz, Shailene Woodley and More Hand Their Instagrams Over to Doctors." *Rolling Stone*, May 20, 2020, rollingstone.com/culture/culture-news/pass-the-mic-celebrities-doctors-instagram-covid-19–1002922/. Accessed September 11, 2020.

61. Bui, Quoctrung, et al. "How Dr. Fauci Found Himself Talking to Julia Roberts, Lil Wayne and Just About Any Podcaster Who Asked." *The New York Times*, August 27, 2020, nytimes.com/interactive/2020/08/27/upshot/fauci-media-appearances.html. Accessed September 13, 2020.

62. Bui.

63. Gunter, p. 171–192.

64. Gunter, p. 179.

65. Osborne, Mark. "Tom Hanks, Rita Wilson Say They Have Coronavirus." *ABC News*, March 12, 2020, abcnews.go.com/Entertainment/tom-hanks-rita-wilson-coronavirus/story?id=69547484. Accessed September 14, 2020.

66. Sims.

67. Avlon, John. "In Coronavirus Crisis, Tom Hanks Is More of a Role Model than Donald Trump." *CNN.com*, March 12, 2020, cnn.com/2020/03/12/opinions/tom-hanks-more-of-a-role-model-in-crisis-than-

donald-trump-avlon/index.html. Accessed September 9, 2020.

68. Specter, Emma. "Tom Hanks Posts a Coronavirus Update, Remains Perfect." *Vogue*, March 13, 2020, vogue.com/article/tom-hanks-coronavirus-update-instagram. Accessed September 10, 2020.

69. Smith, Sabrina. "Tom Hanks' Typewriter Obsession Makes Him the Proud Owner of More than 250 Models." *Showbiz Cheat Sheet*, August 17, 2020, cheatsheet.com/entertainment/tom-hanks-typewriter-obsession-makes-him-the-proud-owner-of-more-than-250-models.html/. Accessed September 14, 2020.

70. Bruney, Gabrielle. "Tom Hanks Was the Perfect Surprise Guest Host for *Saturday Night Live*'s First Digital Episode." *Esquire*, April 12, 2020, esquire.com/entertainment/tv/a32118571/saturday-night-live-at-home-coronavirus-tom-hanks/. Accessed September 14, 2020.

71. Calvario, Liz. "Tom Hanks Shares Update After Returning Home After Coronavirus Diagnosis." *ET News*, March 28, 2020, etonline.com/tom-hanks-shares-update-after-returning-home-after-coronavirus-diagnosis-143845. Accessed September 16, 2020.

72. *Wait Wait ... Don't Tell Me!* National Public Radio, April 18, 2020, npr.org/2020/04/18/837682956/we-call-to-check-in-on-tom-hanks-and-ask-him-to-play-not-my-job /. Accessed September 10, 2020.

73. Henderson, Cydney. "'Plasmatic!' Tom Hanks Shares Picture of Himself Donating Plasma to Combat COVID-19." *USA Today*, May 27, 2020, usatoday.com/story/entertainment/celebrities/2020/05/27/tom-hanks-donates-plasma-combat-covid-19-and-shares-photo/5271559002/. Accessed September 9, 2020.

74. Bruney.

75. Freeman, Hadley. "Tom Hanks on Surviving Coronavirus: 'I Had Crippling Body Aches, Fatigue and Couldn't Concentrate.'" *The Guardian*, July 6, 2020, theguardian.com/film/2020/jul/06/tom-hanks-on-surviving-coronavirus-i-had-crippling-body-aches-fatigue-and-couldnt-concentrate. Accessed September 9, 2020.

76. Steinmetz, Katy. "You've Tested Positive for COVID-19. Who Has a Right to Know?" *Time*, March 26, 2020, time.com/5810231/covid19-test-sharing-positive-result/. Accessed September 16, 2020.

77. Coyle, Jake. "Tom Hanks on COVID-19, 'Greyhound' and Wartime Mentality." *Associated Press*, July 6, 2020, apnews.com/ba58fe517346a0164013b37622476b00. Accessed September 14, 2020.

78. Coyle.

79. Jacob, Ayesha. "The Narratives that Define the Coronavirus Pandemic Will Influence Its Outcome." *The Mail & Guardian*, March 16, 2020, mg.co.za/article/2020-03-16-the-narratives-that-define-the-coronavirus-pandemic-will-influence-its-outcome/. Accessed September 17, 2020.

80. Locker, Melissa. "Tom Hanks Gave His Corona Typewriter to a Kid Bullied Over Having the Name Corona." *Time*, April 24, 2020, time.com/5826972/tom-hanks-typewriter-letter/. Accessed September 16, 2020.

Chapter 11

1. Jenkins, Sally. "At U.S. Open, Power of Serena Williams and Naomi Osaka Is Overshadowed by an Umpire's Power Play." *The Washington Post*, September 8, 2018, washingtonpost.com/sports/tennis/at-us-open-power-of-serena-williams-and-naomi-osaka-is-overshadowed-by-an-umpires-power-play/2018/09/08/edbf46c8-b3b4-11e8-a20b-5f4f84429666_story.html. Accessed June 20, 2019. King, Billie Jean. "Billie Jean King: Serena Is Still Treated Differently than Male Athletes." *The Washington Post*, September 9, 2018, washingtonpost.com/outlook/2018/09/09/serena-is-still-treated-differently-than-male-athletes/. Accessed September 18, 2020.

2. Fendrich, Howard. "Analysis: Naomi Osaka Is Poised to Lead Tennis On, Off Court." *Associated Press*, September 13, 2020, apnews.com/ac3b328d9352aa6bdf-bc33f007053361. Accessed September 13, 2020.

3. Wallace, Ava. "U.S. Open Champion Naomi Osaka Lets Her Masks Do the Talking. In the End, She Wanted to Know What We Heard." *The Washington Post*, September 12, 2020, washingtonpost.com/sports/2020/09/12/naomi-osaka-us-open-message/. Accessed September 13, 2020.

4. Gay, Jason. "Naomi Osaka's Big

Summer." *The Wall Street Journal,* September 14, 2020. wsj.com/articles/the-meaningful-summer-of-naomi-osaka-11600002023. Accessed September 14, 2020.

5. Wallace.

6. Lipari, Lisbeth. *Listening, Thinking, Being: Toward an Ethics of Attunement.* Pennsylvania State University Press, 2014, p. 2.

7. Parks, Elizabeth S. *The Ethics of Listening: Creating Space for Sustainable Dialogue.* Lexington Books, 2019, p. 1.

8. Lipari, p. 2.

9. Tannen, Deborah. *The Argument Culture: Stopping America's War of Words.* Ballantine Books, 1998.

10. Lacey, Kate. *Listening Publics: The Politics and Experience of Listening in the Media Age.* Polity Press, 2013, p. 3.

11. Lacey, p. 166.

12. Ward, Stephen J.A., and Herman Wasserman. "Open Ethics: Towards a Global Media Ethics of Listening." *Journalism Studies,* vol. 16, no. 6, 2015, pp. 834–849, doi:10.1080/1461670X.2014.950882, p. 837.

13. Parks, p. vii.

14. Mill, John Stuart. *On Liberty,* edited by Elizabeth Rappaport. Hackett Publishing, 1978, p. 50.

15. Lacey, p. 165.

16. Lacey, p. 187.

17. Schudson, Michael. *The Good Citizen: A History of American Civic Life.* Harvard University Press, 1998, p. 310.

18. Schudson, p. 311.

19. Parks, p. 1.

20. Lipari, p. 50.

21. Lipari, p. 177.

22. Lacey, p. 195.

23. Parks, p. 32.

24. Carter, Stephen L. *Civility: Manners, Morals, and the Etiquette of Democracy.* Basic Books, 1998, p. 138.

25. Barthold, Lauren Swayne. "Giving Birth in the Public Square: The Political Relevance of Dialogue." *The Good Society,* vol. 26, nos. 2–3, 2017, pp. 290–304, doi: 10.5325/goodsociety.26.2–3.0290, p. 293.

26. Barthold, p. 294.

27. Dreher, Tanya. "Listening Across Difference: Media and Multiculturalism Beyond the Politics of Voice." *Continuum: Journal of Media & Cultural Studies,* vol. 23, no. 4, August 2009, pp. 445–458, doi: 10.1080/10304310903015712, p. 451.

28. Dreher, p. 451.

29. Lipari, p. 53.

30. Stauffer, Jill. *Ethical Loneliness: The Injustice of Not Being Heard.* Columbia University Press, 2015, p.1.

31. Stauffer, p. 80.

32. Lacey, p. 187.

33. Maben, Sarah K., and Christopher C. Gearhart. "Organizational Social Media Accounts: Moving Toward Listening Competency." *International Journal of Listening,* vol. 32, 2018, pp. 101–114, doi: 10.1080/10904018.2017.1330658, p. 103.

34. Crawford, Kate. "Following You: Disciplines of Listening in Social Media." *Continuum: Journal of Media & Cultural Studies,* vol. 23, no. 4, August 2009, pp. 525–535, doi:10.1080/10304310903003270, p. 526.

35. Crawford, p. 527.

36. Crawford, p. 528.

37. Nichols, Michael P. *The Lost Art of Listening.* Guilford Press, 1995, p. 113.

38. Billings, Andrew. "Power in the Reverberation: Why Twitter Matters, but Not the Way Most Believe." *Communication & Sport,* vol. 2, no. 2, 2014, pp. 107–112, doi: 10.1177/2167479514527427, p. 110.

39. McCombs, Maxwell. "The Agenda-Setting Function of the Press." *The Press,* edited by Geneva Overholser and Kathleen Hall Jamieson, Oxford University Press, 2005, p. 160.

40. Patterson, Thomas, and Philip Seib. "Informing the Public." *The Press,* edited by Geneva Overholser and Kathleen Hall Jamieson, Oxford University Press, 2005, p. 193.

41. Clarey, Christopher. "Naomi Osaka, While Rallying for Social Justice, Wins U.S. Open Title." *The New York Times,* September 12, 2020, nytimes.com/2020/09/12/sports/tennis/naomi-osaka-us-open-title.html. Accessed September 13, 2020.

42. Maine, D'Arcy. "Naomi Osaka Cements Her Status as Leader On and Off the Court with U.S. Open Run." *ESPN,* September 13, 2020, espn.com/tennis/story/_/id/29869802/naomi-osaka-cements-status-leader-the-court-2020-us-open-run. Accessed September 14, 2020.

43. Kambhampaty, Anna Purna. "Naomi Osaka's U.S. Open Masks Showcase One of an Athlete's Most Powerful Tools for Protest." *Time,* September 11, 2020, time.com/5888072/sports-style-protest/. Accessed September 12, 2020.

44. Patterson and Seib, p. 193.

45. McCann, Michael. "Colin Kaepernick and Eric Reid Settle Collusion Grievance with the NFL: What's the Significance?" *Sports Illustrated*, February 15, 2019, si.com/nfl/2019/02/15/colin-kaepernick-nfl-collusion-grievance-settlement-eric-reid. Accessed June 17, 2019.

46. Witz, Billy. "This Time, Colin Kaepernick Takes a Stand by Kneeling." *The New York Times*, September 1, 2016, nytimes.com/2016/09/02/sports/football/colin-kaepernick-kneels-national-anthem-protest.html. Accessed January 8. 2020.

47. Dreher, p. 447.

48. O'Donnell, Penny. "Journalism, Change and Listening Practices." *Continuum: Journal of Media & Cultural Studies*, vol. 23, no. 4, August 2009, pp. 503–517, doi: 10.1080/10304310903015720.

49. Kovach, Bill, and Tom Rosenstiel. *The Elements of Journalism: What Newspeople Should Know and the Public Should Expect.* 3rd ed. Three Rivers Press, 2016, p. 169.

50. O'Donnell.

51. Feyer, Thomas. "Women, Please Speak Out." *The New York Times*, February 14, 2020, nytimes.com/2020-02-14/opinion/letters/letters-editor-nytimes-gender.html. Accessed February 15, 2020.

52. Probolus, Kimberly. "Men, You Need to Listen to Women." *The New York Times*, February 14, 2020, nytimes.com/2020/02/14/opinion/letters/nytimes-letters-women.html. Accessed February 15, 2020.

53. King.

54. Gay.

55. Osaka, Naomi. "I Never Would've Imagined Writing This Two Years Ago." *Esquire*, July 1, 2020, esquire.com/sports/a33022329/naomi-osaka-op-ed-george-floyd-protests/. Accessed September 12, 2020.

56. Osaka.

57. Denyer, Simon. "Japanese Tennis Player Naomi Osaka Speaks Out for Black Lives Matter, Faces Backlash." *The Washington Post*, June 8, 2020, washingtonpost.com/world/asia_pacific/japanese-tennis-player-naomi-osaka-speaks-out-for-black-lives-matter-faces-backlash/2020/06/08/f8432ca0-a92f-11ea-a43b-be9f6494a87d_story.html. Accessed June 9, 2020.

58. Futterman, Matthew. "Naomi Osaka Returns after Protest Prompts Tournament's Pause." *The New York Times*, August 28, 2020, nytimes.com/2020/08/28/sports/tennis/naomi-osaka.html. Accessed August 28, 2020.

59. Elliott, Helene. "Naomi Osaka Stood Tall, and Alone, in Protest Following Jacob Blake Shooting." *The Los Angeles Times*, August 27, 2020, latimes.com/sports/story/2020–08–27/naomi-osaka-stood-tall-and-alone-in-withdrawing-from-tennis-tournament. Accessed August 28, 2020.

60. Wolken, Dan. "Opinion: Naomi Osaka Nearing Icon Status, and It's Not Just Because of Her Tennis." *USA Today*, September 11, 2020, usatoday.com/story/sports/columnist/dan-wolken/2020/09/11/naomi-osaka-tennis-superstar-voice-for-change/3471156001/. Accessed September 12, 2020.

61. Associated Press. "Japan Celebrates Naomi Osaka; Sponsors Cautious about Activism." *Honolulu Star-Advertiser*, September 15, 2020, staradvertiser.com/2020/09/15/sports/sports-breaking/japan-celebrates-naomi-osaka-sponsors-cautious-about-activism. Accessed September 16, 2020.

62. Osaka.

63. Elliott.

64. Gay.

65. Elliott.

66. Futterman.

67. Boren, Cindy. "Naomi Osaka Brought Seven Face Masks to the U.S. Open, Each One Honoring a Victim of Violence." *The Washington Post*, September 1, 2020, washingtonpost.com/sports/2020/09/01/naomi-osaka-facemask-us-open/. Accessed September 2, 2020.

68. Gay.

69. Boren, Cindy. "Parents of Trayvon Martin, Ahmad Arbery Thank Naomi Osaka in Video after U.S. Open Win." *The Washington Post*, September 9, 2020, washingtonpost.com/sports/2020/09/09/naomi-osaka-mask-us-open/. Accessed September 11, 2020.

70. Carayol, Tumaini. "Naomi Osaka Proves Herself a Champion On and Off the Court." *The Guardian*, September 13, 2020, theguardian.com/sport/2020/sep/13/naomi-osaka-proves-herself-a-champion-on-and-off-the-court. Accessed September 19, 2020.

71. Ley, Tom. "Naomi Osaka Asked the Right Question." *Defector Media*, September 13, 2020, defector.com/naomi-osaka-asked-the-right-question/. Accessed September 15, 2020.

72. Carayol.

73. "'A Real Pro': Naomi Osaka's Anti-Racism Message Resonates with Japan Youth." *The Mainichi*, September 25, 2020, mainichi.jp/english/articles/20200924/p2a/00m/0dm/022000c. Accessed September 25, 2020.

74. Bengel, Chris. "Naomi Osaka Fires Back at Critics Who Told Her to 'Keep Politics Out of Sports' at U.S. Open." *CBS Sports*, September 16, 2020, cbssports.com/tennis/news/naomi-osaka-fires-back-at-critics-who-told-her-to-keep-politics-out-of-sports-at-us-open/. Accessed September 17, 2020.

75. Smith, Grady. "Is Country Music Ready to Forgive the Dixie Chicks?" *The Guardian*, November 19, 2015, theguardian.com/music/2015/nov/19/the-dixie-chicks-tour-is-country-music-ready-to-forgive. Accessed February 23, 2020.

76. "The Dixie Chicks on Turning Their Bad Times into Ballads." *CBS News*, March 8, 2020, cbsnews.com/news/the-dixie-chicks-natalie-maines-martie-maguire-emily-strayer/. Accessed March 9, 2020.

77. "The Dixie Chicks on Turning Their Bad Times into Ballads."

78. Gotrich, Lars. "Dixie Chicks Announce First Album in 14 Years, 'Gaslighter,' Share Title Track." *NPR*, March 4, 2020, npr.org/2020/03/04/812018782/dixie-chicks-gaslighter-first-album-14-years-release-single. Accessed March 15, 2020.

79. "The Dixie Chicks on Turning Their Bad Times into Ballads."

80. Horton, Adrian. "Shut Up and Sing: Why the Chicks' 2006 Documentary Means More Now Than Ever." *The Guardian*, July 21, 2020, theguardian.com/culture/2020/jul/21/the-chicks-2006-documentary-means-more-now-than-ever. Accessed August 11, 2020.

81. Tatum, Beverly Daniel. *Why Are All the Black Kids Sitting Together in the Cafeteria? And Other Conversations about Race.* Basic Books, 2017, p. 342.

82. White, Judith. "NGO Leaders on the Edge: The Moral Courage to Fight for Human Rights." *Moral Courage in Organizations: Doing the Right Thing at Work*, edited by Debra R. Comer and Gina Vega. M.E. Sharpe, Inc., 2011, pp. 103–104.

83. Gentile, Mary C. "Giving Voice to Values: Building Moral Competence." *Moral Courage in Organizations: Doing the Right Thing at Work*, edited by Debra R. Comer and Gina Vega. M.E. Sharpe, Inc., 2011, p. 118.

84. Gentile, p. 118.

85. Kidder, Rushworth M. *How Good People Make Tough Choices: Resolving the Dilemmas of Ethical Living.* HarperCollins, 2003, p. 48.

86. Gentile, p. 119.

87. Kidder, p. 192.

88. Bird, Frederick Bruce. *The Muted Conscience: Moral Silence and the Practice of Silence in Business.* Quorum Books, 1996, pp. 1–4.

89. Martin, Mike W. *Meaningful Work: Rethinking Professional Ethics.* Oxford University Press, 2000, p. 204.

90. Becker, Lawrence C., and Charlotte B. Becker, editors. *Encyclopedia of Ethics.* Garland Publishing, 2nd ed., 2001, pp. 405–406.

91. Shirky, Clay. *Here Comes Everybody: The Power of Organizing without Organizations.* Penguin, 2008, pp. 105–106.

92. Shirky, p. 79.

93. Shirky, p. 89.

94. Macsai, Dan. "Taylor Swift on Going Pop, Ignoring the Gossip and the Best (Worst) Nickname She's Ever Had." *Time*, October 19, 2012, entertainment.time.com/2012/10/19/taylor-swift-on-going-pop-ignoring-the-gossip-and-the-best-worst-nickname-shes-ever-had/. Accessed November 28, 2018.

95. Yahr, Emily. "As the Chicks Take the Democratic Convention Stage, Three Generations of Country Singers Challenge the Genre's Conservative Stereotypes." *The Washington Post*, August 20, 2020, washingtonpost.com/arts-entertainment/2020/08/20/chicks-dnc-taylor-swift-dolly-parton/. Accessed August 20, 2020.

96. Charles, Ashley. *Outraged: Why Everyone Is Shouting and No One Is Talking.* Bloomsbury Publishing, 2020, p. 126.

97. Charles, p. 127.

98. Nichols, Tom. *The Death of Expertise: The Campaign Against Established*

Knowledge and Why It Matters. Oxford University Press, 2017, p. 111.

99. Nossel, Suzanne. *Dare to Speak: Defending Free Speech for All.* HarperCollins, 2020, p. 123.

100. Nossel, pp. 124–126.

101. Snapes, Laura. "The Chicks: 'We Were Used and Abused by Everybody Who Wanted to Make Money Off Us." *The Guardian*, July 18, 2020, theguardian.com/music/2020/jul/18/dixie-chicks-used-and-abused-by-everybody-who-wanted-to-make-money-off-us. Accessed July 18, 2020.

Works Cited by Chapter

Introduction

Boswell, Thomas. "It's Not Which Sports Figures Are Speaking Out That's Telling. It's How Many." *The Washington Post*, June 10, 2020, washingtonpost.com/sports/2020/06/10/its-not-which-sports-figures-are-speaking-out-thats-telling-its-how-many/. Accessed June 10, 2020.

Bryant, Howard. *The Heritage: Black Athletes, a Divided America, and the Politics of Patriotism*. Beacon Press, 2018.

Bryson, Donna. "Taylor Swift Was Groped by Radio Host, Jury Finds." *The New York Times*, August 14, 2017, nytimes.com/2017/08/14/arts/music/taylor-swift-trial-jury-verdict.html. Accessed February 21, 2020.

Caulfield, Timothy. *Is Gwyneth Paltrow Wrong about Everything? How the Famous Sell Us Elixirs of Health, Beauty and Happiness*. Beacon Press, 2015.

Coleman, Nancy. "Why We're Capitalizing Black." *The New York Times*, July 5, 2020, nytimes.com/2020/07/05/insider/capitalized-black.html. Accessed July 6, 2020.

Daniszewski, John. "Why We Will Lowercase White." The Associated Press, July 20, 2020, blog.ap.org/announcements/why-we-will-lowercase-white?utm_campaign. Accessed July 20, 2020.

Farzan, Antonia Noori. "'I Just Knew I Wasn't Going to Help': Taylor Swift Finally Explains Why She Didn't Endorse Hillary Clinton." *The Washington Post*, August 9, 2019, washingtonpost.com/nation/2019/08/09/taylor-swift-hillary-clinton-trump-vogue-interview/. Accessed February 21, 2020.

Finan, Eileen. "Taylor Swift Votes for First Time 'With My Gut." *People*, October 31, 2008, people.com/celebrity/taylor-swift-votes-for-first-time-with-my-gut/. Accessed November 28, 2018.

"Full Text of Brokaw's Interview with Bush." *The New York Times*, April 25, 2003, nytimes.com/2003/04/25/international/world special/full-text-of-brokaws-interview-with-bush.html. Accessed July 20, 2020.

Gunter, Barrie. *Celebrity Capital: Assessing the Value of Fame*. Bloomsbury, 2014.

Haag, Matthew. "Voter Registrations Spike as Deadlines Loom. Taylor Swift Had Something to Do with It." *The New York Times*, October 9, 2018, nytimes.com/2018/10/09/us/politics/taylor-swift-voter-registration.html. Accessed November 28, 2018.

Hill, Evan, et al. "How George Floyd Was Killed in Police Custody." *The New York Times*, May 31, 2020, Updated July 28, 2020, nytimes.com/2020/05/31/us/George-Floyd-investigation.html. Accessed August 7, 2020.

Holden, Stephen. "In an Instant, Country Stars Became Political Casualties." *The New York Times*, October 27, 2006, nytimes.com/2006/10/27/movies/in-an-instant-country-stars-became-political-casualties.html. Accessed February 23, 2020.

Hotez, Peter J. *Vaccines Did Not Cause Rachel's Autism: My Journey as a Vaccine Scientist, Pediatrician, and Autism Dad*. Johns Hopkins University Press, 2018.

Leeds, Jeff. "Grammy Sweep by Dixie Chicks Is Seen as a Vindication." *The New York Times*, February 13, 2007, nytimes.com/2007/02/13/arts/music/13gram.html. Accessed February 23, 2020.

Macsai, Dan. "Taylor Swift on Going Pop, Ignoring the Gossip and the Best (Worst) Nickname She's Ever Had." *Time*, October 19, 2012, entertainment.time.com/2012/10/19/taylor-swift-on-going-pop-ignoring-the-gossip-and-the-best-worst-nickname-shes-ever-had/. Accessed November 28, 2018.

Mnookin, Seth. *The Panic Virus: A True Story of Medicine, Science, and Fear.* Simon & Schuster, 2011.

Offit, Paul A. *Bad Advice: Or Why Celebrities, Politicians, and Activists Aren't Your Best Source of Health Information.* Columbia University Press, 2018.

Pareles, Jon. "The Dixie Chicks: America Catches Up with Them." *The New York Times*, May 21, 2006, nytimes.com/2006/05/21/arts/music/21pare.html. Accessed February 23, 2020.

Sanneh, Kelefa. "It's Dixie Chicks vs. Country Fans, but Who's Dissing Whom? *The New York Times*, May 25, 2006, nytimes.com/2006/05/25/arts/music/25sann.html. Accessed November 28, 2018.

Smith, Grady. "Is Country Music Ready to Forgive the Dixie Chicks?" *The Guardian*, November 19, 2015, theguardian.com/music/2015/nov/19/the-dixie-chicks-tour-is-country-music-ready-to-forgive. Accessed February 23, 2020.

Swift, Taylor. "I'm writing this post about the upcoming midterm elections ..." *Instagram*, October 7, 2018, instagram.com/p/BopoXpYnCes/?hl=en. Accessed November 28, 2018.

Williamson, Nigel. "Free the Dixie Three." *The Guardian*, August 21, 2003, theguardian.com/music/2003/aug/22/1. Accessed February 23, 2020.

Willman, Chris. "Taylor Swift: No Longer 'Polite at All Costs.'" *Variety*, January 21, 2020, variety.com/2020/music/features/taylor-swift-politics-sundance-documentary-miss-americana-1203471910/. Accessed February 23, 2020.

Yahr, Emily. "After the Trump-Putin News Conference, Here's Why People Are Talking about the Dixie Chicks." *The Washington Post*, July 17, 2018, washingtonpost.com/news/arts-and-entertainment/wp/2018/07/17/after-the-trump-putin-news-conference-heres-why-people-are-talking-about-the-dixie-chicks/. Accessed November 28, 2018.

Chapter 1

Academy Awards Acceptance Speech Database. aaspeechesdb.oscars.org/link/035-1/. Accessed February 9, 2019.

Academy Awards Acceptance Speech Database. aaspeechesdb.oscars.org/link/044-3/. Accessed February 8, 2019.

Academy Awards Acceptance Speech Database. aaspeechesdb.oscars.org/link/045-1/. Accessed February 8, 2019.

Anderson, Joel. "Why the NFL Is Suddenly Standing Up for Black Lives." *Slate*, June 7, 2020, slate.com/culture/2020/06/nfl-roger-goodell-black-lives-matter-players-video-kaepernick.html. Accessed July 21, 2020.

Andrews, David L., and Steven J. Jackson. "Introduction: Sports Celebrities, Public Culture, and Private Experience." *Sports Stars: The Cultural Politics of Sporting Celebrity*, edited by David L. Andrews and Steven J. Jackson. Routledge, 2001.

Associated Press. "Political Oscars Speeches Started with Marlon Brando." *Page Six*, February 27, 2018, pagesix.com/2018/02/27/political-oscar-speeches-started-with-marlon-brando/. Accessed February 8, 2019.

Baum, Matthew A., and Angela S. Jamison. "The Oprah Effect: How Soft News Helps Inattentive Citizens Vote Consistently." *The Journal of Politics*, vol. 68, no. 4, November 2006, pp. 946–959, doi:10.1111/j.1468–2508.2006.00482.x.

Bembry, Jerry. "Athletes Getting Back in the Protest Game." *The Undefeated,* August 25, 2016, theundefeated.com/features/athletes-getting-back-in-the-protest-game. Accessed March 2, 2019.

Boorstin, Daniel. *The Image: A Guide to Pseudo-Events in America.* Harper & Row, Harper Colophon edition, 1961.

Bonesteel, Matt. "Stephen Curry's Endorsement of Joe Biden a Natural Step in NBA Star's Political Progression." *The Washington Post*, August 21, 2020, washingtonpost.com/sports/2020/08/21/stephen-Curry's-endorsement-joe-biden-natural-step-nba-stars-political-progression/. Accessed August 21, 2020.

Boren, Cindy. "LeBron James on Ahmaud Arbery Shooting: 'We're Literally Hunted Everyday.'" *The Washington Post*, May 7, 2020, washingtonpost.

com/sports/2020/05/07/lebron-james-ahmaud-arbery-shooting-were-literally-hunted-everyday/. Accessed June 2, 2020.

Bradner, Eric. "Top Takeaways from the Democratic National Convention." *CNN Politics*, August 21, 2020, cnn.com/2020/08/21/politics/dnc-2020-takeaways/index.html. Accessed August 23, 2020.

Buchanan, Larry, Quoctrung Bui and Jugal K. Patel. "Black Lives Matter May Be the Largest Movement in U.S. History." *The New York Times*, July 3, 2020, nytimes.com/interactive/2020/07/03/us/george-floyd-protests-crowd-size.html. Accessed August 7, 2020.

"Celebrity Endorsement Tracker." *Los Angeles Times*, April 12, 2016, graphics.latimes.com/celebrity-presidential-endorsements/. Accessed February 8, 2019.

Cheong, Wayne. "A Special Interview and Shoot with John Legend in These COVID Times." *Esquire*, June 19, 2020, esquiresg.com/features/john-legend-interview-chrissy-teigen-lockdown-a-special-interview-and-shoot-in-these-covid-times/. Accessed August 18, 2020.

Choi, Chong Ju, and Ron Berger. "Ethics of Celebrities and Their Increasing Influence in 21st Century Society." *Journal of Business Ethics*, vol. 91, 2010, pp. 313–318, doi: 10.1007/s10551-009-0090-4.

Couldry, Nick, and Tim Markham. "Celebrity Culture and Public Connection: Bridge or Chasm?" *International Journal of Cultural Studies*, vol. 10, no. 4, 2007, pp. 403–421, doi: 10.1177/1367877907083077.

Deb, Sopan. "Robert De Niro's Anti-Trump Screed and Meryl Streep's Ode to Men." *The New York Times*, January 10, 2018, nytimes.com/2018/01/10/arts/robert-de-niro-meryl-streep-national-board-of-review.html. Accessed February 16, 2019.

Deb, Sopan. "Stephen and Ayesha Curry Endorse Biden at Democratic National Convention." *The New York Times*, August 20, 2020, nytimes.com/2020/08/20/us/politics/Stephen-Ayesha-curry-endorse-Biden.html. Accessed August 21, 2020.

Ember, Sydney, and Lisa Lerer. "Julia Louis-Dreyfus Caps a Week of Starring Roles for 4 Actresses." *The New York Times*, August 20, 2020, nytimes.com/2020/08/20/us/politics/julia-louis-dreyfus-dnc.html. Accessed August 20, 2020.

"Forbes Most Powerful Women in the World in 2016." *Telegraph*, June 13, 2016, telegraph.co.uk/business/2016/06/06/the-most-powerful-women-in-the-world/oprah-winfrey/. Accessed February 9, 2019.

Furedi, Frank. "Celebrity Culture." *Society*, vol. 47, 2010, pp. 493–497, doi: 10.1007/s12115-010-9367-6.

Garthwaite, Craig, and Timothy J. Moore. "Can Celebrity Endorsements Affect Political Outcomes? Evidence from the 2008 US Democratic Presidential Primary." *The Journal of Law, Economics, and Organization*, vol. 29, no. 2, February 10, 2012, pp. 355–384, doi: 10.1093/jleo/ewr031.

Goldsmith, Reid. "Stephen Curry, Chris Paul, Other NBA Stars React to Ahmaud Arbery Killing." *ClutchPoints*, May 7, 2020, clutchpoints.com/nba-news-stephen-curry-chris-paul-other-nba-stars-react-to-ahmaud-arbery-killing/. Accessed August 19, 2020.

Harrington, Jim. "Should Artists Speak Out on Politics? John Legend Weighs In on Subject." *Marin Independent Journal*, July 14, 2020. marinij.com/2020/07/14/should-artists-speak-out-on-politics-john-legend-weighs-in-on-subject/. Accessed July 15, 2020.

Hedges, Chris. *Empire of Illusion: The End of Literacy and the Triumph of Spectacle.* Nation Books, 2009.

Hill, Evan, et al. "How George Floyd Was Killed in Police Custody." *The New York Times*, May 31, 2020, Updated July 28, 2020, nytimes.com/2020/05/31/us/George-Floyd-investigation.html. Accessed August 7, 2020.

Hsu, Hua. "The Political Athlete: Then and Now." *The New Yorker*, March 22, 2017, newyorker.com/culture/cultural-comment/the-political-athlete-then-and-now. Accessed June 24, 2019.

"Instagram Accounts with the Most Followers Worldwide as of February 2020 (in Millions)." *Statista*, statista.com/statistics/421169/most-followers-instagram/. Accessed August 18, 2020.

Jones, Jeffrey M. "As Industry Grows, Percentage of U.S. Sports Fans Steady," *Gallup*, June 17, 2015, news.gallup.com/poll/183689/industry-grows-percentage-sports-fans-steady.aspx. Accessed June 24, 2019.

La Ferla, Ruth. "The Land of the Oscars, the Home of the Dove." *The New York Times*, March 25, 2003, nytimes.com/2003/03/25/us/the-land-of-the-oscars-the-home-of-the-dove.html. Accessed February 15, 2019.

Marshall, P. David. *Celebrity and Power: Fame in Contemporary Culture*. 1997. University of Minnesota Press, 2014.

May, William F. *Beleaguered Rulers: The Public Obligation of the Professional*. Westminster John Knox Press, 2001.

"Most Popular Facebook Fan Pages as of June 2020, Based on Number of Fans (in Millions)." *Statista*, statista.com/statistics/269304/international-brands-on-facebook-by-number-of-fans/. Accessed August 18, 2020.

Norman, Jim. "Football Still Americans' Favorite Sport to Watch," *Gallup*, January 4, 2018, news.gallup.com/poll/224864/football-americans-favorite sport-watch. aspx. Accessed June 24, 2019.

"Number of Monthly Active Facebook Users Worldwide as of 2nd Quarter 2020 (in Millions)." *Statista*, statista.com/statistics/264810/number-of-monthly-active-facebook-users-worldwide/. Accessed August 18, 2020.

"Politics at the Oscars." *The New York Times*, March 1, 2014, nytimes.com/2014/03/01/us/politics/politics-at-the-oscars.html. Accessed February 15, 2019.

Puente, Maria. "The 'Oprah Effect': Does Everything She Touch Turn to Gold?" *USA Today*, October 19, 2015, usatoday.com/story/life/tv/2015/10/19/oprah-effect-does-everything-she-touches-turn-gold/74211636/. Accessed February 9, 2019.

Rabidoux, Greg R. *Hollywood Politicos, Then and Now: Who They Are, What They Want, Why It Matters*. University Press of America, 2009.

Raymond, Emilie. *Stars for Freedom: Hollywood, Black Celebrities, and the Civil Rights Movement*. University of Washington Press, 2015.

Rhoden, William C. *Forty Million Dollar Slaves: The Rise, Fall, and Redemption of the Black Athlete*. Three Rivers Press, 2006.

Russonello, Giovanni. "Read Oprah Winfrey's Golden Globes Speech." *The New York Times*, January 7, 2018. nytimes.com/2018/01/07/movies/oprah-winfrey-golden-globes-speech-transcript.html. Accessed February 16, 2019.

Scribner's, Herb. "Twitter Goes Wild for Steph and Ayesha Curry During the Democratic National Convention." *MSN*, August 21, 2020, msn.com/en-us/sports/nba/twitter-goes-wild-for-steph-and-ayesha-curry-during-the-democratic-national-convention/at-BB18di6g?. Accessed August 22, 2020.

Tamblyn, Amber. "Amber Tamblyn: Redefining the Red Carpet." *The New York Times*, January 7, 2018, nytimes.com/2018/01/07/opinion/sunday/amber-tamblyn-golden-globes-metoo.html. Accessed February 15, 2019.

"Twitter Accounts with the Most Followers Worldwide as of May 2020 (in Millions)." *Statista*, statista.com/statistics/273172/twitter-accounts-with-the-most-followers-worldwide. Accessed August 183, 2020.

Ugwu, Reggie. "President Oprah? After the Golden Globes, Some Have a 2020 Vision." *The New York Times*, January 8, 2018, nytimes.com/2018/01/08/movies/oprah-winfrey-lifetime-achievement-golden-globes.html. Accessed February 16, 2019.

van Elteren, Mel. "Celebrity Culture, Performative Politics, and the Spectacle of 'Democracy' in America," *The Journal of American Culture*, vol. 36, no. 4, December 21, 2013, pp. 263–283, doi: 10.1111/jacc.12049.

Victor, Daniel, and Giovanni Russonello. "Meryl Streep's Golden Globes Speech." *The New York Times*, January 8, 2017, nytimes.com/2017/01/08/arts/television/meryl-streep-golden-globes-speech.html. Accessed February 16, 2019.

Wanshel, Elyse. "John Legend Becomes First Black Man to Reach EGOT Status." *HuffPost*, September 10, 2018, huffpost.com/entry/john-legend-first-black-man-with-egot_n_5b9693fce4b0511db3e4ce6d. Accessed August 18, 2020.

Wheeler, Mark. *Celebrity Politics: Image and Identity in Contemporary Political Communications*. Polity Press, 2013.

Willman, Chris. "Taylor Swift: No Longer 'Polite at All Costs.'" *Variety*, January 21, 2020, variety.com/2020/music/features/taylor-swift-politics-sundance-

documentary-miss-americana-12034
71910/. Accessed February 23, 2020.

Wyatt, Wendy N., and Kristie Bunton. "The Ethics of Speaking Out." *Ethics in Entertainment: Essays on Media Culture and Media Morality,* edited by Howard Good and Sandra L. Borden. McFarland, 2010, pp. 9–22.

"Year in Sports Media Report, U.S. 2017." *Nielsen,* nielsen.com/us/en/insights/report/2018/2017-year-in-sports-media/. Accessed June 24, 2019.

Zeleny, Jeff. "Oprah Endorses Obama." *The New York Times,* May 3, 2007, thecaucus-blogs.nytimes.com/2007/05/03/oprah-endorses-Obama-2/. Accessed February 9, 2019.

Zubcevic-Basic, Nives. "US Election: What Impact Do Celebrity Endorsements Really Have?" *The Conversation,* October 4, 2016, theconversation.com/us-election-what-impact-do-celebrity-endorsements-really-have-66204. Accessed February 9, 2019.

Chapter 2

@StephenCurry30. "Twitter Profile: @StephenCurry30." *Twitter,* mobile.twitter.com/stephencurry30. Accessed February 22, 2019.

Aliko, Carter. "Stephen Curry Church Realization Should Signal Public Endorsement of LGBT Rights." *Forbes,* March 31, 2016, forbes.com/sites/alikocarter/2016/03/31/stephen-curry-church-realization-should-signal-public-endorsement-of-lgbt-rights/#6a43084419b0. Accessed February 23, 2019.

"Ambassadors: Stephen Curry," *Nothing But Nets,* nothingbutnets.net/about/. Accessed February 23, 2019.

Andrews, Travis M. "'How Do I Explain This to My Children?': Van Jones Gives Voice to the 'Nightmare' Some Are Feeling." *The Washington Post,* November 9, 2016, washingtonpost.com/news/morning-mix/wp/2016/11/09/how-do-i-explain-this. Accessed March 3, 2019.

Associated Press. "Steph Curry Hopes for Changes to LGBT Law in North Carolina." *USA Today,* September 15, 2016, usatoday.com/story/sports/nba/2016/09/15/steph-curry-hopes-for-changes-to-lgbt-law-in-north-carolina/9043 8676/. Accessed February 23, 2019.

Associated Press. "Steph Curry Doesn't Want to Visit the White House, and Trump, in a Tweet, Withdraws the Invitation." *Los Angeles Times,* September 23, 2017 latimes.com/sports/sportsnow/la-sp-curry-trump-20170923-story.html. Accessed March 5, 2019.

Barker, Jeff. "Under Armour Has Stories to Tell about Its Celebrity Athletes." *Baltimore Sun,* November 13, 2015, baltimoresun.com/business/bs-by/under-armour-athletes-20151113-story.html. Accessed February 23, 2019.

Becker, Jon. "Is Steph Curry the Most Likable Star in Bay Area Sports History?" *The Mercury News,* March 15, 2018, mercurynews.com/2018/03/15/is-steph-curry-the-most-likable-star-in-bay-area-pro-sports-history-2/. Accessed February 23, 2019.

Bonesteel, Matt. "Warriors Skip the White House, Meet with Former President Barack Obama Instead." *The Washington Post,* January 25, 2019, washingtonpost.com/sports/2019/01/25/warriors-skip-white-house-meet-with-former-president-barack-obama-i nstead/. Accessed March 9, 2019.

Bontemps, Tim. "Stephen Curry Has Long Been Reluctant to Speak Out. Then Along Came Donald Trump." *The Washington Post,* September 22, 2017, washingtonpost.com/news/sports/wp/2017/09/22/stephen-curry-has-long-been-reluctant-to-speak-out-then-along-came-donald-trump/. Accessed February 23, 2019.

Bontemps, Tim. "It's Surreal, to Be Honest,' Stephen Curry Says of President Trump Uninviting Warriors to the White House." *The Washington Post,* September 23, 2017, washingtonpost.com/news/sports/wp/2017/09/23/stephen-curry-steve-kerr-and-the-warriors-respond-to-president-trump/. Accessed February 22, 2019.

Curry, Stephen. "Underrated." *The Players Tribune,* January 2, 2019, theplayerstribune.com/en-us/articles/stephen-curry-underrated. Accessed February 25, 2019.

DePaula, Nick. "Decoding the Sneaker Scribbles of NBA Stars." *ESPN,* March 22, 2018, espn.com/nba/story/_id/2283

5960/decoding-sneaker-scribbles-nba-st ars. Accessed February 23, 2019.

Disbrow, Bill. "Warriors MVP Stephen Curry Says He'll Take Clinton over Trump." *SFGate*, September 14, 2016, sfgate.com/politics/article/Warriors-MVP-Stephen-Curry-says-he-ll-take-9222970.php. Accessed March 2, 2019.

Dowd, Katie. "After Years of Silence, Steph Curry Is Finally Getting Political." *SFGate*, November 9, 2016, sfgate.com/elections/article/After-years-of-silence-Steph-Curry-gets-political-10604186.php. Accessed February 22, 2019.

Glidden, Paige. "3 Facts About Steph Curry After His 3rd Championship Win." *Nothing But Nets,* June 12, 2018, nothingbutnets.net/press-release/3-facts-about-steph-curry. Accessed February 23, 2019.

Golliver, Ben. "Grades: Warriors Lavish Stephen Curry with Record-Setting $201 Million Max Deal." *Sports Illustrated*, June 30, 2017, si.com/nba/2017/07/01/warriors-stephen-curry-contract-nba-free-agency-signing-kevin-durant. Accessed February 23, 2019.

Heath, Thomas. "Under Armour, Stephen Curry and the Risk of Celebrity Endorsementsl" *The Washington Post*, February 13, 2017, washingtonpost.com/business/economy/under-armour-steph-curry-and-the-risk-of-celebrity-endorsements/2017/02/13/d418dbea-f208–11e6-b9c9-e83fce42fb61_story.html. Accessed March 2, 2019.

Hoffman, Benjamin. "LeBron James and Stephen Curry Unite Against White House Visits." *The New York Times,* June 5, 2018, nytimes.com/2018/06/05/sports/lebron-james-stephen-curry-trump.html. Accessed March 9, 2019.

Kroichick, Ron. "Stephen Curry at 30: From Baby-Faced Warriors Guard to Basketball Revolutionary and Beyond." *San Francisco Chronicle*, March 8, 2018, sfchronicle.com/warriors/article/Stephen-Curry-at-30-From-baby-faced-Warriors-12736239.php. Accessed February 23, 2019.

Letourneau, Connor. "Stephen Curry, Barack Obama Discuss Trials of Their Youth at Oakland Event." *San Francisco Chronicle*, February 19, 2019, sfchronicle.com/warriors/article/Stephen-Curry-Barack-Obama-discuss-trials-of-13629222.php. Accessed February 23, 2019.

Martin, Nick. "President Obama Helps Curry Out with His Jumpshot in 'The Mentorship.'" *The Washington Post*, April 16, 2016 washingtonpost.com/news/early-lead/wp/2016/04/16/president-obama-helps-curry-out-with-his-jumpshot-in-the-mentorship/?utm_term=.30c4b2f88e65. Accessed February 28, 2019.

Medina, Mark. "Stephen Curry's Mother Proud of How He Has Handled White House Controversy." *The Mercury News*, October 12, 2017, mercurynews.com/2017/10/12/stephen-currys-mother-proud-of-how-he-has-handled-white-house-controversy/. Accessed February 23, 2019.

Nakamura, David, and Cindy Boren. "Warriors Visit White House to See Steph Curry's Friend President Obama." *The Washington Post*, February 4, 2016, washingtonpost.com/news/early-lead/wp/2016/02/04/watch-live-as-warriors-visit-white-house-a-place-stephen-curry-knows-well/. Accessed February 23, 2019.

"NBA MVP Award Winners." *NBA.com,* nba.com/history/awards/mvp. Accessed February 23, 2019.

Plaisance, Patrick Lee. *Media Ethics: Key Principles for Responsible Practice.* Sage, 2009, p. 3.

"Remarks by the President at Visit of the 2015 NBA Champion Golden State Warriors." *White House Office of the Press Secretary*, February 4, 2016, obamawhitehouse.archives.gov/the-press-office/2016/02/04/remarks-president-visit. Accessed March 2, 2019.

Shekhar, Rishabh. "NBA: 10 Most Popular Current Players on Social Media." *Sportskeeda*, December 20, 2019, sportskeeda.com/basketball/10-most-popular-current-players-on-social-media/5. Accessed March 3, 2020.

Shipnuck, Alan. "Exclusive: Stephen Curry and Wife Ayesha on Marriage, Kids and Their Matching Tattoos." *Parents*, June 2016, parents.com/parenting/celebrity-parents-moms-dads/exclusive-stephen-curry-and-wife-ayesha-on-marriage-kids-and/. Accessed February 23, 2019.

Simmons, Rusty. "Curry's Good Deeds Earn

Visit with President Obama." *SFGate,* February 25, 2015, sfgate.com/warriors/article/Curry-meets-Obama-tours-White-House-6101475.php. Accessed February 23, 2019.

Strauss, Ben. "'This Era of Athlete Is Unfraid': Stephen Curry Speaks Up in D.C., Again without White House Trip." *The Washington Post,* January 24, 2019, washingtonpost.com/sports/2019/01/24/this-era-athlete-is-unafraid-stephen-curry-speaks-up-dc-again-without-white-house-trip/. Accessed February 22, 2019.

Thompson, Marcus. "Warriors' Stephen Curry Talks North Carolina Transgender Law, But He Answered Already without Words." *Mercury News,* April 5, 2016, blogs.mercurynews.com/thompson/2016/04/05/warriors-stephen-curry-talks-north-carolina-transgender-law-answered-already-without-words/. Accessed February 23, 2019.

Thrush, Glenn. "New Outcry as Trump Rebukes Charlottesville Racists 2 Days Later." *The New York Times,* August 14, 2017, nytimes.com/2017/08/14/us/politics/trump-charlottesville-protest.html. Accessed March 5, 2019.

"Warriors' Stephen Curry Wins 2015–16 Kia NBA Most Valuable Player Award." *NBA Communications,* May 10, 2016, pr.nba.com/stephen-curry-2015–16-kia-nba-mvp-award-warriors/. Accessed February 23, 2019.

"What Is Malaria?" *Nothing But Nets,* nothingbutnets.net/about-malaria/. Accessed February 23, 2019.

"Why Stephen Curry's Latest Shoe Release Is Designed to Save Souls." *Nothing But Nets,* December 27, 2017, nothingbutnets.net/press-releases/stephen-curry-latest-shoe-release-is-designed-save-souls. Accessed February 23, 2019.

Zillgitt, Jeff. "Openly Gay NBA Executive Decides to Particpate in All-Star Weekend in Charlotte." *USA Today,* February 17, 2019, usatoday.com/story/sports/nba/allstar/2019/02/17/openly-gay-nba-executive-attend-all-star-weekend-charlotte/2898930002/. Accessed February 23, 2019.

Chapter 3

Bieler, Des. "Kyrie Irving Sorry for Saying Earth Is Flat, Blames it on a YouTube 'Rabbit Hole.'" *The Washington Post,* October 1, 2018, washingtonpost.com/sports/2018/10/02/kyrie-irving-sorry-saying-earth-is-flat-blames-it-youtube-rabbit-hole/?noredirect=on. Accessed March 23, 2019.

Bogage, Jacob. "Steph Curry Says He Was Joking about Not Believing in the Moon Landing and Everything Is Fine." *The Washington Post,* December 12, 2018, washingtonpost.com/sports/2018/12/12/steph-curry-says-he-was-joking-about-not-believing-moon-landing-everything-is-fine/. Accessed March 16, 2019.

Bogage, Jacob. "Stephen Curry, Now Very Sure of the Moon Landing, Interviews Astronaut Scott Kelly." *The Washington Post,* December 15, 2018, washingtonpost.com/sports/2018/12/15/stephen-curry-now-very-sure-moon-landing-interviews-astronaut-scott-kelly/. Accessed March 16, 2019.

Bok, Sissela Bok. *Lying: Moral Choice in Public and Private Life.* Vintage Books, 1989.

Bunnin, Nicholas, and Jiyuan Yu. *The Blackwell Dictionary of Western Philosophy.* John Wiley & Sons, 2004.

Curry, Stephen. "Stephen Curry: Small Gestures Can Make All the Difference in Times of Crisis." *Time,* April 16, 2020, https://time.com/collection/finding-hope-coronavirus-pandemic/5820660/steph-curry-helping-coronavirus/. Accessed July 4, 2020.

Curry, Stephen. "The Noise," *The Players' Tribune,* November 11, 2017, theplayerstribune.com/en-us/articles/stephen-curry-veterans-day. Accessed February 22, 2019.

Davis, Scott. "ESPN's Michael Wilbon and Tony Kornheiser Blast Stephen Curry for Saying the Moon Landing Was Fake: 'Does That Mean You Don't Believe in Slavery?'" *Business Insider,* December 12, 2018, businessinsider.com/steph-curry-moon-landing-comments-blasted-espn-pardon-the-interruption-2018–12. Accessed February 22, 2019.

Friedell, Nick. "Warriors' Stephen Curry Says He Was Joking About Moon Landing, Will Visit NASA." *ESPN,* December 18, 2018 espn.com/nba/story/_/id/25518468/stephen-curry-golden-state-warriors-says-joking-moon-landing-accept-nasa-invitation. Accessed March 16, 2019.

Friedell, Nick. "Stephen Curry Never Lost Sight of His Charlotte Roots." *ESPN*, February 25, 2019, espn.com/nba/story/_/id/26057432/stephen-curry-never-lost-sight-charlotte-roots. Accessed March 16, 2019.

Hearit, Keith, and Sandra Borden. "Apologetic Ethics." *Crisis Management by Apology: Corporate Repsonse to Allegations of Wrongdoing*, edited by Keith Hearit. Lawrence Earlbaum, 2006, pp. 58–78.

Hoffman, Benjamin. "Stephen Curry Doubts Moon Landings. NASA Offers to Show Him the Rocks." *The New York Times*, December 10, 2018, nytimes.com/2018/12/10/sports/stephen-curry-moon-landing.html. Accessed February 22, 2019.

Jaramillo, Antonia. "NASA, Boeing and Others Pounce on Stephen Curry after He Said Moon Landing Was a Hoax." *Florida Today*, December 12, 2018, floridatoday.com/story/tech/science/space/2018/12/12/nasa-boeing-and-others-pounce-step. Accessed March 25, 2019.

Joseph, Andrew. "Kyrie Irving Apologized for Saying Earth Is Flat." *USA Today*, October 1, 2018, usatoday.com/story/sports/ftw/2018/10/01/kyrie-irving-apologized-for-saying-the-earth-is-flat-i-was-huge-into-conspiracies/38012367/. Accessed March 23, 2019.

Joseph, Andrew. "How the Science Community Reacted to Steph Curry's Moon-Landing Conspiracy." *USA Today*, December 11, 2018 ftw.usatoday.com/2018/12012/stephen-curry-moon-landing-fake-conspiracy-nasa-scien. Accessed March 25, 2019.

Kleinschmidt, Jessica. "Warriors' Stephen Curry 'Moon Landing' Shoes Auctioned Off for $58,000." *NBC Sports*. January 14, 2019, nbcsports.com/bayarea/warriors/warriors-stephen-curry-moon-landing-shoes-auctioned-58000. Accessed March 31, 2019.

Lawrence, Andrew. "Fake Moon Landings and a Flat Earth: Why Do Athletes Love Conspiracy Theories?" *The Guardian*, December 27, 2018, theguardian.com/sport/2018/dec/27/stephen-curry-kyrie-irving-conspiracy-theories-nba. Accessed March 16, 2019.

May, William F. *Beleaguered Rulers: The Public Obligation of the Professional*. Westminster John Knox Press.

McIntyre, Lee. *Post-Truth*. The MIT Press, 2018.

Medina, Mark. "Opinion: Stephen Curry's Coronavirus Interview with Dr. Anthony Fauci Is Most Significant Move of His Career." *USA Today*, March 26, 2020, usatoday.com/story/sports/nba/columnist/mark-Medina/2020/02/36/stephen-curry-coronavirus-interview-anthony-fauci-most-significant-move/2922652001/. Accessed July 4, 2020.

"NASA Head Claps Back at Steph Curry, We Went to Moon Six Times!" *TMZSports*, December 11, 2018, tmz.com/2018/12/11/jim-bridenstine-nasa-steph-curry-moon-landing-nba. Accessed March 25, 2019.

New York Times Co. v. Sullivan, 376 U.S. 254 (1964).

Russell, Jake. "Kyrie Irving Believes the Earth Is Flat. It Is Not." *The Washington Post*, February 17, 2017, washingtonpost.com/news/early-lead/wp/2017/02/17/kyrie-irving-believes-the-earth-is-flat-it-is-not/?smid=nytcore-ios-share. Accessed March 23, 2019.

Sprung, Schlomo. "Vince Carter, Kent Bazemore Discuss Winging It Podcast, Steph Curry Moon Landing Incident," *Forbes*, January 25, 2019, forbes.com/sites/shlomosprung/2019/01/25/vince-carter-kent-bazemore-discuss-popular-winging-it-podcast-steph-curry-moon-landing-incident/#20339e0d20a3. Accessed March 25, 2019.

Tavag, Yasmin. "Steph Curry Called Out by Educators for Spreading Moon Landing Conspiracy." *Inverse*, December 11, 2018, inverse.com/article/51671-steph-curry-the-moon-landing-is-real. Accessed March 25, 2019.

Taylor, Derrick Bryson. "A Timeline of the Coronavirus Pandemic." *The New York Times*, August 6, 2020, nytimes.com/article/coronavirus-timeline.html. Accessed August 20, 2020.

The Observer Editorial Board, "Did Stephen Curry Really Say the Moon Landings Were Fake? We Hope Not." *The Charlotte Observer*, December 10, 2018, charlotteobserver.com/opinion/article222902600.html. Accessed March 31, 2019.

Usher, Nikki, and Janel S. Schuh. "'I'm Sorry, oh, So Sorry': Celebrity Apologies and Public Ethics." *Ethics in Entertainment: Essays on Media Culture and Media Morality,* edited by Howard Good and Sandra L. Borden. McFarland, 2010, pp. 23–40.

Wall, Mike. "Steph Curry Tells Former Astronaut Scott Kelly Moon-Landing Comment Was 'Made in Jest.'" *Space,* December 17, 2018, space.com/42763-steph-curry-moon-landing-scott-kelly.html. Accessed March 16, 2019.

Wallace, Ava. "Stephen Curry and Anthony Fauci Chatted on Instagram. Thousands Watched, Including Barack Obama." *The Washington Post,* March 26, 2020, washingtonpost.com/sports/2020/03/26/stephen-curry-anthony-fauci-chatted-instagram-thousands-watched-including-barack-obama/. Accessed July 4, 2020.

Wolfman-Arent, Avi. "The Ongoing Battle between Science Teachers and Fake News." *National Public Radio,* July 28, 2017, npr.org/sections/ed/2017/07/28/537907951/the-ongoing-battle-between-science-teachers-and-fake-news?smid=nytcore-ios-share. Accessed March 23, 2019.

Wong, Wilson. "Latest to Interview Fauci on Coronavirus? NBA's Steph Curry, on Instagram." NBC News, March 26, 2020, nbcnews.com/news/nbcblk/latest-interview-fauci-coronavirus-nba-s-steph-curry-instagram-n1169746. Accessed June 2, 2020.

Wootson, Cleve R., Jr. "Stephen Curry Says the U.S. Never Landed on the Moon. NASA Cries Foul." *The Washington Post,* December 11, 2018, washingtonpost.com/sports/2018/12/11/stephen-curry-says-us-never-landed-moon-nasa-cries-foul/. Accessed February 22, 2019.

Wyatt, Wendy N., and Kristie Bunton. "The Ethics of Speaking Out." *Ethics in Entertainment: Essays on Media Culture and Media Morality,* edited by Howard Good and Sandra L. Borden. McFarland, 2010, pp. 9–22.

Chapter 4

Adams, Guy. "The Serious Side of Jon Stewart: The Man Who Is Famous for Lampooning Politicians Is Now Forging a Reputation as a Political Campaigner Himself." *The Independent,* December 30, 2010, independent.co.uk/news/people/news/the-serious-side-of-jon-stewart-2171794.html. Accessed June 22, 2019.

Andrews-Dyer, Helena. "'No Selfies If You're Not on the Bill': Jon Stewart's Day on the Hill." *The Washington Post,* September 16, 2015, washingtonpost.com/news/reliable-source-wp/2015/09/16/no-selfies-if-youre-not-on-the-bill-jon-stewarts-day-on-the-hill/?utm_term=.fe9c4dcbaaeb. Accessed June 30, 2019.

Associated Press. "Obama Signs Sept. 11 First Responders Bill." *NBC News,* January 2, 2011, nbcnews.com/id/40879753/ns/politics-white-house/t/obama-signs-sept-first-responders-bill/#.XRkM-0MpOmhA. Accessed June 30, 2019.

Barrett, Devlin. "After Emotional Testimony from 9/11 Responders, House Panel Votes to Replenish Victims Fund." *The Washington Post,* June 12, 2019, washingtonpost.com/world/national-security/after-emotional-testimony-from-911-responders-house-panel-votes-to-replenish-victim-fund/2019/06/12/826ffa1e-8d27–11e9–8f69-a2795fca3343_story.html?utm_term=.4669d265c146. Accessed June 16, 2019.

Berenson, Tessa. "Watch Jon Stewart's 5 Greatest Daily Show Moments." *Time,* August 4, 2015, time.com/3704285/the-daily-show-finale-jon-stewart-best-moments/. Accessed June 29, 2019.

Blakemore, Erin. "9/11 Memorial Glade: A Monument to Responders, Survivors Who Paid for the Attacks with Their Health." *The Washington Post,* June 8, 2019, washingtonpost.com/health/911-memorial-glade-a-monument-to-responders-survivors-who-paid-for-the-attacks-with-their-health/2019/06/07/7f411d66–87b7–11e9-a870-b9c411dc4312_story.html?utm_term=.2db56a9ae945. Accessed June 16, 2019.

Bowers, Peggy. "Charles Taylor's Practical Reason." *Moral Engagement in Public Life,* edited by Sharon Bracci and Clifford Christians. Peter Lang, 2002.

Boyle, Brian. "Jon Stewart Just Reminded Us How Outrage Is Supposed to Work." *Los Angeles Times,* June 11, 2019, latimes.com/opinion/enterthefray/

la-ol-jon-stewart-911-outrage-congress-20190611-story.html. Accessed June 21, 2019.

Bunnin, Nicholas, and Jiyuan Yu. *The Blackwell Dictionary of Western Philosophy.* John Wiley & Sons, 2004.

Butler, Bethonie. "Jon Stewart's 'Daily Show' Changed How We Consume News. His Political Influence Still Endures." *The Washington Post,* June 19, 2019, washingtonpost.com/arts-entertainment/2019/06/19/jon-stewarts-daily-show-changed-how-we-consume-news-his-political-influence-still-endures/?utem_term=.e2d27a4cd5e9. Accessed June 20, 2019.

Carter, Bill, and Brian Stelter. "In 'Daily Show' Role on 9/11 Bill, Echoes of Murrow." *The New York Times,* December 26, 2010, nytimes.com/2010/12/27/business/media/27stewart.html. Accessed June 16, 2019.

Chiu, Allyson. "'I'm Bent Out of Shape for Them': Jon Stewart Roasts Mitch McConnell over 9/11 Victims Fund." *The Washington Post,* June 18, 2019, washingtonpost.com/nation/2019/06/18/jon-stewart-mitch-mcconnell-stephen-colbert-funding/?utm_term=.5ee6e-5a7d5e0. Accessed June 18, 2019.

Compton, Josh. "Introduction: Surveying Scholarship on The Daily Show and The Colbert Report." *The Stewart/Colbert Effect: Essays on the Real Impacts of Fake News,* edited by Amarnath Amarasingam. McFarland, 2011, p. 9.

Daugherty, Owen. "McConnell Says Senate Will Vote on 9/11 Responders Bill after Jon Stewart Criticism." The Hill.com, June 25, 2019, thehill.com/homenews/senate/45039-mcconnell-says-senate-will-vote-on-9–11-compensation-fund-after-criticism. Accessed June 27, 2019.

Dowd, Maureen. "Jon Stewart and Stephen Colbert: America's Anchors." *Rolling Stone,* November 16, 2006, rollingstone.com/tv/tv-news/jon-stewart-and-stephen-colbert-americas-anchors-247689/. Accessed June 22, 2019.

Egner, Jeremy. "Jon Stewart's Notable Moments on 'The Daily Show.'" *The New York Times,* February 11, 2015 artsbeat.blogs.nytimes.com/2015/02/11/jon-stewarts-notable-moments-on-the-daily-show/. Accessed June 29, 2019.

Heritage, Stuart. "Jon Stewart's 10 Best Moments." *The Guardian,* February 11, 2015, theguardian.com/tv-and-radio/2015/feb/11/jon-stewarts-10-best-moments. Accessed June 29, 2019.

"House Panel Approves Funds for Sept. 11 First Responders." *National Public Radio,* June 13, 2019, npr.org/2019/06/13/732270815/house-panel-approves-funds-for-sept-11-first-responders. Accessed July 1, 2019.

Kakutani, Michiko. "Is Jon Stewart the Most Trusted Man in America?" *The New York Times,* August 15, 2008, nytimes.com/2008/08/17/arts/television/17kaku.html. Accessed June 22, 2019.

Kilby, Allaina. "Jon Stewart: Journey from Satirist to Political Advocate Is No Laughing Matter." *The Conversation,* June 14, 2019, theconversation.com/jon-stewart-journey-from-satirist-to-political-advocate-is-no-laughing-matter-118784. Accessed June 22, 2019.

McAuliff, Michael. "Jon Stewart and 9/11 Responders Walk the Halls of Congress." *HuffPost,* September 16, 2015, huffpost.com/entry/jon-stewart-911-responders_n_55f950bce4b0b48f67014d60. Accessed June 30, 2019.

McCullough, Thomas E. *The Moral Imagination and Public Life: Raising the Ethical Question.* Chatham House Publishers, Inc., 1991.

Moore, Mark. "Read Jon Stewart's Full Testimony Supporting the 9/11 Victims Fund." *New York Post,* June 12, 2019, nypost.com/2019/06/12/read-jon-stewarts-full-testimony-supporting-the-9–11-victims-fund/. Accessed June 29, 2019.

Pallotta, Frank. "Stephen Colbert 'Trumps Up' Jon Stewart on 'Late Show." *CNN Money,* December 11, 2015, money.cnn.com/2014/12/11/media/stephen-colbert-jon-stewart-donald-trump/index.html. Accessed July 1, 2019.

Rogak, Lisa. *Angry Optimist: The Life and Times of Jon Stewart.* Thomas Dunne Books, 2015.

Samuelsohn, Darren. "Jon Stewart's Next Act: Lobbyist?" *Politico,* July 31, 2015, politico.com/agenda/story/2015/07/jon-stewarts-next-act-lobbyist-000179. Accessed June 22, 2019.

Serfaty, Sunlen, and Paul LeBlanc. "'We Pay for That Shit': 9/11 First Responder

Goes Off on Congress after McConnell Commits to Vote on Victims Fund Extension." *CNN*, June 25, 2019, cnn.com/2019/06/25/politics/mitch-mcconnell-first-responders-meeting/index.html. Accessed June 27, 2019.

Smith, Chris. *The Daily Show (The Book): An Oral History*. Grand Central Publishing, 2016.

Sonmez, Felicia. "McConnell: I Don't Know Why Jon Stewart Is 'All Bent Out of Shape' on 9/11 Victims Fund." *The Washington Post*, June 14, 2019, washingtonpost.com/politics/mcconnell-i-dont-know-why-jon-stewart-is-all-bent-out-of-shape-on-911-victims-fund/2019/06/17/193143bc-913e-11e9-b570-6416efdc0803_story.html?utm_term=.6bf06320e648. Accessed June 18, 2019.

Stelter, Brian. "Jon Stewart, the Advocate, on the 9/11 Health Bill." *The New York Times*, December 17, 2010, mediadecoder.blogs.nytimes.com. Accessed June 16, 2019.

VanMetre, Elizabeth. "Jon Stewart's Most Memorable Moments on 'The Daily Show.'" *New York Daily News*, Feb. 10, 2015, nydailynews.com/entertainment/tv/jon-stewart-top-10-daily-show-moments-article-1.2110423. Accessed June 29, 2019.

Wyatt, Wendy N., and Kristie Bunton. "The Ethics of Speaking Out." *Ethics in Entertainment: Essays on Media Culture and Media Morality*, edited by Howard Good and Sandra L. Borden. McFarland, 2010, pp. 9–22.

Chapter 5

Aguilera, Jasmine, and Tara Law. "9/11 First Responder Luis Alvarez Has Died, 18 Days After Testifying Before Congress With Jon Stewart." *Time*, June 29, 2019, time.com/5613357/9-11-first-responder-luis-alvarez-dies-jon-stewart/. Accessed June 29, 2019.

Barrett, Devlin. "Tears, Anger at Congressional Hearing Seeking Extension of Victim Fund for 9/11 Responders." *The Washington Post*, June 11, 2019, washingtonpost.com/world/national-security/tears-anger-at-congressional-hearing-seeking-extension-of-victim-fund-for-911-responders/2019/06/11/20d7c254–

8c51–11e9-adf3-f70f78c156e8_story.html. Accessed June 22, 2019.

Becker, Lawrence C., and Charlotte B. Becker, editors. *Encyclopedia of Ethics*. Garland Publishing, 2nd ed., 2001.

Bird, Frederick Bruce. *The Muted Conscience: Moral Silence and the Practice of Ethics in Business*. Quorum Books, 1996.

Bok, Sissela. *Lying: Moral Choice in Public and Private Life*. Vintage Books Edition, 1989.

boyd, danah. *It's Complicated: The Social Lives of Networked Teens*. Yale University Press, 2014.

Chiu, Allyson. "Jon Stewart Accuses Rand Paul of 'Fiscal Responsibility Virtue Signaling' in Stalling 9/11 Victims Funding." *The Washington Post*, July 18, 2019, washingtonpost.com/nation/2019/07/18/jon-stewart-rand-paul-mike-lee-victims-fund-delay/. Accessed July 18, 2019.

Cole, Devan. "Jon Stewart Says 9/11 First Responders Fund Is the 'Least' Lawmakers Can Do 'for the Best of Us' after Bill's Passage." *CNN Wire*, July 24, 2019, cnn.com/2019/07/24/politics/john-feal-jon-stewart-9–11-fund-cnntv/index.html. Accessed July 24, 2019.

Drumwright, Minette E., and Patrick E. Murphy. "How Advertising Practitioners View Ethics: Moral Muteness, Moral Myopia, and Moral Imagination." *Journal of Advertising*, vol. 33, no. 2, 2004, pp. 7–24, doi: 10.1080/00913367.2004.10639158.

Edelman, Adam. "Trump Signs Bill Ensuring 9/11 Victims Fund Will Never Run Out of Money." *NBC News*, July 29, 2019, nbcnews.com/politics/white-house/trump-signs-bill-ensuring-9–11-victims-fund-will-never-n1035656. Accessed July 29, 2019.

Editorial Board. "Give Sept. 11 Survivors the Help They Deserve." *The New York Times*, Feb. 28, 2019 nytimes.com/2019/02/28/opinion/9–11-first-responders-fund.html. Accessed June 16, 2019.

Flynn, Meagan. "Again, 9/11 First Responders Are Pleading with Congress to Fund Their Health Care. Again, Jon Stewart Is Joining Them." *The Washington Post*, February 26, 2019, washingtonpost.com/nation/2019/02/26/again-first-responders-are-pleading-with-congress-fund-their-health-care-again-jon-stewart-is-joining-them/?utm_term=.c9a2e1b3203d. Accessed June 16, 2019.

Gallucci, Nicole. "Watch a Tearful Jon Stewart Receive a Touching Gift from 9/11 First Responders." *Mashable*, June 14, 2019, mashable.com/video/jon-stewart-cries-september-11-first-responders-friend-bunker-coat/ (accessed September 6, 2019).

Gert, Bernard. *Common Morality: Deciding What to Do.* Oxford University Press, 2007.

Hernandez, Raymond. "Senate Passes 9/11 Health Bill as Republicans Back Down." *The New York Times*, December 22, 2010, nytimes.com/2010/12/23/nyregion/23health.html. Accessed September 6, 2019.

"House Panel Approves Funds for Sept. 11 First Responders." *National Public Radio*, June 13, 2019, npr.org/2019/06/13/732270815/house-panel-approves-funds-for-sept-11-first-responders. Accessed July 1, 2019.

Hyde, Marina. *Celebrity: How Entertainers Took Over the World and Why We Need an Exit Strategy.* Vintage Books, 2010.

Iati, Marisa. "'You Should Be Ashamed of Yourselves': Watch Jon Stewart Tear into Congress Over 9/11 Victims Fund." *The Washington Post*, June 12, 2019, washingtonpost.com/politics/2019/06/11/jon-stewart-blasts-congress-first-responders-fund/. Accessed June 16, 2019.

Jackson, Hallie. "'This One's for Them': 9/11 First Responder Dedicates Funding Bill to Memory of Those Who Died." *MSNBC*, July 29, 2019, msnbc.com/hallie-jackson/watch/-this-ones-for-them-9-11-first-responder-dedicates-funding-bill-to-memory-of-those-who-died-64800837639. Accessed July 29, 2019.

Kant, Immanuel. *Groundwork on the Metaphysic of Morals.* Translated by H.J. Patton, Harper Torchbooks, 1964.

Kidder, Rushworth M. *How Good People Make Tough Choices: Resolving the Dilemmas of Ethical Living.* HarperCollins, 2003.

Kilby, Allaina. "Jon Stewart: Journey from Satirist to Political Advocate Is No Laughing Matter." *The Conversation*, June 14, 2019, theconversation.com/jon-stewart-journey-from-satirist-to-political-advocate-is-no-laughing-matter-118784. Accessed June 22, 2019.

Lim, Naomi. "Jon Stewart: Trump's Justice Department 'Doing an Excellent Job' on 9/11 Fund." *Washington Examiner*, February 25, 2019, washingtonexaminer.com/news/jon-stewart-trumps-justice-department-doing-an-excellent-job-on-9-11-fund. Accessed August 30, 2019.

McAuliff, Michael. "The Inside Story of How a 9/11 First Responder Pounded McConnell into Action." *The Daily Beast*, July 23, 2019, thedailybeast.com/the-inside-story-of-how-911-first-responder-john-feal-pounded-mitch-mcconnell-into-action. Accessed September 6, 2019.

McAuliff, Michael. "Jon Stewart Sticks By Praise for Trump Administration's Handling of 9/11 Fund." *New York Daily News*, March 3, 2019, nydailynews.com/new-york/ny-pol-stewart-trump-praise-20190303-story.html. Accessed September 10, 2019.

McGraw, Meridith. "Trump Signs 9/11 Victim Compensation Fund Bill for First Responders." *ABC News*, July 29, 2019, abcnews.go.com/Politics/trump-signs-911-victim-compensation-fund-bill-responders/story?id=64630468. Accessed July 29, 2019.

Mongolian, Lorena, and Jackie Salo. "Hundreds Pay Respects at Funeral of 9/11 Hero Luis Alvarez," *New York Post*, July 3, 2019, nypost.com/2019/03/03/hundreds-pay-respects-at-funeral-of-9-11hero-luis-alvarez/. Accessed July 29, 2019.

Nichols, Tom. *The Death of Expertise: The Campaign Against Established Knowledge and Why It Matters.* Oxford University Press, 2017.

Pierce, Charles P. "Jon Stewart's Outrage Forced Washington to Actually Do Something Good." *Esquire*, July 23, 2019, esquire.com/news-politics/politics/a28485934/9-11-first-responders-bill-jon-stewart-rand-paul/. Accessed Aug. 2, 2019.

Rabidoux, Greg R. *Hollywood Politicos, Then and Now: Who They Are, What They Want, Why It Matters.* University Press of America, 2009.

"Remarks by President Trump at Signing of H.R. 1327, an Act to Permanently Authorize the September 11th Victim Compensation Fund." *White House Briefings and*

Statements, July 29, 2019, whitehouse. gov/briefings-statements/remarks-president-trump-signing-h-r-1327-act-permanently-authorize-september-11th-victim-compensation-fund/. Accessed July 29, 2019.

Royce, Josiah. *The Philosophy of Loyalty.* Macmillan, 1914.

Salant, Jonathan D. "Trump Signs 9/11 First Responders Bill Championed by Jon Stewart." *NJ.com*, July 29, 2019, nj.com/politics/2019/07/trump-signs-911-first-responders-bill-championed-by-jon-stewart.html. Accessed July 29, 2019.

Sonmez, Felicia. "Jon Stewart Calls Rand Paul a 'Scalawag' and 'Ragamuffin' Amid Feud over 9/11 Bill." *The Washington Post*, July 24, 2019, washingtonpost.com/politics/jon-stewart-calls-rand-paul-a-scalawag-and-ragamuffin-amid-feud-over-911-bill/2019/07/24/6f2e56e6-ae2c-11e9-bc5c-e73b603e7f38_story.html. Accessed July 24, 2019.

Stewart, Jon. "Jon Stewart: What 9/11 Heroes Need from Congress. Make the Victim Compensation Fund Permanent, and Fund It." *New York Daily News*, February 25, 2019, nydailynews.com/opinion/ny-oped-what-911-heroes-need-from-congress-20190222-story.html. Accessed September 6, 2019.

Stieglitz, Brian. "Zadroga Act Renamed to Honor Pfeifer, Alvarez." *Long Island Herald*, July 12, 2019, liherald.com/stories/zadroga-act-renamed-to-honor-pfeifer-alvarez. Accessed September 6, 2019.

Wehner, Peter. *The Death of Politics: How to Heal Our Frayed Republic After Trump.* HarperCollins, 2019.

Wyatt, Wendy N., and Kristie Bunton. "The Ethics of Speaking Out." *Ethics in Entertainment: Essays on Media Culture and Media Morality,* edited by Howard Good and Sandra L. Borden. McFarland, 2010, pp. 9–22.

Chapter 6

@serenawilliams. *Instagram*. instagram.com/serenawilliams/?hl=en. Accessed August 23, 2020.

@serenawilliams. *Twitter*. twitter.com/serenawilliams. Accessed August 23, 2020.

@SerenaWilliams. *Facebook*. Facebook. com/SerenaWilliams/. Accessed August 23, 2020.

Associated Press. "Serena Williams Withdraws From S.C. Event." *The Washington Post*, April 13, 2000, washingtonpost.com/archive/sports/2000/04/13/citing-flag-serena-williams-withdraws-from-sc-event/a4967b46-4831-488f-b7bb-1f870de3dd55/. Accessed September 20, 2019.

Baym, Nancy K., and danah boyd. "Socially Mediated Publicness: An Introduction." *Journal of Broadcasting & Electronic Media*, vol. 56, no. 3, 2012, pp. 320–329, doi: 10.1080/08838151.2012.075200.

Becker, Lawrence C., and Charlotte B. Becker, editors. *Encyclopedia of Ethics.* Garland Publishing, 1992, 2nd ed. 2001, p. 652.

Bieler, Des. "'Silence Is Betrayal': Serena Williams Vows to Speak Out on Racial Injustice." *The Washington Post*, September 28, 2016, washingtonpost.com/news/early-lead/wp/2016/09/27/silence-is-betrayal-serena-williams-vows-to-speak-out-on-racial-injustice/. Accessed June 20, 2019.

Boren, Cindy. "Serena Williams Reacts to Shooting of Unarmed College Football Player." *The Washington Post*, August 9, 2015, washingtonpost.com/news/early-lead/wp/2015/08/09/serena-williams-reacts-to-shooting-of-unarmed-college-football-player/. Accessed September 21, 2019.

boyd, danah. *It's Complicated: The Social Lives of Networked Teens.* Yale University Press, 2014.

Crouch, Ian. "Serena Williams Is America's Greatest Athlete." *The New Yorker*, September 9, 2014, newyorker.com/sports/sporting-scene/serena-williams-americas-greatest-athlete. Accessed June 22, 2019.

Culpepper, Chuck. "At the U.S. Open, Serena Williams's Story Line Eclipses All Others." *The Washington Post*, August 25, 2019, washingtonpost.com/sports/tennis/at-the-us-open-serena-williams-story-line-eclipses-all-others/2019/08/23/9333d37c-c5b5-11e9-9986-1fb3e4397be4_story.html. Accessed August 26, 2019.

Dadich, Scott. "The Battle for Equity is a WIRED Issue." *WIRED*, October 27, 2015, wired.com/2015/10/editor-letter-november-2015/. Accessed September 17, 2019.

Desmond-Harris, Jenee. "Despite Decades of Racist and Sexist Attacks, Serena Williams Keeps Winning." *Vox*, January 28, 2017, vox.com/2017/1/28/14424624/serena-williams-wins-australian-open-venus-record-sexist-attacks. Accessed September 17, 2019.

Douglas, Delia D. "Venus, Serena, and the Inconspicuous Consumption of Blackness: A Commentary on Surveillance, Race Talk, and New Racism(s)." *Journal of Black Studies*, vol. 43, no. 2, 2012, pp. 127–145, doi: 10.1177/0021934711410880.

Feather, A.J. "Top 15 Issues That Have Americans Worried." *ABC News*, March 19, 2015, abcnews.go.com/Politics/top-15-issues-americans-worried-/story?id=29758744. Accessed September 20, 2019.

Gert, Bernard. *Common Morality: Deciding What to Do*. Oxford University Press, 2007.

Gibbs, Lindsay. "Serena Williams' First Tweet After Reaching Wimbledon Was On the Murder of Philando Castile." *ThinkProgress*, July 7, 2016, thinkprogress.org/serena-williams-first-tweet-after-reaching-wimbledon-final-was-on-the-murder-of-philando-castile-c74b312f972.e. Accessed September 17, 2019.

Gopnik, Adam. *A Thousand Small Sanities: The Moral Adventure of Liberalism*. Basic Books, 2019.

Harwitt, Sandra. "Serena Williams on Why Social Media Matters." *USA Today*, January 19, 2017, usatoday.com/story/sports/tennis/aus/2017/01/19/serena-williams-caroline-wozniacki-social-media/9676 5240/. Accessed September 12, 2019.

Hayat, Tsahi, Yair Galily and Tal Samuel-Azran. "Can Celebrity Athletes Burst the Echo Chamber Bubble? The Case of LeBron James and Lady Gaga." *International Review for the Sociology of Sport*, vol. 55, no. 7, June 2019, pp. 900–914, doi: 10.1177/1012690219855913.

Hyde, Marina. *Celebrity: How Entertainers Took Over the World and Why We Need an Exit Strategy*. Vintage Books, 2010.

Jenkins, Sally. "Serena Williams Finds Her Path to History Narrowing to a Tightrope." *The Washington Post*, July 13, 2019, washingtonpost.com/sports/tennis/serena-williams-finds-her-path-to-history-narrowing-to-a-tightrope/2019/07/13/c18df4ac-a5ab-11e9-b732–41a79c2551bf_story.html. Accessed July 15, 2019.

Jenkins, Sally. "Serena Williams Has Her Greatest, Most Hard-Won Title: Champion of Women." *The Washington Post*, July 14, 2018, washingtonpost.com/sports/tennis/serena-williams-has-her-greatest-most-hard-won-title-champion-of-women/2018/07/14/a14ea062–8796–11e8–8553-a3ce89036c78_story.html. Accessed June 20, 2019.

Kedmey, Dan. "J.K. Rowling Just Crafted the Perfect Response to a Serena Williams Hater." *Time*, July 11, 2015, time.com/3954611/jk-rowling-twitter-serena-williams/. Accessed September 17, 2019.

Newman, Elizabeth. "No Room for Body Image Criticism in Serena Williams' Grand Slam Chase." *Sports Illustrated*, July 14, 2015, si.com/tennis/2015/07/14/serena-williams-body-image-wta-tennis. Accessed September 17, 2019.

Nichols, Tom. *The Death of Expertise: The Campaign Against Established Knowledge and Why It Matters*. Oxford University Press, 2017.

Price, S.L. "Serena Williams Is Sports Illustrated's 2015 Sportsperson of the Year." December 14, 2015, si.com/sportsperson/2015/12/14/serena-williams-si-sportsperson-year. Accessed June 21, 2019.

Proudfoot, Jenny. "Serena Williams' Heartbreaking Words on Inequality Are Going Viral." *Marie Claire*, June 5, 2020. marieclaire.co.uk/news/serena-williams-racial-injustice-message-700141. Accessed August 25, 2020.

Rankine, Claudia. "The Meaning of Serena Williams." *The New York Times*, August 25, 2015, nytimes.com/2015/08/30/magazine/the-meaning-of-serenawilliams.html. Accessed June 20, 2019.

Soong, Kalyn. "Here's Just How Rare Serena Williams's SI's Sportsperson of the Year Award Is." *The Washington Post*, December 14, 2015, washingtonpost.com/news/early-lead/wp/2015/12/14/heres-just-how-rare-serena-williamss-sis-sportsperson-of-the-year-award-is/. Accessed June 20, 2019.

Stone, Christian. "Why Serena Williams Is SI's 2015 Sportsperson of the Year." *Sports*

Illustrated, December 14, 2015, si.com/ sportsperson/2015/12/14/why-serena-williams-is-sportsperson-of-theyear. Accessed September 16, 2019.

Thomas, Etan. *We Matter: Athletes and Activism.* Edge of Sports/Akashic Books, 2018.

Tignor, Steve. "The 50 Greatest Players of the Open Era (W): No. 1, Serena Williams." *Tennis,* tennis.com/ pro-game/2018/03/50-greatest-players-open-era-w-no-1-serena-williams/724 77/. Accessed June 22, 2019.

Tognotti, Chris. "What Does 'Serena Slam' Mean? Serena Williams Just Notched Another One." *Bustle,* July 11, 2015, bustle.com/articles/96572-what-does-serena-slam-mean-serena-williams-just-notched-another-one. Accessed September 17, 2019.

Townes, Cecilia. "Dawn Staley, Natasha Cloud Reaction to George Floyd's Death Shows Women's Sports Link to Racial Inequality." *Forbes Sports-Money,* June 1, 2020, forbes.com/sites/ ceceliatownes/2020/06/01/george-floyds-killing-has-everything-to-do-with-womens-sports/#11f1e2ca5b55. Accessed August 23, 2020.

Williams, Serena. "Serena Williams: I'm Going Back to Indian Wells." *Time,* February 4, 2015, time.com/3694659/serena-williams-indian-wells/. Accessed June 21, 2019.

Williams, Serena. "The Ball Is In Your Court," *WIRED,* November 2015, wired. com/2015/10/serena-williams-guest-editor-race-gender-equality/. Accessed September 17, 2019.

Williams, Serena. "Today I Asked My 18 Year Old Nephew ..." *Facebook,* September 27, 2016, facebook.com/Seren-aWilliams/posts/10154607381941834. Accessed September 21, 2019.

Williams, Serena, with Daniel Paisner. *On The Line.* Grand Central Publishing, 2009.

Wyatt, Wendy N., and Kristie Bunton. "The Ethics of Speaking Out." *Ethics in Entertainment: Essays on Media Culture and Media Morality,* edited by Howard Good and Sandra L. Borden. McFarland, 2010, pp. 9–22.

Yates, Clinton. "Serena Williams Breaks Her Silence: In Powerful Facebook Post, Williams Addresses Police Brutality." *The Undefeated,* September 27, 2016, theun-defeated.com/whew/serena-williams-breaks-her -silence/. Accessed June 21, 2019.

Zirin, Dave. "Serena Williams, Indian Wells and Rewriting the Future." *The Nation,* February 6, 2015, thenation.com/ article/serena-williams-indian-wells and-rewriting-future/. Accessed September 20, 2019.

Chapter 7

Abrams v. U.S., 250 U.S. 616 (1919).

Allen, Danielle. "Reconceiving Public Spheres: The Flow Dynamics Model." *From Voice to Influence: Understanding Citizenship in a Digital Age,* edited by Danielle Allen and Jennifer S. Light. University of Chicago Press, 2015, pp. 178–207.

Allen, David S. "Jurgen Habermas and the Search for Democratic Principles." *Moral Engagement in Public Life,* edited by Sharon Bracci and Clifford Christians. Peter Lang, 2002.

Antonio, Robert J., and Douglas Kellner. "Communication, Modernity, and Democracy in Habermas and Dewey." *Symbolic Interaction,* vol. 15, no. 3, Fall 1992, pp. 277–297, doi: 10.1525/ si.1992.15.3.277.

Associated Press. "Serena Williams Withdraws at Indian Wells and Will Lose No. 1 Ranking." *The New York Times,* March 8, 2017, nytimes.com/2017/03/08/sports/ tennis/serena-williiams-indian-wells-withdrawal.html. Accessed October 14, 2019.

Azzimonti, Marina, and Marcos Fernandes. "Social Media Networks, Fake News, and Polarization." *National Bureau of Economic Research Working Paper Series,* March 2018, nber/org/papers/w24462. Accessed September 28, 2019.

Badenhausen, Kurt. "Inside Serena Williams' Plan to Ace Venture Investing." *Forbes,* June 3, 2019, forbes.com/sites/ kurtbadenhausen/2019/06/03/inside-serena-williams-plan-to-ace-venture-investing/#62c75d587787. Accessed June 20, 2019.

Barthold, Lauren Swayne. "Giving Birth in the Public Square: The Political Relevance of Dialogue." *The Good Society,* vol. 26, nos. 2–3, 2017, pp. 290–304. *Project MUSE* muse.jhu.edu/article/702185.

Bissinger, Buzz. "Serena Williams's Love Match." *Vanity Fair*, August 2017, vanityfair.com/style/2017/06/serena-williams-cover-story. Accessed June 22, 2019.

boyd, danah, *It's Complicated: The Social Lives of Networked Teens.* Yale University Press, 2014.

Carter, Stephen L. *Civility: Manners, Morals, and the Etiquette of Democracy.* Basic Books, 1998.

Chandler, Daniel, and Rod Munday. *A Dictionary of Social Media.* Oxford University Press, 2016, doi: 10.1093/acref/9780191803093.001.0001.

Chiu, Allyson. "Beyonce, Serena Williams Open Up About Potentially Fatal Child births, A Problem Especially for Black Mothers." *The Washington Post*, August 7, 2018, washingtonpost.com/news/morning-mix/wp/2018/08/07/beyonce-serena-williams-open-up-about-potentially-fatal-childbirths-a-problem-especially-for-black-mothers/?utm_term=.796c08631822. Accessed June 21, 2019.

Coombs, Danielle Sarver, and Simon Collister, editors. *Debates for the Digital Age: The Good, the Bad, and the Ugly of Our Online World.* Praeger, 2016.

Cuccinello, Hayley C. "From Taylor Swift to Katrina Lake, America's Richest Self-Made Women Under 40." *Forbes*, June 4, 2019, forbes.com/sites/hayleycuccinello/2019/06/04/from-taylor-swift-to-katrina-lake-americas-richest-self-made-women-under-40/#41f8acc5753a. Accessed June 22, 2019.

Culpepper, Chuck. "Serena Williams Stands Alone Atop Modern Tennis After Winning Australian Open." *The Washington Post*, January 28, 2019, washingtonpost.com/sports/tennis/serena-williams-stands-alone-atop-modern-tennis-after-beating-sister-to-win-australian-open/2017/01/28/b4422ed4-e542-11e6-a453-19ec4b3d09ba_story.html. Accessed October 9, 2019.

Dewey, John Dewey. *The Public and its Problems: An Essay in Political Inquiry,* edited by Melvin L. Rogers. Swallow Press, 2016.

Geren, Peggy Ruth. "Public Discourse: Creating the Conditions for Dialogue Concerning the Common Good in a Postmodern Heterogeneous Democracy." *Studies in Philosophy and Education*, vol. 20, 2001, pp. 191–199, doi: 1023/A:10103676511519.

Gordon, Jill. "John Stuart Mill and the 'Marketplace of Ideas.'" *Social Theory and Practice*, vol. 23, no. 2, Summer 1997, pp. 235–249.

Gouinlock, James. *Excellence in Public Discourse: John Stuart Mill, John Dewey, and Social Intelligence.* Teachers College Press, 1986.

Gouinlock, James, editor. *The Moral Writings of John Dewey.* Prometheus Books, 1994.

Haglage, Abby. "Serena Williams's HBO Series 'Being Serena' Is Shedding Light on the Crisis of Black Maternal Mortality." *Yahoo! Lifestyle*, May 10, 2018, yahoo.com/lifestyle/serena-williams-hbo-series-serena-shedding-light-crisis-black-maternal-mortality-110036121.html. Accessed October 13, 2019.

Harvey, Chelsea. "Here's How Scientific Misinformation, Such as Climate Doubt, Spreads through Social Media." *Washington Post*, January 4, 2016, washingtonpost.com/news/energy-environment/wp/2016/01/04/heres-how-scientific-misinformation-such-as-climate-doubt-spreads-through-social-media/. Accessed September 28, 2019.

Haskell, Rob. "Serena Williams on Motherhood, Marriage, and Making Her Comeback." *Vogue*, January 2018, vogue.com/article/serena-williams-vogue-cover-interview-february-2018. Accessed June 21, 2019.

Kemp, Simon. "Digital 2020: Global Digital Overview." *DataReportal*, January 30, 2020, datareportal.com/reports/digital-2020-global-digital-overview. Accessed August 26, 2020.

Kemp, Simon. "Digital 2020: The United States of America." *DataReportal*, February 11, 2020, datareportal.com/reports/digital-2020-united-states-of-america. Accessed August 26, 2020.

Kroll, Luisa, and Kerry A. Dolan. "America's Richest Self-Made Women." *Forbes*, June 4, 2019, forbes.com/self-made-women/#5677d3e16d96. Accessed June 20, 2019.

Levy, Leonard W. *Emergence of a Free Press.* Oxford University Press, 1985.

McCullough, Thomas E. *The Moral Imagination and Public Life: Raising the Ethical Question.* Chatham House Publishers, 1991.

Meadows-Fernandez, Rochaun. "Beyonce and Serena Speaking Out About Their Birth Experiences Is Good For All Black Women." *The Washington Post,* August 8, 2018, washingtonpost.com/news/parenting/wp/2018/08/08/beyonce-and-serena-speaking-out-about-their-birth-experiences-is-good-for-all-black-women/. Accessed June 20, 2019.

Murray, Cori. "The Future of Serena Williams: The Tennis Superstar and Designer Is Ready to Conquer More." *Essence,* August 8, 2019, essence.com/feature/serena-williams-essence-magazine-cover-story-September-2019/. Accessed September 13, 2019.

Nossel, Suzanne. *Dare to Speak: Defending Free Speech for All.* HarperCollins, 2020.

Nussbaum, Martha C. *The Monarchy of Fear: A Philosopher Looks at our Political Crisis.* Simon & Schuster, 2018.

Payne, Marissa. "It's a Girl: Serena Williams Reportedly Gives Birth to Her First Child." *The Washington Post,* September 1, 2017, washingtonpost.com/news/early-lead/wp/2017/09/01/its-a-girl-serena-williams-reportedly-gives-birth-to-her-first-child/. Accessed October 9, 2019.

Philby, Charlotte. "Serena Williams and the Realities of the 'Maternal Mortality Crisis.'" *The Guardian,* February 21, 2018, theguardian.com/lifeandstyle/shortcuts/2018/feb/21/serena-williams-maternal-mortality-crisis. Accessed October 12, 2019.

Reinstein, Julia. "Black Women Are Speaking Out After Serena Williams Revealed She Faced Life-Threatening Birth Complications." *BuzzFeed News,* January 11, 2018, buzzfeednews.com/article/juliareinstein/serena-williams-birth-complications. Accessed October 14, 2019.

Russmann, Uta, and Anne B. Lane. "Doing the Talk: Discussion, Dialogue, and Discourse in Action." *International Journal of Communication,* vol. 19, 2016, pp. 4034–4039.

Salam, Maya. "For Serena Williams, Childbirth Was a Harrowing Ordeal. She's Not Alone." *The New York Times,* January 11, 2018, nytimes.com/2018/01/11/sports/tennis/serena-williams-baby-vogue.html. Accessed June 15, 2019.

Saraiya, Sonia. "We've Never Seen an Athlete's Story Quite Like Serena Williams's HBO Docuseries." *Vanity Fair,* May 2, 2018, vanityfair.com/hollywood/2018/05/serena-williams-hbo-review. Accessed October 13, 2019.

Schroeder, Jared. "The Future of Discourse in Online Spaces." *Social Media and the Law: A Guidebook for Communication Students and Professionals,* edited by Daxton R. Stewart. Routledge, 2017, 2nd ed., pp. 255–274.

Schroeder, Jared. "Toward a Discursive Marketplace of Ideas: Reimaging the Marketplace Metaphor in the Era of Social Media, Fake News, and Artificial Intelligence." *First Amendment Studies,* vol. 52, nos. 1–2, 2018, pp. 38–60, doi: 10.1080/21689725.2018.1460215.

Shamsian, Jacob. "Serena Williams and Her Husband Made a Video About Her Pregnancy and It'll Make You Cry." September 13, 2017, insider.com/serena-williams-baby-video-photo-alexis-olympia-ohanian-2017-9. Accessed October 12, 2019.

Spohr, Dominic. "Fake News and Ideological Polarization: Filter Bubbles and selective Exposure on Social Media." *Business Information Review,* vol. 34, no. 3, 2017, pp. 150–160, doi: 10.1177/0266382117722446.

Toole, Tucker. "Serena Williams Invests in Project Aimed at Improving Women's Maternal Health." *The Undefeated,* July 18, 2019, theundefeated.com/features/serena-williams-invests-in-project-aimed-at-improving-womens-maternal-health/. Accessed September 13, 2019.

Tornberg, Petter. "Echo Chambers and Viral Misinformation: Modeling Fake News as Complex Contagion." *PLoS ONE,* vol. 13., no. 9, September 20, 2018, e0203956, doi.org/10.1371/journal.pone.0203958. Accessed September 28, 2019.

Williams, Serena. "I Didn't Expect that Sharing ..." *Facebook,* January 15, 2018, m.facebook.com/SerenaWilliams/videos/10156086135726834/. Accessed June 21, 2019.

Williams, Serena. "Serena Williams: What

My Life-Threatening Experience Taught Me About Giving Birth." *CNN.com*, February 20, 2018, cnn.com/2018/02/20/opinions/protect-mother-pregnancy-williams-opinion-index.html. Accessed June 21, 2019.

Wyatt, Wendy N., and Kristie Bunton. "The Ethics of Speaking Out." *Ethics in Entertainment: Essays on Media Culture and Media Morality*, edited by Howard Good and Sandra L. Borden. McFarland, 2010, pp. 9–22.

Chapter 8

Abdul-Jabbar, Kareem. "Abdul-Jabbar: Insulting Colin Kaepernick Says More About Our Patriotism Than His." *The Washington Post*, August 30, 2016, washingtonpost.com/posteverything/wp/2016/08/30/insulting-colin-kaepernick-says-more-about-our-patriotism-than-his/. Accessed January 2, 2020.

"Allyson Felix on Breaking Gold Medal Record 10 Months after Giving Birth." *CBS News*, October 9, 2019, cbsnews.com/news/allyson-felix-record-usain-bolt-winning-most-world-championship-gold-medals-10-months-after-giving-birth/. Accessed January 6, 2020.

Anderson, Monica, et al. "#BlackLivesMatter Surges on Twitter after George Floyd's Death." *Fact Tank: News in the Numbers*, June 10, 2020, pewresearch.org/fact-tank/2020/06/10/blacklivesmatter-surges-on-twitter-after-george-floyds-death/. Accessed July 6, 2020.

Bembry, Jerry. "Athletes Getting Back in the Protest Game." *The Undefeated*, August 25, 2016, theundefeated.com/features/athletes-getting-back-in-the-protest-game/. Accessed March 2, 2019.

Blake, James, with Carol Taylor. *Ways of Grace: Stories of Activism, Adversity, and How Sports Can Bring Us Together.* HarperCollins, 2017.

Boswell, Thomas. "It's Not Which Sports Figures Are Speaking Out That's Telling. It's How Many." *The Washington Post*, June 10, 2020, washingtonpost.com/sports/2020/06/10/its-not-which-sports-figures-are-speaking-out-thats-telling-its-how-many/. Accessed June 10, 2020.

Brown, DeNeen L. "'Shoot Them for What?' How Muhammad Ali Won His Greatest Fight." *The Washington Post*, June 16, 2018, washingtonpost.com/news/retropolis/wp/2018/06/15/shoot-them-for-what-how-muhammad-ali-won-his-greatest-fight/. Accessed December 29, 2019.

Bryant, Howard. *The Heritage: Black Athletes, a Divided America, and the Politics of Patriotism.* Beacon Press, 2018.

Burrow, Gwen. "Not Just a Game: The Impact of Sports on U.S. Economy." *Economic Modeling*, July 9, 2013, economicmodeling.com/2013/07/09/not-just-a-game-the-impact-of-sports-on-u-s-economy/. Accessed October 31, 2019.

Carlos, John, with Dave Zirin. *The John Carlos Story: The Sports Moment that Changed the World.* Haymarket Books, 2001.

Cohen, Patricia and Ben Casselman. "Minority Workers Who Lagged in a Boom Are Hit Hard in a Bust." *The New York Times*, June 6, 2020, https://www.nytimes.com/2020/06/06/business/economy/jobs-report-minorities.html. Accessed August 31, 2020.

Dougherty, Jesse. "Sean Doolittle on Declining White House Invite: 'I Don't Want to Hang Out with Somebody Who Talks Like That.'" *The Washington Post*, November 2, 2019, washingtonpost.com/sports/2019/11/01/sean-doolittle-declining-white-house-invite-i-dont-want-hang-out-with-somebody-who-talks-like-that/. Accessed November 4, 2019.

Feinstein, John. "'Sticking to Sports' Isn't Just Pointless. It's Inhuman." *The Washington Post*, August 7, 2019, washingtonpost.com/sports/sticking-to-sports-isnt-just-pointless-its-inhuman/2019/08/06/781ea97e-b88e-11e9-b3b4-2bb69e8c4e39_story.html. Accessed August 7, 2019.

Felix, Allyson, et al. "Allyson Felix: My Own Nike Pregnancy Story." *The New York Times*, May 22, 2019, nytimes.com/2019/05/22/opinion/allyson-felix-pregnancy-nike.html. Accessed January 4, 2020.

Frank, Noah. "Nats' Sean Doolittle and Wife, Eireann Dolan, Defy Baseball Convention." *WTOP*, April 5, 2018, wtop.com/washington-nationals/2018/04/

eireann-dolan-sean-doolittle-defy-baseball-convention/. Accessed January 1, 2020.

Frederick, Evan L., et al. "Divided and United: Perceptions of Athlete Activism at the ESPYS." *Sport in Society*, November 2018, doi: 10.1080/17430437.2018.1530220.

Freed, Benjamin. "Nationals Pitcher Speaks Out Against Charlottesville Rally and Trump's Response." *The Washingtonian*, August 14, 2017, washingtonian.com/2017/08/14/washington-nationals-sean-doolittle-charlottesville-trump/. Accessed January 1, 2020.

Gregory, Sean. "A New Era for Athletes." *Time*, June 25, 2020, time.com/5859194/athlete-activism/. Accessed July 19, 2020.

Hall, Stefan. "This Is How COVID-19 Is Affecting the World of Sports." *World Economic Forum Agenda*, April 9, 2020, weforum.org/agenda/2020/04/sports-covid19-coronavirus-excersise-specators-media-coverage/. Accessed August 30, 2020.

Hill, Evan, et al. "How George Floyd Was Killed in Police Custody." *The New York Times*, May 31, 2020, Updated July 28, 2020, nytimes.com/2020/05/31/us/George-Floyd-investigation.html. Accessed August 7, 2020.

Hsu, Hua. "The Political Athlete Then and Now." *The New Yorker*, March 22, 2017, newyorker.com/culture/cultural-comment/the-political-athlete-then-and-now. Accessed March 2, 2019.

Janes, Chelsea. "Sean Doolittle and Eireann Dolan May Be Baseball's Most 'Woke' Couple." *The Washington Post*, March 27, 2018, washingtonpost.com/sports/nationals/sean-doolittle-and-eireann-dolan-may-be-baseballs-most-woke-couple/2018/03/27/646b32ca-2dda-11e8-8688-e053ba58f1e4_story.html. Accessed January 1, 2020.

Jenkins, Sally. "China Is Getting Exactly What It Wants from LeBron James and the NBA: Capitulation." *The Washington Post*, October 16, 2019, washingtonpost.com/sports/nba/china-is-getting-exactly-what-it-wants-from-lebron-james-and-the-nba-capitulation/2019/10/16/364df696-efa5-11e9-b648-76bcf86eb67e_story.html. Accessed October 21, 2019.

Jones, Jeffrey M. "As Industry Grows, Percentage of U.S. Sports Fans Steady."

Gallup, June 17, 2015, news.gallup.com/poll/183689/industry-grows-percentage-sports-fans-steady.aspx. Accessed June 24, 2019.

Kepner, Tyler. "Off the Mound, Sean Doolittle Brings Relief to the Ostracized." *The New York Times*, March 12, 2016, nytimes.com/2016/03/13/sports/baseball/off-the-mound-sean-doolittle-brings-relief-to-the-ostracized.html. Accessed January 1, 2020.

Kidwai, Aman. "Etan Thomas Addressed Social Issues Before It Was the Popular Thing to Do." *Washington City Paper*, December 26, 2018, washingtoncity-paper.com/sports/article/21038546/etan-thomas-addressed-social-issues-before-it-was-the-popular-thing-to-do. Accessed January 2, 2020.

Kilgore, Adam. "As a Runner, Allyson Felix Didn't Want to Speak Out. As a Mom, She Felt She Had to." *The Washington Post*, July 31, 2019, washingtonpost.com/sports/2019/07/31/runner-allyson-felix-didnt-want-speak-out-mom-she-felt-she-had/. Accessed January 4, 2020.

Luker, Rich. "Sports Spending Not on Pace with Economic Growth." *Sports Business Journal*, February 22, 2016, sportsbusinessdaily.com/Journal/Issues/2016/02/22/Research-and-Ratings/Up-Next-with-Rich-Luker.aspx?hl=rich+luker&sc=0. Accessed October 31, 2019.

Mather, Victor. "Alejandro Bedoya Spoke Out on Gun Violence. It Helped Make Him M.L.S.'s Player of the Week." *The New York Times*, August 7, 2019, nytimes.com/2019/08/05/sports/alejandro-bedoya-mls-gun-violence.html. Accessed January 1, 2020.

Montaño, Alysia, et al. "Nike Told Me to Dream Crazy, Until I Wanted a Baby." *The New York Times*, May 12, 2019, nytimes.com/2019/05/12/opinion/nike-maternity-leave.html. Accessed January 4, 2020.

O'Neal, Lonnae. "Olympic Champion Allyson Felix Tells Congress About the Black Maternal Health Crisis." *The Undefeated*, May 16, 2019, theundefeated.com/whhw/olympic-medalist-allyson-felix-tells-congress-about-the-black-maternal-health-crisis/. Accessed January 7, 2020.

Paulsen. "ESPY Awards a Mixed Bag."

Sports Media Watch, July 12, 2019, sports-mediawatch.com/2019/07/espy-awards-ratings-viewership-abc/. Accessed January 6, 2020.

Pugmire, Lance. "Muhammad Ali Defied the Draft—and Polarized the Nation—49 Years Ago Today." *The Los Angeles Times,* April 28, 2016, latimes.com/sports/sportsnow/la-sp-sn-muhammad-ali-refused-draft-20160428-story.html. Accessed December 31, 2019.

Rhoden, William C. *Forty Million Dollar Slaves: The Rise, Fall, and Redemption of the Black Athlete.* Three Rivers Press, 2006.

Rhoden, William C. "Hodges Criticizes Jordan for His Silence on Issues." *The New York Times,* June 5, 1992, nytimes.com/1992/06/05/sports/basketball-hodges-criticizes-jordan-for-his-silence-on-issues.html. Accessed December 31, 2019.

Serazio, Michael. *The Power of Sports: Media and Spectacle in American Culture.* New York University Press, 2019.

Shy, Leta. "Allyson Felix Wants to Save Black Mothers." *Self,* July 30, 2019, self.com/story/allyson-felix. Accessed January 6, 2020.

Simon, Robert L., et al. *Fair Play: The Ethics of Sport.* Westview Press, 2015, 4th ed.

Smith, Johnny. "The Reign of Lew Alcindor in the Age of Revolt." *The Undefeated,* March 30, 2018, theundefeated.com/features/lew-alcindor-kareem-abdul-jabbar-ucla-boycot-1968-olympics/ Accessed January 4, 2020.

Spears, Marc J. "Carmelo Anthony: 'The System Is Broken. It Takes a Lot to Fix It.'" *The Undefeated,* July 19, 2016, theundefeated.com/features/carmelo-anthony-the-system-is-broken-it-takes-a-lot-to-fix-it/. Accessed January 6, 2020.

Streeter, Kurt. "Is Slavery's Legacy in the Power Dynamics of Sports?" *The New York Times,* August 16, 2019, nytimes.com/2019/08/16/sports/basketball/slavery-anniversary-basketball-owners.html. Accessed October 21, 2019.

Strings, Sabrina. "It's Not Obesity. It's Slavery. We Know Why Covid-19 Is Killing So Many Black People." *The New York Times,* May 25, 2020, nytimes.com/2020/05/25/opinion/coronavirus-race-obesity.html. Accessed August 31, 2020.

Svrulga, Barry. "For World Series Champion Nats, the Team That Wouldn't Die, There Was No Doubt, Just Hope." *The Washington Post,* October 30, 2019, washingtonpost.com/sports/nationals/for-world-champion-nats-the-team-that-wouldnt-die-there-was-no-doubt-just-hope/2019/10/31/6a758d56-fb4b-11e9-8906-ab6b60de9124_story.html. Accessed October 31, 2019.

Taylor, Derrick Bryson. "A Timeline of the Coronavirus Pandemic." *The New York Times,* August 6, 2020, nytimes.com/article/coronavirus-timeline.html. Accessed August 20, 2020.

Thomas, Etan. *We Matter: Athletes and Activism.* Akashic Books, 2018.

Trenaman, Calum and Amanda Davies. "Becoming a Mother Inspired Allyxon Felix to Fight for 'Voiceless.'" *CNN,* June 15, 2020, cnn.com/2020/06/12/sport/allyson-felix-race-protests-mother-daughter-cmd-spt-intl/index.html. Accessed September 1, 2020.

Trimbur, Lucia. "Taking a Knee, Making a Stand: Social Justice, Trump America, and the Politics of Sport." *Quest,* 2018, doi: 10.1080/00336297.2018.1551806.

Tsui, Bonnie. "Meet the Women Who Are Changing What It Means to Be a Mom and a Professional Athlete." *Sports Illustrated,* December 13, 2019, si.com/more-sports/2019/12/13/female-athlete-mothers-speaking-out-serena-felix-montano-goucher. Accessed January 6, 2020.

Vasilogambros, Matt. "When Athletes Take Political Stands." *The Atlantic,* July 12, 2016, theatlantic.com/news/archive/2016/07/when-athletes-take-political-stands/490967/. Accessed March 2, 2019.

Villarosa, Linda. "Why America's Black Mothers and Babies Are in a Life-or-Death Crisis." *The New York Times Magazine,* April 11, 2018, nytimes.com/2018/04/11/magazine/black-mothers-babies-death-maternal-mortality.html. Accessed October 14, 2019.

Wagner, Laura. "'Republicans Buy Sneakers, Too.' That Quote Has Haunted Michael Jordan for Decades. But Did He Really Say It?" *Slate,* July 28, 2016, slate.com/culture/2016/07/did-michael-jordan-really-say-republicans-buy-sneakers-too.html. Accessed November 21, 2018.

Will, George F. "Poor Bat Behavior Is a

Stain on Baseball's Unwritten Standards." *The Washington Post*, October 30, 2019, washingtonpost.com/opinions/poor-bat-behavior-is-a-stain-on-baseballs-unwritten-standards/2019/10/30/8ff1d55c-fb42–11e9–8190–6be4deb56e01_story.html. Accessed November 4, 2019.

Wyatt, Wendy N., and Kristie Bunton. "The Ethics of Speaking Out." *Ethics in Entertainment: Essays on Media Culture and Media Morality*, edited by Howard Good and Sandra L. Borden. McFarland, 2010, pp. 9–22.

"Year in Sports Media, U.S." *Nielsen*, nielsen.com/us/en/insights/report/2018/2017-year-in-sports-media/. Accessed June 24, 2019.

Chapter 9

Armour, Nancy. "Opinion: Truth Is, NFL Thriving While Players Take Action on Social Injustice." *USA Today*, September 17, 2020, https://www.usatoday.com/story/sports/columnist/nancy-armour/2020/09/17/protests-no-threat-nfls-status-americas-favorite-pastime/5811211002/. Accessed September 17, 2020.

Balz, Dan. "The Politics of Race Are Shifting, and Politicians Are Struggling to Keep Pace." *The Washington Post*, July 5, 2020, washingtonpost.com/graphics/2020/politics/race-reckoning/. Accessed July 6, 2020.

Belson, Ken. "N.F.L. Kicks Off Season with Nods to Unrest and Focus on Anthem." *The New York Times*, September 13, 2020, nytimes.com/2020/09/13/sports/football/nfl-protests.html. Accessed September 14, 2020.

Belson, Ken. "N.F.L. Settlement with Kaepernick and Reid Is Said to Be Much Less than $10 Million." *The New York Times*, March 21, 2019, nytimes.com/2019/03/21/sports/colin-kaepernick-nfl-settlement.html. Accessed January 13, 2020.

Boren, Cindy. "Giants Manager Takes a Knee During Anthem and Trump Tweets 'The Game Is Over for Me.'" *The Washington Post*, July 21, 2020, washingtonpost.com/sports/2020/07/21/giants-manager-takes-knee-during-anthem-trump-tweets-game-is-over-me/. Accessed July 21, 2020.

Boren, Cindy. "LeBron James on Ahmaud Arbery Shooting: 'We're Literally Hunted Everyday.'" *The Washington Post*, May 7, 2020, washingtonpost.com/sports/2020/05/07/lebron-james-ahmaud-arbery-shooting-were-literally-hunted-everyday/. Accessed June 2, 2020.

Branch, John. "The Awakening of Colin Kaepernick." *The New York Times*, September 7, 2017, nytimes.com/2017/09/07/sports/colin-kaepernick-nfl-protests.html. Accessed January 9, 2020.

Branch, John. "The Anthem Debate Is Back. But Now It's Standing That's Polarizing." *The New York Times*, July 4, 2020, nytimes.com/2020/07/04/football/anthem-kneeling-sports.html. Accessed July 5, 2020.

Brewer, Jerry. "A New Day in Sports: Owners Don't Have to Agree with Players, But They Must Listen." *The Washington Post*, July 22, 2020, washingtonpost.com/sports/2020/07/22/new-day-sports-owners-dont-have-agree-with-players-they-must-listen/. Accessed July 22, 2020.

Brewer, Jerry. "For Black Athletes, Social Unrest Is Not a Game, and This Historic Action Is an Urgent Plea." *The Washington Post*, August 26, 2020, washingtonpost.com/sports/2020/08/26/black-america-nba-strike/. Accessed August 28, 2020.

Brewer, Jerry. "Protesters Often Win History's Long Game. Ask Tommie Smith and John Carlos." *The Washington Post*, October 20, 2018, washingtonpost.com/sports/olympics/protesters-often-win-historys-long-game-ask-tommie-smith-and-john-carlos/2018/10/20/b4aef406-d48d-11e8–83d6–291fcead2ab1_story.html. Accessed December 13, 2018.

Brewer, Jerry. "Sports Used to Be an Escape from the World. Now They're a Window into It." *The Washington Post*, August 5, 2020, washingtonpost.com/sports/2020/08/05/sports-used-be-an-escape-world-now-theyre-window-into-it/. Accessed August 6, 2020.

Brewer, Jerry. "Taking a Stand Isn't New for the WNBA. It's a Way of Life." *The Washington Post*, August 7, 2020, washingtonpost.com/sports/2020/

08/07/taking-stand-isnt-new-wnba-its-way-life/. Accessed August 7, 2020.

Brockell, Gillian. "A National Anthem Protest Ruined His NBA Career. Now Abdul-Rauf Is Being Honored by LSU." *The Washington Post*, July 23, 2019, washingtonpost.com/history/2019/07/23/national-anthem-protest-ruined-his-nba-career-now-abdul-rauf-is-being-honored-by-lsu/. Accessed July 24, 2019.

Carlos, John, with Dave Zirin. *The John Carlos Story: The Sports Moment that Changed the World*. Haymarket Books, 2011.

Davis, Amira Rose. "Sixty Years Ago She Refused to Stand for the Anthem." *Zora*, September 26, 2019, zora.medium.com/sixty-years-ago-she-refused-to-stand-for-the-anthem-cf443b4e75c7. Accessed January 10, 2020.

Deb, Sopan. "As Protests Spur Posts from Athletes, N.B.A. Players Take to the Streets." *The New York Times*, June 1, 2020, nytimes.com/2020/06/01/sports/basketball/george-floyd-nba-protests.html. Accessed June 2, 2020.

Draper, Kevin, and Julie Creswell. "Colin Kaepernick 'Dream Crazy' Ad Wins Nike an Emmy." *The New York Times*, September 16, 2019, nytimes.com/2019/09/16/sports/football/colin-kaepernick-nike-emmy.html. Accessed January 13, 2020.

Eastland, Terry, editor. *Freedom of Expression in the Supreme Court: The Defining Cases*. Rowman & Littlefield Publishers, 2000.

Eig, Jonathan. "The NBA's Short Playoff Halt Was the Sports's World's Boldest Push for Racial Justice in Decades." *The New York Times*, August 27, 2020, washingtonpost.com/opinions/2020/08/27/nbas-short-playoff-halt-was-sports-worlds-boldest-push-racial-justice-decades/. Accessed August 28, 2020.

Eligon, John. "Chiefs Fans, Used to Chops and Cheers, React to N.F.L.'s New Climate." *The New York Times*, September 11, 2020, nytimes.com/2020/09/11/sports/football/nfl-chiefs-texans.html. Accessed September 11, 2020.

Grewal, Zareena. "Taking a Stand By Sitting Down: Kaepernick, Abdul-Rauf and the National Anthem." *The Undefeated*, August 30, 2016, theundefeated.com/features/taking-a-stand-by-sitting-down-kaepernick-abdul-rauf-and-the-national-anthem/. Accessed January 13, 2020.

Kahn, Ronald. "Symbolic Speech." *The First Amendment Encyclopedia*, 2009, mtsu.edu/First-amendment/article/1022/symbolic-speech. Accessed January 5, 2020.

Longman, Jere. "Kaepernick's Knee and Olympic Fists Are Linked by History." *The New York Times*, September 6, 2018, nytimes.com/2018/09/06/sports/kaepernick-nike-kneeling.html. Accessed January 10, 2020.

Mahoney, Brian and Tim Reynolds. "Boycott: NBA Playoff Games Called Off Amid Player Protest," *Associated Press*, August 26, 2020, apnews.com/313150f407d5d68eaa60f93554a5f43e. Accessed August 26, 2020.

McCann, Michael. "Colin Kaepernick and Eric Reid Settle Collusion Grievance with the NFL: What's the Significance?" *Sports Illustrated*, February 15, 2019, si.com/nfl/2019/02/15/colin-kaepernick-nfl-collusion-grievance-settlement-eric-reid. Accessed June 17, 2019.

McGoldrick, James M., Jr. "Symbolic Speech: A Message from Mind to Mind," *Oklahoma Law Review*, vol. 61. No. 1, Spring 2008, pp. 1–82.

Powell, Michael. "Colin Kaepernick Is Silenced by a Settlement, but His Knee Spoke Volumes." *The New York Times*, February 15, 2019, nytimes.com/2019/02/15/sports/colin-kaepernick-nfl-human-rights.html. Accessed January 8, 2020.

Putnam, Lara, Jeremy Pressman and Erica Chenoweth. "Black Lives Matter Beyond America's Big Cities." *The Washington Post*, July 8, 2020, washingtonpost.com/politics/2020/07/08/black-lives-matter-beyond-americas-big-cities/. Accessed July 13, 2020.

Rosen, Jody. "Who's Better at Image Management: Colin Kaepernick or the N.F.L.?" *The New York Times Magazine*, December 12, 2019, nytimes.com/2019/12/12/magazine/colin-kaepernick-nfl-video.html. Accessed December 20, 2019.

Sanderson, et al. "When Athlete Activism Clashes with Group Values: Social Identity Threat Management via Social Media." *Mass Communication and*

Society, vol. 19, 2016, pp. 301–322, doi: 10.1080/15205436.2015.1128549.

Serazio, Michael. *The Power of Sports: Media and Spectacle in American Culture.* New York University Press, 2019.

Shpigel, Ben. "Does Colin Kaepernick Still Need Football?" *The New York Times*, November 14, 2019, nytimes.com/2019/11/14/sports/football/colin-kaepernick-workout-nfl.html. Accessed November 18, 2019.

Solomon, Stephen. "From Liberty Tree to Taking a Knee: America's Founding Era Sheds Light on the NFL Controversy." *First Amendment Watch*, firstamendmentwatch.org/deep-dive/from-liberty-tree-to-taking-a-knee-americas-founding-era-sheds-light-on-the-nfl-controversy/. Accessed January 10, 2020.

Solomon, Stephen D. *Revolutionary Dissent: How the Founding Generation Created the Freedom of Speech.* St. Martin's Press, 2016.

Stein, Marc, Sopan Deb and Alan Blinder. "One N.B.A. Team Walked out. A Generation of Athletes Followed." *The New York Times*, August 27, 2020, nytimes.com/2020/08/27/sports/basketball/nba-resume.html. Accessed August 28, 2020.

Thomas, Etan. *We Matter: Athletes and Activism.* Akashic Books, 2018.

Tiersma, Peter Meijes. "Nonverbal Communication and the Freedom of 'Speech.'" *Wisconsin Law Review*, 1993, pp. 1525–1589.

Vasilogambros, Matt. "When Athletes Take Political Stands." *The Atlantic*, July 12, 2016, theatlantic.com/news/archive/2016/07/when-athletes-take-political-stands/490967/. Accessed March 2, 2019.

Wagner, James. "After a Long Lull, Protesting Is Taking Hold Across Baseball." *The New York Times*, August 28, 2020, nytimes.com/2020/08/28/sports/baseball/mlb-protest-canceled-games.html. Accessed August 30, 2020.

Waszak, Dennis, Jr. "9 NFL Teams Cancel Practice in Response to Blake Shooting." *Associated Press*, August 27, 2020, apnews.com/6406e0a34e55173e995885fea58a97f8. Accessed September 7, 2020; Wawrow, John. "NHL Players Use Pause to Focus on Racial Injustice Concerns." *Associated Press*, August 28, 2020, apnews.com/89370c875517020a48976f7a24547074. Accessed September 7, 2020.

West, Jenna. "NWSL Challenge Cup Players Kneel in Mass During National Anthem." *Sports Illustrated*, June 27, 2020, si.com/soccer/2020/06/27/nwsl-players-kneeling-national-anthem-courage-thorns. Accessed September 5, 2020.

Widmer, Ted. "Why Two Black Athletes Raised Their Fists During the Anthem." *The New York Times*, October 16, 2018, nytimes.com/2018/10/16/opinion/why-smith-and-carlos-raised-their-fists.html. Accessed December 13, 2018.

Williams, J. Corey. "The Oppressive Seeds of the Colin Kaepernick Backlash." *Protesting on Bended Knee: Race, Dissent, and Patriotism in 21st Century America*, edited by Eric Burn. The Digital Press at the University of North Dakota, 2018.

Wilson, Stephen. "Olympian Wyomia Tyus Sprinted to Gold and Spoke Out in Mexico City. America Forgot Her." *The Washington Post*, September 22, 2020, washingtonpost.com/sports/2020/09/22/wyomia-tyus-olympic-sprinter-gold-medals/. Accessed September 23, 2020.

Witz, Billy. "Kneeling During the Anthem at Ole Miss: 'I Needed to Stand Up for My Rights.'" *The New York Times*, February 27, 2019, nytimes.com/2019/02/27/sports/ole-miss-kneeling.html. Accessed March 2, 2019.

Witz, Billy. "This Time, Colin Kaepernick Takes a Stand by Kneeling." *The New York Times*, September 1, 2016, nytimes.com/2016/09/02/sports/football/colin-kaepernick-kneels-national-anthem-protest.html. Accessed January 8. 2020.

Wood, Josh and Tim Craig. "As Breonna Taylor Protests Stretch into 12th Week, Calls for Officers' Arrests Intensify." *The Washington Post*, August 18, 2020, washingtonpost.com/national/as-breonna-taylor-protests-stretch-into-12th-week-calls-for-officers-arrests-intensify/2020/08/18/ce6f2b9a-d823-11ea-930e-d88518c57dcc_story.html. Accessed September 4, 2020.

Wyatt, Wendy N., and Kristie Bunton. "The Ethics of Speaking Out." *Ethics in Entertainment: Essays on Media Culture and Media Morality*, edited by Howard Good and Sandra L. Borden. McFarland, 2010, pp. 9–22.

Zillgitt, Jeff. "Full List of the Messages NBA Players Will Wear on Their Jerseys as Season Restarts." *USA Today*, July 30, 2020, usatoday.com/story/sports/nba/2020/07/30/what-message-nba-players-will-wear-on-back-of-jerseys/5536311002/. Accessed September 4, 2020.

Chapter 10

Andrews, Travis M. "Madonna Keeps Making Controversial Covid-19 Claims, Calling a Misinformation-Spreading Doctor Her 'Hero.'" *The Washington Post*, July 29, 2020, washingtonpost.com/technology/2020/07/29/madonna-instagram-covid-coronavirus-stella-immanuel-bathtub/. Accessed July 29, 2020.

Avlon, John. "In Coronavirus Crisis, Tom Hanks Is More of a Role Model than Donald Trump." *CNN.com*, March 12, 2020, cnn.com/2020/03/12/opinions/tom-hanks-more-of-a-role-model-in-crisis-than-donald-trump-avlon/index.html. Accessed September 9, 2020.

Barthold, Lauren Swayne. "Giving Birth in the Public Square: The Political Relevance of Dialogue." *The Good Society*, vol. 26, nos. 2–3, 2017, pp. 290–304. *Project MUSE* muse.jhu.edu/article/702185.

Beck, Christina S., et al. "Blurring Personal Health and Public Priorities: An Analysis of Celebrity Health Narratives in the Public Sphere." *Health Communication*, vol. 29, 2014, pp. 244–256, doi: 10.1080/10410236.2012.741669.

Bruney, Gabrielle. "Tom Hanks Was the Perfect Surprise Guest Host for *Saturday Night Live*'s First Digital Episode." *Esquire*, April 12, 2020, esquire.com/entertainment/tv/a32118571/saturday-night-live-at-home-coronavirus-tom-hanks/. Accessed September 14, 2020.

Bui, Quoctrung, et al. "How Dr. Fauci Found Himself Talking to Julia Roberts, Lil Wayne and Just About Any Podcaster Who Asked." *The New York Times*, August 27, 2020, nytimes.com/interactive/2020/08/27/upshot/fauci-media-appearances.html. Accessed September 13, 2020.

Calvario, Liz. "Tom Hanks Shares Update After Returning Home After Coronavirus Diagnosis." *ET News*, March 28, 2020, etonline.com/tom-hanks-shares-update-after-returning-home-after-coronavirus-diagnosis-143845. Accessed September 16, 2020.

Cohen, Patricia and Gillian Friedman. "Unemployment Claims Show Layoffs Continue to Batter Economy." *The New York Times*, September 3, 2020, nytimes.com/2020/09/03/business/economy/unemployment-claims.html. Accessed September 13, 2020.

"Covid in the U.S.: Latest Map and Case Count." *The New York Times*, September 13, 2020, nytimes.com/interactive/2020/us/coronavirus-us-cases.html. Accessed September 13, 2020.

Coyle, Jake. "Tom Hanks on COVID-19, 'Greyhound' and Wartime Mentality." *Associated Press*, July 6, 2020, apnews.com/ba58fe517346a0164013b37622476b00. Accessed September 14, 2020.

Elkins, Chris. "Celebrities Team with Big Pharma to Promote Drugs, Disease Awareness." *Drugwatch*, August 30, 2019, drugwatch.com/news/2015/11/09/celebrity-and-big-pharma-drug-promotion/. Accessed January 30, 2020.

Fisher, Marc and Rachel Weiner. "With Little Clarity on Coronavirus, Americans Crowdsource How to Live in a Pandemic." *The Washington Post*, July 20, 2020, washingtonpost.com/politics/with-little-clarity-on-coronavirus-americans-crowdsource-how-to-live-in-a-pandemic/2020/07/20/6abcb8ea-c5f6-11ea-b037-f9711f89ee46_story.html. Accessed July 21, 2020.

Freeman, Hadley. "Tom Hanks on Surviving Coronavirus: 'I Had Crippling Body Aches, Fatigue and Couldn't Concentrate.'" *The Guardian*, July 6, 2020, theguardian.com/film/2020/jul/06/tom-hanks-on-surviving-coronavirus-i-had-crippling-body-aches-fatigue-and-couldnt-concentrate. Accessed September 9, 2020.

Gert, Bernard. *Common Morality: Deciding What to Do*. Oxford University Press, 2007.

Gunter, Barrie. *Celebrity Capital: Assessing the Value of Fame*. Bloomsbury, 2014.

Hamilton, David P. "Celebrities Help 'Educate' Public About the Virtues of New Drugs." *The Wall Street Journal*, April 22, 2002, wsj.com/articles/

SB1019433329579504640. Accessed January 28, 2020.

Henderson, Cydney. "'Plasmatic!' Tom Hanks Shares Picture of Himself Donating Plasma to Combat COVID-19." *USA Today*, May 27, 2020, usatoday.com/story/entertainment/celebrities/2020/05/27/tom-hanks-donates-plasma-combat-covid-19-and-shares-photo/5271559002/. Accessed September 9, 2020.

Hess, Amanda. "Celebrity Culture Is Burning." *The New York Times*, March 30, 2020, nytimes.com/2020/03/30/arts/virus-celebrities.html. Accessed June 2, 2020.

Hoffman, Steven J., and Charlie Tan. "Following Celebrities' Medical Advice: Meta-Narrative Analysis." *BMJ*, December 17, 2013, doi: 10.1136/bmj/f7151;

Jacob, Ayesha. "The Narratives that Define the Coronavirus Pandemic Will Influence Its Outcome." *The Mail & Guardian*, March 16, 2020, mg.co.za/article/2020-03-16-the-narratives-that-define-the-coronavirus-pandemic-will-influence-its-outcome/. Accessed September 17, 2020.

Johnson, Sharilyn. "Julia Louis-Dreyfus Has 'Nothing But Regret' for Elaine's *Seinfeld* Fashion." *Vanity Fair*, December 8, 2019, vanityfair.com/hollywood/2019/12/julia-louis-dreyfus-stephen-colbert. Accessed January 19, 2020.

Jolie, Angelina. "My Medical Choice." *The New York Times*, May 14, 2013, nytimes.com/2013/05/14/opinion/my-medical-choice.html. Accessed January 18, 2020.

Karni, Annie and Maggie Haberman. "In Rare Oval Office Speech, Trump Voices New Concerns and Old Themes." *The New York Times*, March 12, 2020, nytimes.com/2020/03/12/us/politics/trump-coronavirus-address.html. Accessed September 15, 2020.

Kluger, Jeffrey, et al. "The Angelina Effect." *Time*, May 27, 2013, time.com/3450368/the-angelina-effect. Accessed January 18, 2020.

Levy, Ariel. "Julia Louis-Dreyfus Acts Out." *The New Yorker*, December 10, 2018, newyorker.com/magazine/2018/12/17/julia-louis-dreyfus-acts-out. Accessed January 19, 2020.

Liede, Alexander, et al. "Risk-Reducing Mastectomy Rates in the US: A Closer Examination of the Angelina Jolie Effect." *Breast Cancer Research and Treatment*, vol. 171, 2018, pp. 435–442, doi: 10.1007/s10549-018-4824-9.

Locker, Melissa. "Tom Hanks and Rita Wilson Had Very Different Reactions to COVID-19." *Time*, July 6, 2020, time.com/5863326/tom-hanks-coronavirus-reaction/. Accessed September 9, 2020.

Locker, Melissa. "Tom Hanks Gave His Corona Typewriter to a Kid Bullied Over Having the Name Corona." *Time*, April 24, 2020, time.com/5826972/tom-hanks-typewriter-letter/. Accessed September 16, 2020.

Neel, Joe. "NPR Poll: Financial Pain from Coronavirus Pandemic 'Much, Much Worse' than Expected." National Public Radio, September 9, 2020, npr.org/sections/health-shots/2020/09/09/909669760/npr-poll-financial-pain-from-coronavirus-pandemic-much-much-worse-than-expected. Accessed September 9, 2020.

Nichols, Tom. *The Death of Expertise: The Campaign Against Established Knowledge and Why It Matters*. Oxford University Press, 2017.

Noguchi, Yuki. 'I Try So Hard Not to Cry': Nearly Half of U.S. Households Face a Financial Crisis." National Public Radio, September 10, 2020, npr.org/sections/health-shots/2020/09/10/910724801/overview-of-poll-data-on-pandemics-damage. Accessed September 13, 2020.

Offit, Paul A. *Bad Advice: Or Why Celebrities, Politicians, and Activists Aren't Your Best Source of Health Information*. Columbia University Press, 2018.

Oppel, Richard A., Jr., et al. "The Fullest Look Yet at the Racial Inequity of Coronavirus." *The New York Times*, July 5, 2020, nytimes.com/interactive/2020/07/05/us/coronavirus-latinos-african-americans-cdc-data.html. Accessed September 13, 2020.

Osborne, Mark. "Tom Hanks, Rita Wilson Say They Have Coronavirus." *ABC News*, March 12, 2020, abcnews.go.com/Entertainment/tom-hanks-rita-wilson-coronavirus/story?id=69547484. Accessed September 14, 2020.

Paquette, Danielle. "The Angelina Jolie Effect: When a Sex Symbol Removes Her Ovaries to Prevent Cancer, Women More Likely to Follow." *The Washington*

Post, March 24, 2015, washingtonpost. com/news/wonk/wp/2015/03/24/the-angelina-jolie-effect-when-a-sex-symbol-removes-her-ovaries-to-pre vent-cancer-other-women-more-likely-to-follow/. Accessed January 23, 2020.

Pavelko, Rachelle L., et al. "Public Reactions to Celebrity Cancer Disclosures via Social Media: Implications for Campaign Message Design and Strategy." *Higher Education Journal,* vol. 76, no. 4, 2017, doi: 10.1177/0017896917696122.

Pitt, Angelina Jolie. "Angelina Jolie Pitt: Diary of a Surgery," *The New York Times,* March 24, 2015, nytimes. com/2015/03/24/opinion/angelina-jolie-pitt-diary-of-a-surgery.html. Accessed January 18, 2020.

Rao, Sonia. "Ellen DeGeneres Removes YouTube Video in Which She Compares Social Distancing to 'Being in Jail.'" *The Washington Post,* April 8, 2020, washingtonpost.com/arts-entertain ment/2020/04/08/ellen-degeneres-jail-coronavirus-video-backlash/. Accessed June 2, 2020.

Robinson, Eugene. "The Original Sin in the U.S. Response to Coronavirus Is Lack of Testing." *The Washington Post,* March 12, 2020, washingtonpost. com/opinions/the-original-sin-in-the-us-response-to-coronavirus-is-lack-of-testing/2020/03/12/dff208c2-648a-11ea-acca-80c22bbee96f_story. html. Accessed September 9, 2020.

Salam, Maya. "Julia Louis-Dreyfus Shares Breast Cancer Diagnosis." *The New York Times,* September 28, 2017, nytimes. com/2017/09/28/arts/television/breast-cancer-julia-louis-dreyfus.html. Accessed January 19, 2020.

Shaffer, Claire. "Penelope Cruz, Shailene Woodley and More Hand Their Instagrams Over to Doctors." *Rolling Stone,* May 20, 2020, rollingstone.com/culture/culture-news/pass-the-mic-celebrities-doctors-instagram-covid-19-1002922/. Accessed September 11, 2020.

Sims, David. "The Strange Weight of Tom Hanks's Coronavirus Diagnosis." *The Atlantic,* March 12, 2020, theatlan tic.com/culture/archive/2020/03/tom-hanks-rita-wilson-coronavirus/607888/. Accessed September 14, 2020.

Smith, Sabrina. "Tom Hanks' Typewriter Obsession Makes Him the Proud Owner of More than 250 Models." *Showbiz Cheat Sheet,* August 17, 2020, cheatsheet.com/entertainment/tom-hanks-typewriter-obsession-makes-him-the-proud-owner-of-more-than-250-models.html/. Accessed September 14, 2020.

Specter, Emma. "Tom Hanks Posts a Coronavirus Update, Remains Perfect." *Vogue,* March 13, 2020, vogue.com/article/tom-hanks-coronavirus-update-instagram. Accessed September 10, 2020.

Steinmetz, Katy. "You've Tested Positive for COVID-19. Who Has a Right to Know?" *Time,* March 26, 2020, time. com/5810231/covid19-test-sharing-positive-result/. Accessed September 16, 2020.

Sterling, Nicole. "Emmys Extra Cover: Julia Louis-Dreyfus, Out of Office." *Vanity Fair,* August 8, 2019, vanityfair.com/hollywood/2019/08/julia-louis-dreyfus-emmys-cover-story. Accessed January 19, 2020.

Taylor, Derrick Bryson. "A Timeline of the Coronavirus Pandemic." *The New York* Times, August 6, 2020, nytimes. com/article/coronavirus-timeline.html. Accessed August 20, 2020.

Trepany, Charles. "Jamie Foxx, Ellen Pompeo and Other Stars in Mask Up Campaign as More Celebs Encourage Face Masks." *USA Today,* July 16, 2020, usatoday.com/story/entertainment/celebrities/2020/07/16/what-tom-hanks-jamie-foxx-more-celebs-saying-face-masks/5456283002/. Accessed September 9, 2020.

Vos, Sarah C., et al. "Celebrity Cancer on Twitter: Mapping a Novel Opportunity for Cancer Prevention." *Cancer Control,* vol. 26, 2019, pp. 1–8, doi: 10.1177/1073274819825826.

Yasmin, Seema and Craig Spencer. "'But I Saw It on Facebook': Hoaxes Are Making Doctors' Jobs Harder." *The New York Times,* August 28, 2020, nytimes. com/2020/08/28/opinion/sunday/coronavirus-misinformation-faceboook. html. Accessed August 30, 2020.

Yerramilli, Divya, et al. "How Should Clinicians Respond When Patients Are Influenced by Celebrities' Cancer Stories?" *AMA Journal of Ethics,* vol. 20, no. 11, November 2018, doi: 10.1001/amajethics.2018.1075.

"Wait Wait ... Don't Tell Me!" *National*

Public Radio, April 18, 2020, npr. org/2020/04/18/837682956/we-call-to-check-in-on-tom-hanks-and-ask-him-to-play-not-my-job /. Accessed September 10, 2020.

Wyatt, Wendy N., and Kristie Bunton. "The Ethics of Speaking Out." *Ethics in Entertainment: Essays on Media Culture and Media Morality,* edited by Howard Good and Sandra L. Borden. McFarland, 2010, pp. 9–22.

Zillgitt, Jeff. "NBA Shuts Down after Rudy Gobert Tests Positive for Coronavirus." *USA Today,* March 11, 2020, usatoday.com/story/sports/nba/2020/03/11/coronavirus-nba-shuts-down-after-rudy-gobert-tests-positive/5028026002/. Accessed September 15, 2020.

Chapter 11

"'A Real Pro': Naomi Osaka's Anti-Racism Message Resonates with Japan Youth." *The Mainichi,* September 25, 2020, mainichi.jp/english/articles/20200924/p2a/00m/0dm/022000c. Accessed September 25, 2020.

Associated Press. "Japan Celebrates Naomi Osaka; Sponsors Cautious about Activism." *Honolulu Star-Advertiser,* September 15, 2020, staradvertiser.com/2020/09/15/sports/sports-breaking/japan-celebrates-naomi-osaka-sponsors-cautious-about-activism. Accessed September 16, 2020.

Barthold, Lauren Swayne. "Giving Birth in the Public Square: The Political Relevance of Dialogue." *The Good Society,* vol. 26, nos. 2–3, 2017, pp. 290–304, doi: 10.5325/goodsociety.26.2–3.0290.

Bengel, Chris. "Naomi Osaka Fires Back at Critics Who Told Her to 'Keep Politics Out of Sports' at US Open." *CBS Sports,* September 16, 2020, cbssports.com/tennis/news/naomi-osaka-fires-back-at-critics-who-told-her-to-keep-politics-out-of-sports-at-us-open/. Accessed September 17, 2020.

Billings, Andrew. "Power in the Reverberation: Why Twitter Matters, but Not the Way Most Believe." *Communication & Sport,* vol. 2, no. 2, 2014, pp. 107–112, doi: 10.1177/2167479514527427.

Boren, Cindy. "Naomi Osaka Brought Seven Face Masks to the U.S. Open, Each One Honoring a Victim of Violence." *The Washington Post,* September 1, 2020, washingtonpost.com/sports/2020/09/01/naomi-osaka-facemask-us-open/. Accessed September 2, 2020.

Boren, Cindy. "Parents of Trayvon Martin, Ahmad Arbery Thank Naomi Osaka in Video after U.S. Open Win." *The Washington Post,* September 9, 2020, washingtonpost.com/sports/2020/09/09/naomi-osaka-mask-us-open/. Accessed September 11, 2020.

Carayol, Tumaini. "Naomi Osaka Proves Herself a Champion On and Off the Court." *The Guardian,* September 13, 2020, theguardian.com/sport/2020/sep/13/naomi-osaka-proves-herself-a-champion-on-and-off-the-court. Accessed September 19, 2020.

Carter, Stephen L. *Civility: Manners, Morals, and the Etiquette of Democracy.* Basic Books, 1998.

Clarey, Christopher. "Naomi Osaka, While Rallying for Social Justice, Wins U.S. Open Title." *The New York Times,* September 12, 2020, nytimes.com/2020/09/12/sports/tennis/naomi-osaka-us-open-title.html. Accessed September 13, 2020.

Crawford, Kate. "Following You: Disciplines of Listening in Social Media." *Continuum: Journal of Media & Cultural Studies,* vol. 23, no. 4, August 2009, pp. 525–535, doi:10.1080/10304310903003270.

Denyer, Simon. "Japanese Tennis Player Naomi Osaka Speaks Out for Black Lives Matter, Faces Backlash." *The Washington Post,* June 8, 2020, washingtonpost.com/world/asia_pacific/japanese-tennis-player-naomi-osaka-speaks-out-for-black-lives-matter-faces-backlash/2020/06/08/f8432ca0-a92f-11ea-a43b-be9f6494a87d_story.html. Accessed June 9, 2020.

Dreher, Tanya. "Listening Across Difference: Media and Multiculturalism Beyond the Politics of Voice." *Continuum: Journal of Media & Cultural Studies,* vol. 23, no. 4, August 2009, pp. 445–458, doi: 10.1080/10304310903015712.

Elliott, Helene. "Naomi Osaka Stood Tall, and Alone, in Protest Following Jacob Blake Shooting." *The Los Angeles Times,* August 27, 2020, latimes.com/sports/story/2020-08-27/naomi-osaka-stood-tall-and-alone-in-withdrawing-from-tennis-tournament. Accessed August 28, 2020.

Fendrich, Howard. "Analysis: Naomi Osaka Is Poised to Lead Tennis On, Off Court." *Associated Press*, September 13, 2020, apnews.com/ac3b328d9352aa6bdf-bc33f007053361. Accessed September 13, 2020.

Feyer, Thomas. "Women, Please Speak Out." *The New York Times*, February 14, 2020, nytimes.com/2020-02-14/opinion/letters/letters-editor-nytimes-gender.html. Accessed February 15, 2020.

Futterman, Matthew. "Naomi Osaka Returns after Protest Prompts Tournament's Pause." *The New York Times*, August 28, 2020, nytimes.com/2020/08/28/sports/tennis/naomi-osaka.html. Accessed August 28, 2020.

Gay, Jason. "Naomi Osaka's Big Summer." *The Wall Street Journal*, September 14, 2020. wsj.com/articles/the-meaningful-summer-of-naomi-osaka-11600002023. Accessed September 14, 2020.

Jenkins, Sally. "At U.S. Open, Power of Serena Williams and Naomi Osaka Is Overshadowed by an Umpire's Power Play." *The Washington Post*, September 8, 2018, washingtonpost.com/sports/tennis/at-us-open-power-of-serena-williams-and-naomi-osaka-is-overshadowed-by-an-umpires-power-play/2018/09/08/edbf46c8-b3b4-11e8-a20b-5f4f84429666_story.html. Accessed June 20, 2019.

Kambhampaty, Anna Purna. "Naomi Osaka's U.S. Open Masks Showcase One of an Athlete's Most Powerful Tools for Protest." *Time*, September 11, 2020, time.com/5888072/sports-style-protest/. Accessed September 12, 2020.

King, Billie Jean. "Billie Jean King: Serena Is Still Treated Differently than Male Athletes." *The Washington Post*, September 9, 2018, washingtonpost.com/outlook/2018/09/09/serena-is-still-treated-differently-than-male-athletes/. Accessed September 18, 2020.

Kovach, Bill, and Tom Rosenstiel. *The Elements of Journalism: What Newspeople Should Know and the Public Should Expect.* 3rd ed. Three Rivers Press, 2016.

Lacey, Kate. *Listening Publics: The Politics and Experience of Listening in the Media Age.* Polity Press, 2013.

Ley, Tom. "Naomi Osaka Asked the Right Question." *Defector Media*, September 13, 2020, defector.com/naomi-osaka-asked-the-right-question/. Accessed September 15, 2020.

Lipari, Lisbeth. *Listening, Thinking, Being: Toward an Ethics of Attunement.* The Pennsylvania State University Press, 2014.

Maben, Sarah K., and Christopher C. Gearhart. "Organizational Social Media Accounts: Moving Toward Listening Competency." *International Journal of Listening,* vol. 32, 2018, pp. 101–114, doi: 10.1080/10904018.2017.1330658.

Maine, D'Arcy. "Naomi Osaka Cements Her Status as Leader On and Off the Court with US Open Run." *ESPN*, September 13, 2020, espn.com/tennis/story/_/id/29869802/naomi-osaka-cements-status-leader-the-court-2020-us-open-run. Accessed September 14, 2020.

McCann, Michael. "Colin Kaepernick and Eric Reid Settle Collusion Grievance with the NFL: What's the Significance?" *Sports Illustrated*, February 15, 2019, si.com/nfl/2019/02/15/colin-kaepernick-nfl-collusion-grievance-settlement-eric-reid. Accessed June 17, 2019.

McCombs, Maxwell. "The Agenda-Setting Function of the Press." *The Press*, edited by Geneva Overholser and Kathleen Hall Jamieson. Oxford University Press, 2005, pp. 156–168.

Mill, John Stuart. *On Liberty,* edited by Elizabeth Rappaport. Hackett Publishing, 1978.

Nichols, Michael P. *The Lost Art of Listening.* Guilford Press, 1995.

O'Donnell, Penny. "Journalism, Change and Listening Practices." *Continuum: Journal of Media & Cultural Studies,* vol. 23, no. 4, August 2009, pp. 503–517, doi: 10.1080/10304310903015720.

Osaka, Naomi. "I Never Would've Imagined Writing This Two Years Ago." *Esquire*, July 1, 2020, esquire.com/sports/a33022329/naomi-osaka-op-ed-george-floyd-protests/. Accessed September 12, 2020.

Parks, Elizabeth S. *The Ethics of Listening: Creating Space for Sustainable Dialogue.* Lexington Books, 2019.

Patterson, Thomas, and Philip Seib. "Informing the Public." *The Press*, edited by Geneva Overholser and Kathleen Hall Jamieson. Oxford University Press, 2005, pp. 189–193.

Probolus, Kimberly. "Men, You Need to Listen to Women." *The New York Times*, February 14, 2020, nytimes.com/2020/02/14/opinion/letters/nytimes-letters-women.html. Accessed February 15, 2020.

Schudson, Michael. *The Good Citizen: A History of American Civic Life*. Harvard University Press, 1998.

Stauffer, Jill. *Ethical Loneliness: The Injustice of Not Being Heard*. Columbia University Press, 2015.

Tannen, Deborah. *The Argument Culture: Stopping America's War of Words*. Ballantine Books, 1998.

Wallace, Ava. "U.S. Open Champion Naomi Osaka Lets Her Masks Do the Talking. In the End, She Wanted to Know What We Heard." *The Washington Post*, September 12, 2020, washingtonpost.com/sports/2020/09/12/naomi-osaka-us-open-message/. Accessed September 13, 2020.

Ward, Stephen J.A., and Herman Wasserman. "Open Ethics: Towards a Global Media Ethics of Listening." *Journalism Studies*, vol. 16, no. 6, 2015, pp.834–849, doi:10.1080/1461670X.2014.950882.

Witz, Billy. "This Time, Colin Kaepernick Takes a Stand by Kneeling." *The New York Times*, September 1, 2016, nytimes.com/2016/09/02/sports/football/colin-kaepernick-kneels-national-anthem-protest.html. Accessed January 8. 2020.

Wolken, Dan. "Opinion: Naomi Osaka Nearing Icon Status, and It's Not Just Because of Her Tennis." *USA Today*, September 11, 2020, usatoday.com/story/sports/columnist/dan-wolken/2020/09/11/naomi-osaka-tennis-superstar-voice-for-change/3471156001/. Accessed September 12, 2020.

Wyatt, Wendy N., and Kristie Bunton. "The Ethics of Speaking Out." *Ethics in Entertainment: Essays on Media Culture and Media Morality*, edited by Howard Good and Sandra L. Borden. McFarland, 2010, pp. 9–22.

Conclusion

Becker, Lawrence C., and Charlotte B. Becker, editors. *Encyclopedia of Ethics*. Garland Publishing, 2nd ed., 2001.

Bird, Frederick Bruce. *The Muted Conscience: Moral Silence and the Practice of Silence in Business*. Quorum Books, 1996.

Charles, Ashley. *Outraged: Why Everyone Is Shouting and No One Is Talking*. Bloomsbury Publishing, 2020.

Gentile, Mary C. "Giving Voice to Values: Building Moral Competence." *Moral Courage in Organizations: Doing the Right Thing at Work*, edited by Debra R. Comer and Gina Vega. M.E. Sharpe, Inc., 2011, pp. 117–129.

Gotrich, Lars. "Dixie Chicks Announce First Album in 14 Years, 'Gaslighter,' Share Title Track." *NPR*, March 4, 2020, npr.org/2020/03/04/812018782/dixie-chicks-gaslighter-first-album-14-years-release-single. Accessed March 15, 2020.

Horton, Adrian. "Shut Up and Sing: Why the Chicks' 2006 Documentary Means More Now than Ever." *The Guardian*, July 21, 2020, theguardian.com/culture/2020/jul/21/the-chicks-2006-documentary-means-more-now-than-ever. Accessed August 11, 2020.

Kidder, Rushworth M. *How Good People Make Tough Choices: Resolving the Dilemmas of Ethical Living*. HarperCollins, 2003.

Macsai, Dan. "Taylor Swift on Going Pop, Ignoring the Gossip and the Best (Worst) Nickname She's Ever Had." *Time*, October 19, 2012, entertainment.time.com/2012/10/19/taylor-swift-on-going-pop-ignoring-the-gossip-and-the-best-worst-nickname-shes-ever-had/. Accessed November 28, 2018.

Martin, Mike W. *Meaningful Work: Rethinking Professional Ethics*. Oxford University Press, 2000.

Nichols, Tom. *The Death of Expertise: The Campaign Against Established Knowledge and Why It Matters*, Oxford University Press, 2017.

Nossel, Suzanne. *Dare to Speak: Defending Free Speech for All*. HarperCollins Books, 2020.

Shirky, Clay. *Here Comes Everybody: The Power of Organizing without Organizations*. Penguin, 2008.

Smith, Grady. "Is Country Music Ready to Forgive the Dixie Chicks?" *The Guardian*, November 19, 2015, theguardian.com/music/2015/nov/19/the-dixie-chicks-tour-is-country-music-ready-to-forgive. Accessed February 23, 2020.

Snapes, Laura. "The Chicks: 'We Were Used and Abused by Everybody Who Wanted to Make Money Off Us.'" *The*

Guardian, July 18, 2020, theguardian. com/music/2020/jul/18/dixie-chicks-used-and-abused-by-everybody-who-wanted-to-make-money-off-us. Accessed July 18, 2020.

Tatum, Beverly Daniel. *Why Are All the Black Kids Sitting Together in the Cafeteria? And Other Conversatios about Race.* Basic Books, 2017.

"The Dixie Chicks on Turning Their Bad Times into Ballads." *CBS News*, March 8, 2020, cbsnews.com/news/the-dixie-chicks-natalie-maines-martie-maguire-emily-strayer/. Accessed March 9, 2020.

White, Judith. "NGO Leaders on the Edge: The Moral Courage to Fight for Human Rights." *Moral Courage in Organizations: Doing the Right Thing at Work*, edited by Debra R. Comer and Gina Vega. M.E. Sharpe, Inc., 2011, pp. 103–104.

Yahr, Emily. "As the Chicks Take the Democratic Convention Stage, Three Generations of Country Singers Challenge the Genre's Conservative Stereotypes." *The Washington Post*, August 20, 2020, washingtonpost.com/arts-entertainment/2020/08/20/chicks-dnc-taylor-swift-dolly-parton/. Accessed August 20, 2020.

Index

Abdhul-Jabbar, Kareem 34, 130
Abdul-Rauf, Mahmoud 145, 146, 153
Academy Awards 19, 20, 21, 22
Academy of Country Music Awards 8
accountability 27, 165
achieved, ascribed and attributed celebrity 13, 14, 124
agenda setting function 179, 180
Ali, Muhammad 24, 130, 133
Allen, Danielle 107, 114
Allen, David 113
Alvarez, Luis 77, 78, 88
American flag 139, 141, 142, 143, 145, 147, 148, 149, 152
amplification of speaking out 13, 149, 179, 180, 186, 189, 195
Andrews, David 30
"Angelina effect" 160, 166
Aniston, Jennifer 168
Anthony, Carmelo 128
apology 59, 194, 195
application of speaking out principles to ordinary people 11, 12, 14, 189, 192, 194, 195
Arbery, Ahmaud 27, 28, 151, 185, 186
artificially intelligent communicators 7, 110
Azarenka, Victoria 173

Barthold, Lauren Swayne 106, 118, 166, 177
Baym, Nancy 95
Beatty, Warren 17
Becker, Charlotte 79, 80, 92, 93
Becker, Lawrence 79, 80, 92, 93
Bedoya, Alejandro 129
Belafonte, Harry 17, 19
Bembry, Jerry 130
Berger, Ron 27
Berkus, Nate 17
Beyonce 28, 118
Biden, Joseph 23
Bieber, Justin 28
Biles, Simone 104
Billings, Andrew 179
Bird, Frederick Bruce 82
Bird, Larry 34

black athletes and racial representation 51, 119, 128, 129, 130, 147, 153
Black Lives Matter 13, 25, 26, 100, 101, 102, 104, 136, 145, 151, 152, 153, 183, 185, 192
black maternal mortality crisis 91, 106, 114, 115, 116, 117, 118, 119, 135, 136, 191, 192
Blackburn, Marsha 5, 6
Blake, Jacob 153, 183
Blake, James 129, 130, 135
Bloomberg, Michael 70
Bogart, Humphrey 17
Bok, Sissela 57, 83
Bono 29
Bono, Sonny 18
Boorstin, Daniel 26, 27
Boswell, Thomas 137
Bowers, Peggy 75
boyd, danah 95
Bradley, Bill 18
Branch, John 151, 152
Brando, Marlon 19, 20
Bredesen, Phil 6
Brewer, Jerry 138, 150, 153
Bridenstine, Jim 53
Brokaw, Tom 66
Brown, Michael 97, 145
Bryant, Howard 8, 122, 128, 130, 133
Bunnin, Nicholas 59, 66
Bunton, Kristie 57, 61, 68, 79, 106, 107, 129, 143, 159
burden of racial representation 51, 153
Bush, George W. 8, 9, 11, 16, 125, 134, 188

cancer disclosures of celebrities 160, 162, 163, 164, 165, 166
capitalization of Black 198n34
Carlos, John 24, 25, 130, 133, 134, 138, 139, 141, 142, 144, 145, 146, 147, 148, 149, 150, 191, 195
Carter, Stephen 111, 177
Castile, Philando 103, 145
"celebocracy" 80, 81
celebrity health capital 168, 169
celebrity influence 26, 27, 30, 31, 32, 52, 55, 81, 125, 158, 159, 160, 164, 165, 168, 169

261

celebrity politicians 18, 19
Chamberlain, Wilt 34
Charles, Ashley 194
Chicks 189, 194, 195
Choi, Chong Ju 27
civil rights 17, 19, 130, 144, 147, 148, 189
Clinton, Bill 17
Clinton, Hillary 7, 10, 17, 18, 41, 42, 55, 193
Cohen, Paul 142
Colbert, Stephen 72, 74
confirmation bias 110, 111
context 111, 129, 148
Cooper, Anderson 66
Cooper, Jim 6
coronavirus pandemic 13, 26, 49, 60, 61, 62,
    135, 136, 150, 151, 153, 154, 155, 156, 157, 166,
    167, 168, 169, 170, 171, 172, 173, 182, 185, 193
Couldry, Nick 30, 31
Crawford, Kate 179
cross-expertise violations 81, 100, 160, 161
Curry, Ayesha 23, 34
Curry, Stephen 23, 27, 28, 33, 34, 35, 36, 37, 38,
    39, 40, 41, 42, 43, 44, 45, 46, 47, 48, 49, 50,
    51, 52, 53, 54, 55, 56, 57, 58, 59, 60, 61, 62, 159

Davis, Ossie 19
Davis, Sammy, Jr. 19
Davis, Wade 149
deception 161
Dee, Ruby 19
DeGeneres, Ellen 29, 168
De Vries, Corona 172
Dewey, John 112, 113, 114, 117, 177
dialogue 106, 110, 117, 118, 119, 134, 140, 143,
    149, 150, 165, 166, 175, 177
Diesel, Vin 29
discourse 112, 113, 114, 175, 176, 177
discursive marketplace of ideas 112, 113, 194
discursive power of celebrity athletes and
    entertainers 30, 31, 53, 100, 113, 114
Dixie Chicks 7, 8, 9, 10, 11, 16, 159, 188, 189,
    193, 194, 195
Doolittle, Sean 124, 125, 126, 127, 128
Dowd, Maureen 66
Dreher, Tanya 177, 178, 181
Drumwright, Minette 82

Eastland, Terry 140
echo chambers 110, 111
Eckhardt, Christopher 142
Eig, Jonathan 153
election campaigns 6, 7, 13, 16
ESPY awards 25, 128
ethical fitness 82, 83, 190
ethical loneliness 178
ethical obligation not to speak out 80, 108
ethically salient characteristics of speaking
    out 37, 65, 66, 67, 68, 126, 127, 128, 129,
    158, 159
expertise 26, 27, 55, 68, 81, 100, 157, 158, 161

Fairbanks, Douglas 16
fallibility 177, 194
Fauci, Anthony 61, 62, 169
Feal, John 72, 74, 78, 79, 84, 85, 86, 87, 89
Felix, Allyson 14, 104, 131, 132, 135, 136, 137,
    159, 191, 192
filter bubbles 110, 111
First Amendment rights to expression 9, 49,
    82, 107, 109, 140
Flood, Curt 132, 133
Floyd, George 13, 25, 26, 104, 136, 137, 150,
    151, 183
Fonda, Jane 19
forgiveness 97, 98, 194
Foster, Brian 150
framing function 179, 180, 186
Franken, Al 19
Franks, Trent 71
Furedi, Frank 27

Garland, Judy 17
Garner, Eric 145
gatekeeping function 109, 179, 192
Gentile, Mary 190
Gere, Richard 20
Geren, Peggy Ruth 113
Gert, Bernard 83, 88, 92, 93, 100, 102, 161,
    162, 164
Gibson, Althea 98, 104
Gillibrand, Kirsten 71
Goldberg, Whoopi 20
Golden Globes awards 21, 22
Gomez, Selena 28
Gopnik, Adam 92, 94
Gordon, Jill 108
Gouinlock, James 112
Grammy awards 5, 7, 8
Grande, Ariana 28
Gray, Freddie 128
Gregory, Dick 19
Gregory, Sean 137
Grewal, Zareena 145, 149
Griffith-Joyner, Florence 104
gun violence 93, 94, 129
Gunter, Barrie 157, 169
Gurol, Nick 54, 55
Guthrie, Kamari 6

Habermas, Jurgen 112, 113, 117
Hager, Peter 123, 124
Hanks, Tom 156, 157, 169, 170, 171, 172, 193
Harding, Warren 16
harm 11, 62, 83, 88, 92, 93, 94, 100, 102, 103,
    108, 132, 134, 143, 146, 147, 148, 149, 157, 162,
    163, 165, 192, 194, 195
Hayworth, Rita 17
health experiences of celebrities 157, 159, 160,
    162, 163, 166, 168, 169, 170, 171, 193
Hedges, Chris 26
Hodges, Craig 133, 134

Holmes, Oliver Wendell 107, 110
Hsu, Hua 25, 134
Hyde, Marina 80, 81

Indian Wells, California, tennis
   tournament 91, 96, 97
intent 38, 40, 67, 79, 128, 141, 142, 143, 148,
   158, 169
Irving, Kyrie 51, 52, 53, 54, 55

Jackson, Steven 30
Jacub, Ayesha 172
James, LeBron 25, 27, 28, 30, 34, 45, 101, 128,
   145, 178, 192
Jenkins, Sally 123
Jenner, Kylie 28
Jolie, Angelina 160, 161, 162, 164, 165, 166
Jolson, Al 16
Johnson, Dwayne "The Rock" 28
Johnson, Gregory 142
Johnson, Magic 34
Jones, Van 41, 42
Jordan, Michael 34, 133, 136, 144
journalism's relationship to speaking out 13,
   28, 30, 31, 40, 52, 68, 72, 83, 86, 88, 89, 96,
   99, 104, 116, 117, 139, 144, 145, 148, 149, 163,
   166, 173, 179, 180, 181, 186, 187
justification test for speaking out 57, 58, 59,
   61, 62, 79, 92, 106, 107, 129, 143, 147, 148,
   159

Kaepernick, Colin 13, 24, 26, 41, 138, 139, 141,
   146, 147, 148, 149, 150, 151, 152, 154, 178, 180,
   192, 195
Kant, Immanuel 79, 191
Kapler, Gabe 152
Kardashian West, Kim 28
Keith, Toby 8
Kelly, Scott 54, 59
Kemp, Jack 18
Kennedy, John F. 17
Kidder, Rushworth 82, 84, 190
Kilby, Allaina 75, 89
King, Billie Jean 182, 185
King, Martin Luther 103, 134, 148, 189, 192
King, Rodney 133
Kornheiser, Tony 50, 51, 54

Lacey, Kate 175, 176, 178
Lady Gaga 28, 168
Lee, Harper 20
Legend, John 31, 32
Leslie, Lisa 104
Ley, Tom 186
Lipari, Lisbeth 174, 176, 177, 178
listening as an ethical act 106, 174, 175, 176,
   177, 178, 179, 181, 182, 186, 189, 195
Lizzo 168
Longoria, Eva 23
Lopez, Jennifer 168

Louis-Dreyfus, Julia 23, 162, 163, 164
loyalty 84, 87

Madonna 168
Maguire, Martie 7, 10
Maines, Natalie 7, 8, 9, 10, 188, 195
Major League Baseball positions on speaking
   out 152
Malcolm X 147
marketplace of ideas 107, 108, 109, 110, 111, 112,
   175, 176, 186, 194
Markham, Tim 30, 31
Marshall, P. David 31
Martin, Mike 191
Martin, Trayvon 145, 185
May, William F. 31, 32, 53
McCombs, Maxwell 179
McConaughey, Matthew 169
McConnell, Mitch 65, 70, 72, 73, 74, 88, 89
McCullough, Thomas 76, 113
McEntire, Reba 8
McGoldrick, James 142, 148
McGovern, George 17
McIntyre, Lee 58, 59
Me Too movement 21, 22
Meadows-Fernandez, Rochaun 118
Medina, Mark 61
Messi, Leo 28, 29
Mill, John Stuart 92, 94, 107, 108, 110, 112, 175
Milton, John 107, 110, 111
Montano, Alysia 131
moon landings 49, 50, 51, 52, 53, 54, 55, 56,
   58, 59, 189
moral agent 56, 57, 59, 66, 67, 75, 79, 163, 189,
   190, 195
moral blindness, deafness and muteness 82
moral competence 190
moral consistency 84, 85, 104, 171, 174, 188,
   190, 191, 193
moral courage 10, 13, 14, 24, 40, 103, 122, 150,
   174, 189, 190
moral justification 46, 57
moral voicing 82, 188, 190, 191
motive 9, 57, 58, 74, 76, 79, 80, 83, 89, 98, 131,
   143, 148, 158, 161, 162
Murphy, Patrick 82

national anthem 24, 26, 41, 138, 139, 141, 144,
   145, 146, 147, 148, 149, 150, 151, 152, 154, 155,
   178, 180
National Basketball Association positions on
   speaking out 42, 45, 46, 145, 151
National Football League positions on
   speaking out 26, 154
National Women's Soccer League positions on
   speaking out 151
networked publics 108, 109, 110
Neymar 28
Nichols, Michael 179
Nichols, Tom 81, 85, 100, 101, 194

Nixon, Cynthia 19
Nixon, Richard 17
Nossel, Suzanne 111, 194
Nussbaum, Martha 111

Obama, Barack 6, 17, 28, 36, 37, 39, 40, 41, 42, 70
Obama, Michelle 37, 39, 40
O'Brien, David 142
O'Donnell, Penny 181
offense 93, 94, 142, 143, 149, 194
Offitt, Paul 159
Ohanian, Alexis 115
Olympic Games 24, 25, 130, 131, 134, 136, 138, 141, 144, 148, 154, 182, 191
"Oprah effect" 17
Orman, Suze 17
Osaka, Naomi 173, 174, 179, 180, 182, 183, 184, 185, 186, 187, 192, 195
outrage 193, 194

paid speaking 38, 161
parasocial relationships 164
Parks, Elizabeth 174, 175, 176, 177
participatory media 109, 179
Patterson, Thomas 180
Paul, Chris 128
Paul, Rand 88, 89
Peck, Gregory 20
Perry, Katy 28, 168
Pfeifer, Ray 77, 78, 87
Pickford, Mary 16
Plaisance, Patrick 46
Plank, Kevin 43, 44
platforms of celebrity athletes and entertainers 23, 24, 25, 38, 43, 48, 49, 80, 83, 100, 101, 106, 108, 118, 131, 153, 159, 162, 169, 192
Poitier, Sidney 19
political conventions 23
political endorsements 17, 18, 23, 27, 29, 31, 41
politics in sports 125, 126, 127, 133, 134, 137, 139, 144, 152, 153, 187
post-truth culture 58, 59
power and privilege differentials of celebrity athletes and entertainers 13, 49, 51, 52, 53, 55, 56, 62, 101, 118, 192, 193
Price, Yetunde 91
privacy 93, 163
Probolus, Kimberly 181, 182

Rabidoux, Greg 20, 24
racial injustice 41, 42, 45, 92, 96, 97, 101, 102, 103, 106, 122, 128, 129, 130, 136, 138, 139, 147, 149, 150, 151, 152, 153, 154, 173, 174, 178, 180, 183, 184, 185, 186, 187, 188, 192, 195
racism and sexism in tennis 90, 91, 96, 97, 98, 99, 104, 182, 183, 184
Rapinoe, Megan 151
Rather, Dan 66

Raymond, Emilie 19
Reagan, Ronald 18, 142
respect for human dignity 11, 119, 172, 177, 179, 191, 192, 193, 194
Reynolds, Ryan 168
Rhoden, William 132, 133
"right doing" vs. wrongdoing 14, 190
Rihanna 28
Rinaldi, Tom 186, 187
risks of speaking out 13, 38, 103, 104, 125, 128, 130, 131, 132, 133, 134, 138, 139, 145, 147, 149, 153, 163, 164, 183, 184
Robbins, Tim 20
Roberts, Julia 169
Robinson, Emily 7
Robinson, Eroseanna 144
Robinson, Jackie 13, 17, 129, 130
Rodriguez, Alex 168
role-related expectations 9, 21, 37, 38, 39, 41, 42, 50, 66, 71, 79, 96, 113, 117, 126, 147, 158, 174
Ronaldo, Cristiano 28, 29
Roosevelt, Franklin 16
Ross, Tracee Ellis 23
Rowling, J.K. 99
Royce, Josiah 84, 85
Rudolph, Wilma 104
Russell, Bill 34

Sarandon, Susan 20
Schroeder, Jared 107, 108, 109, 110, 112, 113
Schudson, Michael 176
Schwarzenegger, Arnold 18
"seeing, talking" practitioners of ethics 82
Seib, Philip 180
selective exposure 110, 111
Serazio, Michael 122, 123, 124, 126, 144
Shakira 29
Shirky, Clay 192
Shuh, Janel 59
"shut up and play" or "stick to sports" expectation 122, 125, 132, 133, 147, 176, 178, 183, 187
"shut up and sing" expectation 9, 178
Silver, Adam 45
Simon, Robert 123, 124
Sinatra, Frank 17
Smith, Johnny 130
Smith, Tommie 24, 130, 133, 134, 138, 139, 141, 142, 144, 145, 146, 147, 148, 149, 191, 195
social and digital media power 12, 28, 29, 61, 74, 83, 95, 101, 109, 141, 163, 167, 169, 170, 192
social media characteristics 95, 109, 110, 111, 193
Solomon, Stephen 140
speaking truth to power 73, 83, 113
Specht, Kenny 70, 72
Spence, Harold 142
spheres of influence 189, 195
Spohr, Dominic 110
sport: economic power 125, 126, 131, 132,

133, 144, 154, 155; popularity and cultural importance 24, 122, 123; teaching of moral values 123, 124, 125
Stauffer, Jill 178
Stewart, Jon 64, 65, 66, 67, 68, 69, 70, 71, 72, 73, 74, 75, 76, 78, 79, 84, 85, 86, 87, 88, 89, 159, 190, 191
Strayer, Emily 188
Streep, Meryl 21
Streeter, Kurt 133
Streisand, Barbara 17
Svrulga, Barry 124
Swift, Taylor 5, 6, 7, 9, 10, 11, 16, 27, 28, 29, 30, 193
symbolic speech acts 41, 138, 139, 140, 141, 142, 143, 144, 145, 146, 147, 148, 149, 150, 151, 152, 153, 154, 155, 173, 174, 180, 183, 185, 186, 187

Tamblyn, Amber 22
Tannen, Deborah 175
Tatum, Beverly Daniel 189
Taylor, Breonna 151
Taylor, Charles 75
Taylor, Christian 102
teaching function of celebrities 31, 52, 53, 162, 163, 169
terror attacks on United States 8, 64, 65, 67, 68, 69, 70, 71, 77, 78, 85, 86, 88, 89, 147, 189, 191
Thomas, Etan 125
Tiersma, Peter 148
Time's Up movement 22
Tinker, John 142
Tinker, Mary Beth 142
Tornberg, Petter 110
Torres, Cesar 123, 124
Trump, Donald 7, 10, 11, 18, 21, 22, 24, 28, 31, 41, 42, 43, 44, 45, 46, 48, 61, 72, 77, 78, 79, 86, 87, 124, 127, 139, 147, 152, 156, 159, 193
truth and fact 56, 58, 59, 61, 62, 83, 111, 167, 168
Tyus, Wyomia 144

United States invasion of Iraq 7, 9, 10, 16, 22, 125, 188, 194
Usher, Nikki 59

Ventura, Jesse 18
viral cascades of information 111
volume of celebrity voices 100, 159, 193
voter registration 6, 193
vulnerable stakeholders 59, 84, 89, 93, 98, 104, 117, 127, 136, 148, 177

Wade, Dwayne 128
Ward, Stephen 175
Washington, Kerry 23, 168
Wasserman, Herman 175
Wayne, John 17
Wehner, Peter 88
Welts, Rick 42
Wheeler, Mark 17
White House sports championship visits 40, 41, 44, 45, 46, 48, 124, 127, 134
Widmer, Ted 138
Wilbon, Michael 50, 51, 54, 103
Will, George 124
willful ignorance 58
Williams, Brian 66
Williams, J. Corey 147
Williams, Jayson 145
Williams, Serena 14, 90, 91, 92, 93, 94, 95, 96, 97, 98, 99, 100, 101, 102, 103, 104, 105, 106, 114, 115, 116, 117, 118, 119, 135, 159, 173, 182, 191, 192
Williams, Venus 90, 97, 104, 114
Wilson, Rita 156, 157, 169, 170
Winfrey, Oprah 17, 18, 21, 29
Witherspoon, Reese 168
Wolken, Dan 184
Women's National Basketball Association positions on speaking out 151
Wyatt, Wendy 57, 61, 68, 79, 106, 107, 129, 143, 159

Yu, Jiyuan 59, 66

Zadroga, James 77, 78
Ziemer, Timothy 36, 37